CASENOTE® Legal Briefs®

DEBTORS AND CREDITORS

Keyed to Courses Using

Warren, Westbrook, Porter, and Pottow's
The Law of Debtors and Creditors
Eighth Edition

Authored by: Publisher's Editorial Staff

Wolters Kluwer

This publication is designed to provide accurate and authoritative information in regard to the subject matter covered. It is sold with the understanding that the publisher is not engaged in rendering legal, accounting, or other professional services. If legal advice or other expert assistance is required, the services of a competent professional person should be sought.

— From a Declaration of Principles adopted jointly by a Committee of the American Bar Association and a Committee of Publishers and Associates

Published by Wolters Kluwer in New York.

Wolters Kluwer Legal & Regulatory U.S. serves customers worldwide with CCH, Aspen Publishers, and Kluwer Law International products. (www.WKLegaledu.com)

To contact Customer Service, e-mail customer.service@wolterskluwer.com, call 1-800-234-1660, fax 1-800-901-9075, or mail correspondence to:

Wolters Kluwer
Attn: Order Department
P.O. Box 990
Frederick, MD 21705

Printed in the United States of America.

1 2 3 4 5 6 7 8 9 0

ISBN 978-1-5438-1567-2

About Wolters Kluwer Legal & Regulatory U.S.

Wolters Kluwer Legal & Regulatory U.S. delivers expert content and solutions in the areas of law, corporate compliance, health compliance, reimbursement, and legal education. Its practical solutions help customers successfully navigate the demands of a changing environment to drive their daily activities, enhance decision quality, and inspire confident outcomes.

Serving customers worldwide, its legal and regulatory portfolio includes products under the Aspen Publishers, CCH Incorporated, Kluwer Law International, ftwilliam.com, and MediRegs names. They are regarded as exceptional and trusted resources for general legal and practice-specific knowledge, compliance and risk management, dynamic workflow solutions, and expert commentary.

Format for the Casenote® Legal Brief

Nature of Case: This section identifies the form of action (e.g., breach of contract, negligence, battery), the type of proceeding (e.g., demurrer, appeal from trial court's jury instructions) or the relief sought (e.g., damages, injunction, criminal sanctions).

Fact Summary: This is included to refresh your memory and can be used as a quick reminder of the facts.

Rule of Law: Summarizes the general principle of law that the case illustrates. It may be used for instant recall of the court's holding and for classroom discussion or home review.

Facts: This section contains all relevant facts of the case, including the contentions of the parties and the lower court holdings. It is written in a logical order to give you a clear understanding of the case. The plaintiff and defendant are identified by their proper names throughout and are always labeled with a (P) or (D).

Issue: The issue is a concise question that brings out the essence of the opinion as it relates to the section of the casebook in which the case appears. Both substantive and procedural issues are included if relevant to the decision.

Party ID: Quick identification of the relationship between the parties.

Concurrence/Dissent: All concurrences and dissents are briefed whenever they are included by the casebook author.

Analysis: This last paragraph gives you a broad understanding of where the case "fits in" with other cases in the section of the book and with the entire course. It is a hornbook-style discussion indicating whether the case is a majority or minority opinion and comparing the principal case with other cases in the casebook. It may also provide analysis from restatements, uniform codes, and law review articles.

Holding and Decision: This section offers a clear and in-depth discussion of the rule of the case and the court's rationale. It is written in easy-to-understand language and answers the issue presented by applying the law to the facts of the case. When relevant, it includes a thorough discussion of the exceptions to the case as listed by the court, any major cites to the other cases on point, and the names of the judges who wrote the decisions.

Quicknotes: Conveniently defines legal terms found in the case.

Palsgraf v. Long Island R.R. Co.

Injured bystander (P) v. Railroad company (D)

N.Y. Ct. App., 248 N.Y. 339, 162 N.E. 99 (1928).

NATURE OF CASE: Appeal from judgment affirming verdict for plaintiff seeking damages for personal injury.

FACT SUMMARY: **Helen Palsgraf (P) was injured on R.R.'s (D) train platform when R.R.'s (D) guard helped a passenger aboard a moving train, causing his package to fall on the tracks. The package contained fireworks which exploded, creating a shock that tipped a scale onto Palsgraf (P).**

RULE OF LAW

The risk reasonably to be perceived defines the duty to be obeyed.

FACTS: Helen Palsgraf (P) purchased a ticket to Rockaway Beach from R.R. (D) and was waiting on the train platform. As she waited, two men ran to catch a train that was pulling out from the platform. The first man jumped aboard, but the second man, who appeared as if he might fall, was helped aboard by the guard on the train who had kept the door open so they could jump aboard. A guard on the platform also helped by pushing him onto the train. The man was carrying a package wrapped in newspaper. In the process, the man dropped his package, which fell on the tracks. The package contained fireworks and exploded. The shock of the explosion was apparently of great enough strength to tip over some scales at the other end of the platform, which fell on Palsgraf (P) and injured her. A jury awarded her damages, and R.R. (D) appealed.

ISSUE: Does the risk reasonably to be perceived define the duty to be obeyed?

HOLDING AND DECISION: (Cardozo, C.J.) Yes. The risk reasonably to be perceived defines the duty to be obeyed. If there is no foreseeable hazard to the injured party as the result of a seemingly innocent act, the act does not become a tort because it happened to be a wrong as to another. If the wrong was not willful, the plaintiff must show that the act as to her had such great and apparent possibilities of danger as to entitle her to protection. Negligence in the abstract is not enough upon which to base liability. Negligence is a relative concept, evolving out of the common law doctrine of trespass on the case. To establish liability, the defendant must owe a legal duty of reasonable care to the injured party. A cause of action in tort will lie where harm, though unintended, could have been averted or avoided by observance of such a duty. The scope of the duty is limited by the range of danger that a reasonable person could foresee. In this case, there was nothing to suggest from the appearance of the parcel or otherwise that the parcel contained fireworks. The guard could not reasonably have had any warning of a threat to Palsgraf (P), and R.R. (D) therefore cannot be held liable. Judgment is reversed in favor of R.R. (D).

DISSENT: (Andrews, J.) The concept that there is no negligence unless R.R. (D) owes a legal duty to take care as to Palsgraf (P) herself is too narrow. Everyone owes to the world at large the duty of refraining from those acts that may unreasonably threaten the safety of others. If the guard's action was negligent as to those nearby, it was also negligent as to those outside what might be termed the "danger zone." For Palsgraf (P) to recover, R.R.'s (D) negligence must have been the proximate cause of her injury, a question of fact for the jury.

ANALYSIS

The majority defined the limit of the defendant's liability in terms of the danger that a reasonable person in defendant's situation would have perceived. The dissent argued that the limitation should not be placed on liability, but rather on damages. Judge Andrews suggested that only injuries that would not have happened but for R.R.'s (D) negligence should be compensable. Both the majority and dissent recognized the policy-driven need to limit liability for negligent acts, seeking, in the words of Judge Andrews, to define a framework "that will be practical and in keeping with the general understanding of mankind." The Restatement (Second) of Torts has accepted Judge Cardozo's view.

Quicknotes

FORESEEABILITY A reasonable expectation that change is the probable result of certain acts or omissions.

NEGLIGENCE Conduct falling below the standard of care that a reasonable person would demonstrate under similar conditions.

PROXIMATE CAUSE The natural sequence of events without which an injury would not have been sustained.

Note to Students

Wolters Kluwer Legal & Regulatory U.S. is proud to offer *Casenote® Legal Briefs*—continuing thirty years of publishing America's best-selling legal briefs.

Casenote® Legal Briefs are designed to help you save time when briefing assigned cases. Organized under convenient headings, they show you how to abstract the basic facts and holdings from the text of the actual opinions handed down by the courts. Used as part of a rigorous study regimen, they can help you spend more time analyzing and critiquing points of law than on copying bits and pieces of judicial opinions into your notebook or outline.

Casenote® Legal Briefs should never be used as a substitute for assigned casebook readings. They work best when read as a follow-up to reviewing the underlying opinions themselves. Students who try to avoid reading and digesting the judicial opinions in their casebooks or online sources will end up shortchanging themselves in the long run. The ability to absorb, critique, and restate the dynamic and complex elements of case law decisions is crucial to your success in law school and beyond. It cannot be developed vicariously.

Casenote® Legal Briefs represents but one of the many offerings in Legal Education's Study Aid Timeline, which includes:

- *Casenote® Legal Briefs*
- *Emanuel® Law Outlines*
- Emanuel® *Law in a Flash* Flash Cards
- Emanuel® *CrunchTime®* Series

Each of these series is designed to provide you with easy-to-understand explanations of complex points of law. Each volume offers guidance on the principles of legal analysis and, consulted regularly, will hone your ability to spot relevant issues. We have titles that will help you prepare for class, prepare for your exams, and enhance your general comprehension of the law along the way.

To find out more about our law school tools for success, visit us at *www.WKLegaledu.com* or e-mail us at *legaledu@wolterskluwer.com*. We'll be happy to assist you.

How to Brief a Case

A. Decide on a Format and Stick to It

Structure is essential to a good brief. It enables you to arrange systematically the related parts that are scattered throughout most cases, thus making manageable and understandable what might otherwise seem to be an endless and unfathomable sea of information. There are, of course, an unlimited number of formats that can be utilized. However, it is best to find one that suits your needs and stick to it. Consistency breeds both efficiency and the security that when called upon you will know where to look in your brief for the information you are asked to give.

Any format, as long as it presents the essential elements of a case in an organized fashion, can be used. Experience, however, has led *Casenote*® *Legal Briefs* to develop and utilize the following format because of its logical flow and universal applicability.

NATURE OF CASE: This is a brief statement of the legal character and procedural status of the case (e.g., "Appeal of a burglary conviction").

There are many different alternatives open to a litigant dissatisfied with a court ruling. The key to determining which one has been used is to discover *who is asking this court for what.*

This first entry in the brief should be kept as *short as possible.* Use the court's terminology if you understand it. But since jurisdictions vary as to the titles of pleadings, the best entry is the one that addresses who wants what in this proceeding, not the one that sounds most like the court's language.

RULE OF LAW: A statement of the general principle of law that the case illustrates (e.g., "An acceptance that varies any term of the offer is considered a rejection and counteroffer").

Determining the rule of law of a case is a procedure similar to determining the issue of the case. Avoid being fooled by red herrings; there may be a few rules of law mentioned in the case excerpt, but usually only one is *the* rule with which the casebook editor is concerned. The techniques used to locate the issue, described below, may also be utilized to find the rule of law. Generally, your best guide is simply the chapter heading. It is a clue to the point the casebook editor seeks to make and should be kept in mind when reading every case in the respective section.

FACTS: A synopsis of only the essential facts of the case, i.e., those bearing upon or leading up to the issue.

The facts entry should be a short statement of the events and transactions that led one party to initiate legal proceedings against another in the first place. While some cases conveniently state the salient facts at the beginning of the decision, in other instances they will have to be culled from hiding places throughout the text, even from concurring and dissenting opinions. Some of the "facts" will often be in dispute and should be so noted. Conflicting evidence may be briefly pointed up. "Hard" facts must be included. Both must be *relevant* in order to be listed in the facts entry. It is impossible to tell what is relevant until the entire case is read, as the ultimate determination of the rights and liabilities of the parties may turn on something buried deep in the opinion.

Generally, the facts entry should not be longer than three to five *short* sentences.

It is often helpful to identify the role played by a party in a given context. For example, in a construction contract case the identification of a party as the "contractor" or "builder" alleviates the need to tell that that party was the one who was supposed to have built the house.

It is always helpful, and a good general practice, to identify the "plaintiff" and the "defendant." This may seem elementary and uncomplicated, but, especially in view of the creative editing practiced by some casebook editors, it is sometimes a difficult or even impossible task. Bear in mind that the *party presently* seeking something from this court may not be the plaintiff, and that sometimes only the cross-claim of a defendant is treated in the excerpt. Confusing or misaligning the parties can ruin your analysis and understanding of the case.

ISSUE: A statement of the general legal question answered by or illustrated in the case. For clarity, the issue is best put in the form of a question capable of a "yes" or "no" answer. In reality, the issue is simply the Rule of Law put in the form of a question (e.g., "May an offer be accepted by performance?").

The major problem presented in discerning what is *the* issue in the case is that an opinion usually purports to raise and answer several questions. However, except for rare cases, only one such question is really the issue in the case. Collateral issues not necessary to the resolution of the matter in controversy are handled by the court by language known as *"obiter dictum"* or merely *"dictum."* While dicta may be included later in the brief, they have no place under the issue heading.

To find the issue, ask *who wants what* and then go on to ask *why did that party succeed or fail in getting it.* Once this is determined, the "why" should be turned into a question.

The complexity of the issues in the cases will vary, but in all cases a single-sentence question should sum up the issue. *In a few cases,* there will be two, or even more rarely, three issues of equal importance to the resolution of the case. Each should be expressed in a single-sentence question.

Since many issues are resolved by a court in coming to a final disposition of a case, the casebook editor will reproduce the portion of the opinion containing the issue or issues most relevant to the area of law under scrutiny. A noted law professor gave this advice: "Close the book; look at the title on the cover." Chances are, if it is Property, you need not concern yourself with whether, for example, the federal government's treatment of the plaintiff's land really raises a federal question sufficient to support jurisdiction on this ground in federal court.

The same rule applies to chapter headings designating sub-areas within the subjects. They tip you off as to what the text is designed to teach. The cases are arranged in a casebook to show a progression or development of the law, so that the preceding cases may also help.

It is also most important to remember to *read the notes and questions* at the end of a case to determine what the editors wanted you to have gleaned from it.

HOLDING AND DECISION: This section should succinctly explain the rationale of the court in arriving at its decision. In capsulizing the "reasoning" of the court, it should always include an application of the general rule or rules of law to the specific facts of the case. Hidden justifications come to light in this entry: the reasons for the state of the law, the public policies, the biases and prejudices, those considerations that influence the justices' thinking and, ultimately, the outcome of the case. At the end, there should be a short indication of the disposition or procedural resolution of the case (e.g., "Decision of the trial court for Mr. Smith (P) reversed").

The foregoing format is designed to help you "digest" the reams of case material with which you will be faced in your law school career. Once mastered by practice, it will place at your fingertips the information the authors of your casebooks have sought to impart to you in case-by-case illustration and analysis.

B. Be as Economical as Possible in Briefing Cases

Once armed with a format that encourages succinctness, it is as important to be economical with regard to the time spent on the actual reading of the case as it is to be economical in the writing of the brief itself. This does not mean "skimming" a case. Rather, it means reading the case with an "eye" trained to recognize into which "section" of your brief a particular passage or line fits and having a system for quickly and precisely marking the case so that the passages fitting any one particular part of the brief can be easily identified and brought together in a concise and accurate manner when the brief is actually written.

It is of no use to simply repeat everything in the opinion of the court; record only enough information to trigger your recollection of what the court said. Nevertheless, an accurate statement of the "law of the case," i.e., the legal principle applied to the facts, is absolutely essential to class preparation and to learning the law under the case method.

To that end, it is important to develop a "shorthand" that you can use to make marginal notations. These notations will tell you at a glance in which section of the brief you will be placing that particular passage or portion of the opinion.

Some students prefer to underline all the salient portions of the opinion (with a pencil or colored underliner marker), making marginal notations as they go along. Others prefer the color-coded method of underlining, utilizing different colors of markers to underline the salient portions of the case, each separate color being used to represent a different section of the brief. For example, blue underlining could be used for passages relating to the rule of law, yellow for those relating to the issue, and green for those relating to the holding and decision, etc. While it has its advocates, the color-coded method can be confusing and time-consuming (all that time spent on changing colored markers). Furthermore, it can interfere with the continuity and concentration many students deem essential to the reading of a case for maximum comprehension. In the end, however, it is a matter of personal preference and style. Just remember, whatever method you use, underlining must be used sparingly or its value is lost.

If you take the marginal notation route, an efficient and easy method is to go along underlining the key portions of the case and placing in the margin alongside them the following "markers" to indicate where a particular passage or line "belongs" in the brief you will write:

N (NATURE OF CASE)
RL (RULE OF LAW)
I (ISSUE)
HL (HOLDING AND DECISION, relates to the RULE OF LAW behind the decision)
HR (HOLDING AND DECISION, gives the RATIONALE or reasoning behind the decision)
HA (HOLDING AND DECISION, applies the general principle(s) of law to the facts of the case to arrive at the decision)

Remember that a particular passage may well contain information necessary to more than one part of your brief, in which case you simply note that in the margin. If you are using the color-coded underlining method instead of marginal notation, simply make asterisks or checks in the margin next to the passage in question in the colors that indicate the additional sections of the brief where it might be utilized.

The economy of utilizing "shorthand" in marking cases for briefing can be maintained in the actual brief writing process itself by utilizing "law student shorthand" within the brief. There are many commonly used words and phrases for which abbreviations can be substituted in your briefs (and in your class notes also). You can develop abbreviations that are personal to you and which will save you a lot of time. A reference list of briefing abbreviations can be found on page x of this book.

C. Use Both the Briefing Process and the Brief as a Learning Tool

Now that you have a format and the tools for briefing cases efficiently, the most important thing is to make the time spent in briefing profitable to you and to make the most advantageous use of the briefs you create. Of course, the briefs are invaluable for classroom reference when you are called upon to explain or analyze a particular case. However, they are also useful in reviewing for exams. A quick glance at the fact summary should bring the case to mind, and a rereading of the rule of law should enable you to go over the underlying legal concept in your mind, how it was applied in that particular case, and how it might apply in other factual settings.

As to the value to be derived from engaging in the briefing process itself, there is an immediate benefit that arises from being forced to sift through the essential facts and reasoning from the court's opinion and to succinctly express them in your own words in your brief. The process ensures that you understand the case and the point that it illustrates, and that means you will be ready to absorb further analysis and information brought forth in class. It also ensures you will have something to say when called upon in class. The briefing process helps develop a mental agility for getting to the *gist* of a case and for identifying, expounding on, and applying the legal concepts and issues found there. The briefing process is the mental process on which you must rely in taking law school examinations; it is also the mental process upon which lawyers rely in serving their clients and in making a living.

Abbreviations for Briefs

acceptance ... acp
affirmed ... aff
answer ... ans
assumption of risk ... a/r
attorney ... atty
beyond a reasonable doubt ... b/r/d
bona fide purchaser ... BFP
breach of contract ... br/k
cause of action ... c/a
common law ... c/l
Constitution ... Con
constitutional ... con
contract ... K
contributory negligence ... c/n
cross ... x
cross-complaint ... x/c
cross-examination ... x/ex
cruel and unusual punishment ... c/u/p
defendant ... D
dismissed ... dis
double jeopardy ... d/j
due process ... d/p
equal protection ... e/p
equity ... eq
evidence ... ev
exclude ... exc
exclusionary rule ... exc/r
felony ... f/n
freedom of speech ... f/s
good faith ... g/f
habeas corpus ... h/c
hearsay ... hr
husband ... H
injunction ... inj
in loco parentis ... ILP
inter vivos ... I/v
joint tenancy ... j/t
judgment ... judgt
jurisdiction ... jur
last clear chance ... LCC
long-arm statute ... LAS
majority view ... maj
meeting of minds ... MOM
minority view ... min
Miranda rule ... Mir/r
Miranda warnings ... Mir/w
negligence ... neg
notice ... ntc
nuisance ... nus
obligation ... ob
obscene ... obs
offer ... O
offeree ... OE
offeror ... OR
ordinance ... ord
pain and suffering ... p/s
parol evidence ... p/e
plaintiff ... P
prima facie ... p/f
probable cause ... p/c
proximate cause ... px/c
real property ... r/p
reasonable doubt ... r/d
reasonable man ... r/m
rebuttable presumption ... rb/p
remanded ... rem
res ipsa loquitur ... RIL
respondeat superior ... r/s
Restatement ... RS
reversed ... rev
Rule Against Perpetuities ... RAP
search and seizure ... s/s
search warrant ... s/w
self-defense ... s/d
specific performance ... s/p
statute ... S
statute of frauds ... S/F
statute of limitations ... S/L
summary judgment ... s/j
tenancy at will ... t/w
tenancy in common ... t/c
tenant ... t
third party ... TP
third party beneficiary ... TPB
transferred intent ... TI
unconscionable ... uncon
unconstitutional ... unconst
undue influence ... u/e
Uniform Commercial Code ... UCC
unilateral ... uni
vendee ... VE
vendor ... VR
versus ... v
void for vagueness ... VFV
weight of authority ... w/a
weight of the evidence ... w/e
wife ... W
with ... w/
within ... w/i
without ... w/o
without prejudice ... w/o/p
wrongful death ... wr/d

Table of Cases

Note: There are no principal cases in Chapter 1 of the casebook.

CHAPTER 2

Collecting from Consumer Debtors

Quick Reference Rules of Law

Henson v. Santander Consumer USA, Inc.

Consumers (P) v. Bank (D)

137 S. Ct. 1718 (2017)

NATURE OF CASE: Appeal from Fourth Circuit ruling that Santander Consumer USA, Inc. (D) did not qualify as a debt collector under the Fair Debt Collection Practices Act.

FACT SUMMARY: Consumers (P) accused Santander Consumer USA, Inc. (Santander) (D) of violating the Fair Debt Collection Practices Act (FDCPA) with regard to its debt collection practices. Santander (D) argued that it is not a debt collector subject to the FDCPA because it had purchased the loans from the originating entity instead of collecting on the debt on behalf of another entity.

RULE OF LAW

A company that purchases defaulted debts and regularly attempts to collect on them does not qualify as a debt collector under the Fair Debt Collection Practices Act.

FACTS: CitiFinancial Auto loaned money to consumers in order to buy cars. Santander Consumer USA, Inc. (Santander) (D) purchased loans from CitiFinancial Auto that had been defaulted on by consumers (P). Santander (D) then proceeded to collect on its debts. Consumers (P) argued that Santander's (D) debt collection practices were in violation of the Fair Debt Collection Practices Act (FDCPA). Santander (D) argued that the Act did not apply to its practices because it is not a debt collector under the FDCPA's definitions.

ISSUE: Is a company that purchases defaulted debts and regularly attempts to collect on them qualified as a debt collector under the Fair Debt Collection Practices Act?

HOLDING AND DECISION: (Gorsuch, J.) No. A company that purchases defaulted debts and regularly attempts to collect on them does not qualify as a debt collector under the Fair Debt Collection Practices Act (FDCPA). The FDCPA defines debt collectors as those who regularly seek to collect debts "owed . . . another." The plain language of the FDCPA defines a debt collector as a third-party collection agency that works on behalf of a debt owner; the definition does not include a debt owner collecting on its own debts. Consumers (P) argued that because the statute states "owed" in its definition of a debt collector, it indicates that the statute did not include loan originators but embraced purchasers such as Santander (D). However, this argument is not compelling because the English language often uses past participle verbs [here, "owed"] to describe present states. Because Santander (D) collects debt for its own accounts and not the accounts of a third party, it is not a debt collector under the Act. Affirmed.

ANALYSIS

In *Henson*, Santander [D] was accused of making false statements to consumers and communicating directly with consumers who were represented by counsel. Consumer groups have since argued that the decision in *Henson* permitted the ongoing use of a loophole, where companies that service their own debt are able to employ abusive tactics without repercussions.

Quicknotes

DEFAULT Failure to carry out a legal obligation.

McCollough v. Johnson, Rodenburg & Lauinger

Pro se debtor (P) v. Debt collection law firm (D)

637 F.3d 939 (9th Cir. 2011)

NATURE OF CASE: Appeal from summary judgment for plaintiff in action asserting violations of the Fair Debt Collection Practices Act (FDCPA).

FACT SUMMARY: Johnson, Rodenburg & Lauinger (JRL) (D), a debt collection law firm, contended that it was not liable for violating the Fair Debt Collection Practices Act (FDCPA) because it maintained procedures reasonably adapted to avoid violations of the Act, and because the FDCPA should not be read to cover discovery procedures, such as requests for admission. McCollough (P), a former debtor who was sued by JRL (D), contended, inter alia, that JRL (D) violated the FDCPA by filing a time-barred lawsuit against him, and that JRL's (D) service on him of false requests for admission violated the FDCPA as a matter of law.

RULE OF LAW

(1) Under the Fair Debt Collection Practices Act, a debt collector does not have a bona fide error defense where its reliance on the creditor's representations is unreasonable as a matter of law, and it otherwise does not maintain procedures reasonably adapted to avoiding the violation at issue.

(2) Under the Fair Debt Collection Practices Act, a debt collector's service of requests for admission containing false information upon a pro se defendant without an explanation that the requests would be deemed admitted after thirty days constitutes "unfair or unconscionable" or "false, deceptive, or misleading" means to collect a debt.

FACTS: McCollough (P) had a little over $3,000 in credit card debt, which the issuing bank charged off in 2000. CACV of Colorado, Ltd. (CACV) purchased the debt in 2001 and brought suit against McCollough (P) in 2005 attempting to collect the debt. After McCollough (P), acting pro se, responded that the statute of limitations barred the action, CACV dismissed the action. Then, in 2006, CACV's parent company, Collect America, Ltd., hired Johnson, Rodenburg & Lauinger (JRL) (D), a debt collection law firm, to pursue collection of McCollough's (P) outstanding debt. The contract between JRL (D) and Collect America provided that Collect America made no warranty as to the accuracy or validity of data provided, and it expressly made JRL (D) responsible to determine its legal and ethical ability to collect the accounts. JRL's (D) screening procedures flagged a statute of limitations problem with McCollough's (P) account, noting that the limitation period was up in August 2005. JRL (D) sought documentation that might extend the limitations period, and CACV incorrectly informed JRL (D) that McCollough (P) had made a payment in 2004—which would have extended the limitations period to 2009. Instead, as reflected in the electronic file that had been provided to JRL (D), the event that took place in 2004 was in fact the return of court costs to CACV for a collection complaint and summons that CACV had prepared in 2003. Nevertheless, JRL (D) filed a collection suit against McCollough (P) in 2007, and McCollough (P) responded pro se around two months later asserting a statute of limitations defense. McCollough (P) also informed JRL (D) that he would be seeking summary judgment on that basis. A couple of months later, CACV informed JRL (D) that McCollough (P) had not made a payment in 2004. JRL (D) continued to prosecute the suit, and a few months later served on McCollough (P) a list of 22 requests for admission that would have had McCollough (P) admitting that he owed the debt, that he had made a payment in 2004, and that all assertions in the complaint were true. JRL (D) did not, however, inform McCollough (P) the requests would be deemed admitted if he did not respond within 30 days. After McCollough (P) hired an attorney, JRL (D) dismissed its suit. McCollough (P) then brought suit in federal district court asserting violations of the Fair Debt Collection Practices Act (FDCPA). At trial, before a jury, evidence was presented that JRL's (D) mistake in McCollough's (P) case had been caused by its "factory" approach of "mass producing default judgments." The jury awarded him the $1,000 statutory maximum for violations of the FDCPA; $250,000 for emotional distress; and $60,000 in punitive damages. The court granted summary judgment against JRL (D) on the FDCPA claims, and JRL (D) appealed. The court of appeals granted review.

ISSUE:

(1) Under the Fair Debt Collection Practices Act, does a debt collector have a bona fide error defense where its reliance on the creditor's representations is unreasonable as a matter of law, and it otherwise does not maintain procedures reasonably adapted to avoiding the violation at issue?

(2) Under the Fair Debt Collection Practices Act, does a debt collector's service of requests for admission containing false information upon a pro se defendant without an explanation that the requests would be deemed admitted after thirty days constitutes "unfair or unconscionable" or "false, deceptive, or misleading" means to collect a debt?

Continued on next page.

HOLDING AND DECISION: (Thomas, J.)

(1) No. Under the Fair Debt Collection Practices Act (FDCPA), a debt collector does not have a bona fide error defense where its reliance on the creditor's representations is unreasonable as a matter of law, and it otherwise does not maintain procedures reasonably adapted to avoiding the violation at issue. As a threshold matter, JRL (D) is covered by the FDCPA, which covers lawyers who regularly collect debts through litigation. To qualify for the bona fide error defense, the defendant must prove that (1) it violated the FDCPA unintentionally; (2) the violation resulted from a bona fide error; and (3) it maintained procedures reasonably adapted to avoid the violation. Here, JRL's (D) error was caused not by its failure to catch time-barred cases (in fact, it initially spotted the limitations period problem), but by relying without verification on CACV's representation and by overlooking contrary information in its electronic file. The bona fide error defense does not protect a debt collector whose reliance on a creditor's representation is unreasonable, and here, JRL's (D) reliance on CACV's initial representation about McCollough's (P) having made a payment in 2004 was unreasonable as a matter of law, since its contract with the creditor expressly disclaimed the accuracy or validity of data provided by the creditor; JRL's (D) electronic file indicated the true nature of the 2004 credit, which was not a payment by McCollough (P); the electronic file also indicated that McCollough (P) had asserted a statute of limitations defense in 2005 to the same debt; and McCollough (P) had informed JRL (D) that the debt fell outside the limitations period both in his answer to JRL's (D) complaint and in a phone call. Affirmed as to this issue.

(2) Yes. Under the Fair Debt Collection Practices Act (FDCPA), a debt collector's service of requests for admission containing false information upon a pro se defendant without an explanation that the requests would be deemed admitted after thirty days constitutes "unfair or unconscionable" or "false, deceptive, or misleading" means to collect a debt. As a threshold matter, the FDCPA applies to discovery procedures, such as requests for admission, as it applies to the litigation activities of lawyers. Here, considering JRL's (D) conduct from the standpoint of the least sophisticated debtor, the service of requests for admission containing false information upon McCollough (P), effectively asking him to admit facts that were not true, without informing him that failure to respond would be deemed an admission of those false facts, thus conceding JRL's (D) entire case, was "unfair or unconscionable" or "false, deceptive, or misleading." The least sophisticated debtor cannot be expected to anticipate that a response within 30 days was required to prevent the court from deeming the requests admitted. Therefore, summary judgment on this claim was properly granted. Affirmed as to this issue.

ANALYSIS

This case demonstrates that the FDCPA applies to lawyers and law firms that may be considered debt collectors. Thus, where a significant portion of legal work is debt collection, even routine legal work, such as filing a complaint and summons on a debtor, may trigger the FDCPA's requirements. However, if debt collection work is a relatively small part of a lawyer's or law firm's practice, the FDCPA may be found inapplicable. In any event, as this case points out, there is no exception in the FDCPA for litigation—which is why the requests for admission filed by JRL (D) were subject to the Act.

Quicknotes

DECEIT A false statement made either knowingly or with reckless disregard as to its truth and which is intended to induce the plaintiff to act in reliance thereon to his detriment.

PRO SE An individual appearing on his or her own behalf.

STATUTE OF LIMITATIONS A law prescribing the period in which a legal action may be commenced.

United States v. Ashcraft

Federal government (P) v. Convicted criminal owing restitution (D)

732 F.3d 860 (8th Cir. 2013)

NATURE OF CASE: Appeal from district court denial of objection to the garnishment of disability payments.

FACT SUMMARY: Ashcraft (D) was required to pay restitution after pleading guilty to criminal charges. Ashcraft (D) received long-term disability payments from a former employer, which she argued were "earnings" under the Consumer Credit Protection Act (Act). The Act places limitation on the garnishment of earnings.

RULE OF LAW

Long-term disability payments qualify as "earnings" under the Consumer Credit Protection Act (Act), and are therefore, subject to the Act's limitations on garnishment.

FACTS: Joyce Ashcraft (D) pleaded guilty to several criminal charges and was sentenced to a jail term and restitution in 2004. In 2012, Ashcraft (D) was released from custody. Prior to her incarceration, Ashcraft (D) worked for Amana Refrigeration (Amana), which provided her with long-term disability insurance through Principal Life Insurance Company (Principal). While working for Amana, Ashcraft (D) aggravated a medical condition. Because the condition rendered her unable to work, she began receiving disability payments from Principal, which would continue until she reached the age of 65 in 2016. As part of Ashcraft's (D) restitution, the Government (P) sought to garnish her disability payments. The district court ruled that the disability payments were not "earnings" under the Consumer Credit Protection Act (Act) and therefore could be garnished as restitution.

ISSUE: Do long-term disability payments qualify as "earnings" under the Consumer Credit Protection Act (Act), making them subject to the Act's limitations on garnishment?

HOLDING AND DECISION: (Melloy, J.) Yes. Long-term disability payments qualify as earnings under the Consumer Credit Protection Act (Act), and are therefore, subject to the Act's limitations on garnishment. The Act states, in relevant part, that "earnings" are "compensation paid or payable for personal services, whether denominated as wages, salary, commission, bonus or otherwise, and includes periodic payments pursuant to a pension or retirement program." In *Kokoszka v. Belford*, 417 U.S. 642 (1974), the United States Supreme Court determined that income tax refunds did not constitute "earnings" under the Act, because "earnings" do not include "every asset that is traceable in some way to such compensation." Under the plain language of the Act, Ashcraft's (D) disability payments constitute earnings because they are from Ashcraft's (D) former employer and are designed to function as wage substitutes. Accordingly, they are not merely "traceable in some way" to her compensation but instead, are a direct component of Ashcraft's (D) compensation in return for personal services. Reversed.

ANALYSIS

In 2019, the Department of Labor's Wage and Hour Division (WHD) issued an opinion regarding whether employers' contributions to employees' health savings accounts (HSAs) would similarly qualify as "earnings" under the Consumer Credit Protection Act (Act). The WHD determined that if an employer does not permit the employee to receive HSA earnings as cash instead of a contribution directly to their account, then the funds are exempt from the Act's definition of "earnings" and are not subject to its limitations on garnishment.

Quicknotes

GARNISHMENT Satisfaction of a debt by deducting payments directly from the debtor's wages before the wages are paid to the debtor by his or her employer; due process requires that the debtor be first given notice and an opportunity to be heard.

CHAPTER 3

The Bankruptcy Estate and the Automatic Stay

Quick Reference Rules of Law

Prochnow v. Apex Properties, Inc. (d/b/a ReMax)

Realtor (P) v. Real estate broker (D)

467 B.R. 656 (C.D. Ill. 2012)

NATURE OF CASE: Appeal from summary judgment denying motion to reopen a Chapter 7 bankruptcy case.

FACT SUMMARY: Prochnow (P), who had worked as a realtor for Apex Properties Inc., d/b/a Remax Choice of Bloomington, Illinois (ReMax) (D), a real estate broker, contended that commissions paid to ReMax (D) after his Chapter 7 bankruptcy had closed had not been part of the bankruptcy estate, so that he was entitled to payment of those commissions. ReMax (D) contended that the commissions—which Prochnow (P) had not disclosed in bankruptcy—were part of the bankruptcy estate, and that Prochnow (P) was judicially estopped from claiming an interest in the commissions.

RULE OF LAW

(1) Real estate commissions become part of a realtor's Chapter 7 bankruptcy estate where the real estate company/broker earns the commissions prepetition, notwithstanding a contract between the realtor and broker that provides that the realtor earns the commissions only when the transaction closes and the broker collects the commissions.

(2) A debtor is estopped from asserting an interest in property where the debtor has failed to disclose the interest at the time of filing, notwithstanding that the interest was contingent at that time.

FACTS: Prochnow (P) worked as a realtor for Apex Properties Inc., d/b/a Remax Choice of Bloomington, Illinois (ReMax) (D), a real estate broker, until January 2010. The agreement pursuant to which Prochnow (P) earned commissions provided that "No commissions shall be considered earned or payable to [Prochnow] until the transaction has been completed and the commission has been collected by [ReMax]." In August 2009, Prochnow (P) filed for Chapter 7 bankruptcy, and affirmatively represented that he had no contingent claims. Several months after his bankruptcy case was closed in February 2010, Prochnow (P) moved to reopen the case, asserting that he was entitled to payment by ReMax (D) of commissions from transactions that had closed after he had filed for bankruptcy in August 2009. The bankruptcy court granted summary judgment to ReMax (D), finding that Prochnow (P) had earned the commissions prepetition, so that they were part of the bankruptcy estate, and that Prochnow (P) was judicially estopped from claiming an interest in the funds, since he had not revealed them with his petition. Prochnow (P) appealed, and the district court granted review.

ISSUE:

(1) Do real estate commissions become part of a realtor's Chapter 7 bankruptcy estate where the real estate company/broker earns the commissions prepetition, notwithstanding a contract between the realtor and broker that provides that the realtor earns the commissions only when the transaction closes and the broker collects the commissions?

(2) Is a debtor estopped from asserting an interest in property where the debtor has failed to disclose the interest at the time of filing, notwithstanding that the interest was contingent at that time?

HOLDING AND DECISION: (Myerscough, J.)

(1) Yes. Real estate commissions become part of a realtor's Chapter 7 bankruptcy estate where the real estate company/broker earns the commissions prepetition, notwithstanding a contract between the realtor and broker that provides that the realtor earns the commissions only when the transaction closes and the broker collects the commissions. State law determines the nature of a debtor's interest in property at issue, whereas federal bankruptcy law determines whether that interest is included in the bankruptcy estate. Here, under state law, the interest created by the contract between Prochnow (P) and ReMax (D) was a contingent interest. That is because under state law a broker earns a commission when he procures a buyer who is ready, willing, and able to purchase the real estate on the terms prescribed by the seller, and when any contingencies in the contract for sale are met. Here, ReMax (D) earned the commissions at issue prepetition. Thus, Prochnow (P) had a contingent interest in his portion of those commissions when he filed for bankruptcy protection. Under bankruptcy law, a debtor's contingent interest in future income is property of the estate. Here, although Prochnow's (P) interest in the commissions vested postpetition, he had done all he needed to do to receive the commission even though the commission was contingent on the transaction actually being completed. Moreover, the test for determining whether postpetition income is property of the bankruptcy estate depends on whether the income accrues from prepetition or postpetition services. Prochnow (P) did not perform any postpetition services that would require

Continued on next page.

allocating the commission between pre- and postpetition services. Accordingly, the bankruptcy court properly found that Prochnow's (D) portion of the commissions at issue was property of the bankruptcy estate as a matter of law. Affirmed as to this issue.

(2) Yes. A debtor is estopped from asserting an interest in property where the debtor has failed to disclose the interest at the time of filing, notwithstanding that the interest was contingent at that time. Prochnow (P) was required to disclose any assets on his schedule when he filed his bankruptcy petition, regardless of whether the interest in those assets was reduced to judgment, liquidated, unliquidated, fixed, contingent, matured, unmatured, disputed, undisputed, legal, equitable, secured, or unsecured. Because a debtor-in-bankruptcy who denies owning an asset, including a chose in action or other legal claim, cannot realize on that concealed asset after the bankruptcy ends, and because that is what Prochnow (P) is attempting to do here, the bankruptcy court did not abuse its discretion by finding Prochnow (P) was judicially estopped from pursuing the commissions. Affirmed as to this issue.

ANALYSIS

Section 541(a)(1) of the Bankruptcy Code defines "property of the estate" to include "all legal or equitable interests of the debtor in the property as of the commencement of the case." This definition of property of the estate is broad—"including interests of all types and degrees of contingency"—but is generally limited to interests in existence at the time of the commencement of the case. Although § 541(a)(6) expands this basic definition of property of the estate to include certain property interests that are acquired after the commencement of the case, it contains an express exception, exempting "earnings from services performed by an individual debtor after the commencement of the case." Here, Prochnow (P) was not able to take advantage of this exception, since, as the court observes, he did not perform any postpetition services to earn the commissions but had done everything required to earn the commissions prepetition.

Quicknotes

CONTINGENCY INTEREST An interest that is based on the uncertain happening of another event.

POSTPETITION After bankruptcy petition has been filed.

PREPETITION Before bankruptcy petition has been filed.

VESTED INTEREST A present right to property, although the right to the possession of such property may not be enjoyed until a future date.

In re Chambers

[Parties not identified.]

451 B.R. 621 (Bankr. N.D. Ga. 2011)

NATURE OF CASE: Bankruptcy proceeding to determine whether certain funds are property of a Chapter 13 bankruptcy estate.

FACT SUMMARY: Debtor, who was running for public office, but who had not incorporated her campaign, filed for Chapter 13 bankruptcy protection in an attempt to free her campaign funds from garnishment, make them available to her campaign, and shield them from the reach of her personal creditors.

RULE OF LAW

Under § 541(a) of the Bankruptcy Code, campaign contributions made to a candidate for public office who files bankruptcy without incorporating the campaign are property of the bankruptcy estate.

FACTS: At the time Debtor filed for Chapter 13 bankruptcy protection, she was running a campaign for re-election as a state representative. She had not, however, incorporated the campaign. The campaign funds were held in an account at Wachovia Bank. Prior to the bankruptcy filing, one of her private creditors, Miami Circle, had sought to garnish Debtor's accounts at Wachovia, including the campaign account. In response, Wachovia froze the accounts. After the filing, Debtor claimed that the campaign account was frozen in violation of § 362 of the Bankruptcy Code and sought to unfreeze the funds therein.

ISSUE: Under § 541(a) of the Bankruptcy Code, are campaign contributions made to a candidate for public office who files bankruptcy without incorporating the campaign property of the bankruptcy estate?

HOLDING AND DECISION: (Mullins, J.) Yes. Under § 541(a) of the Bankruptcy Code, campaign contributions made to a candidate for public office who files bankruptcy without incorporating the campaign are property of the bankruptcy estate. This is an issue of first impression. The scope of § 541(a) is very broad and includes all property in which a debtor had any interest prepetition. In addition, under § 541(c)(1)(A), which is commonly referred to as the "anti-alienation provision," a debtor's interest in property (other than a spendthrift trust pursuant to § 541(c)(2)) becomes property of the estate notwithstanding any provision in applicable nonbankruptcy law that restricts or conditions transfer of such interest by the debtor. Here, Debtor had an interest in the campaign funds, regardless of how restricted that interest was by state election finance laws. Therefore, those funds are part of the estate. Although state law restricts the use of the campaign funds, the anti-alienation provision prevents the state law from excluding the funds from becoming property of the estate. Moreover, there was no evidence that the funds were subject to a spendthrift trust. There was no evidence that the funds were held in a trust of any kind, and there was no evidence that Debtor had no access to the funds—which would be required to show the existence of a spendthrift trust. In fact, state law permits a candidate unfettered access to campaign funds, but only restricts the types of expenses that may be paid with those funds. Accordingly, the campaign funds are part of the estate.

ANALYSIS

Although the bankruptcy court determined that the campaign funds were part of Debtor's bankruptcy estate, the court emphasized that its holding did not determine priority among creditors to those funds, for example, as between the Debtor's personal creditors and campaign creditors. Also, the court did not address whether campaign funds of an incorporated campaign committee could be included in a bankruptcy estate. Arguably, in that scenario, campaign funds would belong to the incorporated entity, so that the candidate would not have any interest them and would not come within the scope of § 541(a).

Quicknotes

ALIENATION Conveyance or transfer of property.

In re Green

[Parties not identified.]

2011 WL 5902502 (Bankr. E.D.N.C. 2011)

NATURE OF CASE: Motion for sanctions for violations of the automatic stay in a Chapter 7 bankruptcy case.

FACT SUMMARY: Debtor claimed that the university she attended, East Carolina University (ECU), willfully violated the automatic stay that arose from her August 2009 Chapter 7 bankruptcy petition by billing her for prepetition debt after the automatic stay was in effect and after notice of the filing had been received by ECU.

RULE OF LAW

A creditor is liable for willfully violating an automatic stay even though the creditor's billing for prepetition debt, after the automatic stay is in effect and the creditor has notice of the bankruptcy petition, is caused by the creditor's inadvertent bureaucratic procedures.

FACTS: Debtor had been a student at East Carolina University (ECU) in the fall of 2007. Debtor filed for Chapter 7 bankruptcy protection in August 2009. She continued attending ECU until she withdrew in the summer of 2010. One source of Debtor's financial aid in the fall of 2007 was a Federal Perkins Loan in the amount of $750, which was managed by the Office of Student Loans at ECU. Throughout her course of study, Debtor became indebted to ECU for various amounts, including the Federal Perkins Loan. At a 2011 hearing, Debtor presented evidence that ECU billed her four times for the $750 Federal Perkins Loan amount after the automatic stay was in place and ECU had notice of it, and she moved for sanctions for each of these instances. While acknowledging sending the bills, ECU contended that the collection attempts were not willful violations of the automatic stay because they were inadvertently sent to Debtor as a result of bureaucratic mix-ups. ECU also introduced evidence that it had since rectified its internal procedures to ensure that no attempt to collect on a debt would be made when an automatic stay was in place.

ISSUE: Is a creditor liable for willfully violating an automatic stay even though the creditor's billing for prepetition debt, after the automatic stay is in effect and the creditor has notice of the bankruptcy petition, is caused by the creditor's inadvertent bureaucratic procedures?

HOLDING AND DECISION: (Doub, J.) Yes. A creditor is liable for willfully violating an automatic stay even though the creditor's billing for prepetition debt, after the automatic stay is in effect and the creditor has notice of the bankruptcy petition, is caused by the creditor's inadvertent bureaucratic procedures. Section 362(a) of the Bankruptcy Code imposes a stay on "any act to collect, assess, or recover a claim against the debtor that arose before the commencement of a case under" title 11. Section 362(k)(1) also provides that any "individual injured by any willful violation of a stay provided by this section shall recover actual damages . . . and in appropriate circumstances, may recover punitive damages." Willfulness does not refer to the intent to violate the automatic stay, but the intent to commit the act that violates the automatic stay. Because East Carolina University (ECU) caused the letters and invoices to be sent and such actions were a violation of the automatic stay, ECU willfully violated the automatic stay. While it is commendable that ECU has established procedures to avoid such violations going forward, it should have done so long ago, especially given that it is a large university and its collection of tuition, loans, and fees involves millions of dollars. For having failed to do so prior to 2010, the imposition of punitive damages is merited (Debtor proved no actual damages), and ECU is ordered to pay $500 for each violation of the automatic stay, for a total of $2,000. The motion for sanctions is granted.

ANALYSIS

This case illustrates the breadth and power of the automatic stay, and that bankruptcy courts will not hesitate to punish even large institutions for inadvertent violations caused by bureaucratic shortcomings. Here, ECU sent only four demands for payment of nondischargeable debts by mail, and the court sanctioned it $500 for each mailing. There have been other cases where the punitive damages were more severe, as where the creditor repeatedly ignored the existence of the debtor's bankruptcy case and the authority of the court. See, e.g., *In re Chavis,* 213 B.R. 462 (Bankr. E.D.N.C. 1997).

Quicknotes

AUTOMATIC STAY Upon the filing of a bankruptcy petition, creditors are prohibited from extrajudicial collection efforts against the debtor or the debtor's property.

Nissan Motor Acceptance Corp. v. Baker

Creditor (D) v. Debtors (P)

239 B.R. 484 (Bankr. N.D. Tex. 1999)

NATURE OF CASE: Appeal of damages award for violation of bankruptcy stay.

FACT SUMMARY: When the Bakers (P) filed for bankruptcy under Chapter 7, the auto finance company repossessed and sold their pickup truck.

RULE OF LAW

After receiving notice of an automatic bankruptcy stay, a secured creditor is required to turn over the collateral without first receiving adequate protection.

FACTS: The Bakers (P) were behind in their payments to Nissan Motor Acceptance Corp. (Nissan) (D) when they filed a Chapter 7 bankruptcy petition. At that time, they stated they intended to reaffirm their debt to Nissan (D). Nissan (D) repossessed the pickup truck. When Nissan (D) was later informed of the bankruptcy, Nissan (D) sought relief from the automatic stay, and then sold the car. The bankruptcy court did not know the car had been sold and eventually granted Nissan's (D) motion. The Bakers (P) claimed that Nissan (D) had violated the stay by selling their truck, and filed an adversary proceeding for damages for violation of the automatic stay. The bankruptcy court found the sale of the car was a willful violation of the stay and awarded actual and punitive damages, as well as attorney fees. Nissan (D) appealed.

ISSUE: After receiving notice of an automatic bankruptcy stay, is a secured creditor required to turn over the collateral without first receiving adequate protection?

HOLDING AND DECISION: (Kendall, J.) Yes. After receiving notice of an automatic bankruptcy stay, a secured creditor is required to turn over the collateral without first receiving adequate protection. Here Nissan's (D) action in selling the car was a violation of its obligation under § 542(a) of the Bankruptcy Code. The bankruptcy court's award of actual damages, punitive damages, and attorney fees was not clearly erroneous. Affirmed.

ANALYSIS

The automatic stay provision of the Bankruptcy Code serves to preserve the status quo. The bankruptcy court had given Nissan (D) the option of satisfying the damages part of the judgment by delivering a new truck to the Bakers (P). The court held that creditors could not engage in self-help to retain property as adequate protection.

Quicknotes

ACTUAL DAMAGES Measure of damages necessary to compensate victim for actual injuries suffered.

AUTOMATIC STAY Upon the filing of a bankruptcy petition, creditors are prohibited from extrajudicial collection efforts against the debtor or the debtor's property.

CHAPTER 7 BANKRUPTCY A legal proceeding whereby a debtor, who is unable to pay his or her debts as they become due, is relieved of the obligation to pay creditors by liquidation and distribution of remaining assets.

COLLATERAL Property that secures the payment of a debt.

PUNITIVE DAMAGES Damages exceeding the actual injury suffered for the purposes of punishment, deterrence, and comfort to plaintiff.

CHAPTER 4

Property Exempt from Seizure

Quick Reference Rules of Law

In re Wilkinson, [M.D.]

[Parties not identified.]

402 B.R. 756 (Bankr. W.D. Tex. 2009)

NATURE OF CASE: Objection to claimed exemption in property in Chapter 7 bankruptcy action.

FACT SUMMARY: Debtors claimed an exemption in certain antique firearms, claiming they should be considered exempted home furnishings. The Chapter 7 trustee (Trustee) objected, asserting the old firearms should not be considered anything other than firearms, only two of which were exempted under state law.

RULE OF LAW

Where a state's property law expressly exempts a specified number of "firearms" from inclusion in the bankruptcy estate, but does not define "firearm," more than the specified number of firearms may not be exempted as home furnishings merely because they are antique firearms.

FACTS: As part of their Chapter 7 bankruptcy, Debtors claimed several antique firearms—all predating 1870—as exemptions, using the state's property law exemptions. The bankruptcy trustee (Trustee) objected, asserting that under state property law Debtors were allowed to exempt only two firearms. However, state property law did not define "firearm." Debtors argued that, due to the age of the guns, they were no longer considered firearms under state law and should be considered home furnishings/heirlooms, which were also exempted under state property law, as each was mounted in Debtor's home on a wood plaque bearing a brass plate that described the weapon. In urging this characterization, the Debtors relied by analogy on the state's penal law, which excluded from the definition of "firearm" firearms manufactured before 1899. The provision of the penal code on which Debtors relied criminalized the possession of "firearms" by felons, so that it would not be a crime for a felon to possess any of the firearms in Debtors' home.

ISSUE: Where a state's property law expressly exempts a specified number of "firearms" from inclusion in the bankruptcy estate, but does not define "firearm," may more than the specified number of firearms be exempted as home furnishings merely because they are antique firearms?

HOLDING AND DECISION: (Clark, J.) No. Where a state's property law expressly exempts a specified number of "firearms" from inclusion in the bankruptcy estate, but does not define "firearm," more than the specified number of firearms may not be exempted as home furnishings merely because they are antique firearms. First, it is inappropriate to look at the state's penal code for a definition of "firearm" in the state's property code since the purpose of the provisions in which that term appears have different purposes. The purpose of the property code provision is to enable citizens to keep certain listed property from the reach of creditors. The penal code provision's purpose is to protect the peace and safety of the state's citizens. Thus, whether a convicted felon may carry an antique firearm does not have much to do at all with whether a creditor may reach that same antique gun for purposes of getting repaid, and it is certainly not a threat to public safety for a debtor to repay his debts by the sale of an antique gun. Thus, the court must look to other sources for the definition of "firearm." The dictionary meaning of the term is a weapon that expels a projectile by the combustion of gunpowder or other explosive. The antique firearms owned by Debtors fit this definition. Also, in ordinary usage, the fact that a firearm or gun is antique would not preclude one from referring to it as a firearm. Even if the term were believed to be ambiguous, the legislative history shows that Debtor's firearms were intended to come within the scope of the state's property code, which, starting in 1870, exempted one "gun" from creditors' reach. At that time, when the state was still a frontier and was being settled by force of arms, it seems that this public policy was in place to provide citizens with the ability to defend their home and provide for their family, and perhaps to be able, regardless their financial circumstances, to answer the call to arms should the militia be called up. The language in the statute changed in 1973 to cover two firearms. While the state was no longer a frontier, it seems that this change was a nod to "[t]he typical hunter serious about his or her sport [since he or she] will have a shotgun for birds and a rifle for other game—two guns." The upshot of this is that exemptions are an explicit, approved list of items that the legislature, for reasons of public policy, has decided debtors should be allowed to keep regardless of what they owe their creditors. Because there is no public policy served in preserving the lifestyles of the rich and bankrupt, Debtors may exempt only two firearms, and no more. The Trustee's objection is sustained.

ANALYSIS

As this decision illustrates, the public policy reasons for exempting specific types of property may change with time. The fundamental reasons for exempting property so it cannot be reached by creditors, however, remain fairly constant over time, including the belief that all persons are

Continued on next page.

entitled to retain some property, no matter how much they might owe to their creditors. Some exemptions are preserved primarily because they truly are necessary to the very survival of the family as an independent economic unit not on the public dole. Others are allowed not so much to assure mere survival as to assure survival with a modicum of dignity. Thus, the purpose underlying exemption legislation is securing to debtors the means to support themselves and their families, with the protection of the family being the main consideration.

Quicknotes

CHAPTER 7 BANKRUPTCY A legal proceeding whereby a debtor, who is unable to pay his or her debts as they become due, is relieved of the obligation to pay creditors by liquidation and distribution of remaining assets.

CLAIM OF EXEMPTION Privilege granted to judgment debtor allowing debtor to hold property of a certain class or to a certain amount free from levy or sale on execution or attachment.

In re King

Trustee (P) v. Debtor (D)

508 B.R. 71 (Bankr. N.D. Ind. 2014)

NATURE OF CASE: Determination from bankruptcy court regarding whether a debtor's earned income tax credit is an exempt asset of the bankruptcy estate.

FACT SUMMARY: King (D) filed for Chapter 7 bankruptcy, and the bankruptcy Trustee filed an objection to King's (D) attempted exemption of her earned income tax credit.

RULE OF LAW

A debtor in a Chapter 7 bankruptcy proceeding may still receive an exemption on an earned income tax credit, even if the credit passes through a tax preparer's account prior to disbursement to the debtor, the funds are called something other than an earned income credit upon disbursement, or the funds are commingled.

FACTS: Margaret Naomi King (D) filed for Chapter 7 bankruptcy in Indiana. Three months after filing, the Trustee for the Chapter 7 estate filed an objection to King's (D) exemptions. Specifically, the Trustee argued that King (D) could not exempt $3,138.63 as earned income credit, because (1) the refund was initially deposited into an account owned by H&R Block, a tax preparation service, before it was distributed to King (D); (2) King (D) received the funds as a "Refund Anticipation Check," their nature was changed and they were no longer an exempt earned income credit; and (3) King (D) commingled the earned income credit with other funds.

ISSUE: May a debtor in a Chapter 7 bankruptcy proceeding still receive an exemption on an earned income tax credit, even if the credit passes through a tax preparer's account prior to disbursement to the debtor, the funds are called something other than an "earned income tax credit" upon disbursement, or the funds are commingled?

HOLDING AND DECISION: (Klingberger, J.) Yes. A debtor in a Chapter 7 bankruptcy proceeding may still receive an exemption on an earned income tax credit, even if the credit passes through a tax preparer's account prior to disbursement to the debtor, the funds are called something other than an "earned income credit" upon disbursement, or the funds are commingled. Indiana Code (I.C.) § 34-55-10-2(c)(11) states that a debtor's interest in a refund or a credit received or to be received under the federal or Indiana state earned income tax credit is exempt property of the bankruptcy estate. The Trustee's argument that the funds were changed into something other than a tax refund when they were initially deposited into H&R Block's account prior to disbursement to the debtor is without merit. The funds remained easily traceable, and the initial transfer into H&R Block's account was for King's (D) benefit. Similarly, even though King (D) entered into an agreement with H&R Block to receive the funds as a "Refund Anticipation Check," the disclosures concerning the transaction and the Stipulation did not change it into something other than a tax refund. Finally, two prior Indiana bankruptcy decisions found that commingling of an earned income credit with other funds does not affect the debtor's ability to claim the statutory earned income credit exemption. Accordingly, the earned income credit portion of King's tax refund is an exempt asset of the bankruptcy estate.

ANALYSIS

Bankruptcy exemptions, such as the one discussed in *In re King*, often lead to "exemption planning" prior to filing bankruptcy in order to protect certain assets and prioritize certain creditors. However, exemption planning can be risky: if the bankruptcy judge views a debtor's actions as manipulation of assets rather than exemption planning, the judge may end up denying the debtor's discharge. Riskier exemption planning strategies may include taking out a loan to acquire exempt property or transferring nonexempt property to other individuals.

Quicknotes

BANKRUPTCY A legal proceeding whereby a debtor, who is unable to pay his or her debts as they become due, is relieved of the obligation to pay creditors either by liquidation and distribution of remaining assets or reorganization and payment from future income.

BANKRUPTCY ESTATE Created by the filing of a petition in bankruptcy and includes all legal and equitable interests of the debtor in property as of that time.

BANKRUPTCY TRUSTEE Individual charged with the administration of the bankruptcy estate.

CHAPTER 5

Property Exemptions II

Quick Reference Rules of Law

In re Reed

Trustee (P) v. Debtor (D)

12 B.R. 41 (Bankr. N.D. Tex. 1981)

NATURE OF CASE: Action to challenge exemptions in bankruptcy.

FACT SUMMARY: Reed (D) sold nonexempt property to close acquaintances and applied the proceeds to liens on exempt property, prompting the trustee to sue to set aside the exemptions to preclude fraudulent transfers.

RULE OF LAW

Nonexempt property may be converted into exempt real property prior to bankruptcy.

FACTS: Just prior to filing bankruptcy, Reed (D) sold items of personal property to friends at far below their value. He applied the proceeds to a lien on his home, thus converting the value of nonexempt property into exempt property. The trustee (P) sued to preclude the conversion as fraudulent.

ISSUE: May the value of nonexempt property be converted into exempt property prior to bankruptcy?

HOLDING AND DECISION: (Brister, J.) Yes. The value of nonexempt property may be converted into exempt real property prior to bankruptcy. Had the conversion been to exempt personal property, it could have been set aside. However, the legislature did not include the exemption as applied to real property in its prohibition of conversion to frustrate creditors. Therefore, the transactions were valid.

ANALYSIS

This case illustrates that some transactions, even if facially fraudulent, may survive debt collection techniques. The case turns upon the perceived sanctity of the homestead and the court's reluctance to establish precedent, which would open the door to jeopardizing the exemption.

Quicknotes

LIEN A claim against the property of another in order to secure the payment of a debt.

In re Reed

Creditor bank (P) v. Debtor (D)

700 F.2d 986 (5th Cir. 1983)

NATURE OF CASE: Appeal from denial of discharge under § 727 of the Bankruptcy Code.

FACT SUMMARY: In Texas Bank's (P) action against Reed (D) for denial of discharge under § 727 of the Bankruptcy Code, Texas Bank (P) alleged that Reed (D) effected transfer designed to convert nonexempt property into exempt property less than two weeks before bankruptcy with the intent to hinder, delay, and defraud creditors.

RULE OF LAW

A debtor may be denied discharge under the Bankruptcy Code if he has transferred property with intent to hinder, delay, or defraud a creditor or has failed to explain satisfactorily any loss of assets.

FACTS: Reed (D) opened a men's wear shop, financing this venture in part by obtaining a loan from Texas Bank (P), which was guaranteed by the Small Business Administration (SBA). After a year, Reed (D) knew that his business was insolvent and met with Texas Bank (P), the SBA, and his major trade creditors. Reed (D) signed an agreement to turn over management of the store to a consulting firm, and the creditors agreed to postpone collection efforts if Reed (D) promised to resume payment on his debts. Reed's (D) business continued to fail, Reed (D) signed a foreclosure agreement surrendering the store to Texas Bank (P), and Reed (D) then filed voluntary petitions for bankruptcy. Just before filing for bankruptcy, Reed (D) sold $19,586.83 in personal assets and applied the proceeds to reduce the mortgages on his family residence, which was exempt from creditor's claims under Texas law. In Texas Bank's (P) action against Reed (D), Texas Bank (P) alleged that Reed (D) had affected the transfer of assets in order to convert nonexempt property to exempt property less than two weeks before filing for bankruptcy with the intent to hinder, delay, and defraud creditors. The bankruptcy judge agreed with Texas Bank's (P) allegations and denied Reed (D) discharge under 11 U.S.C. § 727(a)(5). Reed (D) appealed.

ISSUE: May a debtor be denied discharge under the Bankruptcy Code if he has transferred property with intent to hinder, delay, or defraud a creditor or failed to explain satisfactorily any loss of assets?

HOLDING AND DECISION: (Rubin, J.) Yes. A debtor may be denied discharge under the Bankruptcy Code if he has transferred property with intent to hinder, delay, or defraud a creditor or he has failed to explain satisfactorily any loss of assets. Here, the evidence amply supports the bankruptcy court's findings that Reed (D) had actual intent to defraud. Reed's (D) whole pattern of conduct evinces that intent. His rapid conversion of nonexempt assets to extinguish one home mortgage and to reduce another four months before bankruptcy, after arranging with his creditors to be free of payment obligations until the following year, speaks for itself as a transfer of property in fraud of creditors. Asked to account for the disappearance of $19,586.83, Reed (D) could only respond that he had many business and household expenses, which he paid in cash as they arose. The bankruptcy judge's finding that his did not constitute a satisfactory explanation cannot be faulted. Affirmed.

ANALYSIS

A debtor is not entitled to a discharge as a matter of right, but discharge will be granted unless challenged by the trustee or a creditor. The trustee or creditors may object to the debtor's discharge of particular debts under § 523 of the Bankruptcy Code. A § 523 denial of discharge renders only one debt nondischargeable, while under § 727 of the Code, denial of discharge renders all the debtor's debts nondischargeable.

Quicknotes

DISCHARGE OF DEBTS In bankruptcy, the release of a debtor who is unable to pay his or her debts as they become due from the obligation to pay his or her creditors.

CHAPTER 6

Claims and Distributions

Quick Reference Rules of Law

In re Lanza

Debtor (P) v. Creditor bank (D)

51 B.R. 125 (Bankr. E.D. Pa. 1985)

NATURE OF CASE: Debtor's objection to creditor's proofs of claim.

FACT SUMMARY: Debtor Lanza (P) objected to proofs of claim filed by a bank that had loaned the Lanzas (D) at least $300,000; neither party kept substantial records of the loan.

RULE OF LAW

The party objecting to a proof of claim, which is prima facie evidence of its validity and amount, bears the burden of going forward with proof of the claim's invalidity.

FACTS: When the Lanzas (P), husband and wife, filed for bankruptcy, a bank that had made three loans to them filed proofs of claim. They first claimed an initial debt of $200,000, but after $300,000 was actually advanced to the Lanzas (P) by the bank for home improvement, the loan was restructured for an amount of either $300,000 or $350,000. The second and third claimed debts were, respectively, of $40,282 and $27,689. Mr. Lanza (P) died during bankruptcy, and his widow (P) objected to the first claim. However, neither the bank nor Mrs. Lanza (P) (who professed ignorance of all her husband's financial dealings) had any evidence of the claim. The bankruptcy court held an evidentiary hearing on the validity of the claim.

ISSUE: Does the party objecting to a creditor's proof of claim, which constitutes prima facie evidence of its validity and amount, bear the burden of going forward with proof of the claim's invalidity?

HOLDING AND DECISION: (Goldhaber, J.) Yes. The party objecting to a proof of claim, which is prima facie evidence of its validity and amount, bears the burden of going forward with proof of the claim's invalidity. A creditor's proof of claim executed and filed in accordance with Bankruptcy Rule § 3001(f) constitutes prima facie evidence of the validity and amount of the claim. The burden of going forward with proof is on the objecting party, not the claimant. This burden is not met by merely filing the objection. Here, Lanza (P) was left with no financial records to disprove the bank's claim. She was not entitled to assert that the bank's own management and lack of supporting documentation for the loan alone invalidated its claim. Therefore, the claim must be upheld.

ANALYSIS

Most claims that are presented for payment are paid without question, pro rata, by the trustee. This represents ratification of the creditor's claims without the formal mechanism of adjudication. It is rare that a trustee will object to a claim and conduct an evidentiary hearing on the validity of the claim, and even rarer, as here, for a debtor to object to a claim.

Quicknotes

EVIDENTIARY HEARING Hearing pertaining to the evidence of the case.

PRIMA FACIE EVIDENCE Evidence presented by a party that is sufficient, in the absence of contradictory evidence, to support the fact or issue for which it is offered.

PRO RATA In proportion.

Jones v. Wells Fargo Bank, N.A. (In re Jones)

Mortgagor/debtor (P) v. Mortgagee/creditor (D)

366 B.R. 584 (Bankr. E.D. La. 2007)

NATURE OF CASE: Adversary proceeding in Chapter 13 bankruptcy action to recover property of the estate.

FACT SUMMARY: Jones (Debtor) (P), a mortgagor who filed for Chapter 13 bankruptcy protection, and who owed Wells Fargo Bank, N.A. (Wells Fargo) (D) prepetition arrearages, contended that Wells Fargo (D) had inappropriately, and without disclosure, applied payments he made on his mortgage to prepetition charges and fees, rather than applying them to the postpetition installments for which they were intended, which without justification greatly increased the interest and amount he owed at the time he sought to refinance the mortgage and pay Wells Fargo (D) off. [The complete facts are not presented in the casebook extract.]

RULE OF LAW

Where a creditor assesses postpetition charges and fees without disclosure and then diverts estate funds to their satisfaction without court approval, the creditor will be required to return the amounts improperly assessed, plus interest.

FACTS: Jones (Debtor) (P) had a mortgage with Wells Fargo Bank, N.A. (Wells Fargo) (D). The debt was evidenced by an adjustable-rate note dated in April 2001. Debtor (P) filed for Chapter 13 bankruptcy relief in August 2003. At that time, Wells Fargo (D) filed a proof of claim that totaled $22,259.69. The plan of reorganization required Debtor (P) to pay the Chapter 13 trustee (Trustee) a monthly amount from which Wells Fargo (D) would be paid the arrearages as well as monthly mortgage payments. A few years later, Debtor (P) sought to refinance the mortgage and pay off the Wells Fargo (D) loan. The closing for the refinance was set for January 4, 2006. Debtor (P) believed that the payoff amount he received from Wells Fargo (D) as of that date was excessively high, and he brought an adversary proceeding challenging that amount. Debtor (D) asserted that he was overcharged interest of around $13,000 over the life of the plan because Wells Fargo (D) had charged his account for postpetition charges and fees, and had inappropriately applied his payments to prepetition installments, prepetition costs or fees, and postpetition charges not authorized or disclosed to Debtor (P), the Court, or the Trustee, instead of applying those payments to the postpetition installments for which they were intended. The bankruptcy court conducted an accounting of the amounts Debtor (P) actually owed to Wells Fargo (D) as of the date of the refinancing's closing. [The complete facts are not presented in the casebook extract.]

ISSUE: Where a creditor assesses postpetition charges and fees without disclosure and then diverts estate funds to their satisfaction without court approval, will the creditor be required to return the amounts improperly assessed, plus interest?

HOLDING AND DECISION: (Magner, J.) Yes. Where a creditor assesses postpetition charges and fees without disclosure and then diverts estate funds to their satisfaction without court approval, the creditor will be required to return the amounts improperly assessed, plus interest. First, in reviewing the amount of debt owed by Debtor (P), it appears that Wells Fargo (D) charged less than the contractual floor rate of interest under the note. However, Wells Fargo (D) agreed to waive any claim for additional interest as a result of this error. It also appears that Wells Fargo (D) made errors in calculating Debtor's (P) prepetition debt, such as incorrectly accounting for foreclosure costs and amounts owed for escrow. Once these errors are corrected, as of January 4, 2006, Wells Fargo (D) was owed a prepetition past due balance of $2,251.21. When Wells Fargo (D) learned of the refinancing and a payoff quote was requested, it added additional sheriff's commissions to its debt based on the amounts it anticipated receiving, but it did so without amending its proof of claim or notifying the Trustee or Court. Wells Fargo (D), however, failed to inform the sheriff that the refinancing was part of a bankruptcy; if it had so informed the sheriff, the sheriff's commissions would have been waived. Further, as to postpetition debt, it appears that Wells Fargo's (D) actions caused Debtor (P) to pay almost $13,000 in additional interest charges over the life of the plan. Starting on August 26, 2003, Debtor's (P) loan was current. From that date forward, his past due account was "zeroed out" because the arrearage was payable through the plan. Therefore, his postpetition balance consisted of only principal, or $213,949.06, and Debtor's (P) next installment was due for September 1, 2003. Unfortunately, he suffered a heart attack in November 2003, and he fell behind in his direct payments to Wells Fargo (D). These payments were aggregated into a consent order agreement, once again bringing his account current by agreement. Thereafter, though Debtor (P) made his payments in the amounts directed by Wells Fargo (D), rather than apply the amounts received to the postpetition installments for which they were intended, Wells Fargo (D) applied them to prepetition installments, prepetition costs or fees, and postpetition charges not authorized or disclosed to Debtor (P), the Court, or the Trustee. The result was the addition of significant interest charges not really due and a loan balance out of

Continued on next page.

sync with the actual amounts owed. Although postpetition charges incurred prior to confirmation may be included in the debts necessary to cure a default under a plan, they must be disclosed and are subject to review by the court for reasonableness. Here, Wells Fargo (D) failed to disclose these charges as required. Instead, in violation of the automatic stay, Wells Fargo (D) paid itself out of estate funds delivered to it for the payment of other debt, without notification or approval, with the result that Wells Fargo (D) was improperly assessing postpetition charges and diverting estate funds for their satisfaction. Consequently, the payoff amount of $231,463.97 that Wells Fargo (D) collected at closing must be reduced to $207,013.32. Because Wells Fargo (D) refunded $7,598.64 of the difference, Wells Fargo (D) is ordered to return $16,852.01 plus interest. Debtor's (P) request for damages incurred as a loss of personal time are denied because he did not prove at trial that he suffered any monetary loss as a result of the nights and weekends he spent working on this matter, since he presented no evidence that he missed work or incurred a loss of income due to the time he spent. Judgment for Debtor (P).

ANALYSIS

Because Wells Fargo (D) collected both pre- and postpetition charges from property of the estate without authorization and in contravention of several court orders including, but not limited to, the automatic stay and the order confirming Debtor's (P) plan of reorganization, as well because it delayed returning Debtor's (P) property for over one year, failed to provide a reasonable accounting of the loan history from which the correct amounts due could have been ascertained, and improperly applied payments from the Trustee and Debtor (P) resulting in significant additional and unwarranted interest charges, the court held a separate hearing to consider sanctions for these violations. After the hearing, in lieu of granting punitive sanctions, the court ordered Wells Fargo (D) to revise its accounting procedures, under court monitoring and review.

Quicknotes

AUTOMATIC STAY Upon the filing of a bankruptcy petition, creditors are prohibited from extrajudicial collection efforts against the debtor or the debtor's property.

Jones v. Wells Fargo Bank, N.A. (In re Jones) (*cont'd*)

Mortgagor/debtor (P) v. Mortgagee/creditor (D)

366 B.R. 584 (Bankr. E.D. La. 2007)

NATURE OF CASE: Adversary proceeding in bankruptcy action challenging, inter alia, creditor's assessment of postpetition fees and charges. [The complete nature of the case is not presented in the casebook extract.]

FACT SUMMARY: Jones (Debtor) (P), a mortgagor in bankruptcy, challenged as unreasonable various postpetition, post confirmation fees and charges made by Wells Fargo Bank, N.A. (Wells Fargo) (D), the mortgagee, where Wells Fargo (D) could not produce evidence that explained why the fees and charges were made or otherwise supported the fees and charges.

RULE OF LAW

A creditor's postpetition, post confirmation assessment of fees and charges will not be upheld as reasonable where the creditor cannot adduce evidence as to why the fees and charges were imposed, or that otherwise supports the fees and charges.

FACTS: As part of a bankruptcy adversary proceeding, Jones (Debtor) (D), a mortgagor in bankruptcy, challenged as unreasonable various postpetition, post confirmation fees and charges made by Wells Fargo Bank, N.A. (Wells Fargo) (D) as mortgagee. These were itemized as (1) attorney's fees, (2) statutory expenses, and (3) inspection charges. Under the terms of the Wells Fargo (D) note and mortgage, Wells Fargo (D) was entitled to charge Debtor's (P) account for attorney's fees and inspection charges incurred in connection with the loan. These documents also required that the assessments be reasonable. At trial, Wells Fargo (D) offered no evidence as to the nature of the attorney's fees imposed post confirmation or their reasonableness. It neglected to produce invoices identifying the counsel who performed the services or any description regarding the services performed, time spent, or amounts charged. Wells Fargo (D) also offered no explanation or evidence to support its "statutory charge." Finally, Wells Fargo (D) ordered 16 inspections against Debtor's (P) property during the 29 months the case was pending, but it could not explain why so many inspections were conducted, especially since the evidence showed that the property remained in good condition. Wells Fargo's (D) representative could not list a single reason why an inspection would have been ordered postpetition, nor could she detail any reason why continuous monthly monitoring of the property was necessary or reasonable. [The complete facts of the case are not presented in the casebook extract.]

ISSUE: Will a creditor's postpetition, post confirmation assessment of fees and charges be upheld as reasonable where the creditor cannot adduce evidence as to why the fees and charges were imposed, or that otherwise supports the fees and charges?

HOLDING AND DECISION: (Magner, J.) No. A creditor's postpetition, post confirmation assessment of fees and charges will not be upheld as reasonable where the creditor cannot adduce evidence as to why the fees and charges were imposed, or that otherwise supports the fees and charges. A creditor's right to impose postpetition, post confirmation charges is a matter of state law and the contracts between the parties. Here, those contracts gave Wells Fargo (D) the right to impose the fees and charges, but also required that they be reasonable. Additionally, state law requires that such fees and charges be reasonable. Because the creditor bears the burden of establishing its debt, Wells Fargo (D) bears the burden of proving that its charges and fees were reasonable. Here, the court cannot determine whether the attorneys' fees were reasonable because Wells Fargo (D) presented no evidence as to what services were performed, much less, why they were necessary. Wells Fargo (D) simply failed to meet its burden of proof on this issue. Therefore, these attorney's fees are denied. Similarly, because Wells Fargo (D) offered no explanation or evidence to support its "statutory charge," it is also disallowed. As to the inspection charges, because Wells Fargo (D) appears to have had no policy guidelines regarding the taking of inspections, and its representative could offer nothing approximating a justification for them, it failed to meet its burden as to the inspection charges, which are also denied. Judgment for Debtor (P).

ANALYSIS

Postpetition charges incurred prior to confirmation may be included in the debts necessary to cure a default under a plan. Therefore, they must be disclosed and are subject to review by the bankruptcy court for reasonableness. Such fees and charges must be approved by the court as reasonable under § 506(b) of the Bankruptcy Code. However, fees and charges incurred post confirmation are not governed by § 506(b), which applies only from the date of filing through the confirmation date. Thus, as this decision demonstrates, the reasonableness of the fees and charges must be determined under state law and the contracts between the parties.

In re Stewart

[Parties not identified.]

391 B.R. 327 (Bankr. E.D. La. 2008)

NATURE OF CASE: Objection in bankruptcy action challenging creditor's assessment of various charges, costs, and fees. [The complete nature of the case is not presented in the casebook extract.]

FACT SUMMARY: Debtor, a mortgagor, objected to numerous substantial charges, costs, and fees assessed by Wells Fargo, the mortgagee, but Wells Fargo was unable to reconcile its prior proofs of claim with the amounts claimed on its account history, as it was unable to explain or substantiate most of the items assessed on the Debtor's account. [The complete facts are not presented in the casebook extract.]

RULE OF LAW

Where a creditor is unable to reconcile its proof of claims filed in a bankruptcy action with fees, costs, and charges the creditor has assessed against the debtor's account as a result of the creditor's negligence and failure to remedy known problems with its accounting methodologies, the creditor may be ordered to audit every proof of claim it has filed in the district in any case pending on or filed after the date the accounting problems were known to exist, and to provide a complete loan history on every account.

FACTS: Debtor, a mortgagor, objected to numerous charges, costs, and fees assessed by Wells Fargo, the mortgagee. Due to Wells Fargo's delays—and the unavailability of readily available documents supporting the assessments—it took four months to reconcile Debtor's account. Wells Fargo charged nine broker price opinions (BPOs) to Debtor's account but could only produce two corresponding reports. At least three sets of BPOs were duplicative of each other, and two BPOs were never performed due to Hurricane Katrina. All contained hidden fees for Wells Fargo disguised as costs. Only two BPOs were ultimately accepted as validly performed. Wells Fargo charged Debtor with 44 inspections, only one of which was allowed. Wells Fargo also charged 49 late charges, only ten of which were approved. Almost every disallowed inspection and late fee was imposed while Debtor was making regular monthly payments and was assessed under circumstances contrary to Wells Fargo's stated policies or the note's terms. Substantial legal fees were also claimed without over $1,800.00 in credits being posted. Further, the calculation of Debtor's monthly escrow was almost incomprehensible and virtually incorrect in every instance. Proofs of claim filed by Wells Fargo were so significantly erroneous that reconciliation was not possible, as charges for nonsufficient funds (NSF) fees, tax searches, property preservation fees, and unapproved bankruptcy fees were unexplained and unsubstantiated. Further, these charges never appeared as entries on the account history. [The complete facts are not presented in the casebook extract.]

ISSUE: Where a creditor is unable to reconcile its proof of claims filed in a bankruptcy action with fees, costs, and charges the creditor has assessed against the debtor's account as a result of the creditor's negligence and failure to remedy known problems with its accounting methodologies, may the creditor be ordered to audit every proof of claim it has filed in the district in any case pending on or filed after the date the accounting problems were known to exist, and to provide a complete loan history on every account?

HOLDING AND DECISION: (Magner, J.) Yes. Where a creditor is unable to reconcile its proof of claims filed in a bankruptcy action with fees, costs, and charges the creditor has assessed against the debtor's account as a result of the creditor's negligence and failure to remedy known problems with its accounting methodologies, the creditor may be ordered to audit every proof of claim it has filed in the district in any case pending on or filed after the date the accounting problems were known to exist, and to provide a complete loan history on every account. Although Wells Fargo was specifically asked to reconcile the amounts reflected on its prior proofs of claim with the amounts claimed on its account history, it did not. A review by the court revealed why: the proofs of claim filed in the Debtor's bankruptcies were so significantly erroneous that reconciliation was not possible. Wells Fargo was negligent in its practices and took insufficient remedial action following this court's rulings in *Jones v. Wells Fargo*, 366 B.R. 584 (Bankr. E.D. La. 2007), to remedy problems with its accounting. Accordingly, Wells Fargo is ordered to audit every proof of claim it has filed in this district in any case pending on or filed after April 13, 2007, and to provide a complete loan history on every account. For every debtor with a case still pending in the district, the loan histories shall be filed into the claims register and Wells Fargo is ordered to amend, where necessary, the proofs of claim already on file to comply with the principles established in this case and *Jones*. For closed cases, Wells Fargo is ordered to deliver to Debtor, Debtor's counsel, and Trustee a copy of the accounting. The court reserves the right, if warranted after an initial review of the

Continued on next page.

accountings, proofs of claim and any amended claims filed of record, to appoint experts, at Wells Fargo's expense, to review each accounting and submit recommendations to the court for further adjustments. Judgment for Debtor. [The complete holding and decision are not presented in the casebook extract.]

ANALYSIS

Wells Fargo appealed the relief crafted in this decision by Judge Magner, and, in *Wells Fargo Bank, N.A. v. Stewart (In re Stewart),* 647 F.3d 553 (5th Cir. 2011), the Fifth Circuit invalidated the relief as outside the Bankruptcy Court's jurisdiction, explaining that the relief ranged far beyond the dimensions of the particular case to police a range of cases untested by the adversary process. The court noted that the specific commands were not for the benefit of Debtor, whose injuries were fully remedied without the injunction (through various sanctions and other remedies) but was aimed at other cases in which Wells Fargo had appeared or might appear before the bankruptcy courts. While the court of appeals found that justification for Judge Magner's frustration was plentiful, it concluded that the relief lacked jurisdictional legs. Because the *Jones* case was also on appeal, the similar relief ordered in that case was also vacated. On remand in *Jones,* Judge Magner reconsidered monetary sanctions, as ordered by the court of appeals, and awarded over $3 million in punitive damages against Wells Fargo.

Quicknotes

ESCROW A written contract held by a third party until the conditions therein are satisfied, at which time it is delivered to the obligee.

PROOF OF CLAIM Statement by a creditor under oath, stating the amount of and basis for a claim.

Jones v. Wells Fargo Home Mtg. Inc. (In re Jones)

Mortgagor/debtor (P) v. Mortgagee/creditor (D)

2012 WL 1155715 (Bankr. E.D. La., 2012)

NATURE OF CASE: On remand, reconsideration of sanctions in adversary proceeding in bankruptcy action.

FACT SUMMARY: On remand, the bankruptcy court was directed to consider monetary damages where Wells Fargo Home Mtg. Inc. (Wells Fargo) (D), mortgagee/creditor had violated the automatic stay, overcharged Jones (P), the mortgagor/debtor, by over $24,000, committed numerous accounting errors, engaged in evasive and delaying tactics, denied culpability or liability, refused to voluntarily correct its errors and accounting methodologies, and otherwise engaged in reprehensible conduct.

RULE OF LAW

Where a creditor's conduct towards a bankruptcy debtor and the bankruptcy court has been highly reprehensible, the court may award punitive damages designed to deter such conduct in the future.

FACTS: In a prior decision, related to the bankruptcy of Jones (P), a mortgagor/debtor, the bankruptcy court had ordered Wells Fargo Home Mtg. Inc. (Wells Fargo) (D), a mortgagee/creditor, to adopt certain accounting procedures for all cases in which Wells Fargo (D) was a party in the district, both retroactively and prospectively. The court of appeals held that the application of those accounting procedures to all debtors in the district would be an improper exercise of authority beyond the bounds of the *Jones* case. Because the bankruptcy court had ordered the accounting procedures relief in lieu of punitive sanctions, the mandate on remand directed that the bankruptcy court consider monetary relief. The bankruptcy court noted that Wells Fargo (D) had, inter alia, overcharged Jones (P) by over $24,000, committed numerous accounting errors, engaged in evasive and delaying tactics, denied culpability or liability, and refused to voluntarily correct its errors and accounting methodologies. In fact, Wells Fargo's (D) initial legal position denied any responsibility to refund payments demanded in error. The cost to Jones (P) was hundreds of thousands of dollars in legal fees and five years of litigation.

ISSUE: Where a creditor's conduct towards a bankruptcy debtor and the bankruptcy court has been highly reprehensible, may the court award punitive damages designed to deter such conduct in the future?

HOLDING AND DECISION: (Magner, J.) Yes. Where a creditor's conduct towards a bankruptcy debtor and the bankruptcy court has been highly reprehensible, the court may award punitive damages designed to deter such conduct in the future. Wells Fargo (D) has taken the position that every debtor in the district should be made to challenge, by separate suit, the proofs of claim or motions for relief from the automatic stay it files. It has steadfastly refused to audit its pleadings or proofs of claim for errors and has refused to voluntarily correct any errors that come to light except through threat of litigation. Moreover, Wells Fargo's (D) conduct is clandestine, as it refuses to provide debtors with a complete history of their debts on an ongoing basis, and completely stops communicating with them when it deems them in default. Thus, debtors can discover unwarranted charges and fees in their accounts only through extensive litigation discovery. However, the great majority of Wells Fargo (D) debtors in bankruptcy court do not have the resources to demand the production of a simple accounting for their loans, much less verify its accuracy, through a litigation process—which, with Wells Fargo (D), takes several months and several court hearings. Thus, not only has Wells Fargo (D) taken advantage of its borrowers and violated its contractual obligations to them, more disturbingly it refuses to correct its errors or voluntarily relinquish gains obtained through improper accounting methods. To add insult to injury, when exposed, it revealed its true corporate character by denying any obligation to correct its past transgressions and mounting a legal assault ensured it never had to. In sum, Wells Fargo's (D) conduct has been highly reprehensible. Accordingly, an award of punitive damages of $3,171,154.00 is warranted to deter Wells Fargo (D) from similar conduct in the future. Judgment for plaintiff.

ANALYSIS

Section 362(k) of the Bankruptcy Code allows for the award of actual damages, including costs and attorneys' fees, as a result of a stay violation, and punitive damages "in appropriate circumstances." Punitive damages are warranted when the conduct in question is willful and egregious, or when the defendant acted "with actual knowledge that he was violating the federally protected right or with reckless disregard of whether he was doing so." Here, the court found that Wells Fargo (D) had acted both willfully and egregiously, because, despite assessing postpetition charges, Wells Fargo (D) withheld this fact from its borrower and diverted payments made by the trustee and Debtor (P) to satisfy claims not authorized by the plan or court. Wells Fargo (D) admitted that these actions were part of its normal course of conduct, practiced in perhaps thousands of cases, but refused to voluntarily rectify this conduct. The punitive damages

Continued on next page.

awarded were upheld in *Jones v. Wells Fargo Home Mtg. Inc.,* 489 B.R. 645 (E.D. La. March 19, 2013).

Quicknotes

AUTOMATIC STAY Upon the filing of a bankruptcy petition, creditors are prohibited from extrajudicial collection efforts against the debtor or the debtor's property.

PUNITIVE DAMAGES Damages exceeding the actual injury suffered for the purposes of punishment of the defendant, deterrence of the wrongful behavior, or comfort to the plaintiff.

Note: There are no principal cases in Chapter 7 of the casebook.

CHAPTER 8

Discharge

Quick Reference Rules of Law

In re Henry

[Parties not identified.]

266 B.R. 457 (Bankr. C.D. Cal. 2001)

NATURE OF CASE: [The nature of the case is not presented in the casebook extract.]

FACT SUMMARY: [The facts are not presented in the casebook extract.]

RULE OF LAW

As to secured property, a discharge in a Chapter 7 bankruptcy shields the debtor from personal liability for the property but leaves intact the creditor's right to proceed in rem against the property under § 542(a) of the Bankruptcy Code.

FACTS: [The facts are not presented in the casebook extract.]

ISSUE: As to secured property, does a discharge in a Chapter 7 bankruptcy shield the debtor from personal liability for the property but leave intact the creditor's right to proceed in rem against the property under § 542 (a) of the Bankruptcy Code?

HOLDING AND DECISION: (Bufford, J.) Yes. As to secured property, a discharge in a Chapter 7 bankruptcy shields the debtor from personal liability for the property but leaves intact the creditor's right to proceed in rem against the property under § 542(a) of the Bankruptcy Code. Although the discharge eliminates a debt as a personal liability, the law has been settled since 1866 that it does not affect a lien that provides security for the debt: such liens survive or pass through bankruptcy unaffected. Thus, for example, a mortgagee may still foreclose on a mortgage, notwithstanding that the underlying debt has been discharged in bankruptcy as a personal debt of the debtor. The effect of the discharge is to convert the loan to a nonrecourse loan. The lien, however, survives, and may be pursued by the creditor once the automatic stay is terminated. In sum, a Chapter 7 discharge only extinguishes one mode of enforcing a claim, an action in personam against the debtor. [The holding and decision are not presented in the casebook extract.]

ANALYSIS

In contrast with the automatic stay, which does not last indefinitely, and which terminates when a discharge is granted or denied, a discharge is permanent and lasts forever as to the discharged debt. However, as this case points out, a discharge, unlike the automatic stay, does not cover attempts to recover secured property through in rem proceedings. In this aspect, a discharge is narrower than the automatic stay, which prohibits essentially all creditor collection activities absent court order. While the automatic stay prohibits any act to enforce a lien against property of the estate, there is no comparable provision in the discharge injunction.

Quicknotes

IN PERSONAM An action against a person seeking a judgment to impose personal liability.

IN REM An action against property.

In re McNamara

Bankruptcy trustee (P) v. Debtor (D)

310 B.R. 664 (Bankr. D. Conn. 2004)

NATURE OF CASE: Petition for discharge.

FACT SUMMARY: McNamara sought discharge in bankruptcy but had a weak explanation for the disappearance of $150,000 from his estate.

RULE OF LAW

A court must grant a debtor's discharge unless the debtor himself or someone acting on his behalf conceals, destroys, transfers, or removes debtor property within one year of the petition filing date with the intent to defraud creditors or the court.

FACTS: McNamara was the sole witness at the trial to discharge his outstanding debts. The trustee suspected McNamara of hiding money to defraud his former wife, who was a significant creditor of McNamara's estate. The trustee cross-examined McNamara on the disappearance of $150,000 from his estate. McNamara had been ordered to place that money in a state court escrow fund, but instead used approximately $11,000 to go on a Caribbean vacation. The rest was unaccounted for, and in the trustee's opinion, in offshore accounts. McNamara testified that he lost most of the money in a poker game, but he was extremely fuzzy on the details of the game or the circumstances surrounding that evening. The court did not find his testimony credible. McNamara testified that he considered the money to be rightfully his and that he could not remember details because of alcohol and poor health. McNamara did not, however, provide any medical records or other documentation to support his claims.

ISSUE: Must a court grant a debtor's discharge if the debtor himself or someone acting on his behalf conceals, destroys, transfers, or removes debtor property within one year of the petition?

HOLDING AND DECISION: (Shiff, J.) No. A court must grant a debtor's discharge unless the debtor himself or someone acting on his behalf conceals, destroys, transfers, or removes debtor property within one year of the petition. A debtor must satisfactorily explain any lost or misplaced estate assets. The plaintiff introduces evidence of the loss and the debtor must prove a reasonable explanation by a preponderance of the evidence. The Trustee introduced her evidence of the missing $150,000, but McNamara's vague, uncorroborated explanation did not meet his burden. Here, McNamara clearly believed the money was his and his creditor ex-wife had no claim to it. His excuses and explanations for removing the property from his estate and her reach are insufficient. "Bankruptcy is a privilege, not a right." Discharge denied.

ANALYSIS

The bankruptcy court has significant discretion when assessing the credibility of an explanation for missing money. A reasonable, plausible explanation will usually suffice.

Quicknotes

DISCHARGEABLE DEBTS Debts subject to discharge in a bankruptcy proceeding.

FRAUD A false representation of facts with the intent that another will rely on the misrepresentation to his detriment.

PREPONDERANCE OF THE EVIDENCE A standard of proof requiring the trier of fact to determine whether the fact sought to be established is more probable than not.

In re Sharpe

Creditor-former friend (P) v. Debtor-former friend (D)

351 B.R. 409 (Bankr. N.D. Tex. 2006)

NATURE OF CASE: Adversary proceeding against debtor objecting to the dischargeability of certain debt pursuant to 11 U.S.C. § 523.

FACT SUMMARY: Ms. Baker (P) contended that loans she had made to Mr. Sharpe (D) should be not be discharged in bankruptcy because Mr. Sharpe (D), who had become her close friend and whose lifestyle and demeanor indicated he was wealthy, had made various oral representations to her about his financial condition that led her to believe that he in fact was wealthy and had the ability to repay the loans, so that he had deliberately misled her so that his actions amounted to fraud.

RULE OF LAW

The trappings of wealth, demeanor, and an extravagant lifestyle, together with an oral representation by the debtor that he has sufficient funds to repay a debt, do not rise to the level of false pretenses, false representation, or actual fraud such that the debt is nondischargeable pursuant to 11 U.S.C. § 523(a)(2)(A).

FACTS: Ms. Baker (P) and Mr. Sharpe (D) had become close friends and spent a lot of time together. Mr. Sharpe (D) seemed to be wealthy, as he dressed in expensive clothing, ate at the most expensive restaurants, flew in a friend's private jet, and otherwise had an extravagant lifestyle and the demeanor of being wealthy. Mr. Sharpe (D) convinced Ms. Baker (P) to lend him a total of $150,000 through several loans for a business venture in which they were both involved. Two of the loans were evidenced by promissory notes; the rest were not. At the same time, and unbeknownst to Ms. Baker, Mr. Sharpe (D) was actually in financial trouble and was planning to file for bankruptcy. Mr. Sharpe (D) also had apparently represented to Ms. Baker (P) at the time the loans were made that he was able to repay the loans because he was essentially hiding assets from his then-current wife to prevent her from obtaining her share of those assets as part of a then-pending divorce settlement. After Mr. Sharpe (D) filed for bankruptcy protection, Ms. Baker (P) brought an adversary proceeding to object to the discharge of her loans, claiming that they were nondischargeable under 11 U.S.C. § 523(a)(2)(A), which provides in part that a debt is not dischargeable "to the extent obtained by false pretenses, a false representation, or actual fraud, other than a statement respecting the debtor's or an insider's financial condition."

ISSUE: Do the trappings of wealth, demeanor, and an extravagant lifestyle, together with an oral representation by the debtor that he has sufficient funds to repay a debt, rise to the level of false pretenses, false representation or actual fraud such that the debt is nondischargeable pursuant to 11 U.S.C. § 523(a)(2)(A)?

HOLDING AND DECISION: (Jernigan, J.) No. The trappings of wealth, demeanor, and an extravagant lifestyle, together with an oral representation by the debtor that he has sufficient funds to repay a debt, do not rise to the level of false pretenses, false representation, or actual fraud such that the debt is nondischargeable pursuant to 11 U.S.C. § 523(a)(2)(A). When the last part of § 523(a)(2)(A), relating to a debtor's statement of financial condition, is read in conjunction with § 523(a)(2)(B), it is clear a statement respecting the debtor's financial condition must be in writing to result in nondischargeability. Here, Ms. Baker (P) relied only on Mr. Sharpe's (D) oral and nonverbal representations. The question thus becomes whether those rise to the level of "false pretenses, false representation, or actual fraud" under § 523 (a)(2)(A). While Mr. Sharpe's (D) representations—both verbal and nonverbal—were indeed misrepresentations, they were all about his financial condition. Therefore, they do not come within the scope of § 523 (a)(2)(A), which expressly excludes from its coverage statements concerning a debtor's financial condition. Because Ms. Baker (P) failed to protect herself by obtaining from Mr. Sharpe (D) a written statement of his financial condition, she is now not entitled to not have her debt discharged. Plaintiff's debt is dischargeable.

ANALYSIS

The Tenth Circuit Court of Appeals has set forth succinctly the policy behind requiring that statements concerning a debtor's financial condition be in writing: [G]iving a statement of financial condition is a solemn part of significant credit transactions; therefore, it is only natural that solemnity be sanctified by a document which the debtor either prepares or sees and adopts. In a world where important decisions relating to the extensions of credit and service will be made upon the contents of a statement relating to financial condition, too much mischief can be done by either party to the transaction were it otherwise. Somewhere in the commercial risk allocation picture, the writing must stand as a bulwark which tends to protect both sides. A creditor, who forsakes that protection, abandoning caution and sound business practices in the name of convenience, may find itself without protection. *Bellco*

Continued on next page.

First Federal Credit Union v. Kaspar (In re Kaspar), 125 F.3d 1358, 1361 (10th Cir. 1997).

Quicknotes

DISCHARGE OF DEBTS In bankruptcy, the release of a debtor who is unable to pay his debts as they become due from the obligation to pay his creditors.

DISCHARGEABLE DEBTS Debts subject to discharge in a bankruptcy proceeding.

In re Hill

Creditor bank (P) v. Debtor (D)

2008 WL 2227359 (Bankr. N.D. Cal. 2008)

NATURE OF CASE: Adversary proceeding against debtor in Chapter 7 objecting to the dischargeability of certain debt pursuant to 11 U.S.C. § 523.

FACT SUMMARY: National City Bank (Bank) (P), a holder of a junior deed of trust on the Hills' (Debtors') (D) home, contended that its $250,000 claim on the deed of trust, which had been foreclosed out, should not be discharged because the Debtors (D) had deliberately and knowingly misrepresented their income on loan application documents, so that the debt was nondischargeable under 11 U.S.C. § 523(a)(2)(B).

RULE OF LAW

Under 11 U.S.C. § 523(a)(2)(B), a creditor's reliance on a fraudulent written representation of a debtor's financial condition is not reasonable where the creditor's normal business practices deviate from reasonable industry standards and where the creditor ignores "red flags" concerning the misrepresentation.

FACTS: The Hills (Debtors) (D) bought a house for $220,000 pursuant to a first deed of trust. As the value of the house increased over 20 years, they refinanced the original first deed of trust to obtain additional cash. They also obtained a junior deed of trust, which they refinanced several times. Mr. Hill (D) earned around $39,000 per year, and Mrs. Hill (D), who was self-employed, earned up to $26,000. In April 2006, they contacted Ellerback, a mortgage broker, about getting more cash out of their house, and he had them apply for a $200,000 equity line of credit with National City Bank (Bank) (P). In the loan application submitted to obtain this loan, Mr. Hill's (D) monthly income was listed as $8,176, or $98,112 on an annual basis, and Mrs. Hill's (D) monthly income was listed as $3,967, or $47,604 on an annual basis for a combined monthly income of approximately $12,143, or $145,716 on an annual basis. Ellerback obtained this information from Mrs. Hill (D) on the telephone. The loan was approved. By October 2006, the Debtors (D) needed more cash. This time, Mrs. Hill (D) called the Bank (P) directly, and on the application for an increase of the line of credit to $250,000, Mr. Hill's (D) annual income was listed as $67,200 and Mrs. Hill's (D) as $123,600, for a total of $190,000 on an annual basis. The Bank's (P) guidelines for loan approval required that for a borrower who was self-employed, the Bank (P) could choose one of three types of verification: (1) a copy of the borrower's business license, (2) a copy of the most recent month's bank statement reflecting liquidity at least equal to one-tenth of the borrower's annual income, or (3) a certified public accountant's (CPA's) letter verifying the existence and ownership of the business. The loan was approved on the basis of a letter verifying the existence and ownership of Mrs. Hill (D). The letter was written on the letterhead of a CPA, but it was signed by someone other than the CPA whose name was on the letterhead. In April 2006, the house had been appraised at $785,000. In October 2006, it was appraised at $856,000. Shortly after the Debtors (D) filed for bankruptcy under Chapter 7 in April 2007, the first deed of trust holder purchased the house at its foreclosure sale for $450,000. The Bank (P) brought an adversary proceeding objecting to the discharge of $250,000 to which it had a claim, contending that the debt was nondischargeable under 11 U.S.C. § 523(a)(2)(B) because the Debtors (D) had knowingly made a material written misrepresentation as to their financial condition on which the Bank (P) reasonably relied.

ISSUE: Under 11 U.S.C. § 523(a)(2)(B), is a creditor's reliance on a fraudulent written representation of a debtor's financial condition reasonable where the creditor's normal business practices deviate from reasonable industry standards and where the creditor ignores "red flags" concerning the misrepresentation?

HOLDING AND DECISION: (Tchaikovsky, J.) No. Under 11 U.S.C. § 523(a)(2)(B), a creditor's reliance on a fraudulent written representation of a debtor's financial condition is not reasonable where the creditor's normal business practices deviate from reasonable industry standards and where the creditor ignores "red flags" concerning the misrepresentation. To establish a debt as nondischargeable under § 523(a)(2)(B), a creditor must demonstrate that: the debtor made a written representation of respecting the debtor's financial condition; the representation was material; the debtor knew at the time the representation was made that it was false; the representation was made with the intent to deceive the creditor; the creditor relied on the representation; the reliance was reasonable; and the damage suffered by the creditor proximately resulted from the representation. Although the Bank (P) meets all but one of these elements, it fails to establish nondischargeability because it fails to establish that its reliance was reasonable. The Bank (P) established that the Debtors (D) made a false representation to the Bank in writing concerning their financial condition and that the misrepresentation was material, since they overstated their income and would not have received the loan without the falsehood. The evidence also showed that the Debtors (P) knew their representation was fraudulent at the time it was made, and that the representation was made

Continued on next page.

with the intent to deceive the Bank (P). However, when viewed under an objective standard of reasonableness, the Bank (P) either did not rely on the Debtors' (D) representations concerning their income or its reliance was not reasonable. Under an objective test, a lender's reliance is usually reasonable if it follows its normal business practices, but this alone may not be enough if those practices deviate from reasonable industry standards or if the creditor ignores a "red flag" about the debtor's financial condition. Here, the Bank's (P) guidelines required an evaluation of the reasonableness of the salary listed by an employed borrower (here, Mr. Hill (D)) based on job type and geographical area, but there was no indication that the Bank (P) actually conducted such an evaluation. With regard to a self-employed borrower (here, Mrs. Hill (D)), the Bank (P) was supposed to ascertain the existence of the business by verification from a CPA. Here, the Bank (P) failed to question the verification letter supplied by Mrs. Hill (D), which, although on a CPA's letterhead, was not signed by a CPA. Further, the Bank (P) could have checked its file for the April 2006 loan against the information it received for the October 2006 loan, but failed to. If it had, it would have discovered significant discrepancies in listed incomes that purportedly occurred in just six months. The minimal verification required by the loan at issue, known as an "income stated" loan, suggests that in reality the Bank (P) made the loan principally in reliance on the value of the house as reflected by appraisals thereof. Subsequent events strongly suggest that the appraisals were inflated. Therefore, the Debtors (D) cannot be blamed for the Bank's (D) loss, and the Bank's (D) claim should be discharged notwithstanding that the Debtors (D) made a material false representation concerning their financial condition to the Bank (P) with knowledge of its falsity and the intent to deceive the Bank (P). The Bank's (P) claim is discharged.

ANALYSIS

The type of loan involved in this case, known as a "stated income" loan, does not require that the applicant's statement of income be verified by pay stubs, income tax returns, or similar documents or proof of income. As this case demonstrates, during a period of artificially inflated home values, banks were eager to make such loans, and they were widely available. However, as this case also demonstrates, because the usual verification methods are lacking with such loans (given the nickname "liar's loans" by some), having a minimally verified written finance statement may not be enough to protect the lender's claim from discharge.

Quicknotes

CHAPTER 7 BANKRUPTCY A legal proceeding whereby a debtor, who is unable to pay his or her debts as they become due, is relieved of the obligation to pay creditors by liquidation and distribution of remaining assets.

DEED OF TRUST A legal document that acts as a mortgage, placing a security interest in the deeded property with a trustee to insure the payment of a debt.

DISCHARGE OF DEBTS In bankruptcy, the release of a debtor who is unable to pay his or her debts as they become due from the obligation to pay his or her creditors.

Thomas v. Department of Education

Debtor (P) v. Loan servicer (D)

931 F.3d 449 (5th Cir. 2019)

NATURE OF CASE: Appeal from bankruptcy court's denial of discharge of debtor's student loan debt.

FACT SUMMARY: Thomas (P) filed for Chapter 7 bankruptcy and sought to have her federal student loan debt discharged along with other personal debts. Thomas (P) has a physical disability and was unemployed when she filed for bankruptcy.

RULE OF LAW

Student loan debt may not be discharged in Chapter 7 bankruptcy unless the debtor demonstrates a total incapacity to repay the debt now or in the future.

FACTS: Vera Frances Thomas (P), filed for Chapter 7 bankruptcy in 2017. Thomas (P) suffers from diabetic neuropathy and is unemployed; she receives income from public assistance and private charity. Prior to filing, in 2012, Thomas (P) was working at a call center and enrolled in a local community college to improve her career prospects. Thomas (P) obtained two loans totaling $7,000 from the Department of Education (D), one for each semester of college she attended. Thomas (P) made two payments on the loans in 2014, until her health began to decline, and she received a diabetic neuropathy diagnosis. In 2016, Thomas (P) was terminated from her job for rule violations and moved to Texas, where she worked three separate odd jobs but struggled with the physical requirements and eventually became unemployed in 2017. Thomas (P) sought discharge of her student loan debt and other debts in bankruptcy. The bankruptcy court determined that she failed to demonstrate that she would be incapable of repaying her student loan debt. Thomas (P) appealed, and the lower appellate court agreed with the bankruptcy court's denial of the discharge of her student loan debt. Thomas (P) initiated an adversary complaint against the Department of Education.

ISSUE: Can student loan debt be discharged in Chapter 7 bankruptcy without demonstrating the debtor's total incapacity to repay the debt now or in the future?

HOLDING AND DECISION: (Jones, J.) No. Student loan debt may not be discharged in Chapter 7 bankruptcy unless the debtor demonstrates a total incapacity to repay the debt now or in the future. The Bankruptcy Code requires a debtor to show that the debt would cause an "undue hardship" if it were not discharged. In its trial, the bankruptcy court applied the Second Circuit Court of Appeals' decision in *Brunner v. New York State Higher Education Services Corp.*, 831 F.2d 395 (2d Cir. 1987), in which the court established a three-prong test for evaluating an undue hardship claim. The bankruptcy court concluded that Thomas (P) had satisfied the first prong of *Brunner* by showing an inability to maintain a minimal standard of living if forced to repay the loan because her monthly expenses exceeded her monthly income. However, the bankruptcy court concluded that Thomas (P) failed to satisfy the second prong of the *Brunner* test because she could not show that she is incapable of employment now or in the future. The second prong of the *Brunner* test is especially demanding: it requires the debtor to show a total incapacity to repay the debt at any point. Although Thomas (P) could satisfy the first prong and the third prong of the *Brunner/Gerhardt* test, by Thomas's (P) own admission, she would be capable of gaining and maintaining employment in a sedentary work environment. Accordingly, Thomas's (P) circumstances are not likely to persist, and her student loans cannot be discharged. Affirmed.

ANALYSIS

The three-prong test established by the Second Circuit Court of Appeals in *Brunner v. New York State Higher Education Services Corp.*, 831 F.2d 395 (2d Cir. 1987), and adopted by the Fifth Circuit Court of Appeals in *In re Gerhardt*, 348 F.3d 80 (5th Cir. 2003) are "(1) that the debtor cannot maintain, based on current income and expenses, a 'minimal' standard of living for [herself] and [her] dependents if forced to repay the loans; (2) that additional circumstances exist indicating that this state of affairs is likely to persist for a significant portion of the repayment period of the student loans; and (3) that the debtor has made a good faith effort to repay the loans." *In re Gerhardt*, 348 F.3d at 91 (5th Cir. 2003). While most circuit courts apply the *Brunner* test to determine whether student loan debt can be discharged in bankruptcy, in *Fern v. FedLoan Servicing*, 563 B. R. 1 (8th Cir. BAP 2017), the Eighth Circuit Court of Appeals' Bankruptcy Appellate Panel applied a less-stringent totality of the circumstances test in its decision to discharge a debtor's student loan debt. In *Fern*, the plaintiff was a 35-year-old single mother of three children with $27,000 of student loan debt who was employed but had never earned more than $25,000 a year.

Quicknotes

DISCHARGE OF DEBTS In bankruptcy, the release of a debtor who is unable to pay his or her debts as they become due from the obligation to pay his or her creditors.

United States v. Cluck

Federal government (P) v. Debtor (D)

143 F.3d 174 (5th Cir. 1998)

NATURE OF CASE: Appeal from conviction for bankruptcy fraud.

FACT SUMMARY: **When a tax planning attorney was convicted of bankruptcy fraud, he claimed there was insufficient evidence that he had intentionally committed fraud.**

RULE OF LAW

Circumstances, which may be inconclusive if considered separately, may, by their number and joint operation, be sufficient to constitute conclusive proof.

FACTS: Cluck (D) was an attorney who specialized in legal avoidance of taxes. When a state court rendered judgment against him for $2.9 million, Cluck (D) filed for bankruptcy. Before filing for Chapter 7 liquidation, Cluck (D) had disposed of property by signing a promissory note and pawning some assets. Cluck (D) did not disclose these and other transfers to the bankruptcy court. When the bankruptcy court found Cluck (D) had engaged in intentional concealment, the U.S. Attorney charged Cluck (D) with eight counts of bankruptcy fraud. A jury found Cluck (D) guilty on seven counts, and Cluck (D) appealed.

ISSUE: May circumstances, which may be inconclusive if considered separately, by their number and joint operation, be sufficient to constitute conclusive proof?

HOLDING AND DECISION: (Jolly, J.) Yes. Circumstances, which may be inconclusive if considered separately, may, by their number and joint operation, be sufficient to constitute conclusive proof. Cluck's (D) repeated omissions and questionable transfers formed the kind of circumstances that could constitute conclusive proof. A rational jury could have inferred the existence of an intentional plan to defraud from the bare facts of Cluck's (D) systematic concealment and false statements. Affirmed.

ANALYSIS

The denial of discharge in bankruptcy may lead to criminal prosecution, as well. False oaths, false claims, concealment of assets, and fee fixing may be punishable as crimes. The attorney in this case had some of his accounts paid directly to a Nevada corporation owned by his wife.

Quicknotes

CHAPTER 7 BANKRUPTCY A legal proceeding whereby a debtor, who is unable to pay his or her debts as they become due, is relieved of the obligation to pay creditors by liquidation and distribution of remaining assets.

INTENTIONAL CONCEALMENT A false representation of facts with the intent that another will rely on the misrepresentation to his detriment.

INTENTIONAL FRAUD A false representation of facts with the intent that another will rely on the misrepresentation to his detriment.

CHAPTER 9

The Debtor's Position After Bankruptcy

Quick Reference Rules of Law

In re Husain

Trustee (P) v. Debtors (D)

364 B.R. 211 (Bankr. E.D. Va. 2007)

NATURE OF CASE: Hearing regarding Debtors' (D) request for approval on reaffirmation agreements that were not approved by their attorney.

FACT SUMMARY: Debtors (D) entered into a reaffirmation agreement to keep their two vehicles after the conclusion of their Chapter 7 bankruptcy. Though the Debtors (D) were represented by counsel, their attorney refused to sign the reaffirmation agreement because it would cause an undue hardship, meaning that the Debtors' (D) monthly income minus expenses was less than the scheduled payments on the reaffirmed debt. Because their attorney refused to sign the reaffirmation agreement, Debtor Akhter Husain (D) signed the agreement himself and asked the court to approve it as if Debtors (D) were not represented by counsel.

RULE OF LAW

If a debtor who is represented by counsel signs a reaffirmation agreement that his or her counsel refuses to approve because it will cause undue hardship, the court may still approve the agreement.

FACTS: Debtors (D), Akhter and Farah Husain, filed a joint Chapter 7 bankruptcy case. Following a meeting of creditors, the Chapter 7 trustee filed a report of no distribution after determining that there were no assets to administer for the benefit of unsecured creditors. Debtors (D) initially indicated they planned to redeem their two cars, but later undertook action to reaffirm their obligations on both vehicles. The reaffirmation agreement stated that Debtor Akhter Husain (D) would reaffirm $15,438.92 with the Toyota Motor Credit Corporation, with an interest rate of 15.6%, secured by Debtor's (D) 2003 Toyota Avalon. Though Debtors (D) were represented by competent counsel, Debtors' (D) attorney had refused to sign the reaffirmation agreement because the agreement would cause undue hardship to his client. Under the Bankruptcy Code, counsel's failure to certify a reaffirmation agreement will terminate further consideration of the Debtor's ability to reaffirm the debt. However, Debtor Akhter Husain (D) instead signed his own statement indicating that the agreement would not cause undue hardship, believing that this would allow the court to certify the agreement directly, as if he had not been represented by counsel.

ISSUE: If a debtor who is represented by counsel signs a reaffirmation agreement that his or her counsel refuses to approve because it will cause undue hardship, may the court still approve the agreement?

HOLDING AND DECISION: (Huennekens, J.) Yes. If a debtor who is represented by counsel signs a reaffirmation agreement that his or her counsel refuses to approve because it will cause undue hardship, the court may still approve the agreement. However, in this case, the agreement cannot be affirmed because Debtors (D) failed to provide adequate evidence rebutting the presumption of undue hardship. Under § 524(m) of the Bankruptcy Code, there is a rebuttable presumption that a reaffirmation agreement imposes an undue hardship if the debtor's monthly income minus expenses is less than the scheduled payments on the reaffirmed debt. To enter into a reaffirmation agreement, a debtor's attorney is required to certify that the debtor fully understands the agreement and that it does not impose an undue hardship. If the debtor is not represented by an attorney, the debtor may self-certify, and the court may approve the agreement. Here, the Debtors' (D) attorney did not sign the agreements because they would pose an undue hardship on his clients under section 524(m). However, the attorney nevertheless advocated at the hearing for the agreement to be approved because he believed it was important for the Debtors (D) to be able to keep their vehicles. Debtors (D) provided evidence that Akhter Husain planned to work additional hours in order to close the gap between his income and expenses and was slated to begin a job that would bring $1,000 of additional income. However, because Debtors (D) still had a deficit of expenses over income of approximately $3,000 per month, the evidence was insufficient to overcome the presumption of undue hardship. Motion to reaffirm denied.

ANALYSIS

Debtors often reaffirm vehicle loans during Chapter 7 bankruptcy. However, if a debtor misses payments on a reaffirmed loan, he or she remains liable for the loan, even if the lender repossesses the vehicle and sells it at an auction. Alternatively, the debtor may surrender the vehicle during Chapter 7 bankruptcy but may struggle to secure a loan from a reputable lender following bankruptcy.

Quicknotes

REAFFIRMATION An agreement after the filing of the bankruptcy petition to repay obligations that arose prior to its filing.

UNDUE HARDSHIP Excessive suffering or adversity, especially referring to financial positions that are likely to continue in spite of good faith efforts to overcome the situation.

In re Schwass

[Parties not identified.]

378 B.R. 859 (Bankr. S.D. Cal. 2007)

NATURE OF CASE: Motion for relief from stay in Chapter 7 bankruptcy action.

FACT SUMMARY: In Schwass's (Debtor's) Chapter 7 bankruptcy, Pacific Capital Bancorp dba Santa Barbara Bank & Trust (Movant) sought relief from stay under § 362(h)(1)(B) of the Bankruptcy Code, on the grounds that Debtor had failed to fulfill her obligations under § 521(a)(2)(B) to reaffirm the debt she owed Movant, which was secured by her car, because, although she had filed a timely statement of intention to reaffirm the debt, she did not prepare or sign a reaffirmation agreement.

RULE OF LAW

(1) Where a debtor has timely filed a statement of intent to reaffirm a secured debt under Bankruptcy Code § 521(a)(2)(A), it is the secured creditor's responsibility to prepare the reaffirmation agreement.

(2) Where a debtor has timely filed a statement of intent to reaffirm a secured debt under Bankruptcy Code § 521(a)(2)(A), the debtor's performance under § 521(a)(2)(B) is satisfied where the debtor stands ready and willing to execute the reaffirmation agreement prepared by the secured creditor.

FACTS: Prior to filing her Chapter 7 bankruptcy petition, Schwass (Debtor) had borrowed money from Pacific Capital Bancorp dba Santa Barbara Bank & Trust (Movant); the debt was secured by her car. Debtor filed a Statement of Intention, which indicated that she intended to reaffirm the debt. Counsel for Movant wrote to Debtor's counsel requesting that he prepare the reaffirmation agreement. Debtor's counsel replied that Debtor had no obligation to prepare the agreement, but that he would do so for a fee payable by Movant. Movant replied that it was Debtor's responsibility, and no reaffirmation agreement was prepared. Thirty days elapsed from the date set for the first meeting of creditors with no reaffirmation agreement having been filed. Thereafter, Movant moved for relief from stay on the ground that Debtor did not timely follow through with her intention to reaffirm.

ISSUE:

(1) Where a debtor has timely filed a statement of intent to reaffirm a secured debt under Bankruptcy Code § 521(a)(2)(A), is it the secured creditor's responsibility to prepare the reaffirmation agreement?

(2) Where a debtor has timely filed a statement of intent to reaffirm a secured debt under Bankruptcy Code § 521(a)(2)(A), is the debtor's performance under § 521(a)(2)(B) satisfied where the debtor stands ready and willing to execute the reaffirmation agreement prepared by the secured creditor?

HOLDING AND DECISION: (Bowie, C.J.)

(1) Yes. Where a debtor has timely filed a statement of intent to reaffirm a secured debt under Bankruptcy Code § 521(a)(2)(A), it is the secured creditor's responsibility to prepare the reaffirmation agreement. Here, Debtor has complied with § 521(a)(2)(A), which requires that the statement of intention be filed within 30 days of the petition. Section 521(a)(2)(B) provides that a debtor must perform her stated intention within 30 days after the first date set for the § 341(a) meeting of creditors. The issue, therefore, is what constitutes performance. Reaffirmation of debts and the agreements and disclosures required therefor is governed by §§ 524(c) and (k), but neither of these provisions, nor any other provisions or court decisions specify that one party or the other must prepare the reaffirmation agreement. Nevertheless, the statutory scheme in § 524 makes clear that it is the secured creditor that must prepare the reaffirmation agreement. Section 524(c)(2) provides that a reaffirmed debt is excepted from discharge only if the debtor has received disclosures required by § 524(k) at or before the time at which the debtor signs the agreement. It would only make sense that those disclosures come from the secured creditor, since it would be nonsensical to have the disclosures come from the debtor herself. Further, the information required by § 524(k) to be included in the disclosure statement is most readily supplied by the secured creditor. Also, the disclosure statement is replete with language directed at the debtor, e.g., "if you want to reaffirm." It would make no sense for a debtor to prepare such a disclosure statement with such disclosures to herself. Finally, the reaffirmation agreement itself contains language and requirements, such as certification by debtor's counsel, that make it clear the agreement is directed to, as opposed to prepared by, the debtor. For these reasons, and because the secured creditor is the party that stands to benefit from reaffirmation, it is the secured party that has the responsibility to prepare the affirmation agreement and the accompanying disclosure statement—which the debtor must receive on or before the time the debtor signs the agreement for the agreement to be enforceable. [Judgment for Debtor as to this issue.]

Continued on next page.

(2) Yes. Where a debtor has timely filed a statement of intent to reaffirm a secured debt under Bankruptcy Code § 521(a)(2)(A), the debtor's performance under § 521(a)(2)(B) is satisfied where the debtor stands ready and willing to execute the reaffirmation agreement prepared by the secured creditor. Because it is the secured creditor's responsibility to prepare the affirmation agreement and accompanying disclosure statement, a debtor complies with the requirement to "perform" the intention to reaffirm under § 521(a)(2)(B) by standing ready and willing to execute the reaffirmation agreement prepared by the secured creditor. Accordingly, here, relief from the automatic stay is not warranted because Debtor has not failed to reaffirm. The same result may be reached by finding that Movant, by failing to provide a reaffirmation agreement for Debtor's signature, has refused to agree to reaffirmation on the original terms and thus relief is not warranted. Motion denied.

ANALYSIS

In this case, which held that the debtor had done everything she was supposed to do, the debtor was able to hold on to the collateral and keep making payments to the creditor. If the creditor had obtained a valid reaffirmation agreement, however, that would have revived the debt and made it enforceable in a court of law. Whether the creditor in such circumstance could repossess the collateral after discharge or a lift of the stay, given that the debtor was not in default and was current on payments under the contract, is a question of state law.

Quicknotes

REAFFIRMATION An agreement after the filing of the bankruptcy petition to repay obligations that arose prior to its filing.

In re Wilson

Trustee (P) v. Debtor (D)

2012 WL 2411918 (Bankr. N.D. W. Va. 2012)

NATURE OF CASE: Hearing on motion to approve reaffirmation agreement filed by Debtor.

FACT SUMMARY: Debtor moved to approve a reaffirmation agreement that would cause undue hardship. Debtor's attorney refused to sign the reaffirmation agreement, but instead asked the court to permit the vehicle to "pass through" the bankruptcy case unaffected.

RULE OF LAW

In Chapter 7 bankruptcy, a bankruptcy court may grant a pass-through allowing a debtor's vehicle to remain unaffected when reaffirmation of the vehicle debt would cause undue hardship.

FACTS: Debtor (D), Johnnie Wilson, moved to approve a reaffirmation agreement for a 2001 Dodge Caravan. When Debtor (D) filed the reaffirmation agreement, Debtor (D) indicated he was not represented by counsel so a hearing was set. Debtor (D) was represented by counsel, but his attorney refused to approve the reaffirmation agreement because it would cause undue hardship on his client. Debtor's (D) attorney nevertheless asked the court to permit the vehicle to "pass through" the bankruptcy case unaffected because Debtor (D) had complied with the requirements of 11 U.S.C. §§ 524(c) and 521(a), made consistent payments, and needed the vehicle to take his wife to medical appointments.

ISSUE: In a Chapter 7 bankruptcy, may a bankruptcy court grant a pass-through allowing a debtor's vehicle to remain unaffected when reaffirmation of the vehicle debt would cause undue hardship?

HOLDING AND DECISION: (Flatley, J.) Yes. In Chapter 7 bankruptcy, a bankruptcy court may grant a pass-through allowing a debtor's vehicle to remain unaffected when reaffirmation of the vehicle debt would cause undue hardship. If a debtor's declaration states that his or her monthly income minus monthly expenses is less than the scheduled payments on reaffirmed debt, then there is a presumption of undue hardship. Here, because Debtor's (D) monthly expenses exceed his income by $158.00, there is a presumption of undue hardship. Debtor stated at hearing that his son helps him make payments on his vehicle in exchange for Debtor (D) mowing his lawn, but he did not provide evidence regarding his son's ability to pay for his services. Accordingly, the Debtor (D) failed to rebut the presumption of undue hardship, and the reaffirmation agreement cannot be approved. However, Debtor (D) argues that the court should permit him to retain the vehicle and have it "pass through" the bankruptcy case unaffected. Because Debtor (D) fulfilled his obligations under §§ 521(a) and 362(h), avoided the implications of § 521(d), and stated at hearing that he is current on vehicle payments, the automatic stay and discharge injunction will continue as long as he remains current. Pass-through permitted.

ANALYSIS

The court's decision in *In re Wilson* demonstrates how debtors may struggle to retain certain property in Chapter 7 bankruptcy. Though most states permit those who file for Chapter 7 bankruptcy to exempt property, including vehicles, up to a certain dollar limit, a vehicle with equity beyond that limit may be sold by a trustee to pay unsecured creditors. Alternatively, in Chapter 13 bankruptcy, it is often easier for a debtor to keep his or her vehicle and continue making regular payments or reschedule them as part of the bankruptcy repayment plan.

Quicknotes

CHAPTER 7 BANKRUPTCY A legal proceeding whereby a debtor, who is unable to pay his or her debts as they become due, is relieved of the obligation to pay creditors by liquidation and distribution of remaining assets.

REAFFIRMATION An agreement after the filing of the bankruptcy petition to repay obligations that arose prior to its filing.

UNSECURED CREDITOR A creditor whose loan is not backed by specified collateral or a security agreement.

In re Duke

[Parties not identified.]

79 F.3d 43 (7th Cir. 1996)

NATURE OF CASE: Appeal from affirmance of judgment for creditor in Chapter 7 bankruptcy action.

FACT SUMMARY: Duke, a Chapter 7 debtor, contended that Sears, Roebuck & Co. (Sears), one of his creditors, violated the automatic stay by copying him on a letter, which it sent to his attorney, that offered to extend a line of credit to Duke if he reaffirmed his debt to Sears.

RULE OF LAW

(1) A creditor does not violate the automatic stay by sending to the debtor a letter that contains an offer to extend a line of credit to the debtor if the debtor agrees to reaffirm the prepetition debt.

(2) As a matter of bankruptcy law, it is not inherently coercive, and therefore a violation of the automatic stay, for a creditor to send a copy of a letter to an attorney directly to the debtor-client, for information purposes only.

FACTS: Duke owed Sears, Roebuck & Co. (Sears) $317.10 at the time he filed his Chapter 7 bankruptcy action. After it received notice of the automatic stay, Sears sent a letter to Duke's attorney, with a copy to Duke himself "for information purposes." In the letter, Sears indicated that if Duke reaffirmed his debt to Sears, Sears would extend to Duke a $500.00 line of credit. Sears attached to the letter copies of the proposed reaffirmation agreement. Duke challenged the letter in bankruptcy court as violating the automatic stay by offering to reaffirm a prepetition debt. Duke also argued that, as a matter of law, it is inherently coercive, and therefore a violation of the automatic stay, for a creditor to send a copy of a letter to an attorney directly to the debtor-client, for information purposes only. The bankruptcy court ruled in favor of Sears, and the district court affirmed. The court of appeals granted review.

ISSUE:

(1) Does a creditor violate the automatic stay by sending to the debtor a letter that contains an offer to extend a line of credit to the debtor if the debtor agrees to reaffirm the prepetition debt?

(2) As a matter of bankruptcy law, is it inherently coercive, and therefore a violation of the automatic stay, for a creditor to send a copy of a letter to an attorney directly to the debtor-client, for information purposes only?

HOLDING AND DECISION: (Wood, J.)

(1) No. A creditor does not violate the automatic stay by sending to the debtor a letter that contains an offer to extend a line of credit to the debtor if the debtor agrees to reaffirm the prepetition debt. This case presents a question about the relation between the automatic stay of § 362(a)(6) of the Bankruptcy Code and reaffirmation agreements, which are authorized and regulated by § 524. Although § 362 generally prohibits the creditor from taking "any act" to collect prepetition debts, courts have not read this provision so narrowly as to prohibit any contact between the creditor and the debtor. Instead, courts focus on § 362's anti-harassment purpose. A majority of the bankruptcy courts have found that a creditor's letter to a debtor offering to reaffirm a prepetition debt does not violate § 362, provided that letter is nonthreatening and noncoercive. Duke can prevail here only if all creditor-initiated offers to reaffirm debts violate § 362(a)(6), or, alternatively, while offers to reaffirm in general are permissible if they are not threatening or coercive, the letter at issue falls within the prohibited group. The first proposition has correctly been rejected by a majority of courts. The reaffirmation scheme set forth in § 524, with its detailed rules designed to ensure the fairness of reaffirmation agreements, would be rendered meaningless and empty if creditors were forbidden to engage in any communication whatsoever with debtors who have prepetition obligations. The assumption behind the § 524 provisions is that debtors will be agreeing to enter into some reaffirmation agreements, and that it is important to have in place certain institutional protections to guard against creditor overreaching. Moreover, there is no reason to believe that reaffirmation agreements inevitably disadvantage debtors, who might find the idea of a new credit relationship attractive, since this too can be part of a fresh financial start after bankruptcy. Similarly, creditors like the idea that bankruptcy may not result in a complete write-off of amounts due to them. Under § 524, both parties can enjoy the legitimate benefits of reaffirmations, and the debtor is protected from abuse of the system. For these reasons, Duke cannot prevail under the first proposition. As to the second proposition, Duke did not argue that the letter here was threatening or coercive in its contents. Although the letter extends the "carrot" of a line of credit in exchange for reaffirmation of the debt, and although sometimes the line between withholding of a benefit and imposition of a penalty can be elusive, the letter here is as bare-bones and straightforward as possible. There is not a hint of unfavorable action that would be taken against Duke if he does not reaffirm,

Continued on next page.

and it does not even say that his chances of re-establishing credit with Sears would be prejudiced if he chooses not to reaffirm and then later seeks new credit after his discharge in bankruptcy. For these reasons, Duke cannot prevail under the second proposition. Affirmed as to this issue.

(2) No. As a matter of bankruptcy law, it is not inherently coercive, and therefore a violation of the automatic stay, for a creditor to send a copy of a letter to an attorney directly to the debtor-client, for information purposes only. While the letter here raises potential issues under the state's rules of professional responsibility for attorneys, or under the Fair Debt Collection Practices Act, none of those issues were raised below, and, consequently, are not before the court. Further, there is nothing in the Bankruptcy Code itself that requires a creditor to refrain from copying the debtor on correspondence to the debtor's attorney. Affirmed as to this issue. Affirmed.

ANALYSIS

It should be noted that if Duke had not been represented by an attorney, Sears could have mailed the letter directly to Duke. Additionally, Duke's lawyer had a duty to show the offer to Duke whether or not Sears "cc'd" Duke, since § 524(c)(3)(A) requires an attorney to declare in an affidavit that the debtor's consent to a reaffirmation agreement is "fully informed and voluntary," and since lawyers are under an ethical obligation to keep their clients reasonably informed about the status of a matter. These factors weigh in a finding that copying a debtor on a letter sent to the debtor's attorney is not inherently coercive, and, therefore, such conduct does not violate the automatic stay.

Quicknotes

AUTOMATIC STAY Upon the filing of a voluntary bankruptcy petition, creditors are prohibited from attempting to recover payment from the debtor or his property.

REAFFIRMATION An agreement after the filing of the bankruptcy petition to repay obligations that arose prior to its filing.

CHAPTER 10

Secured Creditors in Chapter 13

Quick Reference Rules of Law

In re Radden

Debtor (P) v. GMAC creditor (D)

35 B.R. 821 (Bankr. E.D. Va. 1983)

NATURE OF CASE: Action to recover repossessed property.

FACT SUMMARY: In Radden's (P) action against GMAC (D), to recover an auto that GMAC (D) repossessed when Radden (P) failed to make payments required by the auto sales contract, Radden (P) contended that the auto was necessary for his reorganization under a Chapter 13 bankruptcy, and thus it should be returned to him.

RULE OF LAW

A debtor may retain property under § 362 of the Bankruptcy Code if that property is necessary for an effective reorganization.

FACTS: Radden (P) purchased an automobile and financed the purchase by a retail sales contract secured by the vehicle. The installment sales agreement was assigned to GMAC (D) pursuant to its agreement with the dealer from whom Radden (P) purchased the car. Radden (P) fell behind on his payments, and GMAC (D) repossessed the car. Radden (P) then filed for relief under Chapter 13 of the Bankruptcy Code. The Chapter 13 plan proposed to pay GMAC (D) in full to the extent of the value of the collateral plus interest. GMAC (D) contended that Radden (P) did not have any equity in the car and that the car was not necessary for Radden's (P) effective reorganization. Radden (P) contended that the car was necessary for his reorganization and that it should be returned to him.

ISSUE: May a debtor retain property under § 362 of the Bankruptcy Code if that property is necessary for an effective reorganization?

HOLDING AND DECISION: (Shelley, J.) Yes. A debtor may retain property under § 362 of the Bankruptcy Code if that property is necessary for an effective reorganization. The debtor bears the burden of proving that the property is necessary for his effective reorganization under § 362. Here, it is obvious an automobile is necessary for an individual's effective reorganization in today's society. Radden (P) testified that he needed the auto to get to and from his job as well as to obtain medical and other necessary services. GMAC (D) will, therefore, have to return the repossessed auto to Radden (P).

ANALYSIS

The secured creditor in a Chapter 13 bankruptcy case is better protected than the unsecured creditor. The debtor's Chapter 13 plan to retain property subject to a security interest often provokes a dispute with the secured party who declares the debtor in default and wants the property back. Whether the creditor can exercise its right to repossession and sale, realizing the value of the collateral and ending the contract with the debtor, depends on the debtor's ability to comply with the provisions of Chapter 13, which are designed to protect secured creditors.

Quicknotes

CHAPTER 13 BANKRUPTCY Debtor may modify plan at any time before the completion of the payments under such plan.

REPOSSESSION The taking back of an item paid for under an installment contract when payment of an installment is not made.

SECURED CREDITOR A creditor, the repayment of whose loan is secured by collateral sufficient to repay the debt owed.

UNSECURED CREDITOR A creditor whose loan is not backed by specified collateral or a security agreement.

Ford Motor Credit Co. v. Dale

Secured creditor/vehicle financier (P) v. Debtor/vehicle purchaser (D)

582 F.3d 568 (5th Cir. 2009)

NATURE OF CASE: Appeal from reversal of judgment for debtor in Chapter 13 bankruptcy action.

FACT SUMMARY: Dale (D), who had purchased a vehicle with secured financing from Ford Motor Credit Co. (Ford) (P), contended that pursuant to the hanging paragraph of § 1325(a) of the Bankruptcy Code, Ford's (P) security interest in the sales contract did not extend to those portions attributable to negative equity, gap insurance, and an extended warranty.

RULE OF LAW

The purchase-money security interest exception contained in the hanging paragraph of § 1325(a) of the Bankruptcy Code applies to those portions of a claim attributable to the pay-off of negative equity in a trade-in vehicle, gap insurance, and an extended warranty.

FACTS: Dale (D) traded in her former vehicle to purchase a new vehicle, which had a cash value of $38,291.42. Ford Motor Credit Company, LLC (Ford) financed the sale under a retail sales contract and retained a security interest in the vehicle. Dale (D) owed $4,760 more on the trade-in vehicle than its then-market value. Ford (P) paid off this negative equity and included the sum in the new vehicle's total sale price, which also included a gap insurance premium of $576.84; taxes not included in the cash price totaling $1,450.03; fees totaling $162.73; and an extended warranty charge of $3,030. Dale (D) financed this entire amount totaling $48,271.02 through Ford (P) at 0 percent interest. Dale (D) filed for bankruptcy less than one year later and submitted a Chapter 13 reorganization plan. Of the $41,834.94 still owed to Ford (P), Dale's Chapter 13 plan proposed to pay $23,900 over 37 months at 10.25 percent interest. Under Dale's (D) proposal, the remaining amount owed would be paid pro-rata with other unsecured claims. Ford (D) objected and filed a proof of claim in the amount of $41,834.94, secured by the vehicle. The bankruptcy court ruled that, under the hanging paragraph of § 1325(a) of the Bankruptcy Code, Ford's (P) purchase-money security interest did not extend to those portions of the vehicle loan attributable to the pay-off of negative equity, the gap insurance premium, and the extended warranty charge. The court deemed these portions of the loan unsecured. Under the Code, a lien creditor generally holds a secured claim only to the extent of the present value of the collateral that the lien encumbers. If the amount of the secured claim exceeds the present value of the collateral, the Code treats the excess amount as a separate, unsecured claim. This process is known as bifurcation or "stripping down" the secured claim to the value of the collateral. The hanging paragraph is an exception to this general rule, preventing bifurcation of a claim when the creditor has a "purchase-money security interest" (securing the claimed debt) in a motor vehicle acquired for the debtor's personal use within 910 days of the debtor's bankruptcy filing. It was undisputed that Dale (D) had purchased the vehicle for personal use within 910 days of her bankruptcy filing. The district court reversed, holding that Ford (P) had a purchase-money security interest in the entire sales contract. The court of appeals granted review.

ISSUE: Does the purchase-money security interest exception contained in the hanging paragraph of § 1325(a) of the Bankruptcy Code apply to those portions of a claim attributable to the pay-off of negative equity in a trade-in vehicle, gap insurance, and an extended warranty?

HOLDING AND DECISION: (Haynes, J.) Yes. The purchase-money security interest exception contained in the hanging paragraph of § 1325(a) of the Bankruptcy Code applies to those portions of a claim attributable to the pay-off of negative equity in a trade-in vehicle, gap insurance, and an extended warranty. The hanging paragraph was enacted as part of the Bankruptcy Abuse Prevention and Consumer Protection Act of 2005 (BAPCPA). Prior to the enactment of BAPCPA, the Code allowed a Chapter 13 debtor to modify the rights of a secured creditor with a purchase-money security interest in a vehicle bifurcating the claim into secured and unsecured portions based on the vehicle's then-market value. The secured claim would be paid in full with interest, while the unsecured claim would be paid pro-rata with other unsecured claims. This is known as "bifurcation and cramdown," since the secured claim is reduced to the present value of the collateral, while the remainder of the debt becomes unsecured, forcing the secured creditor to accept less than the full value of its claim. Because the requirements of the hanging paragraph otherwise are met here, the sole issue is whether Ford (P) has a "purchase-money security interest" securing that portion of the debt attributable to negative equity, gap insurance, and the extended warranty. The term "purchase-money security interest" does not have an ordinary or generally understood meaning, and the Code does not define it. Accordingly, the plain text of the hanging paragraph is insufficient to resolve the issue, and state Uniform Commercial Code (UCC) law must be looked to for a definition of the term. That law defines a "purchase-money security interest" in goods as a security interest in

Continued on next page.

goods that are "purchase-money collateral" and "purchase-money collateral" is in turn defined as goods that secure a "purchase-money obligation." A "purchase-money obligation" is defined as "an obligation . . . incurred as all or part of the price of the collateral or for value given to enable the debtor to acquire rights in or the use of the collateral if the value is in fact so used." This definition of "purchase-money obligation" thus contains two prongs: (1) the price of the collateral, and (2) value given to enable the debtor to acquire rights in or use of the collateral. The UCC drafters elaborated that these two prongs encompass various obligations incurred in obtaining a good, including "freight charges," "demurrage," "administrative charges," "expenses of collection and enforcement," and "attorney's fees." The inclusion of these expenses clarify "price" and "value given" are not limited to the price tag of a given good. Applying these definitions and principles here leads to the conclusion that negative equity and related expenses fit perfectly within the "value given to enable" prong. Also rejected is Dale's (D) argument that negative equity is antecedent debt, and thus cannot be considered value given to enable. Ford (P) extended new credit to pay off the negative equity on the trade-in vehicle, which enabled Dale (D) to purchase the new vehicle. The discharge of the amount owed on the old vehicle was directly related to Dale's (D) acquisition of the new car. The funds used to pay off Dale's (D) negative equity are thus properly considered "value given to enable." For these reasons, Dale's (D) debt may not be bifurcated. Affirmed.

ANALYSIS

While bankruptcy courts across the country have divided on this issue, an emerging majority of circuit courts have held, as did the court here, a creditor's purchase-money security interest encompasses the financing of negative equity, as well as the traditional transaction costs associated with purchasing a new vehicle. This position seems to be in line with the underlying purpose of the hanging paragraph of § 1325(a), which was enacted to protect car dealers from the effect of cramdown, which forced car dealers to sustain a deficiency loss on the unsecured portion of a claim, while also forcing them to wait for payout on a post-cramdown reduced loan balance, with all the attendant risks of default that accompanied the original loan.

Quicknotes

BIFURCATION At trial, the consideration of issues separately.

CRAMDOWN Refers to a court's confirmation of a reorganization plan in a bankruptcy proceeding despite the opposition of creditors.

PURCHASE-MONEY SECURITY INTEREST Security interest taken by a seller of the collateral to secure its purchase price.

Anderson v. Hancock

Debtor (P) v. Mortgage lender (D)

820 F.3d 670 (4th Cir. 2016)

NATURE OF CASE: Judgment regarding whether debtor in Chapter 13 bankruptcy can modify residential mortgage loan.

FACT SUMMARY: Debtors (P) purchased a home as a primary residence. The mortgage loan for the house contained a clause stating that in the event of default, the interest rate would change from the initial five percent to seven percent. Debtors defaulted and the interest rate was raised to seven percent, and they filed for Chapter 13 bankruptcy shortly after the mortgage lender (D) initiated foreclosure proceedings. Debtors' (P) bankruptcy plan sought to revert the interest rate to five percent.

RULE OF LAW

When the rate on a debtor's residential mortgage loan is increased upon default, a "cure" under § 1322(b) of the Bankruptcy Code does not allow the debtor's bankruptcy plan to bring post-petition payments down to the initial rate of interest.

FACTS: Debtors William Robert Anderson, Jr., and Danni Sue Jernigan (P) purchased a home as a primary residence in 2011. The home was financed by a $255,000 loan from Wayne and Tim Hancock (D), the sellers. The promissory note on the loan required monthly payments of $1,368.90 with an interest rate of five percent and a 30-year term, and provided that if the borrower had not made their monthly obligation within 30 days of the due date, the borrower would enter default and the interest rate would increase to seven percent (making the monthly payment $1,696.52) for the duration of the loan term. On April 1, 2013, Anderson and Jernigan (P) failed to make their monthly payment, and the Hancocks (D) notified Anderson and Jernigan (P) that they were in default and the future payments should reflect the seven percent interest rate. On August 30, 2013, after Anderson and Jernigan (P) continued not to make payments, the Hancocks (D) initiated foreclosure proceedings. Shortly thereafter, Anderson and Jernigan (P) filed a Chapter 13 bankruptcy petition, invoking an automatic stay and halting the foreclosure proceedings. Anderson and Jernigan (P) filed a bankruptcy plan, which proposed to pay off pre-petition arrears on the Hancock (D) loan over 60 months. Arrears were calculated using a five percent interest rate. The plan also reinstated the original maturity rate and post-petition payment at a five percent interest rate. The Hancocks (D) objected, contending that post-petition payments should reflect the seven percent interest rate as per the promissory note and that arrears to be paid off over the life of the plan should be calculated with the seven percent rate and beginning in June of 2013.

ISSUE: When the rate on a debtor's residential mortgage loan is increased upon default, does a "cure" under § 1322(b) of the Bankruptcy Code allow the debtor's bankruptcy plan to bring post-petition payments down to the initial rate of interest?

HOLDING AND DECISION: (Wilkinson, J.) No. When the rate on a debtor's residential mortgage loan is increased upon default, a "cure" under § 1322(b) of the Bankruptcy Code does not allow the debtor's bankruptcy plan to bring post-petition payments down to the initial rate of interest. Section 1322(b)(2) provides that a bankruptcy plan may "modify the rights of holders of secured claims, other than a claim secured only by a security interest in real property that is the debtor's principal residence." Plans may also "provide for the curing or waiving of any default[.]" Because the loan is secured by Anderson and Jernigan's (P) principal residence, the Hancocks' (D) rights cannot be modified. Anderson and Jernigan (P) argued that a cure would unravel every consequence of default and return to pre-default conditions. However, courts have interpreted the no-modification provision of § 1322(b)(2) to prohibit fundamental alterations of a debtor's obligations, including lowering monthly payments, converting interest rates, or extending repayment terms. Additionally, Anderson and Jernigan's (P) debt was not accelerated as a result of bankruptcy; curing would revert to a pre-default agreement rather than a pre-bankruptcy agreement. Accordingly, debtors may not modify the terms of their loan, and the interest rate will stay at seven percent.

ANALYSIS

Many debtors use Chapter 13 to avoid home foreclosure. However, a debtor must (1) prove that he or she has adequate income to cure arrears (over three to five years), (2) continue making payments, and (3) pay creditors for nonexempt assets. Accordingly, if the debtor's income is disrupted, it can jeopardize his or her ability to stay in compliance with the bankruptcy plan and ultimately result in failure.

Quicknotes

FORECLOSURE An action to recover the amount due on a mortgage of real property where the owner has failed to

Continued on next page.

meet the mortgage obligations, terminating the owner's interest in the property, which must then be sold to satisfy the debt.

SECURED CLAIM A claim, the repayment of which is secured by collateral sufficient to repay the debt owed.

CHAPTER 11

Unsecured Creditors in Chapter 13

Quick Reference Rules of Law

In the Matter of Wyant

Debtor (P) v. Bankruptcy trustee (D)

217 B.R. 585 (Bankr. D. Neb. 1998)

NATURE OF CASE: Objection to confirmation of a debtor's plan.

FACT SUMMARY: When a debtor increased his projected monthly expenses after his ex-wife died and he no longer had to pay alimony, the bankruptcy trustee claimed that the increases were not reasonable.

RULE OF LAW

Only those expenses that are reasonably necessary may be deducted from a debtor's repayment plan.

FACTS: Wyant (P) filed for Chapter 13 bankruptcy after borrowing money from his employer in return for a security interest in several vehicles he owned. When obliged to pay alimony of $1,100 per month, Wyant (P) appealed the divorce decree. His wife died shortly thereafter, and Wyant (P) filed an amended schedule, excluding the alimony. The court considered whether to confirm the proposed plan.

ISSUE: May only those expenses that are reasonably necessary be deducted from a debtor's repayment plan?

HOLDING AND DECISION: (Minahan, J.) Yes. Only those expenses that are reasonably necessary may be deducted from a debtor's repayment plan. Wyant (P) attempted to preserve assets through extensive pre-bankruptcy planning, to manipulate expenses to minimize payments to unsecured creditors, and to provide for payment of excessive attorney fees. The majority of the increase in projected monthly expenditures was discretionary and not reasonable. Wyant's (P) proposed expenses on veterinary expenses and livestock feed were unreasonable. As between the debtor's elderly horses and dogs and his creditors, the creditors should be paid first. Confirmation is denied, trustee's objection is sustained and application for attorney fees is denied.

ANALYSIS

The court decided that only $100 per month should be allowed for feed and veterinary expenses. The court disallowed $375 of the proposed increase in monthly expenditures. The proposed expenses for the animals were found to be excessive, unreasonable, and not necessary for the maintenance or support of the debtor or his dependents.

Quicknotes

BANKRUPTCY TRUSTEE Individual charged with the administration of the bankruptcy estate.

CHAPTER 13 BANKRUPTCY Debtor may modify plan at any time before the completion of the payments under such plan.

CONFIRMATION Court approval of a bankruptcy reorganization plan.

SECURITY INTEREST An interest in property that may be sold upon a default in payment of the debt.

In re Cleary

[Parties not identified.]

357 B.R. 369 (Bankr. D.S.C. 2006)

NATURE OF CASE: Objection to confirmation of a debtor's Chapter 13 plan.

FACT SUMMARY: The Chapter 13 trustee objected to the confirmation of Cleary's (Debtor's) plan on the grounds that expenditures for private school tuition for the Debtor's six children were not reasonable and necessary expenses, so that not all of Debtor's disposable income would go to repaying unsecured creditors.

RULE OF LAW

For a family, whose income is below the state median, private school tuition for parochial schools is a reasonable and necessary expense under Bankruptcy Code § 1325(b)(2)(A) where the family holds strong religious convictions, has a long history of parochial school enrollment, and lives modestly and sacrifices basic expenses to fund private school tuition.

FACTS: Cleary (Debtor), who had petitioned for Chapter 13 protection, had six children, all of whom except one were in private parochial school (and the one that was in public school was hoping to return to private school). Debtor's wife worked as a teacher's aide at a parochial school, and the bulk of her pay was applied to her children's tuition at the school. The family's median income for a family of eight was just below the applicable state's median income. The family received assistance from the private high school in the form of reduced tuition because of their income and family size. The family lived modestly, had almost no equity in their home, which was security for two mortgages, and had three older cars, one of which was under lien. Additionally, Debtor had two purchase-money furniture accounts, two loans secured by avoidable liens on household goods, and less than $18,000 in unsecured debt, mostly from credit cards. The Clearys held strong religious convictions, and Mrs. Cleary, who herself attended parochial school, worked outside the house only to provide additional income to pay for private school tuition. The family sacrificed other basic expenses to fund private school tuition. Debtor's plan included the private school tuitions, to which the Chapter 13 trustee objected, on the grounds that they were not reasonable and necessary expenses, so that not all of Debtor's disposable income would go to repaying unsecured creditors, as required by § 1325(b)(1)(B) of the Bankruptcy Code. The bankruptcy court considered the trustee's objection in a confirmation hearing.

ISSUE: For a family, whose income is below the state median, is private school tuition for parochial schools a reasonable and necessary expense under Bankruptcy Code § 1325(b)(2)(A) where the family holds strong religious convictions, has a long history of parochial school enrollment, and lives modestly and sacrifices basic expenses to fund private school tuition?

HOLDING AND DECISION: (Duncan, J.) Yes. For a family, whose income is below the state median, private school tuition for parochial schools is a reasonable and necessary expense under Bankruptcy Code § 1325(b)(2)(A) where the family holds strong religious convictions, has a long history of parochial school enrollment, and lives modestly and sacrifices basic expenses to fund private school tuition. The issue presented is a narrow one and must be decided in the context of the estimated average monthly expenses reported on Schedule J. Notwithstanding that Debtor is retaining real estate, paying a one percent dividend to general unsecured creditors, and the children have no special education needs, these factors are outweighed by the facts that: the Debtor and his family have shown long-term enrollment at parochial schools; all of the children attend private school, save one, who plans to return to private school; Mrs. Cleary attended private school; the Clearys have strongly held religious convictions; Mrs. Cleary would not work outside the home (and did not do so for many years) except to provide additional income to pay for private school tuition, and her pay check is reduced by the amount of tuition for the couple's children who attend the elementary school where she works; and the family's sacrifice of other basic expenses to fund private school tuition is noteworthy. Additionally, Debtor could file a Chapter 7 petition and it is likely that he would lose no assets to administration for creditors. He is curing a small arrearage on his home loan through the Chapter 13 plan, but the amount is de minimis. Debtor is giving up furniture secured by purchase-money loans. For these reasons, and under this set of circumstances, private school tuition is a reasonable and necessary expense. This holding is limited very narrowly to the facts of this case. The trustee's objection is overruled, and the plan will be confirmed.

ANALYSIS

Prior to the enactment of the Bankruptcy Code by the Bankruptcy Abuse Prevention and Consumer Protection Act of 2005 (BAPCPA), the courts were split on the subject of the reasonableness of private school tuition as a deduction from income to arrive at disposable income. The majority of the cases rejected private school tuition as a

Continued on next page.

reasonable and necessary expense, at least in the absence of educational necessity or special needs, and earlier decisions expressed the "view that a debtor's creditors should not pay tuition for the debtor's children." The public policy notion that private school tuition is a luxury expense for the purposes of calculating available income under either the Chapter 7 means test or for the disposable income analysis in confirming a Chapter 13 plan has arguably been swept aside by BAPCPA, which provides for some private school tuition as an allowable expense. Thus, for some purposes at least, Congress has set forth the public policy that private school tuition can be a reasonable and necessary expense.

Quicknotes

DE MINIMIS Insignificant; trivial; not of sufficient significance to require legal action.

In re Waechter

[Parties not identified.]

439 B.R. 253 (Bankr. D. Mass. 2010)

NATURE OF CASE: Objection to the confirmation of a Chapter 13 plan.

FACT SUMMARY: The Chapter 13 trustee objected to confirmation of the Debtor's plan on the grounds, inter alia, that the Debtor significantly understated her disposable income in violation of Bankruptcy Code § 1325(b)(1)(B), and that under § 1325(a)(3) it was not proposed in good faith, because under the plan the Debtor would pay a disproportionate amount of her and her nonfiling husband's shared household expenses.

RULE OF LAW

(1) A Chapter 13 debtor does not significantly understate her disposable income for purposes of Bankruptcy Code § 1325(b)(1)(B) where the debtor's nonfiling spouse does not contribute anything to the household expenses, and the debtor's income calculation reflects that the debtor does not receive income from the debtor's spouse.

(2) A Chapter 13 plan is proposed in bad faith under § 1325(a)(3) of the Bankruptcy Code where it effectively gives the debtor's nonfiling spouse a free ride on all marital living expenses.

FACTS: Debtor, prior to filing a voluntary Chapter 13 petition, had entered into a premarital agreement with her nonfiling husband that provided that the couple would keep their property and financial obligations entirely separate throughout their marriage. Each spouse would be responsible only for his or her own debt. However, the agreement did not require that the couple not share general household expenses of the marital home. Title to the marital house was solely in the Debtor's name, and she was solely responsible for the mortgage payments. The Debtor's Schedule I included her husband's net income, but her Schedule J, pursuant to a line item described as "Spouse's prerogative, pursuant to premarital agreement, not to share income," had the effect of offsetting all but $38.57 of the husband's income included in Schedule I thus leaving the Debtor with only $119 per month in disposable income to fund her Chapter 13 plan. The plan provided no dividend to general unsecured creditors. The Chapter 13 trustee objected to confirmation of this plan on the grounds, inter alia, the disposable income figure, which was the basis for the proposed plan payment, was significantly understated, and thus violated § 1325(b)(1)(B) of the Bankruptcy Code, and that the plan was not proposed in good faith, in violation of § 1325(a)(3), because it effectively gave her husband a free ride on all marital living expenses. The bankruptcy court considered the trustee's objection in a confirmation hearing.

ISSUE:

(1) Does a Chapter 13 debtor significantly understate her disposable income for purposes of Bankruptcy Code § 1325(b)(1)(B) where the debtor's nonfiling spouse does not contribute anything to the household expenses, and the debtor's income calculation reflects that the debtor does not receive income from the debtor's spouse?

(2) Is a Chapter 13 plan proposed in bad faith under § 1325(a)(3) of the Bankruptcy Code where it effectively gives the debtor's nonfiling spouse a free ride on all marital living expenses?

HOLDING AND DECISION: (Hoffman, J.)

(1) No. A Chapter 13 debtor does not significantly understate her disposable income for purposes of Bankruptcy Code § 1325(b)(1)(B) where the debtor's nonfiling spouse does not contribute anything to the household expenses, and the debtor's income calculation reflects that the debtor does not receive income from the debtor's spouse. The Bankruptcy Code defines "disposable income" as "current monthly income received" minus certain expenses. To be considered part of the debtor's current monthly income, and, therefore, included in the disposable income calculation, income from a nonfiling spouse to help cover household expenses must actually be received by the debtor. In a typical case where spouses pool some or all of their income to pay for joint household expenses, courts look at the amount of pooled household expenses and assume that the nonfiling spouse contributed a proportional amount of his or her income to the debtor for paying such expenses. Here, however, it has been attested that Debtor's husband does not contribute anything to the household expenses. Therefore, because the Debtor does not actually receive any income from her husband, her plan satisfies the requirements of § 1325(b)(1)(B).

(2) Yes. A Chapter 13 plan is proposed in bad faith under § 1325(a)(3) of the Bankruptcy Code where it effectively gives the debtor's nonfiling spouse a free ride on all marital living expenses. Notwithstanding that Debtor's plan satisfies the requirements of § 1325(b)(1)(B), it must also satisfy the good-faith requirement of § 1325(a)(3). A "totality of the circumstances" test is used to evaluate whether a plan is proposed in good faith. Here, applying that test, the premarital agreement

Continued on next page.

provided that neither party was to be held liable for the debts of the other in any way. Thus, Debtor could in good faith propose a plan in which she was solely responsible for the mortgage payment on the marital home, but could not in good faith, propose a plan in which she purported to pay all other joint household expenses while her husband paid nothing. Because the premarital agreement does not address how the spouses will divide the joint day-to-day expenses of their married life, Debtor may not rely on the agreement as justification for taking full responsibility for paying household expenses, effectively subsidizing her husband's income at the expense of her creditors. If the husband were to contribute a proportional share of his income towards these expenses from which he benefits, the Debtor's projected disposable income would increase to $330 per month. If he were to contribute a full 50 percent share of these expenses, the Debtor's disposable income would jump to $703.50. In either circumstance, the Debtor could propose a plan providing for a significant dividend to her general unsecured creditors. Based on the totality of these circumstances, the plan is not proposed in good faith, and the trustee's objection to confirmation is sustained. Judgment for the trustee.

ANALYSIS

Where questions of good faith arise with respect to a nonfiling spouse's contribution, or lack thereof, to a debtor's disposable income in Chapter 13 cases, some courts have investigated the lifestyle choices of the nonfiling spouse. Thus, for example, if the debtor received income towards household expenses from her nonfiling spouse while at the same time enjoying the benefits of excessive luxury household expenses paid for exclusively by the spouse, courts have denied plan confirmation on the basis of bad faith. See *In re McNichols,* 254 B.R. 422, 430 (Bankr. N.D. Ill. 2000). On the other hand, if it is clear the nonfiling spouse is using his surplus income substantially to pay his own obligations and is not otherwise subsidizing the debtor's luxury lifestyle while the debtor's creditors take it on the chin, then courts will find the debtor's plan to be filed in good faith. See *In re Nahat,* 278 B.R. 108 (Bankr. N.D. Tex. 2002).

Quicknotes

GOOD FAITH An honest intention to abstain from taking advantage of another.

TOTALITY OF THE CIRCUMSTANCES TEST Standard that focuses on all the circumstances of a particular case, instead of individual factors.

In re Drew

[Parties not identified.]

325 B.R. 765 (Bankr. N.D. Ill. 2005)

NATURE OF CASE: Consolidated Chapter 13 trustee's motions to modify debtors' confirmed plans under Bankruptcy Code § 1329(a)(1).

FACT SUMMARY: After various debtors (Debtors) Chapter 13 plans were confirmed, the Chapter 13 trustee (Trustee) moved to modify their plans to increase the dividends payable to the prepetition unsecured creditors as a result of their refinancing of their real properties and receiving a lump sum cash payment as part of the refinancing.

RULE OF LAW

A debtor's confirmed plan may be amended under § 1329 of the Bankruptcy Code to increase the dividends payable to the prepetition unsecured creditors as a result of the debtor's refinancing of the debtor's real property and receiving a lump sum cash payment as part of the refinancing.

FACTS: After their Chapter 13 plans were confirmed, debtors (Debtors) whose real properties appreciated in value since confirmation refinanced the properties with the bankruptcy court's permission. The Debtors obtained lump sum cash payments as a result of the refinancings. One of the Debtors, the Drews, had a plan that required them to pay $350 per month to the Chapter 13 trustee (Trustee) for a minimum term of 36 months (totaling $12,600) for unsecured creditors' allowed claims to receive a minimum 10 percent dividend. The order confirming the plan provided if the unsecured creditors would receive 100 percent of their allowed claims, they could pay less than the aggregate sum of $12,600. On January 19, 2005, the Court granted the Debtors' motions to obtain credit in order to refinance their properties. On January 24, 2005, the Trustee moved to modify the Drews' plan (as well as that of another debtor in a similar situation) to increase the dividends payable to the prepetition unsecured creditors as a result of their refinancing of their real property and receiving a lump sum cash payment as part of the refinancing. At that point, the Drews had not made all the payments required under their plan, but instead had paid only $9,380. In the Drews' case, the Trustee alleged that at the time of confirmation, their real estate was valued at $90,000, and they refinanced it for $105,000. The Trustee's motions were consolidated. The Debtors conceded the valuations of the subject properties that were scheduled at the time of confirmation but asserted that the Trustee was estopped from challenging those valuations at this point. They contended that the higher valuations, for refinancing purposes, showed that the real properties appreciated over the passage of time since confirmation. The Debtors argued that they should be able to keep the surplus equity and should not be required to pay those funds to the unsecured creditors and increase their dividends. The Debtors also contended that granting the Trustee's motions would effectively discourage other debtors from seeking relief under Chapter 13.

ISSUE: May a debtor's confirmed plan be amended under § 1329 of the Bankruptcy Code to increase the dividends payable to the prepetition unsecured creditors as a result of the debtor's refinancing of the debtor's real property and receiving a lump sum cash payment as part of the refinancing?

HOLDING AND DECISION: (Squires, J.) Yes. A debtor's confirmed plan may be amended under § 1329 of the Bankruptcy Code to increase the dividends payable to the prepetition unsecured creditors as a result of the debtor's refinancing of the debtor's real property and receiving a lump sum cash payment as part of the refinancing. As a procedural matter, the Trustee has standing under § 1329 of the Bankruptcy Code to seek post-confirmation modification of the plans to increase the dividends to the unsecured claim holders. In a Chapter 13 bankruptcy, property that a debtor acquires postpetition, like the refinancing proceeds the Debtors received in the cases at bar, becomes property of the estate pursuant to § 1306. This result occurs because § 541 broadly defines property of the estate to include "all legal or equitable interests of the debtor in property as of the commencement of the case," and § 1306(a)(1) includes "all property of the kind specified in § 541 that the debtor acquires after the commencement of the case but before the case is closed, dismissed or converted." Although § 1327(c) provides that property vesting in the debtor includes all property acquired after the petition, and that such property is "free and clear of any claim or interest of any creditor provided for by the plan," some courts have held that the estate continues and can be refilled with property acquired after confirmation. The court of appeals for this district has stated that § 1306(a)(2) provides that upon confirmation, the plan returns so much of the estate to the debtor's control as is not necessary for the fulfilment of the plan. Applying that principle here, the portions of the refinancing proceeds intended by the Debtors to be paid to complete their confirmed plans are part of the continuing estates, and the refinancing proceeds are part of the Debtors' bankruptcy estates post-confirmation because those

Continued on next page.

proceeds were acquired by the Debtors for use in making payments under their confirmed plans. This result is fair, as it is fair to require debtors to share good fortune with creditors, in the same way that it is fair to permit Chapter 13 debtors to reduce payments to creditors when circumstances disable the debtor from completing the original plan. The statute works both ways, and both results are permitted by § 1329. Although the refinancing by the Debtors in these cases involved new debt incurred by them, it is doubtful that the new loans made to the Debtors were at a 100 percent loan to value ratio. Instead, it is more likely that each property's value has increased substantially more than the amounts loaned. Hence, there is likely additional equity in each property that the Debtors enjoy and will retain because the properties are not being sold. The Trustee's motions effectively seek to compel the Debtors to contribute so much of that equity to the unsecured creditors' dividends as the Debtors are cashing out via the refinancing. Finally, there is no evidence presented that supports the Debtors' contention that increasing the dividends to unsecured creditors will somehow discourage debtors from either filing Chapter 13 petitions or serve as a disincentive for debtors to seek to exit the system sooner. To the contrary, the possibility of relief under § 1329 only occurs after a Chapter 13 debtor's plan has achieved the major hurdle of being confirmed in the first instance, and many Chapter 13 cases never get to that point. Moreover, of those that do, the vast majority of § 1329 motions are brought by debtors who seek to lower the dividend to unsecured creditors because of their subsequent adverse circumstances. For all these reasons, the Trustee's motions to modify the Debtors' confirmed plans are granted. Judgment for Trustee.

ANALYSIS

As this case demonstrates, property that a Chapter 13 debtor acquires postpetition, like the refinancing proceeds the Debtors received, becomes property of the estate, and it has been held that a Chapter 13 estate can include gifts, inheritances, and windfalls that are acquired by the debtor postpetition. This contrasts with postpetition acquisitions in Chapter 7 or Chapter 11 bankruptcies, where such acquisitions do not become part of the estate. Thus, for example, if a debtor converted to Chapter 7 after winning a lottery or realizing new income, the postpetition assets and income would belong to the debtor and would not be available for distribution to creditors in the Chapter 7 case. Accordingly, the sharing of postpetition good fortune may be seen by some courts as the cost of the Chapter 13 discharge.

Quicknotes

POSTPETITION After bankruptcy petition has been filed.

PREPETITION Before bankruptcy petition has been filed.

UNSECURED CREDITOR A creditor whose loan is not backed by specified collateral or a security agreement.

CHAPTER 12

The Means Test

Quick Reference Rules of Law

In re Shaw

[Court consideration of bankruptcy petition.]

311 B.R. 180 (Bankr. M.D.N.C. 2003)

NATURE OF CASE: Action in bankruptcy under Chapter 7.

FACT SUMMARY: **The Shaws filed for Chapter 7 bankruptcy in an apparent effort to protect their house and three vehicles from creditors. Over the years, the Shaws had amassed hundreds of thousands of dollars in secured and unsecured debt.**

RULE OF LAW

The court may dismiss a debtor's Chapter 7 petition for "substantial abuse" under the Bankruptcy Code if the debtor has the ability to at least partially repay creditors, but seeks to avoid doing so in order to maintain an excessive lifestyle.

FACTS: The Shaws, husband and wife, had a combined monthly income of approximately $7,800. Although Mrs. Shaw experienced a brief period of unemployment, both Shaws are fully employed. The couple spent years, however, with their consumer spending far exceeding their income, thus amassing hundreds of thousands of dollars in secured and unsecured debt. The Shaw family had three cars, a large home, four telephone lines including two mobile phones, an adult son living rent-free at home, and a daughter in college. In an effort to protect the three cars and their principal residence, the Shaws filed for Chapter 7 bankruptcy. The Shaws submitted a family budget of over $6,000 per month, leaving no disposable income. They stipulated that $130,000 of their debt was consumer debt. The court scheduled the matter to determine whether Chapter 7 bankruptcy petition should be dismissed under § 707(b) of the Code for "substantial abuse."

ISSUE: May the court dismiss a debtor's Chapter 7 petition for "substantial abuse" under the Bankruptcy Code if the debtor has the ability to at least partially repay creditors, but seeks to avoid doing so in order to maintain an excessive lifestyle?

HOLDING AND DECISION: (Carruthers, J.) Yes. The court may dismiss a debtor's Chapter 7 petition for "substantial abuse" under the Bankruptcy Code if the debtor has the ability to at least partially repay creditors, but seeks to avoid doing so in order to maintain an excessive lifestyle. Congress did not define "substantial abuse," but the Fourth Circuit adopted a test in *In re Green,* 934 F.2d 568 (1991). A court must consider the "totality of the circumstances," potential ability to repay the debt, and the five *Green* factors. Here, the Shaws do have the ability to repay at least a portion of the unsecured debt because their income remains high and their expenses can be significantly reduced. Their proposed budget is excessive given that the Shaws have no practical need for such a large principal residence, three cars, four phone lines, or college expenses. The amount of $2,000 per month could go toward a Chapter 13 plan. The Shaws have admittedly lived beyond their means for years and are not filing for bankruptcy after an unexpected or tragic event. Their petition cannot be considered filed in good faith when the Shaws seek to maintain their excessive lifestyle at the expense of their creditors. The court does not find that the Shaws intended to mislead parties with inadvertent discrepancies on their inventory, but their proposed budget is unacceptable. Considering the totality of the circumstances, it is a substantial abuse of the Bankruptcy Code to allow these debtors to file under Chapter 7. They may decide whether a Chapter 13 petition should be filed. Dismissed.

ANALYSIS

The income of the Shaws was approximately six times that of the typical petitioner. Courts tend to look askance at debtors with lavish lifestyles simply seeking to avoid the repayment consequences of a life of excess. Chapter 7 is ideally protection for those in need of asset preservation because of a calamity rather than a lifestyle choice.

Quicknotes

CHAPTER 7 BANKRUPTCY A legal proceeding whereby a debtor, who is unable to pay his or her debts as they become due, is relieved of the obligation to pay creditors by liquidation and distribution of remaining assets.

CHAPTER 13 BANKRUPTCY Debtor may modify plan at any time before the completion of the payments under such plan.

DEBT An obligation incurred by a person who promises to render payment or compensation to another.

GOOD FAITH An honest intention to abstain from taking advantage of another.

SECURED DEBT Debt that is backed by a security interest in a debtor's property.

UNSECURED DEBT Debt that is not backed by collateral.

Johnson v. Zimmer

Debtor/ex-wife (D) v. Creditor/ex-husband (P)

686 F.3d 224 (4th Cir. 2012)

NATURE OF CASE: Direct appeal from bankruptcy court's denial of confirmation of a proposed Chapter 13 plan.

FACT SUMMARY: Johnson (Debtor) (D), who had a blended family that included her children and her husband's children from previous relationships, with the children living for varying amounts of time in the household, contended that the appropriate method of calculating "household" size to be used in determining her disposable income under Bankruptcy Code § 1325 was a "heads on the beds" method that accounted for individuals who lived in the household for any length of time within the relevant period, rather than an "economic unit" approach that assesses the number of individuals in the household who act as a single economic unit, and that, if appropriate, assigns fractional values to each individual and rounds up the total to a whole number.

RULE OF LAW

Where a debtor has a blended family, with some family members living with the debtor only some of the time, it is appropriate in calculating the debtor's "household" size for the purpose of determining the debtor's disposable income under Bankruptcy Code § 1325 to use an "economic unit" approach that assesses the number of individuals in the household who act as a single economic unit, and that, if appropriate, assigns fractional values to each individual and rounds up the total to a whole number.

FACTS: Johnson (Debtor) (D) moved to confirm her Chapter 13 plan, and her ex-husband, Zimmer (Creditor) (P) objected, on the grounds that the proposed plan overstated the Debtor's (D) household size, resulting in an inaccurate calculation of her monthly expenses for the purpose of determining her disposable income. Debtor's (D) two minor children lived with her and her husband for 204 days per year, and the husband's two minor children and 19-year old lived with them 180 days per year. Debtor (D) and Creditor (P) shared expenses for clothing, school supplies, and other incidental expenses for their children based on where the children lived, but out-of-pocket medical expenses were divided equally. Debtor (D) claimed a household of seven members, counting individually each person who resided in her home for any period of time within the past six months (i.e., the Debtor (D), her husband, her two children, and her three stepchildren). The Creditor (P) asserted that the Debtor (D) did not actually have seven members of her household because the five children and stepchildren did not live at her residence full-time. He contended that rather than simply counting the number of "heads on the beds" to determine household size, the Debtor's (D) plan should use a method that better approximated the actual economic impact of each individual on the Debtor's (D) expenses. Because the Bankruptcy Code does not define "household" or direct how to calculate the number of members in a household, the bankruptcy court, after reviewing three methods used to determine "household," decided that an "economic unit" approach would best serve the Code's purpose and would be the most flexible in terms of adapting to an individual debtor's circumstances. In doing so, the bankruptcy court rejected the "heads-on-beds" approach that follows the Census Bureau's broad definition of a household as "all the people who occupy a housing unit," without regard to relationship, financial contributions, or financial dependency, and the court rejected the "income tax dependent" method derived from the Internal Revenue Manual's definition that examines which individuals either are or could be included on the debtor's tax return as dependents. Under the bankruptcy court's economic unit approach, the court assessed the number of individuals whose income and expenses were intermingled with the Debtor's (D), and then calculated how much time any part-time residents were members of the Debtor's (D) household. Applying this approach, the bankruptcy court determined that each of the Debtor's (D) two children constituted .56 members of the Debtor's (D) household, and that each of her three stepchildren constituted .49 members of her household. This resulted in the Debtor (D) having a total of 2.59 children in her household full-time, which the court then rounded up to three children. Accordingly, the court determined that the Debtor (D) had five members in her household (the three children, herself, and her husband)—not seven. Consequently, it denied Debtor's (D) motion to confirm her plan. The court of appeals granted direct review.

ISSUE: Where a debtor has a blended family, with some family members living with the debtor only some of the time, is it appropriate in calculating the debtor's "household" size for the purpose of determining the debtor's disposable income under Bankruptcy Code § 1325 to use an "economic unit" approach that assesses the number of individuals in the household who act as a single economic unit, and that, if appropriate, assigns fractional values to each individual and rounds up the total to a whole number?

Continued on next page.

HOLDING AND DECISION: (Agee, J.) Yes. Where a debtor has a blended family, with some family members living with the debtor only some of the time, it is appropriate in calculating the debtor's "household" size for the purpose of determining the debtor's disposable income under Bankruptcy Code § 1325 to use an "economic unit" approach that assesses the number of individuals in the household who act as a single economic unit, and that, if appropriate, assigns fractional values to each individual and rounds up the total to a whole number. There are multiple dictionary definitions of "household," so resorting to the dictionary does not provide a single plain or common meaning of that term. Statutory context provides some guidance, but ultimately does not resolve the fundamental uncertainty of what Congress intended "household" to mean. Congress used the word "household" as opposed to "family," "dependent child," or "dependent," all of which are used elsewhere in the surrounding and cross-referenced Code provisions. This can be taken to mean that Congress intended the term "household" to mean something other than what those terms mean. Definitions of "household" can overlap with each of these terms to varying degrees, as "household" may or may not be defined to include the concept of familial connection or domestic interconnectedness. In § 707(b) Congress refers to a debtor's "dependents" as opposed to his or her "household." Congress's use of "dependents" tends to suggest that although Congress used "dependent" and "household" at different points, they may nonetheless have related meanings. Looking at the statutory context thus does not provide a definitive definition of "household," which can, therefore, be considered an ambiguous term. To resolve the ambiguity, Congress's intent must be gleaned from extrinsic evidence, such as the legislative history, and the interpretation of the ambiguous term must be as harmonious as possible with the statutory scheme and purpose. Although some courts have adopted the "heads on beds" approach, there is not a clear indication that Congress intended the use of the Census Bureau's broad definition of household in a § 1325(b) calculation. A mere cross-reference to the Census Bureau's median income tables in the statute does not evince such intent, nor does the use of "household" as opposed to "family" or "dependents" in the statute. The Census Bureau's definition is wholly unrelated to any bankruptcy purpose and does not serve the Code's objective of identifying a debtor's deductible monthly expenses and, ultimately, disposable income. It makes little sense to allow debtors to broadly define their "households" to include individuals who have no actual financial impact on the debtor's expenses. Permitting the use of such a definition would also be at odds with the Bankruptcy Abuse Prevention and Consumer Protection Act's (BAPCPA's) stated purpose of implementing an income/expense screening mechanism intended to ensure that debtors repay creditors the maximum they can afford. On the other hand, the use of the economic unit approach is consistent with the Code. It is flexible because it recognizes that a debtor's "household" may include nonfamily members and individuals who could not be claimed as dependents on the debtor's federal income tax return, but who nonetheless directly impact the debtor's financial situation. This definition, which is tailored to reflect a debtor's financial situation, focuses directly upon the Code's ultimate purpose. Further, it is not error under this approach to fractionalize household members where appropriate, as in this case where they reside with the debtor for only part of the year. The Debtor's (D) situation is increasingly common in modern American life, and that the number of individuals with a financial relationship to a debtor may well vary depending on the day of the week and other circumstances. Thus, the bankruptcy court did not err in exercising its discretion to accommodate this reality by representing the individuals as fractional full-time members of the household and then rounding to a whole number. Affirmed.

DISSENT: (Wilkinson, J.) The majority's ruling permitting the fractionalization of individuals contravenes statutory text, allows judges to unilaterally update the Bankruptcy Code, and subjects debtors to needlessly intrusive and litigious proceedings. Undefined statutory terms should be given their ordinary meanings, and the word "individual" ordinarily means "a human being, a person." Also, the bankruptcy court's decision to address the increase in split custody arrangements and blended families without ignoring the economic realities of a debtor's living situation, while laudable, effectively is an attempt to update the Code to reflect social changes—a task that must be left to Congress. Finally, by allowing judges to treat dependents as fractions, the majority opens the door to greater litigation and intrusion. This could arise, for example, where estranged parents dispute the details of their custody arrangements. Thus, the cost of arriving at economic accuracy could be significantly greater litigation costs. Such costs are unnecessary, since Congress chose to tolerate the occasional peculiarity that a brighter-line test produces. Although treating children in joint custody arrangements as whole individuals may lead to some inaccuracies redounding to the benefit of either debtors or creditors, that problem is the inevitable result of a standardized formula like the means test. Since Congress chose to tolerate some inaccuracies in the interest of administrability, and since bankruptcy courts can chose from among multiple ways to calculate a debtor's household size or to take the economic circumstances of a debtor into account, they may not embrace interpretations that co-opt the legislative function.

ANALYSIS

It should be noted that the outcome of this case—permitting an economic unit approach to determine household

Continued on next page.

size—may not ultimately determine the debtor's case where the debtor is an above-median debtor. That could be because the means test set forth in § 707(b)(2) directs a debtor to include herself, her "dependents," and in appropriate cases her spouse, in the required calculations, so that the sum of those individuals may not be the same as her "household" size, depending on how "dependents" and "household" are each defined. Thus, if the case were to turn on the ordinary and common meaning of the word "dependent," the meaning of "household" would be irrelevant. The court here, while acknowledging that "household" size may not be the "dispositive" inquiry in determining an above-median debtor's disposable income, emphasized that the determination of "household" remains a significant component of the § 1325(b) scheme.

In re Scott

[Parties not identified.]

457 B.R. 740 (Bankr. S.D. Ill. 2011)

NATURE OF CASE: [The procedural posture of the case is not presented in the casebook extract.]

FACT SUMMARY: Debtors maintained that they were entitled to claim the entire Internal Revenue Service (IRS) Standard for each of their two vehicles based on a plain language interpretation of Bankruptcy Code § 707(b)(2)(A)(ii)(I). The bankruptcy trustee (Trustee) disagreed and objected, arguing, inter alia, that the Debtors' approach frustrated the Bankruptcy Abuse Prevention and Consumer Protection Act's (BAPCPA's) "overall purpose of ensuring that the debtors repay creditors to the extent that they can." [The full facts of the case are not presented in the casebook extract.]

RULE OF LAW

A debtor whose secured debt payment on a car is less than the IRS Standard can receive the benefit of the full deduction.

FACTS: Debtors who were using Form B22C to calculate their expenses took the full Internal Revenue Service (IRS) Standard for each of their two vehicles, instead of using their actual costs. They contended they were entitled to do so based on a plain language interpretation of § 707(b)(2)(A)(ii)(I), which provides in part that "the debtor's monthly expenses shall be the debtor's applicable monthly expense amounts specified under the National and Local Standards. . . ." Because car payments are listed under the local standards on Form B22C and not as an "Other Necessary Expense[]" (which, under the statute, is limited to a debtor's actual monthly expense), Debtors argued that they were entitled to claim the specified standard amount, despite the fact that their actual monthly vehicle payment was less. The bankruptcy trustee (Trustee) disagreed and objected, arguing, inter alia, that the Debtors' approach frustrated the Bankruptcy Abuse Prevention and Consumer Protection Act's (BAPCPA's) "overall purpose of ensuring that the debtors repay creditors to the extent that they can." [The full facts of the case are not presented in the casebook extract.]

ISSUE: Can a debtor whose secured debt payment on a car is less than the IRS Standard receive the benefit of the full deduction?

HOLDING AND DECISION: (Grandy, J.) Yes. A debtor whose secured debt payment on a car is less than the IRS Standard can receive the benefit of the full deduction. Once the debtors can show that they have a secured car ownership expense, they are entitled to claim the IRS Standard because that is the "applicable" expense. Had Congress intended to limit the car ownership expense to actual cost, it could have said so. Instead, the express language of the statute provides that only "the categories specified as Other Necessary Expenses" are to use actual expenses. There is no provision in the statute for reducing the specified amounts to the debtor's actual expenses. Simply put, the statute makes clear that Debtors are entitled to the full deduction regardless of their actual costs. Additionally, the Trustee's argument that permitting this result would frustrate BAPCPA's overriding purpose of maximizing debtor repayment to creditors, while accurate—the Debtors' disposable income would be increased by more than $100.00 per month if the Debtors were forced to use their actual costs—ignores other policy objectives that Congress sought to promote through BAPCPA. One such objective was the removal of judicial discretion in determining disposable income. Permitting debtors to take the IRS Standard furthers this goal, and, in fact, also furthers the goal of maximizing the return to creditors, but simply does so within the framework prescribed by Congress and Form B22C.

ANALYSIS

This case involved debtors whose actual expenses were less than the IRS Standard. However, using the court's approach of strictly applying the statutory language of § 707(b)(2)(A)(ii)(I), a debtor whose actual expenses exceed the IRS Standards would also be limited to the Standard amount, and could claim an allowance only for the specified sum, rather than for his real expenditures.

CHAPTER 13

Chapter Choice

Quick Reference Rules of Law

In re Deutscher

[Parties not identified.]

419 B.R. 42 (Bankr. N.D. Ill. 2009)

NATURE OF CASE: Motion to dismiss in Chapter 7 action. [The complete procedural posture of the case is not presented in the casebook extract.]

FACT SUMMARY: Because the above-median Deutschers (Debtors), who voluntarily filed for Chapter 7 bankruptcy protection, had a large amount of their debt secured by a yacht, a boat, and an SUV, there was no presumption of abuse under the means test under § 707 of the Bankruptcy Code. The United States Trustee (UST) nevertheless moved to dismiss under the totality of the circumstances test of § 707(b)(3).

RULE OF LAW

Where there is no presumption of abuse under the means test under §§ 707(a) and 707(b)(2) of the Bankruptcy Code, because a large amount of the above-median debtor's secured debt significantly exceeds his unsecured debt, a voluntary Chapter 7 bankruptcy action nevertheless may be dismissed under the totality of the circumstances test of § 707(b)(3) where the secured debt is secured by luxury items purchased shortly prior to the debtor's filing the action.

FACTS: The Deutschers (Debtors), who voluntarily filed for Chapter 7 bankruptcy protection in November 2008, were above-median debtors. They had $336,752 in secured debt, $2,220 in unsecured priority debt, and $61,817 in unsecured nonpriority debt. Their obligations are primarily consumer debts. Over half of their secured debt was from a loan used in September 2007 to purchase a yacht; from the purchase in August 2008 of a boat; and from the purchase of an SUV in June 2008. They did not need any of these vehicles for work, and, apparently these purchases were made when Mr. Deutscher was unemployed. As a result of the large secured debt, there was no presumption of abuse under the means test under §§ 707(a) and 707(b)(2) of the Bankruptcy Code. Nevertheless, the United States Trustee (UST) moved to dismiss under the totality of the circumstances test of § 707(b)(3).

ISSUE: Where there is no presumption of abuse under the means test under §§ 707(a) and 707(b)(2) of the Bankruptcy Code, because a large amount of the above-median debtor's secured debt significantly exceeds his unsecured debt, may a voluntary Chapter 7 bankruptcy action nevertheless be dismissed under the totality of the circumstances test of § 707(b)(3) where the secured debt is secured by luxury items purchased shortly prior to the debtor's filing the action?

HOLDING AND DECISION: (Barbosa, J.) Yes. Where there is no presumption of abuse under the means test under §§ 707(a) and 707(b)(2) of the Bankruptcy Code, because a large amount of the above-median debtor's secured debt significantly exceeds his unsecured debt, a voluntary Chapter 7 bankruptcy action nevertheless may be dismissed under the totality of the circumstances test of § 707(b)(3) where the secured debt is secured by luxury items purchased shortly prior to the debtor's filing the action. Failing the means test simply means that the debtor's petition is not presumed abusive. The petition may still be dismissed if the totality of the circumstances warrant dismissal under § 707(b)(3). Under the totality of the circumstances test, a debtor's ability to pay is a key factor, but a court must also consider: (1) whether the bankruptcy petition was filed because of sudden illness, calamity, disability, or unemployment; (2) whether the debtor incurred cash advances and made consumer purchases far in excess of his ability to pay; (3) whether the debtor's proposed family budget is excessive or unreasonable; and (4) whether the debtor's schedules and statement of current income and expenses reasonably and accurately reflect the true financial condition. Because the ability to pay is also the focus of the means test, when addressing ability to pay under § 707(b)(3), a court must be attentive to the policy choices made by Congress in drafting the means test, including the fact that it gave preferred treatment to secured creditors by allowing scheduled payments of secured debt to be listed as deductions without limitation. Therefore, solely because a debtor has a high amount of secured debt or solely because a debtor intends to reaffirm secured debt is not an indication by itself of abuse. Instead, abuse can be gleaned from the totality of the circumstances where there is evidence that a debtor has manipulated the means test, purchased luxuries on credit on the eve of bankruptcy, altered his expenses in his Schedules, accrued significant debt prior to the petition, or has submitted an excessive or unreasonable budget. Looking at these factors, the vehicles at issue can be considered luxury items, and the purchases thereof demonstrate a pattern by the Debtors of living beyond their means. Their financial situation was not caused by a sudden illness, calamity, or disability. Although much of the cause might have been the economic downturn and its impact on Mr. Deutscher's business, these large purchases, which took place during a period Mr. Deutscher claims to have been unemployed, clearly exacerbated the situation. The Debtors appear to want to continue this lifestyle even after seeking a bankruptcy dis-

Continued on next page.

charge by reaffirming their debt on these luxury items rather than follow the expectation that "when seeking bankruptcy relief, debtors may be expected to do some belt tightening, including, where necessary, foregoing the reaffirmation of those secured debts which are not reasonably necessary for the maintenance and support of the debtor and his family." *In re Harter*, 397 B.R. 860, 864 (Bankr. N.D. Ohio 2008). Motion to dismiss granted.

ANALYSIS

Determination of whether a purchase is "on the eve of bankruptcy" or abusive, is a case-by-case determination, and, for example, the more expensive the purchase, the longer the time frame before petition, it might still be seen as being on the eve of bankruptcy. Also, purchases that cause the debtor to become insolvent generally give rise to a determination of abuse, regardless of the length of time that elapses between the purchase and the bankruptcy filing. Here, the Debtors purchased the boat three months before filing their petition, the SUV five months before petition, and the yacht 14 months before petition. These timeframes likely were too long to count as "on the eve of bankruptcy." However, the fact that they were purchased at a time when the Debtors were likely insolvent, or at least on a rapid slide towards bankruptcy, and at a time Mr. Deutscher was unemployed indicates that they were consumer purchases far in excess of the Debtors' ability to pay, thus satisfying an important factor in the totality of the circumstances test.

Quicknotes

TOTALITY OF THE CIRCUMSTANCES TEST Standard that focuses on all the circumstances of a particular case instead of individual factors.

In re Durczynski

[Parties not identified.]

405 B.R. 880 (Bankr. N.D. Ohio 2009)

NATURE OF CASE: Proceeding in bankruptcy action. [The procedural posture of the case is not presented in the casebook extract.]

FACT SUMMARY: Debtors allocated over 40 percent of their net income to house-related secured debts. Their desire to reaffirm those debts so they could retain the house was challenged as abusive. [The complete facts of the case are not presented in the casebook extract.]

RULE OF LAW

Where a debtor desires to retain a house by reaffirming secured debt at the expense of unsecured debt, and where the debtor's payments on the house far exceed the means test formulation of § 707(b)(2) of the Bankruptcy Code, the debtor's petition is abusive where the debtor's desire to retain the house arises from want rather than need.

FACTS: Debtors, a husband and wife who had a family of five, allocated over 40 percent of their net income to house-related secured debts. This was two times the amount that was allowed under the means test formulation of § 707(b)(2). Debtors wanted to reaffirm their secured debt at the expense of their unsecured debt. There was no indication that retaining the house would contribute to the Debtor's children's health or education. Also, the wife worked part time. The Debtor's desire to retain their house was challenged as abusive based on the Debtors' entire financial situation. [The complete facts of the case are not presented in the casebook extract.]

ISSUE: Where a debtor desires to retain a house by reaffirming secured debt at the expense of unsecured debt, and where the debtor's payments on the house far exceed the means test formulation of § 707(b)(2) of the Bankruptcy Code, is the debtor's petition abusive where the debtor's desire to retain the house arises from want rather than need?

HOLDING AND DECISION: (Speer, J.) Yes. Where a debtor desires to retain a house by reaffirming secured debt at the expense of unsecured debt, and where the debtor's payments on the house far exceed the means test formulation of § 707(b)(2) of the Bankruptcy Code, the debtor's petition is abusive where the debtor's desire to retain the house arises from want rather than need. Debtors may be expected to do some belt tightening, including, where necessary, foregoing the reaffirmation of those secured debts that are not reasonably necessary for the maintenance and support of the debtor and his family. Although the means test is not strictly applicable here, its standards serve to show a significant portion of the expenses associated with the Debtors' residence are not necessary for their basic living needs, but instead constitute a "lifestyle" choice. The purchase of a home is a highly personal choice, and debtors may be afforded some latitude in their choice of a home since their choice involves a moral and value-based judgment. Nevertheless, a court must still assess a debtor's ability to pay under § 707(b)(3), and such an assessment may encroach on the highly personal choices—such as purchasing a house—that all individuals make about how to prioritize their expenses and, on more basic level, how to live their lives. The more an expense involves a moral and value-based judgment on the part of the debtor, the more deference that will be accorded to the debtor's decision. However, such deference is not unlimited. Based on these considerations, it is clear here that the Debtor's desire to retain their house arises more from "want" as opposed to any "need." Therefore, notwithstanding the Debtor's understandable emotional attachment to their house, it would be unjustifiable to overlook their overall financial situation, especially since the wife could earn 20 percent to 30 percent more if she worked full time. [The outcome of the case is not presented in the casebook excerpt.]

ANALYSIS

The court seems to be saying that the Debtors' desire to retain their house in this case, given their entire financial situation, is more like making a financial choice, an example of which the court says is the purchase of cable television, which the court says does not involve a moral or value judgment. Thus, the court, which initially concedes that making a house purchase involves making a normative judgment, thus seems to carve out an exception to that general proposition where debtors seemingly can pay unsecured creditors. This reasoning seems to indicate that the means test is really a normative method of identifying "should-pay" debtors, rather than merely identifying "can-pay" debtors.

Quicknotes

REAFFIRMATION An agreement after the filing of the bankruptcy petition to repay obligations that arose prior to its filing.

In re Crager

[Parties not identified.]

691 F.3d 671 (5th Cir. 2012)

NATURE OF CASE: Appeal from reversal of bankruptcy court's confirmation of a Chapter 13 plan.

FACT SUMMARY: The Trustee objected to confirmation of Crager's Chapter 13 plan on the grounds that it was filed in bad faith and that her attorney's fees were unreasonable.

RULE OF LAW

(1) A Chapter 13 plan that results in the debtor's counsel receiving almost the entire amount paid to the trustee, leaving other unsecured creditors unpaid, does not constitute a per se violation of the good-faith requirement under Bankruptcy Code § 1325.

(2) A trustee does not bear the burden of proving that a "no-look" attorney's fee is unreasonable.

(3) Under Bankruptcy Code § 330, a "no-look" fee is reasonable where the trustee's objection transforms an otherwise routine Chapter 13 matter into a complicated proceeding.

FACTS: Crager, who was unemployed, and whose main source of income was $1,060 per month in Social Security benefits plus $16 per month in food stamps, filed for Chapter 13 bankruptcy protection. Her main asset was her primary residence, and her mortgage payments were $327.10 per month. She also had $7,855.27 in credit card debt, and her minimum monthly payments were $197. Prior to filing her Chapter 13 petition, Crager was current on all mortgage and credit card payments. However, Crager learned that if she continued making the minimum payments on her credit cards, it would take her 17 to 20 years to pay off her balances. She contacted the loss mitigation departments of her credit card companies to seek an interest rate or monthly payment reduction but did not receive either. She filed for Chapter 13, rather than Chapter 7, primarily because it would have taken her over a year to save enough money to pay the up-front costs for a Chapter 7 bankruptcy and to do so she would have needed to stop making her minimum monthly credit card payments. There were other reasons that she preferred Chapter 13 over Chapter 7. Her attorney advanced her court costs of $274. The Trustee objected to confirmation of the plan. The Trustee asserted that Crager's petition and plan were not filed in good faith pursuant §§ 1325(a)(3) and (7) of the Bankruptcy Code and that the amount of attorney's fees sought by Crager's attorney was unreasonable, primarily because, according to the Trustee, Crager's bankruptcy was relatively simple. The bankruptcy court overruled the Trustee's objections. The bankruptcy court did so, in part, because it focused on the rising cost of medical care and suggested Crager had a legitimate fear a future medical problem might leave her in a situation in which she had to take on more debt and might need to file another Chapter 13 petition. The court found that it would "border on malpractice" for Crager's attorney to advise her to file a Chapter 7. The court also approved Crager's counsel's fees pursuant to a "no-look" fee of $2,800 established by a Standing Order of the district. A "no-look" fee is an amount that a court may grant as reasonable in the absence of a detailed fee application, because such a fee is presumptively reasonable. The district court reversed, and the court of appeals granted review.

ISSUE:

(1) Does a Chapter 13 plan that results in the debtor's counsel receiving almost the entire amount paid to the trustee, leaving other unsecured creditors unpaid, constitute a per se violation of the good-faith requirement under Bankruptcy Code § 1325?

(2) Does a trustee bear the burden of proving that a "no-look" attorney's fee is unreasonable?

(3) Under Bankruptcy Code § 330, is a "no-look" fee reasonable where the trustee's objection transforms an otherwise routine Chapter 13 matter into a complicated proceeding?

HOLDING AND DECISION: (Higginbotham, J.)

(1) No. A Chapter 13 plan that results in the debtor's counsel receiving almost the entire amount paid to the trustee, leaving other unsecured creditors unpaid, does not constitute a per se violation of the good-faith requirement under Bankruptcy Code § 1325. A court must look at several factors to determine whether a plan is being filed in bad faith. Here, the district court reversed on the basis that because Crager's counsel would receive almost the entire amount paid to the trustee, thus leaving other unsecured creditors unpaid, the plan was per se filed in bad faith. There is no rule, however, that a plan that works such a result is per se filed in bad faith. Whether such a plan shows an attempt to abuse the spirit of the bankruptcy code is just one of at least seven factors a court must consider, and, here, the record shows that the bankruptcy court had the opportunity to judge Crager's credibility as a witness and found credible her proffered reasons for filing a Chapter 13 petition. Thus, it was not clearly erroneous for the bankruptcy court to find that Crager's plan was not an attempt to abuse Chapter 13, but rather a responsible

Continued on next page.

decision given her particular circumstances. Accordingly, the bankruptcy court is affirmed, and the district court is reversed, as to this issue. Judgment for Crager as to this issue.

(2) No. A trustee does not bear the burden of proving that a "no-look" attorney's fee is unreasonable. Under § 330, the bankruptcy court may award to Crager's attorney reasonable compensation based on several factors that assess the nature, the extent, and the value of the attorney's services. While a "no-look" fee is presumptively reasonable, by its own terms it is not an entitlement, and it may be objected to by a trustee. When such an objection is raised, the court must assess the reasonableness of the fee pursuant to the § 330 factors, as the standing order does not supplant § 330's requirements. Thus, the bankruptcy court erred in failing to review these factors. Judgment for Trustee as to this issue.

(3) Yes. Under Bankruptcy Code § 330, a "no-look" fee is reasonable where the trustee's objection transforms an otherwise routine Chapter 13 matter into a complicated proceeding. The Trustee objected to the bankruptcy court awarding the "no-look" fee on the basis that Crager's bankruptcy was "more simplistic and less complicated" than the average Chapter 13 case. Specifically: (1) no disbursements were to be made to secured creditors; (2) there were only five unsecured creditors; (3) Crager's only sources of income were food stamps and Social Security benefits; (4) Crager had not filed an income tax return for many years; and (5) Crager was judgment-proof and had no seizable assets. Under the circumstances, however, the Trustee's objection was based on the false premise that Crager's case was "more simplistic" than the average Chapter 13 bankruptcy, since the Trustee's own "bad faith" challenge to Crager's plan transformed the case from a routine Chapter 13 matter into a complicated proceeding. Given this added complexity, the Trustee's objection was not sound, and the bankruptcy court did not err in allowing the "no-look" fee. Judgment for Crager as to this issue. The district court judgment is reversed, and the bankruptcy court judgment is affirmed.

ANALYSIS

Under § 330, specific factors a court must assess in determining the reasonableness of attorneys' fees for the attorney's services include: (1) the time spent on such services; (2) the rates charged for such services; (3) whether the services were necessary to the administration of, or beneficial at the time at which the service was rendered toward the completion of, a case; (4) whether the services were performed within a reasonable amount of time commensurate with the complexity, importance, and nature of the problem, issue, or task addressed; (5) with respect to a professional person, whether the person is board certified or otherwise has demonstrated skill and experience in the bankruptcy field; and (6) whether the compensation is reasonable based on the customary compensation charged by comparably skilled practitioners in cases other than cases under the Bankruptcy Code.

Quicknotes

BAD FAITH Conduct that is intentionally misleading or deceptive.

GOOD-FAITH REQUIREMENT An implied warranty that the parties will deal honestly in the satisfaction of their obligations and without an intent to defraud.

Veighlan v. Essex (In re Essex)

Chapter 13 trustee (P) v. Chapter 13 debtor (D)

452 B.R. 195 (W.D. Tex. 2011)

NATURE OF CASE: Appeal from bankruptcy court's confirmation of Chapter 13 plan.

FACT SUMMARY: The Chapter 13 trustee (Appellant) (P) contended that the debtors (Appellees) (D) filed their plan in bad faith because, although they satisfied the requirements of Bankruptcy Code § 1325(b)(3) for retaining their $600,000 house, and met the eligibility limits of § 109(e), their plan, which proposed to provide a one percent dividend to unsecured creditors, including the Internal Revenue Service (IRS) to which they had not paid taxes for four years, proposed to have the debtors spend over four times the amount of the IRS standard for housing and utilities for a family of five in their area. This would result in Appellees (D) paying $6,770.00 towards the mortgage each month, but only $1,366.82 to the IRS.

RULE OF LAW

A debtor's proposed monthly expenditures can be lawful under Bankruptcy Code § 1325(b)(3) yet constitute a violation of good faith under § 1325(a)(3) where, under a totality of the circumstances approach, the presumption that expenses deemed to be reasonably necessary under § 1325(b)(3) are asserted in good faith under § 1325(a)(3) is negated by aggravating circumstances.

FACTS: The Debtors (Appellees) (D) purchased a house secured by a $656,000 mortgage in 2006. They had failed to pay their taxes for 2003 through 2006 and owed the IRS $256,498.97. Appellees (D), who had virtually no equity in their house, filed for Chapter 13 bankruptcy protection in 2010. Of the amount they owed the IRS, $136,681.46 was an unsecured claim. They proposed a plan that called for payments of $3,717.00 for a period of 60 months and payment of a one percent dividend to nonpriority unsecured creditors, totaling no less than $1,956.41. The plan proposed that the Appellees (D) would retain their house. They would do this by paying $6,770.00 towards the mortgage each month, an amount that constituted 51 percent of Appellees' (D) monthly income and represented a mortgage payment that was over four times the amount of the IRS standard for housing and utilities for a family of five in the area. Based on the one percent dividend proposed in Appellees' (D) plan, the IRS would receive $1,366.82 of the unsecured debt. The plan was lawful under Bankruptcy Code § 1325(b)(3). The Chapter 13 trustee (Appellant) (P) objected to confirmation of the plan, asserting that the plan was not made in good faith, focusing on the steep contrast between the high mortgage payments and the minimal dividend that would be paid to unsecured creditors. The bankruptcy court, citing the eligibility limits of § 109(e) in conjunction with the Chapter 13 purpose of allowing debtors to retain their homes during bankruptcy, confirmed the plan over the Appellant's (P) objections. In doing so, the bankruptcy court noted that the de facto number for how much house a debtor can retain in Chapter 13 is set by the eligibility limits. The district court granted review.

ISSUE: Can a debtor's proposed monthly expenditures be lawful under Bankruptcy Code § 1325(b)(3) yet constitute a violation of good faith under § 1325(a)(3) where, under a totality of the circumstances approach, the presumption that expenses deemed to be reasonably necessary under § 1325(b)(3) are asserted in good faith under § 1325(a)(3) is negated by aggravating circumstances?

HOLDING AND DECISION: (Rodriguez, J.) Yes. A debtor's proposed monthly expenditures can be lawful under Bankruptcy Code § 1325(b)(3) yet constitute a violation of good faith under § 1325(a)(3) where, under a totality of the circumstances approach, the presumption that expenses deemed to be reasonably necessary under § 1325(b)(3) are asserted in good faith under § 1325(a)(3) is negated by aggravating circumstances. Section 1325(b)(3) looks to the means test found in §§ 707(b)(2)(A)-(B) for a determination of which expenses are "reasonably necessary." However, § 707(b)(2)(A)(iii)(II) places no reasonableness requirement on the monthly payments necessary to "maintain possession of the debtor's primary residence." Rather, any amount necessary to keep the residence is allowed by § 707, and such an amount is considered "reasonably necessary" under § 1325(b)(3). Here, the bankruptcy court found that that the proposed housing expenses in the Appellees' (D) plan complied with § 1325(b)(3), but, because the court chose to overrule the good-faith objection using § 109(e), it did not reach the question of whether the proposed plan nonetheless violated § 1325(a)(3). Some courts that have considered the issue have held that that compliance with § 1325(b)(3) is not determinative of compliance with § 1325(a)(3), and that debtors still must establish that their plans exhibit the good faith demanded by § 1325(a)(3). Other courts have held that expenditures in compliance with § 1325(b)(3) automatically qualify as expenditures in compliance with § 1325(a)(3) as long as no additional instances of bad faith are alleged. Given that courts in this circuit use a totality of circumstances test to determine good faith, it would be improper to rule that a plan's compliance with

Continued on next page.

§ 1325(b)(3) is a per se compliance with § 1325(a)(3). On the other hand, it would also be improper to find that the Appellees (D) proposed their plan in bad faith even though the housing expenses comply with § 1325(b)(3). The appropriate approach is to presume that expenses deemed to be "reasonably necessary" under § 1325(b)(3) are presumed to be asserted in good faith under § 1325(a)(3), where the presumption of good faith can be negated by aggravating circumstances. Under this approach, the fact that Appellees' (D) proposed monthly mortgage payments are lawful under § 1325(b)(3) is important yet constitutes only one factor to be considered in addition to any "aggravating circumstances" that might arise within the overall "totality of the circumstances" test. Applying this approach here, the Appellant (P) argues that there are aggravating circumstances, namely, that the Appellees (D) chose to live in a luxury home rather than pay their income taxes, and the Appellant (P) questions whether the Appellees (D) living in a $600,000 home while paying next to nothing on $136,681.46 of unsecured tax debt is the bargain that Congress intended between debtors and unsecured creditors. The Appellant (P) is correct that the Appellees' choices constitute aggravating circumstances. Although Appellees' (D) proposed housing expenses satisfy the standards outlined in § 1325(b)(3) and thus are presumed to have been proposed in good faith, the presumption is rebutted by Appellees' (D) proposal to retain a home valued at $600,000 while paying only one percent of the $136,681.46 unsecured debt owed to the IRS. Accordingly, their plan is proposed in bad faith. Additionally, the Appellees (D) have failed to present any reason why it is necessary to retain a home for which the mortgage payments are over four times the amount of the IRS standard for their area despite the extremely low dividend they seek to pay to their unsecured creditors. The Appellees' (D) plan evinces the Appellees' (D) refusal to engage in belt tightening, as well as their desire to maintain their prepetition lifestyle at the expense of their unsecured creditors. There is no reason why the Appellees (D) cannot find more affordable housing and pay their unsecured creditors a reasonable dividend while still living a comfortable lifestyle. Accordingly, based on the totality of the circumstances, the bankruptcy court's order confirming the Appellees' (D) plan is reversed. Reversed.

ANALYSIS

Although the bankruptcy court was correct to emphasize that a purpose of Chapter 13 bankruptcy proceedings is to allow debtors to keep their homes, it is doubtful that Congress intended to protect individuals, like the Appellees (D), who purchased the home during a period when they evaded their income taxes. To allow the Appellees (D) to retain their homestead while paying only one percent of the debt owed to unsecured creditors, including the IRS, would be to allow a bargain that too greatly favors the Appellees (D). In fact, bankruptcy courts increasingly have found Chapter 13 plans that allow debtors to keep highly valued homes in which they have very little equity while paying virtually nothing to unsecured creditors to be proposed in bad faith. See, e.g., *In re Namie*, 395 B.R. 594 (Bankr. D.S.C. 2008); *In re Stitt*, 403 B.R. 694 (Bankr. D. Idaho 2008).

Quicknotes

BAD FAITH Conduct that is intentionally misleading or deceptive.

GOOD-FAITH REQUIREMENT An implied warranty that the parties will deal honestly in the satisfaction of their obligations and without an intent to defraud.

TOTALITY OF THE CIRCUMSTANCES TEST Standard that focuses on all the circumstances of a particular case, instead of individual factors.

In re Puffer

[Parties not identified.]

674 F.3d 78 (1st Cir. 2012)

NATURE OF CASE: Appeal involving a Chapter 13 fee-only plan. [The complete procedural posture of the case is not presented in the casebook extract.]

FACT SUMMARY: [The facts are not presented in the casebook extract.]

RULE OF LAW

[The rule of law of the case is not presented in the casebook extract.]

FACTS: [The facts are not presented in the casebook extract.]

ISSUE: [The issue of the case is not presented in the casebook extract.]

HOLDING AND DECISION: [The holding and decision of the case are not presented in the casebook extract.]

CONCURRENCE: (Lipez, J.) A fee-only plan may achieve the Bankruptcy Code's goal of giving a debtor a fresh start, but such a plan may not achieve the goal of maximizing payments to creditors. Bankruptcy judges should be able to evaluate such plans under the totality of the circumstances test, and they may take into account as one factor under that test whether the plan is consistent with the spirit and purpose of rehabilitation through debt repayment. The majority errs, however, in requiring a special circumstances overlay on top of the totality of the circumstances test, since that will, as a practical matter, impose on debtors the more difficult task of proving that they did not act in bad faith, rather than proving that they acted in good faith. While a fee-only plan may render some debtors vulnerable to attorneys seeking to maximize their fees, a struggling debtor who lacks the resources to pay a Chapter 7 attorney's fee up front has limited options. Proceeding pro se, while theoretically possible, is not a viable alternative given the complexities of bankruptcy proceedings, and that the success rate of pro se filings is quite low. Many errors that pro se debtors make cannot be undone, and legal counsel is often crucial in helping the debtor make an informed decision based on his unique circumstances and the available alternatives. Finally, there is no market for cheap or free bankruptcy-related legal services.

ANALYSIS

In this case, the majority held that a fee-only plan is not per se filed in bad faith, but, as the concurrence notes, the majority crafted a special circumstances requirement for such plans, as part of the totality of the circumstances test for determining whether a plan has been proposed in good faith. In this regard, the majority indicated that while fee-only plans should not be used as a matter of course, there may be special circumstances, albeit relatively rare, in which this type of "odd" arrangement is justified. The court instructed that reviewing courts hew to the overarching principle that the presence or absence of good faith should be ascertained case by case, and the court added that a debtor who submits such a plan carries a heavy burden of demonstrating special circumstances that justify its submission.

Quicknotes

CHAPTER 7 BANKRUPTCY A legal proceeding whereby a debtor, who is unable to pay his or her debts as they become due, is relieved of the obligation to pay creditors by liquidation and distribution of remaining assets.

PRO SE An individual appearing on his or her own behalf.

TOTALITY OF THE CIRCUMSTANCES TEST Standard that focuses on all the circumstances of a particular case, instead of individual factors.

CHAPTER 14

Policy and Practice

Quick Reference Rules of Law

		PAGE
1.	*In re Spickelmier.* A court may impose disgorgement of attorneys' fees under § 329(b) of the Bankruptcy Code for attorney violations of Rule 9011 of the Federal Rules of Bankruptcy Procedure where a court determines that the reasonable value of an attorney's services is zero.	*80*

In re Spickelmier

[Parties not identified.]

469 B.R. 903 (Bankr. D. Nev. 2012)

NATURE OF CASE: Hearing on an order to show cause under Rule 9011 of the Federal Rules of Bankruptcy Procedure.

FACT SUMMARY: The bankruptcy court issued an order to the Chapter 13 debtor's counsel, Mondejar, of the Barry Levinson & Associates law firm, to show cause under Rule 9011 of the Federal Rules of Bankruptcy Procedure (Order to Show Cause) as to why counsel should not be sanctioned for: filing a motion similar to one that counsel had previously filed, and that had been denied; for failing to disclose the prior motion and denial thereof in the subsequent motion; and for other failings.

RULE OF LAW

A court may impose disgorgement of attorneys' fees under § 329(b) of the Bankruptcy Code for attorney violations of Rule 9011 of the Federal Rules of Bankruptcy Procedure where a court determines that the reasonable value of an attorney's services is zero.

FACTS: Debtor's counsel, Mondejar, and his firm, Barry Levinson & Associates law firm (the Levinson firm), had filed a Chapter 13 petition, even though the debtor was clearly not eligible for relief under Chapter 13. The Levinson firm negotiated a stipulation for conversion or dismissal with the Chapter 13 Trustee, but failed to comply with it, resulting in the dismissal of the case. Mondejar then attempted to remedy this failing by moving for reconsideration, but he did not appear at the hearing on the motion. Thereafter, he filed an Order Shortening Time (OST) motion for a motion that had previously been opposed and denied in regular time, without citing to any legal authority that supported the filing. Mondejar had failed to disclose both the previous motion, and the order denying that motion in his OST motion, and he also failed to notify opposing counsel. The dates of notification were also incorrect. Based on these failures, the court issued an order to show cause (Order to Show Cause) to the Levinson firm to appear and show-cause why the filing of the OST motion did not violate Rule 9011 of the Federal Rules of Bankruptcy Procedure. The court specifically instructed counsel to be prepared to address why the OST Motion, which did not contain any information that would help the court find a basis upon which to grant the relief requested, did not violate Rule 9011, and also requested that counsel be prepared to offer specific examples, supported by admissible evidence, of the prejudice referred to in an affidavit submitted by the firm (Levinson Affidavit) in support of the OST. The Order to Show Cause included disgorgement of fees as a possible sanction. Mondejar not only arrived late for the hearing Order to Show Cause, without good reason for doing so, but he was completely unprepared to address the shortcomings that the Order to Show Cause had directed the law firm to be prepared to address. Prior to Mondejar's tardy arrival, the debtor had expressed dissatisfaction with Mondejar, who had missed court appearances, and whose firm had received $5,000 for these "services." During the hearing, Mondejar stared repeatedly at his computer screen and, most times, was unable to answer the simplest of queries. Mondejar floundered throughout the hearing, and even when he did attempt to be responsive, his answers were erroneous. The court bemoaned that "[t]his was the lowest moment in attorney representation the court has ever witnessed." After concluding that Mondejar and the Levinson firm had committed multiple violations of the standards for attorney conduct set forth in Rule 9011, the court addressed sanctions.

ISSUE: May a court impose disgorgement of attorneys' fees under § 329(b) of the Bankruptcy Code for attorney violations of Rule 9011 of the Federal Rules of Bankruptcy Procedure where a court determines that the reasonable value of an attorney's services is zero?

HOLDING AND DECISION: (Markell, J.) Yes. A court may impose disgorgement of attorneys' fees under § 329(b) of the Bankruptcy Code for attorney violations of Rule 9011 of the Federal Rules of Bankruptcy Procedure where a court determines that the reasonable value of an attorney's services is zero. Under § 329(b), the court is authorized to examine the reasonableness of attorneys' fees and to order the return of any payments made for attorney services that exceed the value of those services. The reasonable value of attorneys' fees is a question of fact, determined on a case-by-case basis, and requested compensation may be reduced if the court finds that the work done was excessive or of poor quality. Here, Mondejar's work, and that of the Levinson law firm, was so shoddy, incompetent, and lacking in diligence that it does not deserve to be compensated at all. The attorneys filed a Chapter 13 bankruptcy action for which the debtor was ineligible; they filed unsupported and redundant motions; they were completely unprepared to answer the court's Order to Show Cause; and they otherwise acted incompetently and unprofessionally throughout their representation of the debtor. In other words, the reasonable value of the services

Continued on next page.

rendered is zero. Accordingly, under § 329(b), the fees collected for those services may be ordered to be disgorged. Therefore, the Levinson law firm is ordered to disgorge all monies paid to it by the debtor. [The court also imposed other sanctions under Rule 9011, including referral of the attorneys to the state bar's disciplinary body.]

ANALYSIS

Rule 9011 addresses representations made by all who file or appear in bankruptcy court, and its analog in the Federal Rules of Civil Procedure is Rule 11. Therefore, courts analyzing sanctions under Rule 9011 may appropriately rely on cases interpreting Civil Rule 11. Under Rule 9011(b)(3), bankruptcy courts have the authority to sanction attorneys who present, through signing, filing, submitting, or later advocating, a pleading that is frivolous. A frivolous filing is one that is both baseless—lacks factual foundation—and made without reasonable competent inquiry. An attorney, therefore, has a duty to conduct a reasonable factual investigation as well as to perform adequate legal research that confirms that his position is warranted by existing law (or by a good faith argument for a modification or extension of existing law).

Quicknotes

SHOW CAUSE Generally referred to as an order to show cause or a show cause order. The order is directed to the opposing party to appear and show cause why a certain order should not be enforced or confirmed, or give reason why a court should take or not take a proposed action.

CHAPTER 15

Recovering from Business Debtors

Quick Reference Rules of Law

Office Depot, Inc. v. Zuccarini

Judgment creditor (P) v. Judgment debtor (D)

621 F. Supp. 2d 773 (N.D. Cal. 2007)

NATURE OF CASE: Motion relating to the execution of a money judgment. [The complete procedural posture of the case is not presented in the casebook extract.]

FACT SUMMARY: Office Depot (P) obtained a money judgment against Zuccarini (D) and assigned the judgment to DS Holdings (P), which sought to enforce the judgment by levying upon Zuccarini's (D) interests in domain names. Zuccarini (D) contended that, although the domain name registry was located in the district in which the action was brought, the domain name registrars were outside the district, so that it was inappropriate for the court to oversee levy of the domain names.

RULE OF LAW

A money judgment can be executed against domain names in the district where the domain name registry is located, rather than where the domain name registrars are located.

FACTS: Office Depot (P) obtained a $100,000 money judgment, plus attorneys' fees, against Zuccarini (D) d/b/a "Country Walk," and assigned the judgment to DS Holdings (P). Zuccarini (D) had a sizeable domain name portfolio, and DS Holdings (P) sought to levy upon the domain names. DS Holdings (P) sought a writ of execution in the Northern District of California because the domain name registry, VeriSign, was located there. The domain name registrars, however, were all outside this district in other states and countries. Zuccarini (D) objected to levy in the district, asserting that levy had to be executed where the registrars were located because the registrars handle the day-to-day management of domain names, so that anyone who wants to alter the ownership of a domain name, including a sheriff or marshal seeking to execute a judgment, must do so through the registrars. Nevertheless, VeriSign maintains the records that ultimately determine the existence and ownership of domain names.

ISSUE: Can a money judgment be executed against domain names in the district where the domain name registry is located, rather than where the domain name registrars are located?

HOLDING AND DECISION: (Illston, J.) Yes. A money judgment can be executed against domain names in the district where the domain name registry is located, rather than where the domain name registrars are located. The matter is one of first impression. Under state law, the property to be levied upon must be in the county where the levy is to be made. A threshold issue is whether domain names constitute property. The court of appeals for this district has resolved that question in the affirmative, indicating that a domain name registrant has an intangible property right in his or her domain name. Because under state law all property of the judgment debtor is subject to enforcement of a money judgment, and domain names are intangible property, domain names can be levied upon. Therefore, domain names owned by Zuccarini (D) and existing in the state are subject to levy under a writ of execution. The next question is whether the domain names are located in this district. DS Holdings (P) contends that because the .com and .net registry, VeriSign, is located in this district, the domain names at issue are also located here. Zuccarini (D) counters that the domain names are located where the registrars are located, since, as a practical matter, they handle the day-to-day management of the domain names. Under the Anticybersquatting Consumer Protection Act of 1999 (ACPA), Congress manifested its intent that in rem jurisdiction over domain names inhere in the judicial district either where the registry or registrar of the domain names is located. Domain names are thus property existing in both the location of the registry, and the location of the registrar. Thus, ACPA suggests that it is appropriate for this court to oversee levy of the domain names. Notwithstanding that a registry never interacts with domain name owners—in fact, in this case, DS Holdings (P) has interacted solely with the registrars in its attempts to levy upon the domain names—the registry maintains the records that ultimately determine the existence and ownership of domain names, so that in the internet hierarchy, registrars answer to registries. Thus, if the location of a domain name is determined based on the location of the party with "control" over ownership of the domain name, then the location of the registry is as good as any. Because a domain name exists in the location of both the registrar and the registry, this is the appropriate court to oversee levy upon domain names listed on the VeriSign registry. Judgment for DS Holdings (P).

ANALYSIS

Although the Ninth Circuit has held that a registrant has an intangible property right in a domain name, the Supreme Court of Virginia reached the opposite conclusion in *Network Solutions, Inc. v. Umbro International, Inc.*, 259 Va. 759, 529 S.E.2d 80, 86-87 (Va. 2000), holding that domain name registration creates merely a contract for services, not an intangible property right, and under Virginia law, contractual rights to services cannot be garnished to satisfy a money judgment. Given that one of the registrars of

Continued on next page.

Zuccarini's (D) domain names was located in Virginia, had the court in this case not concluded that it could oversee levy of the domain names based on the location of the registry, DS Holdings (P) likely would not have been able to levy on Zuccarini's (D) domain names managed by the Virginia registrar. Nevertheless, under either analysis, domain names embody property rights that have discernible value and against which secured interests can be perfected under Article 9 of the Uniform Commercial Code. It is well settled that domain names are considered assets of a debtor's bankruptcy estate, and bankruptcy trustees regularly include domain names in asset sales under the supervision of the bankruptcy court. See, *Considerations for Perfecting Liens on Cyber Assets,* 32-8 ABIJ 22 (Sept. 1, 2013).

Quicknotes

LEVY The collection or assessment of a tax; the legal process pursuant to which property is seized and sold in order to satisfy a debt.

Beef & Bison Breeders, Inc. v. Capitol Refrigeration Co., Inc.

Secured creditor (P) v. Lien creditor (D)

N.Y. Sup. Ct., 431 N.Y.S.2d 986 (1980)

NATURE OF CASE: Motions in related actions for orders to determine the priority of creditors.

FACT SUMMARY: In one action, Beef & Bison Breeders, Inc. (Beef & Bison) (P) contended that because it had a perfected security interest in the assets of Kwik Serv, it had priority over Capitol Refrigeration Co., Inc. (Capitol Refrigeration) (D) and Cornell (D), which had levied upon Kwik Serv's assets. The lien creditors disputed that Beef & Bison (P) had in fact perfected its interest. In a second related action, Cornell (P) [now the petitioner], contended that he had priority over Capitol Refrigeration (D) because the Sherriff's levy on Cornell's (P) behalf of Kwik Serv's bank accounts extinguished Capitol Refrigeration's (D) priority, as levies made on Capitol Refrigeration's (D) behalf were made earlier. Capitol Refrigeration (D) contended that it retained priority because it had delivered its execution to the Sherriff prior to Cornell's (P) delivery.

RULE OF LAW

(1) A secured creditor who has failed to perfect its security interest does not have priority over a lien creditor who has subsequently levied on the debtor's property.

(2) As between two judgment creditors seeking to levy against the same judgment debtor, using the same enforcement officer, priority is established by the order of delivery of the writ of execution.

FACTS: Beef & Bison Breeders, Inc. (Beef & Bison) (P) had obtained from Kwik Serv a security agreement that granted Beef & Bison (P) a security interest in all of the personal property, furniture, fixtures, equipment, and vehicles then owned or thereafter acquired by Kwik Serv. Beef & Bison (P) purported to perfect its security interest, but it filed the financing statement in the wrong office on February 20. On April 20, Capitol Refrigeration Co., Inc. (Capitol Refrigeration) (D) obtained a judgment against Kwik Serv for $701.78. On April 16, Capitol Refrigeration (D) delivered a property execution to the Sheriff, and the Sheriff levied upon Kwik Serv's property on August 15. Cornell (D), Kwik Serv's former landlord, obtained a judgment against Kwik Serv on June 30 for $4,469. Based on the judgment, an execution was issued to the Sheriff on July 3. Then, on August 20, Cornell (D) served an execution on the Sheriff that specified Kwik Serv's bank accounts, which collectively contained around $1000. The Sheriff levied on the bank accounts on August 22. In one action, Beef & Bison (P) contended that because it had a perfected security interest in the assets of Kwik Serv, it had priority over Capitol Refrigeration (D) and Cornell (D), the lien creditors. The lien creditors disputed that Beef & Bison (P) had in fact perfected its interest. In a second related action, Cornell (P) [now the petitioner], contended that he had priority over Capitol Refrigeration (D) because the Sheriff's levy on Cornell's (P) behalf of Kwik Serv's bank accounts extinguished Capitol Refrigeration's (D) priority, as levies made on Capitol Refrigeration's (D) behalf were made earlier. Cornell (P) moved for an order directing that Cornell (P) had priority to the bank account assets. Specifically, Cornell (P) conceded that Capitol Refrigeration (D) had priority to the proceeds of levies made on or before August 15, but Cornell (P) contended that he had priority to the proceeds of the bank accounts that were levied upon on August 22, on the theory that Capitol Refrigeration's (D) priority had been extinguished at that point. Capitol Refrigeration (D) contended that it retained priority because it had delivered its execution to the Sheriff prior to Cornell's (P) delivery.

ISSUE:

(1) Does a secured creditor who has failed to perfect its security interest have priority over a lien creditor who has subsequently levied on the debtor's property?

(2) As between two judgment creditors seeking to levy against the same judgment debtor, using the same enforcement officer, is priority established by the order of delivery of the writ of execution?

HOLDING AND DECISION: (Conway, J.)

(1) No. A secured creditor who has failed to perfect its security interest does not have priority over a lien creditor who has subsequently levied on the debtor's property. Beef & Bison (P) failed to perfect its security interest because it filed its financing statement in the wrong office. Therefore, it does not have priority over the lien creditors, and Capitol Refrigeration's (D) levy continues. Beef & Bison's (P) motion is denied. Judgment for the lien creditors as to this issue.

(2) Yes. As between two judgment creditors seeking to levy against the same judgment debtor, using the same enforcement officer, priority is established by the order of delivery of the writ of execution. Thus, the levy by the Sheriff on behalf of Capitol Refrigeration (D) on all of Kwik Serv's personal property, chattels and equipment did not extinguish Capitol Refrigeration's (D) priority with regard to the proceeds in Kwik Serv's bank accounts which were turned over to the Sheriff under the levy on behalf of Cornell (P) since it was not neces-

Continued on next page.

sary for priority purposes that the Sheriff levy under the first execution before the delivery of or levy upon the second or subsequent execution. In general, if a levy is made under a junior execution and the judgment debtor's property is sold, the judgment creditor who first delivered an execution does not lose his priority. Accordingly, because Capitol Refrigeration (D) filed its writ of execution first, it retains its priority, regardless of when that writ was levied upon, or if other levies were subsequently made upon Kwik Serv's assets. Cornell's (P) motion is denied. Judgment for Capitol Refrigeration (D).

ANALYSIS

If a secured creditor succeeds in perfecting its security interest, it will prevail over a subsequent lien creditor, regardless of the timing of that lien creditor's levy. Thus, had Beef & Bison (P) perfected its security interest in this case, it would have won. As this case demonstrates, if a secured creditor fails to perfect its interest, like Beef & Bison (P) here, it will lose to a third-party judgment creditor who properly levies on that property first.

Quicknotes

LEVY The collection or assessment of a tax; the legal process pursuant to which property is seized and sold in order to satisfy a debt.

LIEN A claim against the property of another in order to secure the payment of a debt.

LIEN CREDITOR A creditor whose interest is secured pursuant to a lien on certain property.

PERFECT Execute; enforce; to make marketable.

SECURED CREDITOR A creditor, the repayment of whose loan is secured by collateral sufficient to repay the debt owed.

SECURITY INTEREST An interest in property that may be sold upon a default in payment of the debt.

In re John Richards Homes Building Co.

[Parties not identified.]

291 B.R. 727 (Bankr. E.D. Mich. 2003)

NATURE OF CASE: Request for compensatory and punitive damages for involuntary bankruptcy petition allegedly filed in bad faith.

FACT SUMMARY: John Richards Homes Building Co. (JRH), the debtor in an involuntary bankruptcy that was dismissed, sought compensatory and punitive damages, claiming that Adell, the creditor, had filed the petition in bad faith and knew that his claims were subject to a bona fide dispute, thus violating § 303(b) of the Bankruptcy Code.

RULE OF LAW

Compensatory and punitive damages may be awarded against a creditor who files an involuntary bankruptcy petition in bad faith and with the knowledge, in violation of Bankruptcy Code § 303(b), that his claim is subject to a bona fide dispute.

FACTS: John Richards Homes Building Co. (JRH) and Adell entered a contract for JRH to sell property to, and construct a home for, Adell, who agreed to pay a total of $3,030,000. The contract required that JRH commence construction within a reasonable time. The closing papers showed that Adell agreed to allocate $1,750,000 for the purchase of the property and the balance to the building construction. A few months after closing, two disputes developed. First, Adell asserted that the true value of the real property was $1 million rather than the $1.75 million stated in the closing papers and in the deed. Thus, he contended that the excess of $750,000 was actually an improper initial construction draw to which JRH was not entitled. Second, Adell asserted that delays in commencing construction were unreasonable. On June 6, Adell filed suit against JRH and others asserting numerous claims. On June 18, JRH filed an answer to Adell's claims, affirmative defenses, and numerous counterclaims. Six days later, on June 24, Adell filed an involuntary bankruptcy petition against JRH, alleging that Adell's claim was $800,000 for fraud and breach of contract, and that he was eligible to file the petition under Bankruptcy Code § 303(b), i.e., that his claim was not subject to a bona fide dispute. On July 1, JRH filed a motion to dismiss, asserting that Adell's claim was the subject of a bona fide dispute, and that the petition was filed in bad faith, so that JRH was entitled to substantial compensatory and punitive damages, as well as attorney fees and costs. On July 15, the bankruptcy court dismissed the petition, finding that Adell "knew or surely must have known that his claim was the subject of a bona fide dispute, and therefore that he was not qualified to be a petitioning creditor." The court then held a hearing on the issue of damages.

ISSUE: May compensatory and punitive damages be awarded against a creditor who files an involuntary bankruptcy petition in bad faith and with the knowledge, in violation of Bankruptcy Code § 303(b), that his claim is subject to a bona fide dispute?

HOLDING AND DECISION: (Rhodes, C.J.) Yes. Compensatory and punitive damages may be awarded against a creditor who files an involuntary bankruptcy petition in bad faith and with the knowledge, in violation of Bankruptcy Code § 303(b), that his claim is subject to a bona fide dispute. Here the evidence overwhelmingly indicates that Adell filed the involuntary bankruptcy petition in bad faith and with the knowledge that his claim against JRH was subject to a bona fide dispute. There was evidence that Adell's attorneys knew of JRH's responsive pleadings before Adell filed the petition, and even if they had not informed him of those responsive pleadings, Adell should have known that, given the nature of his claims, he and JRH would have real and substantial legal and factual disputes, and that the litigation to resolve those disputes would be lengthy and costly. Even before JRH filed responsive pleadings, Adell could not have reasonably concluded that JRH would simply admit that it had committed the frauds and the other intentional wrongs that he had alleged. Moreover, at least twice before Adell filed the involuntary petition, JRH's attorneys specifically told Adell's attorneys that JRH would contest Adell's claims and that therefore an involuntary petition would be improper. JRH's attorneys also informed Adell's attorneys that the parties' dispute was "extremely contentious." Further, Adell did not withdraw the petition after learning of the responsive pleadings. The evidence also shows that Adell knew that JRH would suffer significant harm from the filing of an involuntary bankruptcy petition, and that he intended such harm. An indication of this was Adell's extraordinary effort and expense to hire a public relations firm to publicize the bankruptcy filing. Email messages sent to newspaper reporters at three newspapers contained falsehoods and defamatory contents. Adell's attorney also went so far as to outrageously threaten criminal prosecution against JRH. Adell also was unable to substantiate the claim he made in the petition. Another indication of bad faith was that Adell used improper threats and flaunted his wealth in an attempt to solicit creditors to join his petition, telling potential co-creditors that they would get paid only if they joined in the petition. Adell also intimated that he was very wealthy and that he would spare no expense just to get back at someone who made him mad. Adell's testi-

Continued on next page.

mony he filed the petition in reliance on the advice of experienced bankruptcy attorneys and therefore in good faith must be rejected. Although Adell's bankruptcy counsel did some substantial investigation before concluding that an involuntary petition would be proper, it turns out that Adell and Adell's nonbankruptcy attorneys deliberately misinformed bankruptcy counsel as to the amount that was undisputed, notwithstanding bankruptcy counsel's admonitions that there would be serious problems if a certain undisputed amount could not be established. They withheld from bankruptcy counsel significant information that plainly would have, or should have, made a difference on the critical issue of whether JRH either "admitted," or at least did not dispute, any portion of Adell's claim—e.g., JRH's answer and counterclaims. It is a well-established proposition that a client reasonably relies on an attorney's advice only when the client provides to the attorney all the pertinent facts in the client's possession. Given Adell's deliberate omissions, he may not rely on bankruptcy counsel's advice. Finally, Adell falsely testified that in filing the involuntary petition, he was motivated by a concern for JRH's trade creditors. If he were indeed so charitably motivated, he would not have threatened at least two creditors that the only way they would be paid would be to join in the petition. The totality of these circumstances indicates that Adell filed the petition in bad faith in an attempt either to coerce a settlement, or, failing that, to damage JRH's reputation and business. JRH, as a developer of high-end homes, relied heavily on its reputation, and, here, it provided evidence that the involuntary petition damaged its reputation and caused it to lose a significant amount of business. Thus, it is entitled to compensatory damages of $4,100,000 for those losses. Additionally, given that bad faith was involved, punitive damages may also be awarded. In determining such damages, the totality of the circumstances must be considered under § 303(i)(2). Here, evidence of Adell's bad faith was overwhelming; his conduct constituted an extreme case of abuse of the bankruptcy process. Adell's conduct was reprehensible and must be deterred and punished. Punitive damages in the amount of $2 million are necessary and appropriate to achieve that goal, almost one-half of the compensatory damages. Judgment for JRH.

ANALYSIS

This case raises the question of whether a creditor whose debt is only in partial dispute may be considered as a petitioning creditor, since as to the undisputed portion, it is clearly a creditor. However, the Bankruptcy Abuse Prevention and Consumer Protection Act of 2005 (BAPCPA) made clear in §§ 303(b)(1) and (h)(1) that a dispute about either the fact of liability or the amount owed is sufficient to classify the debt as "disputed." Therefore, a creditor cannot validly file an involuntary petition even where a debt is only partially disputed.

Quicknotes

BAD FAITH Conduct that is intentionally misleading or deceptive.

BONA FIDE In good faith.

COMPENSATORY DAMAGES Measure of damages necessary to compensate victim for actual injuries suffered.

INVOLUNTARY BANKRUPTCY Proceedings brought against a debtor by his or her creditors thereby forcing debtor into bankruptcy.

INVOLUNTARY PETITION A bankruptcy petition that is filed by the debtor's creditors forcing debtor into bankruptcy.

PUNITIVE DAMAGES Damages exceeding the actual injury suffered for the purposes of punishment of the defendant, deterrence of the wrongful behavior or comfort to the plaintiff.

CHAPTER 16

Reorganizing Businesses

Quick Reference Rules of Law

In re Cook and Sons Mining, Inc.

[Parties not identified.]

2005 WL 2386238 (E.D. Ky. 2005)

NATURE OF CASE: Cross-appeals in Chapter 11 bankruptcy from order granting administrative expenses and from ruling that debtor could not avoid its contract with creditor for a period of time.

FACT SUMMARY: Cook and Sons Mining, Inc. (Debtor), a debtor-in-possession in a Chapter 11 bankruptcy, contended that a contract it entered postpetition with South Carolina Public Service Authority (Santee Cooper) was not entered into in the ordinary course of business pursuant to Bankruptcy Code § 363(b) and was avoidable under § 549(a), so that it was inappropriate for the bankruptcy court to order administrative expenses to Santee Cooper. Santee Cooper, on the other hand, contended that the bankruptcy court erred in ruling that Debtor could avoid the contract for a period of time.

RULE OF LAW

A transaction by a debtor-in-possession in a Chapter 11 bankruptcy occurs in the ordinary course of the debtor's business for purposes of the vertical dimension test where the goods involved are those the debtor is in the business of selling; the price for the goods is a market price; the debtor entered into similar transactions both prepetition and postpetition; at the time the debtor entered the transaction there was no indication it would not be able to fulfill its obligations; and at the time the debtor entered the transaction, there was no indication that financial costs of the transaction would exceed the possible detriment if the debtor did not enter into the transaction.

FACTS: Cook and Sons Mining, Inc. (Debtor), a mining company, filed for Chapter 11 bankruptcy protection in August 2003. In November 2003, Debtor submitted a proposal to South Carolina Public Service Authority (Santee Cooper), a public utility, to ship to Santee Cooper 60,000 tons of coal per month for a one-year period beginning January 1, 2004, at $35 per ton. Santee Cooper accepted the proposal, and the parties entered a contract based on the proposal. This type of contract was ordinary in the coal industry, and the contract price was a good market price for the coal. Prior to filing its petition, Debtor had been able to provide this quantity of coal to its customers. Postpetition, Debtor entered similar contracts with several other customers, which required it to produce, in the aggregate, 107,000 tons per month. At the time it entered the contracts, it was able to produce 170,000 tons per month. Debtor began shipping coal pursuant to the contract, and did so for three months (January, February, and March 2004), but in no single month did it meet the 60,000-ton requirement. By April 2004, Debtor became administratively insolvent and ceased shipments. In July 2004 Santee Cooper moved for an administrative priority claim in the amount of $10,815,484.62, claiming that this amount represented the damages it incurred as a result of Debtor's breach of the postpetition contract. Debtor defended by contending that Santee Cooper was not entitled to an administrative priority claim in any amount because the postpetition contract was not in the "ordinary course of business" pursuant to Bankruptcy Code § 363(b) and was avoidable under § 549(a), and it moved to avoid the contract on the same basis. The bankruptcy court decided that Debtor could avoid the postpetition contract for the months of July 2004 to December 2004 but not for the months of January 2004 through June 2004, and it further granted Santee Cooper an administrative expense claim of $5,150,284.62, which represented its damages for the months of January to June 2004. The district court granted review.

ISSUE: Does a transaction by a debtor-in-possession in a Chapter 11 bankruptcy occur in the ordinary course of the debtor's business for purposes of the vertical dimension test where the goods involved are those the debtor is in the business of selling; the price for the goods is a market price; the debtor entered into similar transactions both prepetition and postpetition; at the time the debtor entered the transaction there was no indication it would not be able to fulfill its obligations; and at the time the debtor entered the transaction, there was no indication that financial costs of the transaction would exceed the possible detriment if the debtor did not enter into the transaction?

HOLDING AND DECISION: (Caldwell, J.) Yes. A transaction by a debtor-in-possession in a Chapter 11 bankruptcy occurs in the ordinary course of the debtor's business for purposes of the vertical dimension test where the goods involved are those the debtor is in the business of selling; the price for the goods is a market price; the debtor entered into similar transactions both prepetition and postpetition; at the time the debtor entered the transaction there was no indication it would not be able to fulfill its obligations; and at the time the debtor entered the transaction, there was no indication that financial costs of the transaction would exceed the possible detriment if the debtor did not enter into the transaction. Under § 549(a), a debtor-in-possession may avoid certain transfers of property that occur after the commencement of the case if the

Continued on next page.

transfer was unauthorized. Whether a postpetition transaction is authorized is controlled by § 363(b)(1), which provides that a debtor-in-possession's transactions, other than those in the ordinary course of business, must be authorized by the court after notice and a hearing. Whether a transaction occurs in the ordinary course of the debtor's business is a question of fact. Here, given that the bankruptcy court avoided six months of the contract, it must have determined that the contract was made in the ordinary course of Debtor's business. This determination is reviewed for clear error. There are two tests for determining whether a transaction occurs in the ordinary course of business: (1) the horizontal dimension test and (2) the vertical dimension test. The horizontal dimension test is an objective test asking whether, from an industrywide perspective, the transaction is of the sort commonly undertaken by companies in that industry. Here, the parties agree that the contract satisfies the horizontal dimension test for "ordinary," since the contract was the kind typically entered into in the industry. The vertical dimension examines the reasonable expectations of interested parties as to the particular debtor-in-possession, and asks whether, relative to the debtor, the transaction was extraordinary, so that a creditor would have wanted advance notice of it so it could object. One aspect of the test is consideration of whether the proposed transaction imposes a financial cost that exceeds the possible benefit of entering into the agreement, and also, exceeds the possible detriment that will occur if the debtor-in-possession does not enter into the agreement. Here, the facts show that the contract meets the vertical dimension test for "ordinary." First, Debtor was in the business of mining and shipping coal to utilities—the subject of the contract. Given prepetition Debtor was able to fulfill contract obligations similar to those in the contract with Santee Cooper, there were no indications that the size of the Santee Cooper contract was inconsistent with Debtor's prepetition business. Additionally, given that at the beginning of the case Debtor was mining more than enough coal to fulfill its obligations, there was nothing that indicated that, at the time the contract was formed, Debtor was incapable of fulfilling its obligations under the Santee Cooper contract or that those obligations were extraordinary or unexpected. There was also evidence that the contract price was a market price, so that at the time the contract was formed, the purchase price was not extraordinary or unexpected. Further, at the time the parties entered the contract, there was no indication that the financial costs of the agreement would exceed the possible detriment if Debtor did not enter the contract. At the time it appeared Debtor was capable of fulfilling its obligations under the contract, and was trying to and believed that it could continue operating and could reorganize. Thus, there was nothing about the size or nature of the contract that rendered it extraordinary or subjected the creditors to unexpected risks. Accordingly, the contract meets the vertical test for "ordinary course of business." Because the contract meets both the horizontal and vertical dimension tests, the bankruptcy court did not clearly err in concluding that, at the time the contract was formed, it was in the "ordinary course of business." Affirmed as to this issue. [The district court, however, disagreed with some of the bankruptcy court's other rulings, and, accordingly, it affirmed in part and reversed in part.]

ANALYSIS

Under § 363(c)(1) a debtor-in-possession may enter transactions in the ordinary course of business without notice or a hearing. This provides the debtor the flexibility to engage in ordinary transactions without unnecessary creditor and bankruptcy court oversight while protecting creditors by giving them an opportunity to be heard when transactions are not ordinary. The purpose of requiring notice and a hearing for transactions that are not in the ordinary course of business is so that creditors have an opportunity to review the terms of the proposed transaction and to object if they deem the terms and conditions are not in their best interest. The showing of ordinary course of business assures that neither the debtor nor any of its creditors can do anything abnormal either to dissipate assets or gain inappropriate advantage over other creditors.

Quicknotes

DEBTOR-IN-POSSESSION A Chapter 11 bankruptcy debtor who retains control of assets or property pursuant to a plan of reorganization.

ORDINARY COURSE OF BUSINESS The conducting of business in accordance with standard customs and practices.

POSTPETITION After bankruptcy petition has been filed.

PREPETITION Before bankruptcy petition has been filed.

In re Biolitec, Inc.

[Parties not identified.]

2013 WL 1352302 (Bankr. D.N.J. 2013) (not approved for publication)

NATURE OF CASE: Motion for appointment of a Chapter 11 trustee pursuant to Bankruptcy Code § 1104(a).

FACT SUMMARY: AngioDynamics, Inc. moved for appointment of a Chapter 11 trustee pursuant to Bankruptcy Code § 1104(a), contending that cause for such appointment existed based on the conduct of Biolitec, Inc. (Biolitec or Debtor), the debtor, in the bankruptcy proceedings, and Biolitec's management's inability to represent the best interests of Biolitec's creditors. Biolitec countered that AngioDynamics failed to overcome the strong presumption of leaving a debtor in possession of the estate.

RULE OF LAW

(1) "Cause" for purposes of appointment of a Chapter 11 trustee pursuant to Bankruptcy Code § 1104(a) is established by clear and convincing evidence where there is evidence of great acrimony between the creditor and debtor and where the debtor is intimately tied through common ownership and control with a controlling owner and related entities that are the recipients of alleged fraudulent and preferential transfers.

(2) The appointment of a Chapter 11 trustee is in the best interests of creditors and the estate under Bankruptcy Code § 1104(a)(2) where the debtor has insufficient independence from a controlling owner and related entities that allegedly have engaged in conduct adverse to the interests of creditors.

FACTS: Biolitec, Inc. (Biolitec or Debtor), was the U.S. affiliate of the Biolitec Group, a multinational group of companies. Biolitec and these "Related Entities" were controlled by Neuberger. In 2002 AngioDynamics and Biolitec entered into a supply and distribution agreement. In 2008 AngioDynamics sued Biolitec for breach of the indemnification provisions of the agreement in federal district court in New York, which eventually awarded AngioDynamics $23 million in 2012. In the meantime, in 2009 fearing Biolitec was systematically funneling assets to certain of the Related Entities to make any potential judgment uncollectible, AngioDynamics brought suit in federal district court in Massachusetts, alleging that Biolitec, Neuberger, and Related Entities fraudulently removed assets amounting to $18 million from Biolitec to render the Debtor judgment proof. The Massachusetts court issued a permanent injunction in 2012 prohibiting Biolitec from transferring assets. The injunction also prohibited one of the Related Entities, Biolitec AG, from merging with its Austrian subsidiary. The injunction, in part, was based on the court's finding, absent an evidentiary hearing and based solely on the pleadings, of an extraordinarily dramatic diminution in Biolitec's assets, and an increase in its debt, in just three years. On request for reconsideration, the court questioned the defendants' good faith, as there was evidence that Biolitec AG had taken steps to merge with its subsidiary in contravention of the injunction. The court of appeals affirmed the injunction, after which affirmance, the merger was completed. In similar, but separate, litigation, former Biolitec officers brought suit in New Jersey state court alleging—without verification—shareholder oppression, that Neuberger acted fraudulently, and that more than $15 million in cash and assets were fraudulently and illegally transferred from Biolitec. Biolitec filed for Chapter 11 bankruptcy protection in 2013. In that bankruptcy action, AngioDynamics moved for appointment of a Chapter 11 trustee pursuant to Bankruptcy Code § 1104(a), contending that cause for such appointment existed based on the findings of the Massachusetts district court, Biolitec's actions in the bankruptcy case, and the inability of Biolitec's management to represent the best interests of Biolitec's creditors. AngioDynamics argue alternatively, pursuant to § 1104(a)(2), that a trustee would be in the best interests of the creditors. Biolitec opposed the motion on the grounds that AngioDynamics failed to overcome the strong presumption of leaving a debtor in possession of the estate. Specifically, Biolitec argued that the evidence relied on by AngioDynamics amounted to preliminary findings and mere allegations, so that AngioDynamics did not meet its burden of showing clear and convincing evidence of "cause."

ISSUE:

(1) Is "cause" for purposes of appointment of a Chapter 11 trustee pursuant to Bankruptcy Code § 1104(a) established by clear and convincing evidence where there is evidence of great acrimony between the creditor and debtor and where the debtor is intimately tied through common ownership and control with a controlling owner and related entities that are the recipients of alleged fraudulent and preferential transfers?

(2) Is the appointment of a Chapter 11 trustee in the best interests of creditors and the estate under Bankruptcy Code § 1104(a)(2) where the debtor has insufficient independence from a controlling owner and related entities that allegedly have engaged in conduct adverse to the interests of creditors?

Continued on next page.

HOLDING AND DECISION: (Steckroth, J.)

(1) Yes. "Cause" for purposes of appointment of a Chapter 11 trustee pursuant to Bankruptcy Code § 1104(a) is established by clear and convincing evidence where there is evidence of great acrimony between the creditor and debtor and where the debtor is intimately tied through common ownership and control with a controlling owner and related entities that are the recipients of alleged fraudulent and preferential transfers. The determination of whether the moving party has satisfied its burden in showing "cause" is committed to the bankruptcy court's discretion, but the appointment of a trustee is the exception, rather than the rule, and is relief granted only as a last resort, which is why "cause" must be demonstrated by clear and convincing evidence. Here, there is no doubt that there is great acrimony between Biolitec and AngioDynamics, two entities each with roles crucial to a successful reorganization of Biolitec. Most significantly, however, is that Biolitec, as debtor-in-possession, is intimately tied through common ownership and control with Neuberger and the Related Entities, the recipients of alleged fraudulent and preferential transfers. Although Biolitec's management is experienced and has successfully operated Biolitec for many years, it would be naïve to think, however, that it can operate independently from Neuberger's controlling ownership of Neuberger and the commonality of the Related Entities, particularly in light of their prepetition and postpetition conduct. In light of the relationship of the parties and their conduct before this and other courts, "cause" is established, and it clear that the appointment of a trustee is appropriate. Judgment for AngioDynamics as to this issue.

(2) Yes. The appointment of a Chapter 11 trustee is in the best interests of creditors and the estate under Bankruptcy Code § 1104(a)(2) where the debtor has insufficient independence from a controlling owner and related entities that allegedly have engaged in conduct adverse to the interests of creditors. Biolitec, while profitable under current management and control leading up to the current Chapter 11 petition, fails to have sufficient independence from Neuberger and the Related Entities that engaged in conduct adverse to the interests of creditors. Considering the deep-seated conflicts between the parties and their inability to resolve them, the commonality among Biolitec, Neuberger, and the Related Entities will likely be an obstacle to a successful reorganization and, therefore, the appointment of a trustee is in the best interest of creditors and the estate. AngioDynamics's motion for the appointment of a trustee is granted under § 1104(a)(2). Judgment for AngioDynamics as to this issue.

ANALYSIS

Unlike § 1104(a)(1), which provides for mandatory appointment upon a specific finding of cause, § 1104(a)(2) envisions a flexible standard. It gives the court discretion to appoint a trustee when to do so would serve the parties' and estate's interests. Thus, for example, based on the acrimony found between the parties in this case, even if appointment was not mandated under (a)(1), it could fall within the flexible standard of (a)(2). In light of the flexible standard of (a)(2), there is sufficient basis to appoint a trustee where there is a deep-seated conflict between the debtor and its creditors and where the case is sufficiently complex and the parties are sharply divided on many issues, and are presently incapable of resolving them—as was the situation the bankruptcy court faced in this case.

Quicknotes

DEBTOR-IN-POSSESSION A Chapter 11 bankruptcy debtor who retains control of assets or property pursuant to a plan of reorganization.

CHAPTER 17

Getting Started

Quick Reference Rules of Law

In re Burgess

Debtor (P) v. Bankruptcy court (D)

234 B.R. 793 (Bankr. D. Nev. 1999)

NATURE OF CASE: Appeal from denial of debtor's request that the revocation of his license to operate a legal brothel be undone.

FACT SUMMARY: When a bankruptcy court held that a license to operate a brothel was not property for purposes of federal bankruptcy law, the license-holder appealed.

RULE OF LAW

Licenses issued by state agencies are property for bankruptcy purposes.

FACTS: A Debtor (P) who owned and operated a legal brothel in Storey County, Nevada, filed for Chapter 11 bankruptcy. The Storey County Commission and Sheriff did not like the Debtor's (P) continuing association with the Hell's Angels and revoked the Debtor's (P) brothel license soon afterwards. When the Debtor (P) sought to undo the revocation of the license, the Bankruptcy court (D) held that the license was not property, but rather a personal privilege.

ISSUE: Are licenses issued by state agencies property for bankruptcy purposes?

HOLDING AND DECISION: (Reed, J.) Yes. Licenses issued by state agencies are property for bankruptcy purposes. The license at issue in this case has enormous value to the estate; without it, there would be no business left to reorganize. The congressional goal of encouraging reorganizations is met by a broad definition of property. Reversed and remanded.

ANALYSIS

The court found that the license at issue here was similar to a liquor license or a license to operate a casino, which had been held to be property. The very same license had been held to be property for due process purposes in the same debtor's civil rights case. Many state-created privileges are considered property for bankruptcy purposes.

Quicknotes

CHAPTER 11 BANKRUPTCY A legal proceeding whereby a debtor, who is unable to pay his or her debts as they become due, is relieved of the obligation to pay creditors through reorganization and payment from future income.

CHAPTER 11 REORGANIZATION A plan formulated pursuant to Chapter 11 of the Bankruptcy Code whereby a debtor, who is unable to pay his or her debts as they become due, is relieved of the obligation to pay creditors through reorganization and payment from future income.

In re The Majestic Star Casino, LLC

[Parties not identified.]

716 F.3d 736 (3d Cir. 2013)

NATURE OF CASE: Appeal from grant of summary judgment to debtor ordering the avoidance of a postpetition transfer of property in a Chapter 11 bankruptcy.

FACT SUMMARY: Barden Development, Inc. (BDI), Barden, and the Internal Revenue Service (IRS), contended that BDI's election to terminate its status for tax purposes as an "S" corporation (or "S-corp"), thus forfeiting the pass-through tax benefits that it and its debtor subsidiary, Majestic Star Casino II, Inc. (MSC II), had enjoyed, did not constitute an illegal postpetition transfer of property because the election of S-corp status did not constitute "property of the estate" under Bankruptcy Code § 541(a).

RULE OF LAW

A nondebtor company's decision to abandon its classification as an "S" corporation ("S-corp") for federal tax purposes, thus forfeiting the pass-through tax benefits that it and its debtor subsidiary had enjoyed, is not void as a postpetition transfer of property of the bankruptcy estate.

FACTS: Majestic Star Casino II, Inc. (MSC II) filed for Chapter 11 bankruptcy protection in November 2009 and became a debtor-in-possession. MSC II was a subsidiary of Barden Development, Inc. (BDI), which in turn was wholly owned by Barden. BDI did not file for bankruptcy relief. At the time of petition, BDI was, for tax purposes, an "S" corporation (or "S-corp"), which is not taxed at the entity level, but its shareholders are taxed on a pass-through basis. As BDI's subsidiary, MSC II was a qualified subchapter S subsidiary, or "QSub," and it, too, was not taxed at the entity level. Then, postpetition, Barden elected to revoke BDI's S-corp status, which revocation was approved by the Internal Revenue Service (IRS). S-corp status may be revoked if more than half of the corporation's shareholders consent to the revocation. If S-corp status is revoked, the entity cannot elect such status again within five years of the revocation without the consent of the Secretary of the Treasury. Additionally, there are certain events that automatically cause a corporation to lose its S-corp status, e.g., it has more than 100 shareholders. Here, the revocation became effective on January 1, 2010. This had the effect of causing MSC II to lose its QSub status effective that date, and, consequently, MSC II became responsible for filing its own tax returns and paying income taxes on its holdings and operations. MSC II, now controlled by its creditors, did not agree that it should have to shoulder this new tax burden, and it filed an adversary complaint asserting that the revocation of BDI's S-corp status caused an unlawful postpetition transfer of property of the MSC II bankruptcy estate. The bankruptcy court, determining that S-corp status constitutes "property" under Bankruptcy Code § 541(a), granted summary judgment to MSC II and ordered the reinstatement of both BDI's status as an S-corp and MSC II's status as a QSub. The case was certified to the court of appeals on direct appeal.

ISSUE: Is a nondebtor company's decision to abandon its classification as an S corporation for federal tax purposes, thus forfeiting the pass-through tax benefits that it and its debtor subsidiary had enjoyed, void as a postpetition transfer of property of the bankruptcy estate?

HOLDING AND DECISION: (Jordan, J.) No. A nondebtor company's decision to abandon its classification as an S corporation for federal tax purposes, thus forfeiting the pass-through tax benefits that it and its debtor subsidiary had enjoyed, is not void as a postpetition transfer of property of the bankruptcy estate. The key issue here is whether S-corp status constitutes "property" for purposes of § 541(a), which defines "property of the estate" as "all legal or equitable interests of the debtor in property as of the commencement of the case." This definition sweeps very broadly and covers all kinds of property, including tangible or intangible property, and causes of action. An interest is not outside its reach because it is novel or contingent or because enjoyment must be postponed. Even the mere opportunity to receive an economic benefit in the future is covered by the definition. Notwithstanding this broadly sweeping definition, bankruptcy does not create new property rights or value where there previously were none, and the estate is determined at the time of the initial filing of the bankruptcy petition. Ordinarily, property is determined pursuant to state law. However, where federal interests are at stake, property may be determined pursuant to federal law. Here, the Internal Revenue Code (IRC), rather than state law, governs the characterization of entity tax status as a property interest for purposes of the Bankruptcy Code. The IRC itself, however, does not expressly determine whether tax status constitutes a property interest of the taxpayer, and the case law is not entirely clear on this issue. Some courts have concluded that once a corporation elects to be treated as an S corporation, the IRC guarantees and protects the corporation's right to use and enjoy that status until it is terminated, and, therefore, that this right constitutes property. The flaw with this reasoning is that the IRC does not, and cannot, guarantee a corporation's right to S-corp status, because the corpora-

Continued on next page.

tion's shareholders may elect to revoke that status "at will." Even if the shareholders do not vote to revoke their corporation's S-corp status, any individual shareholder may at any time sell his interest to others in a manner that will lawfully increase the total number of shareholders to more than 100. Any of those sales would trigger the automatic revocation of the company's S status. Other courts, recognizing these flaws, have held that S-corp status is "property" because it has value to the estate. Here, the bankruptcy court defined the Debtors' property interest as "the right to prevent a shifting of tax liability from the shareholders to the QSub through a revocation of the 'S' corporation's status." Merely because such a right might have value does not render it a legal or equitable interest. The definition of "property" does not extend to override rights statutorily granted to shareholders to control the tax status of the entity they own; a tax classification over which the debtor has no control is not a legal or equitable interest of the debtor in property for purposes of § 541. Reversed and remanded.

ANALYSIS

Although the constitutional authority of Congress to establish "uniform Laws on the subject of Bankruptcies throughout the United States," U.S. Const., art. I, § 8, cl. 4, could, in theory, encompass a statutory framework defining property interests for purposes of bankruptcy," Congress has deliberately chosen not to establish such a framework, and instead has generally left the determination of property rights in the assets of a bankrupt's estate to state law, or, as this case demonstrates, to federal law where a federal interest requires it. However, it is not always clear whether state or federal law should apply. In this case, for example, the court noted that, on the one hand, the Internal Revenue Code (IRC) does not create property rights but merely attaches consequences, federally defined, to rights created under state law. It observed that, on the other hand, once it has been determined that state law creates sufficient interests in the taxpayer to satisfy the requirements of the federal revenue statute, state law is inoperative, and the tax consequences thenceforth are dictated by federal law. Ultimately, the court opted to look to federal law because the IRC addresses the handling of tax attributes in the bankruptcy context, and the Bankruptcy Code itself defers to the IRC with respect to the creation and character of certain tax attributes of the bankruptcy estate.

Quicknotes

DEBTOR-IN-POSSESSION A Chapter 11 bankruptcy debtor who retains control of assets or property pursuant to a plan of reorganization.

In re Fulton

City of Chicago (P) v. Debtor (D)

926 F.3d 916 (7th Cir. 2019)

NATURE OF CASE: Consolidated appeal of four bankruptcy court orders.

FACT SUMMARY: Four Chapter 13 bankruptcy debtors (D) had outstanding parking tickets with the City of Chicago (P), which sought to ignore the Bankruptcy Code's automatic stay and continue holding the debtors' (D) vehicles until the parking tickets were paid.

RULE OF LAW

A municipality that impounds debtors' vehicles for failure to pay multiple traffic fines is not entitled to an exception to a Chapter 13 automatic stay under § 362(b)(4).

FACTS: Four debtors' vehicles had been impounded by the City of Chicago (City) (P) for failure to pay multiple traffic fines prior to each filing for Chapter 13 bankruptcy. After debtors (D) filed their Chapter 13 petitions, the City (P) refused to return debtors' (D) vehicles, arguing that the City (P) was excepted from the automatic stay. In each case, the bankruptcy courts ordered the City (P) to return the debtors' (D) vehicles and imposed sanctions on the City (P) for violating the stay.

ISSUE: Is a municipality that impounds debtors' vehicles for failure to pay multiple traffic fines entitled to an exception to a Chapter 13 automatic stay under § 362(b)(4)?

HOLDING AND DECISION: (Flaum, J.) No. A municipality that impounds debtors' vehicles for failure to pay multiple traffic fines is not entitled to an exception to a Chapter 13 automatic stay under § 362(b)(4). The City (P) argues that under § 362(b)(4), a Chapter 13 bankruptcy petition does not operate as a § 362(a) automatic stay. Section 362(b)(4) sets out an exception that applies to the enforcement of state laws affecting health, welfare, morals, and safety, but not "regulatory laws that directly conflict with the control of the res or property by the bankruptcy court." The City (P) asserts that its impoundment of vehicles is an exercise of its police power to enforce traffic regulations as a matter of public safety; debtors (D) argue that it is instead a mechanism for the City (P) to collect revenue and is, accordingly, a money judgment that is not exempt under § 362(b)(4). If a state action satisfies either the pecuniary purpose test or the public policy test, then § 362(b)(4) applies. Here, the City (P) fails the pecuniary purpose test because attempting to collect on traffic tickets is focused on the debtor's (D) financial obligation rather than the City's (P) safety concerns. The public policy test considers whether the state action is principally to effectuate public policy or adjudicate private rights. Because (1) the City (P) makes significant revenue from parking and traffic tickets, (2) the tickets in this case are for minor infractions such as parking tickets and failure to display a City tax sticker, and (3) the City (P) imposes a monetary penalty on the owner of the vehicle rather than the driver, the City's (P) public policy case is similarly flimsy. However, even if adjudication of these tickets was a result of the City's (P) exercise of its police or regulatory power, the final determinations of liability constitute "money judgments" under § 362(b)(4) and cannot be enforced without violating the automatic stay. Affirmed.

ANALYSIS

In re Fulton was appealed to the United States Supreme Court, where the Seventh Circuit Court of Appeals' decision was unanimously reversed in *City of Chicago v. Fulton,* 2021 WL 125106, ___ U.S. ___ (January 14, 2021). The Court ruled that the City (P) was not immediately required to return the debtors' cars once the debtors (D) filed their Chapter 13 petitions. Rather, the Court determined that the debtors (D) needed to seek a § 542(a) turnover in order to recover their property.

Quicknotes

AUTOMATIC STAY Upon the filing of a bankruptcy petition, creditors are prohibited from extrajudicial collection efforts against the debtor or the debtor's property.

In re Panther Mountain Land Dev., LLC

[Parties not identified.]

438 B.R. 169 (Bankr. E.D. Ark. 2010)

NATURE OF CASE: Motion for relief from automatic stay, and motion for valuation, in Chapter 11 bankruptcy.

FACT SUMMARY: National Bank of Arkansas (National Bank) contended that it was entitled to relief from the automatic stay in the Chapter 11 bankruptcy of Panther Mountain Land Development, LLC (Debtor) because there was a lack of adequate protection with regard to two real estate tracts, primarily as the result of inadequate equity cushions.

RULE OF LAW

In a Chapter 11 bankruptcy, a creditor is not entitled to relief from the automatic stay on the grounds there is a lack of adequate protection where, although postpetition interest may erode the equity cushion, there is evidence the value of the collateral will continue to increase, there is a likelihood the debtor's plan of reorganization will be confirmed, and the debtor has an aggressive marketing plan to affect an expedient sale of the collateral.

FACTS: Panther Mountain Land Development, LLC (Debtor) owned and managed two real estate tracts. One, Sunset Lake, was an approximately 126-acre tract of land that was held for future development in the form of vacant, undeveloped acreage and was zoned for both residential and commercial use. The other, Panther Mountain, was an approximately 79-acre tract of land held in the form of a developed subdivision, consisting of a total of 25 residential lots and an approximately 15-acre tract of undeveloped land. These tracts were security for notes held by National Bank of Arkansas (National Bank). Debtor filed for Chapter 11 bankruptcy protection. The next day, National Bank moved for relief from the automatic stay. This motion was denied, but within five months, National Bank filed another motion for relief, as well as a motion for valuation. At the time of filing, Debtor owed $1,206,736.65 on the loan secured by the Sunset Lake property and $689,442.11 on the loan secured by the Panther Mountain property. Before filing, Debtor had sold eight of the original 25 lots in Panther Mountain. National Bank contended that it was entitled to relief from the automatic stay because there was a lack of adequate protection, i.e., that the collateral for its loans would lose value as a result of the bankruptcy filing, based on an inadequate equity cushion. An "equity cushion" is a term of art defined as the amount by which the value of the collateral exceeds the liens—equity—that will operate as a shield to protect the creditor's interest—cushion—if the property value declines during the bankruptcy case. National Bank argued that the equity cushion would be depleted as a result of postpetition interest accruing on the claim. The Debtor countered by presenting evidence that the value of the properties was likely to continue to increase; that there was a contract for the sale of a large portion of the Sunset Lake property; that the Debtor was putting in place an aggressive marketing effort to sell lots in Panther Mountain within two years and sell unsold lots at public auction thereafter; and that there was a likelihood that Debtor's plan of reorganization would be confirmed.

ISSUE: In a Chapter 11 bankruptcy, is a creditor entitled to relief from the automatic stay on the grounds there is a lack of adequate protection where, although postpetition interest may erode the equity cushion, there is evidence the value of the collateral will continue to increase, there is a likelihood the debtor's plan of reorganization will be confirmed, and the debtor has an aggressive marketing plan to affect an expedient sale of the collateral?

HOLDING AND DECISION: (Evans, J.) No. In a Chapter 11 bankruptcy, a creditor is not entitled to relief from the automatic stay on the grounds there is a lack of adequate protection where, although postpetition interest may erode the equity cushion, there is evidence the value of the collateral will continue to increase, there is a likelihood the debtor's plan of reorganization will be confirmed, and the debtor has an aggressive marketing plan to affect an expedient sale of the collateral. Relief from the automatic stay may be granted for cause under Bankruptcy Code § 362(d)(1), which sets forth one reason for "cause" as lack of adequate protection. The purpose of adequate protection is to guard a secured creditor's interest from a decline in the value of the collateralized property. In exchange for providing protective assurances against a decline in property value, the debtor is allowed to retain the protections provided by the Bankruptcy Code. To establish a prima facie case of lack of adequate protection, the creditor must show that the value of the collateral is declining, or at least threatened, as a result of the automatic stay. Once a creditor establishes a prima facie case, the debtor must either persuasively refute the evidence of the decline, or in the alternative, show that there are sufficient protections in place to guard against it. The methods of providing adequate protection for a secured creditor fall broadly into one of three categories: cash payments, replacement liens, or any other form of protection that provides the creditor with the "indubitable equivalent" of

Continued on next page.

its interest. Of these, a sufficient equity cushion is often determinative, and the sufficiency of the equity cushion is determined on a case-by-case basis. Here, National Bank makes out a prima facie case of lack of adequate protection. Its argument that postpetition interest will erode the equity cushion, by itself, is insufficient to establish a prima facie case, since even at a colossal interest rate, it is unlikely the accrual of interest after a debtor declares bankruptcy, on its own, could ever cause a lack of adequate protection. Because postpetition interest accruals are only allowed to the extent of the value of the collateral, they can erode the equity cushion, possibly even in its entirety, but can never actually impede the creditor's interest in the collateral given the division of a creditor's secured and unsecured claims. Also rejected is National Bank's broad argument that there must be a minimum equity cushion, because it does not follow that even the tiniest equity cushion would automatically fail to provide adequate protection if the chances of jeopardizing the creditor's interest were also tiny. However, National Bank implies that the equity cushion in this case—which is eroding as a result of postpetition interest—is insufficient on the particular facts of this case, and that implication is sufficient to establish National Bank's prima facie case. Accordingly, the burden to prove National Bank is adequately protected shifts to Debtor. In contrast to National Bank's evidence as to the adequacy of the equity cushion, which was based on the speculative outcome of yet undetermined events, Debtor presented persuasive evidence that there is an adequate cushion. First, credible witnesses testified that the value of the properties has increased and will continue to do so. Although the fact that none of the properties have sold in the last year weighs against the Debtor, the fact that there is a contract for the sale of a portion of the Sunset Lake property weighs in Debtor's favor. Not only is there an equity cushion, there is also evidence that National Bank's interest is adequately protected. There was evidence that an aggressive marketing campaign has producing interest in the properties, and potential purchasers. Debtor also has given the court good cause to believe that the plan of reorganization will be confirmed, since the plan places deadlines on the sale of the properties so that if the properties are not sold within a two-year period they will be sold at a public auction. This evidence demonstrates that adequate measures are being taken to sell the property as quickly and efficiently as possible, which will provide protection to National Bank. Taken together, all these factors likewise indicate that notwithstanding the potential erosion of the equity cushion as a consequence of postpetition interest, National Bank's interest will be adequately protected. Motion for relief from the automatic stay is denied.

ANALYSIS

For purposes of demonstrating lack of adequate protection, the most direct and convincing proof that the value is declining, or at least threatened, comes from a comparison of the property value at the time of the hearing to the property value on the date of filing of the bankruptcy petition. Nonetheless, a creditor may meet the prima facie case requirement by presenting evidence, in any form, effectively demonstrates its position in the collateral is in jeopardy—as did National Bank here. As the case illustrates, however, establishing a prima facie case is not tantamount to prevailing on a motion for relief from the automatic stay, since the debtor can adduce evidence of adequate protection, and the parties can present disparate valuations as to whether there is a sufficient equity cushion.

Quicknotes

AUTOMATIC STAY Upon the filing of a bankruptcy petition, creditors are prohibited from extrajudicial collection efforts against the debtor or the debtor's property.

PRIMA FACIE EVIDENCE Evidence, presented by a party, that is sufficient, in the absence of contradictory evidence, to support the fact or issue for which it is offered.

Chrysler LLC v. Plastech Engineered Prods.

Automobile maker/creditor (P) v. Automobile components supplier/debtor (D)

382 B.R. 90 (Bankr. E.D. Mich. 2008)

NATURE OF CASE: Motion, under §§ 362(d)(1) and (d)(2) for relief from automatic stay in Chapter 11 bankruptcy.

FACT SUMMARY: Chrysler LLC (P), an automobile manufacturer, contended that there was cause under § 362(d)(1) of the Bankruptcy Code to lift the automatic stay in Plastech Engineered Prods., Inc.'s (Debtor's) (D) Chapter 11 bankruptcy, and that, under § 362(d)(2), Debtor's (D) tooling (property that it is used to make metal or plastic parts for an automobile) was not necessary to an effective reorganization of Debtor (D), an automobile components supplier.

RULE OF LAW

(1) Under Bankruptcy Code § 362(d)(1), there is no "cause" to lift the automatic stay where not lifting the stay will result in economic harm to the movant creditor, but lifting the stay will economically harm the debtor; the case is in its infancy; and there are many other parties who have legitimate and substantial interests in the case that will be greatly affected if not destroyed by a lift of the automatic stay.

(2) Under Bankruptcy Code § 362(d)(2) a debtor's property is necessary to an effective reorganization where, although the debtor has no equity in the property, the debtor is making a good faith and intensive effort to restructure, the debtor has a chance of restructuring, and permitting a creditor to take possession of the property will likely destroy the possibilities of an effective reorganization.

FACTS: Plastech Engineered Prods., Inc. (Debtor) (D) was in the business of manufacturing products and components primarily for use in the automotive industry. Its primary customers included the nation's top automobile manufacturers (Major Customers), including Chrysler LLC (P). Debtor's (D) financing was comprised essentially of a revolving credit facility with various lenders and first and second lien term loans involving various lenders. In 2007 and 2008, Debtor (D) obtained certain financial accommodations from its Major Customers. In exchange for these accommodations, Debtor (D) granted to the Major Customers certain rights in the tooling used in the Debtor's (D) manufacture of components parts for the Major Customers. Generally speaking, tooling is property used to make metal or plastic parts for an automobile. Although Chrysler (P) typically owned tooling once it had paid for it, the additional rights Debtor (D) granted to Chrysler (P) were an acknowledgment that neither the Debtor (D) nor any other party had an interest in the tooling that Chrysler had paid for; that Chrysler (P) had the right to demand immediate possession of the tooling paid for by Chrysler (P) at Chrysler's (P) choosing; that Debtor (D) would cooperate with Chrysler (P) in taking possession of such tooling, including allowing access to the Debtor's (D) facilities; and that notwithstanding a dispute over payment for tooling, Chrysler (P) could take possession of the tooling while the dispute was resolved. On February 1, 2008, Chrysler (P) terminated its contracts with Debtor (D) and demanded the return of all of Chrysler's (P) tooling. This was based on Chrysler's (P) having given Debtor (D) close to $7 million it had not been obligated to provide to Debtor (D), as well as on Chrysler's (P) assessment that Debtor (D) was in "meltdown" and insolvent. Chrysler (P) also obtained a restraining order and order of possession requiring Debtor (D) to immediately deliver possession of all the tooling that it utilized in the production of Chrysler's (P) parts. Later that day, Debtor (D) filed for Chapter 11 bankruptcy protection. The next day, Chrysler (P) moved under §§ 362(d)(1) and (d)(2) for relief from the automatic stay. Chrysler (P) argued that under § 362(d)(1) there was "cause" to lift the stay. It also argued that under § 362(d)(2) Debtor (D) did not have any equity in the tooling and that such tooling would not be necessary to an effective reorganization. Evidence showed that if Chrysler (P) did not promptly receive its tooling, it would be forced to either continue to purchase parts from the Debtor (D) on some basis that could require it to make additional accommodations going forward or, alternatively, close many of its plants and idle many of its employees while it began the process of resourcing with new suppliers. Either alternative would harm Chrysler (P) economically. Evidence also showed that if Debtor (D) were forced to provide the tooling to Chrysler (P), Debtor (D) would have to shutter many plants and, also, suffer substantial economic harm. Additionally, other creditors, and other Major Customers also claimed interests in the tooling that Chrysler (P) sought. Further, the evidence showed that Debtor (D) did not have any equity in the tooling. Finally, at the time of filing, Debtor (D) did not have any agreements in place that would enable it to reorganize, though it was making efforts to do so.

ISSUE:

(1) Under Bankruptcy Code § 362(d)(1), is there "cause" to lift the automatic stay where not lifting the stay will

Continued on next page.

result in economic harm to the movant creditor, but lifting the stay will economically harm the debtor; the case is in its infancy; and there are many other parties who have legitimate and substantial interests in the case that will be greatly affected if not destroyed by a lift of the automatic stay?

(2) Under Bankruptcy Code § 362(d)(2), is a debtor's property necessary to an effective reorganization where, although the debtor has no equity in the property, the debtor is making a good faith and intensive effort to restructure, the debtor has a chance of restructuring, and permitting a creditor to take possession of the property will likely destroy the possibilities of an effective reorganization?

HOLDING AND DECISION: (Shefferly, J.)

(1) No. Under Bankruptcy Code § 362(d)(1), there is no "cause" to lift the automatic stay where not lifting the stay will result in economic harm to the movant creditor, but lifting the stay will economically harm the debtor; the case is in its infancy; and there are many other parties who have legitimate and substantial interests in the case that will be greatly affected if not destroyed by a lift of the automatic stay. Whether there is "cause" under § 362(d)(1) is determined on a case-by-case basis in the court's equitable discretion. Here, the record shows that Chrysler (P) will suffer economic harm if the stay is not lifted. On the other hand, the record shows Debtor (D) will suffer economic harm if the stay is lifted. These potential hardships to the respective parties are tempered by other factors. First, the case is in its infancy, and it is a large case with 36 manufacturing facilities, 7,700 employees, and many business entities who are suppliers to the Debtor (D) and depend themselves upon the Debtor's (D) business. The Debtor has approximately $500,000,000 of secured debt. It has projected annual sales of over $1 billion to its other Major Customers, without even considering the Chrysler (P) sales volume. It is an important supplier to major automobile manufacturers, and there are other creditors who claim an interest in the tooling Chrysler (P) seeks to take. Thus, there are many parties who have legitimate and substantial interests in this case that will be greatly affected if not destroyed by a lift of the automatic stay at this point in the case. Chrysler's (P) rights and interests are valid and important, but so are those of the Debtor (D) and the other constituents. A balancing of these various factors and potential impacts on the various parties, in light of the overarching goals of the Bankruptcy Code, leads to the conclusion that Chrysler (P) has failed to demonstrate "cause." Chrysler's (P) motion to lift the automatic stay under § 362(d)(1) is denied.

(2) Yes. Under Bankruptcy Code § 362(d)(2) a debtor's property is necessary to an effective reorganization where, although the debtor has no equity in the property, the debtor is making a good faith and intensive effort to restructure, the debtor has a chance of restructuring, and permitting a creditor to take possession of the property will likely destroy the possibilities of an effective reorganization. Relief under § 362(d)(2) requires a showing of both a lack of the debtor's equity in the property and that the property is not necessary for an effective reorganization. Here, it is clear Debtor (D) has no equity in the tooling. Equity is the value, above all secured claims against the property, which can be realized from the sale of the property for the benefit of the unsecured creditors. The tooling, as a result of its unique nature, would have no value other than as scrap to any party other than Chrysler (P). Also, the various lenders and tool makers have claims aggregating around $500 million of security in the tooling. Thus, Chrysler (P) has met its burden to show that the Debtor (D) does not have any equity in the tooling that Chrysler (P) paid for. To show that property is necessary for an effective reorganization, it must be shown not only that if there is conceivably to be an effective reorganization, the property will be needed for it, but that the property is essential for an effective reorganization that is in prospect, which means that there must be a reasonable possibility of a successful reorganization within a reasonable time. Here, as of the date of filing, Debtor (D) has no commitments for future financial accommodations from its customers, nor has it accomplished a restructuring. Moreover, it is in breach of financial covenants with its secured lenders, and it has no agreement with its secured lenders for them to forbear from enforcing their rights and remedies against it. Nevertheless, it has been engaged in good faith and intensive negotiations to try to reach an agreement for a restructuring plan. Evidence was also presented that Debtor (D) has a "top line" of $1.2 billion or $1.3 billion, a proven capability of producing components for substantial customers, significant contracts, a strong work force, and a supportive group of lenders. These factors suggest that there are ingredients from which a successful reorganization may be created. Permitting Chrysler (P) to take possession of its tooling at this time would likely destroy the possibilities for an effective reorganization, as it would cause the immediate closing of many of Debtor's (D) plants, and the resulting inability of Debtor (D) to provide components for its Major Customers other than Chrysler (P). The Debtor (D) does not have to show that it will affect a successful reorganization, but merely that it has a prospect for an effective reorganization and that the tooling that Chrysler seeks to take at this time are necessary to an effective reorganization. It is too early in the case to say whether such a reorganization will in fact occur, or what it will look like, but, at this point in the case, Debtor (D) has met its burden of showing that the

Continued on next page.

tooling is necessary to an effective reorganization: without the tooling, Debtor's (D) prospect of a reorganization is destroyed; with the tooling, Debtor (D) has a chance at building an effective reorganization. That is all the law requires at this early stage in the case. Chrysler's (P) motion to lift the automatic stay under § 362 (d)(2) is denied.

ANALYSIS

Under Bankruptcy Code § 362(d)(1), "cause" is an elastic concept. As this case demonstrates, if the relief from stay is requested at the early stages of the bankruptcy case, the burden upon the debtor is less stringent. If, however, relief from stay is requested later in the case, the debtor's showing is scrutinized more closely. The longer the case goes on, the more the analysis may change, and the balance of competing interests may compel a different result. As this case illustrates, in a case in its earliest stages, where the consequences of lifting the stay are shown by the evidence to be so devastating to the debtor and virtually all other parties in interest, it is unlikely a court will be persuaded absent extenuating circumstances that the balancing of the various interests in the case supports a finding that there is "cause" to lift the automatic stay.

Quicknotes

AUTOMATIC STAY Upon the filing of a bankruptcy petition, creditors are prohibited from extrajudicial collection efforts against the debtor or the debtor's property.

CHAPTER 18

Running the Business

Quick Reference Rules of Law

In re Colad Group, Inc.

[Parties not identified.]

324 B.R. 208 (Bankr. W.D.N.Y. 2005)

NATURE OF CASE: Court's rulings on first day motions in Chapter 11 bankruptcy action.

FACT SUMMARY: After Colad Group, Inc. (Colad) filed for Chapter 11 bankruptcy protection the bankruptcy court addressed first day motions.

RULE OF LAW

In a Chapter 11 bankruptcy, first day motions will be granted where the requested relief is limited to that which is minimally necessary to maintain the existence of the debtor, until such time as the debtor can effect appropriate notice to creditors and parties in interest, provided that the orders granting such relief will effect no unanticipated or untoward consequences, will provide no substitute for the procedural and substantive protections of the plan confirmation process, and will not violate or disregard the substantive rights of parties, in ways not expressly authorized by the Bankruptcy Code.

FACTS: The Colad Group, Inc. (Colad) filed for Chapter 11 bankruptcy protection and made first day motions. The court held a hearing that interested parties attended, including Continental Plants Group, LLC (Continental), the primary secured creditor. The bankruptcy court orally ruled on many of the motions, and its oral decisions were memorialized in written orders, including an order for interim financing. Left to be decided were issues and motions related to a final order for postpetition financing. The court disposed of motions for, inter alia, payments to employees and taxing authorities; postpetition utility services; authority to implement a key employee retention and incentive program; approval of a restructuring consultant; appointment of counsel; and approval of a cash management system.

ISSUE: In a Chapter 11 bankruptcy, will first day motions be granted where the requested relief is limited to that which is minimally necessary to maintain the existence of the debtor, until such time as the debtor can effect appropriate notice to creditors and parties in interest, provided that the orders granting such relief will effect no unanticipated or untoward consequences, will provide no substitute for the procedural and substantive protections of the plan confirmation process, and will not violate or disregard the substantive rights of parties, in ways not expressly authorized by the Bankruptcy Code?

HOLDING AND DECISION: (Bucki, J.) Yes. In a Chapter 11 bankruptcy, first day motions will be granted where the requested relief is limited to that which is minimally necessary to maintain the existence of the debtor, until such time as the debtor can effect appropriate notice to creditors and parties in interest, provided that the orders granting such relief will effect no unanticipated or untoward consequences, will provide no substitute for the procedural and substantive protections of the plan confirmation process, and will not violate or disregard the substantive rights of parties, in ways not expressly authorized by the Bankruptcy Code. As to Colad's motions to pay prepetition wages and benefits, and prepetition use and sales taxes, Colad represented that nearly all of the wages, benefits, and taxes would constitute priority claims; that it had incurred these obligations in its ordinary course of operations; that the outstanding wages and benefits were prepetition obligations that were not yet payable; that a disruption of wage and benefit payments could affect its ability to maintain its work force; and that the outstanding tax liabilities were ordinary obligations for use taxes and for sales taxes that it had collected from its customers. The principal concern in ruling on these motions is prejudice to the rights of creditors. Here, Continental consented to Colad's proposed distribution. Based upon that consent and upon Colad's various representations the motions are granted in substantial part. With respect to employee wages and benefits, however, the distribution may not exceed the priority limits of Bankruptcy Code §§ 507(a)(3) and (4), except for a certain de minimis amount and with restrictions on payments to an insider. As to postpetition utility services, § 366 addresses this issue, so that Colad's request for additional creditor assurances at this time is premature, and, therefore, rejected. As to implementation of a key employee retention and incentive program, which is outside Colad's ordinary course of business, the motion is approved as it meets the requirements of § 503(c). As to a restructuring consultant, Colad had, prepetition, hired Getzler Henrich & Associates LLC (Getzler Henrich) as a restructuring consultant in response to Continental's request for such a consultant. The continued retention of the firm will involve the use of resources outside the ordinary course of Colad's business. Accordingly, Colad has properly moved for court approval of Getzler Henrich's appointment. The court initially approved only an interim retention, with direction for final hearing on notice to the 20 largest creditors and others who might request service. At that final hearing, Colad's counsel demonstrated the need for a consultant and that Colad had exercised sound discretion in its selection of Getzler Henrich. For these reasons, final approval to the retention proposal is granted.

Continued on next page.

As to retention of counsel for the debtor in possession, absent opposition from the U.S. Trustee, this motion is ordinarily granted. As to Colad's cash management system, for which Colad sought authority to maintain, Colad had established a cash management system that required the deposit of receipts into a lockbox and the transfer of those funds to Continental, on account of its secured position, thus facilitating Colad's revolving credit agreement. For reasons of convenience, Colad may retain all its accounts, but is ordered to obtain new checks indicating its status as a debtor in possession. The processing of extant checks is also approved, in order to avoid disruption of relationships with employees who in any event can claim priority for the amount of their uncashed checks. [Additional dispositions of first day motions were omitted from the casebook extract.]

ANALYSIS

In bankruptcy practice, the phrase "first day motions" (also "first day orders") refers generally to any of a variety of requests made shortly after the filing of a Chapter 11 petition, for prompt authorizations needed to facilitate the operation of the debtor's business. As this case demonstrates many of the motions relate to matters that might threaten the debtor's continued operations if not promptly addressed (e.g., paying employees, retaining key employees, keeping utility services going, etc.). These motions are typically entered ex parte, with only a handful of key-creditors present, if that, since at this point in the proceedings there has not been time to provide notice to all stakeholders. As this case also demonstrates, judges often use interim orders to avoid rushing to final judgment without the input of those stakeholders and enter final orders only once all stakeholders have had an opportunity to be heard.

Quicknotes

POSTPETITION After bankruptcy petition has been filed.

PREPETITION Before bankruptcy petition has been filed.

In re Carbone Companies, Inc.

[Parties not identified.]

395 B.R. 631 (Bankr. N.D. Ohio 2008)

NATURE OF CASE: Motion under Bankruptcy Code § 363(c)(2)(B) for authorization to use cash collateral.

FACT SUMMARY: **Carbone Companies, Inc. (or alternatively "R.P. Carbone"), along with related entities (collectively "Debtors"), which were debtors-in-possession in Chapter 11 bankruptcies, moved for authorization to use cash collateral pursuant to Bankruptcy Code § 363(c)(2)(B). Debtors' secured lender, Fifth Third Bank (Bank), objected on the basis that it was not adequately protected.**

RULE OF LAW

A Chapter 11 debtor will be authorized to use cash collateral under Bankruptcy Code § 363(c)(2)(B) where the evidence demonstrates that an objecting creditor has adequate protection.

FACTS: Carbone Companies, Inc. (or alternatively "R. P. Carbone"), along with related entities (collectively "Debtors"), were debtors-in-possession in Chapter 11 bankruptcies. Debtors were in the construction business. Their main clients were the Ohio School Facilities Commission (OSFC) and McTech Corporation (McTech). In 2004, R.P. Carbone obtained a $15 million loan from Fifth Third Bank (Bank). The loan was secured by, inter alia, Debtors' accounts. R.P. Carbone defaulted on the loan on June 17, 2008. Allegedly, the Bank agreed to forbearance and proposed a budget for Debtors. When Debtors made several changes to the budget, the Bank ceased negotiations and swept Debtors' accounts, after which Debtors were unable to pay their operating expenses, including payroll and taxes. On August 1, 2008, the Bank obtained a judgment on the loan, and the Bank notified Carbone Companies it was executing the judgment. The next day, Debtors filed their respective Chapter 11 petitions and continued to operate their businesses as debtors-in-possession (DIPs). Debtors had multiple projects in progress, as well as several startup projects, at the time of filing. Debtors were granted limited use of cash collateral (cash and accounts receivable) while the Bank received replacement liens on the Debtors' postpetition assets. Debtors moved for final court approval for continued use of cash collateral under § 363(c)(2)(B), since the Bank refused consent to continued use of its cash collateral. The Bank opposed the relief sought on the grounds that it was not adequately protected. Specifically, the Bank alleged that the Debtors were maintaining an inadequate cash management system, that their budgets were excessive, and that they made improper transfers to insiders and affiliates. As a remedy for the inadequate protection of its security interest, the Bank proposed liens on potential avoidance actions that the Debtors could bring in their bankruptcy proceedings. Debtors presented evidence from Goddard, a turnaround specialist, who held that Debtors' net cash flows for the ensuing quarter would be positive and would increase by almost $90,000 since the petitions were filed, and that their accounts receivable for the same period would increase by close to $62,000. Thus, there was evidence cash collateral would increase. Goddard also opined that Debtors would be profitable going forward. Debtors supported this position with a report showing that they had exceeded their projections (i.e., more cash and accounts receivable, and fewer expenses) for the previous month. Evidence was also presented that Debtors' principal clients, OSFC and McTech, had indicated they would continue to do business with Debtors notwithstanding Debtors' pending bankruptcy proceedings. In support of its objection, the Bank alleged a diminution of Debtors' assets through a questionable transfer by McTech to an affiliate of the Debtor, Carbone Audubon, and to one of Carbone Audubon's law firms. However, the Bank was not able to show that the transfers by McTech involved any transfer of assets belonging to the Debtors. Instead, it turned out that the transfers were of McTech's own assets.

ISSUE: Will a Chapter 11 debtor be authorized to use cash collateral under Bankruptcy Code § 363(c)(2)(B) where the evidence demonstrates that an objecting creditor has adequate protection?

HOLDING AND DECISION: (Baxter, J.) Yes. A Chapter 11 debtor will be authorized to use cash collateral under Bankruptcy Code § 363(c)(2)(B) where the evidence demonstrates that an objecting creditor has adequate protection. Debtors bear the burden of proof on the issue of adequate protection, which, although not defined in the Code, means that the debtor may give cash, additional or replacement liens, or other relief that will result in the indubitable equivalent of the objecting party's interest in such property. Thus, the test is whether the secured party's interest is protected from diminution or decrease as a result of the proposed use of cash collateral. Here, the evidence presented by Debtors showed that cash and accounts receivable would increase, and that Debtors would be profitable. This shows that the Bank is adequately protected because its cash collateral will not diminish during Debtors' proposed use, but instead will increase as a result of Debtors' use. There is further protection of the Bank's cash collateral because the Bank is entitled to postpetition re-

Continued on next page.

placement liens on its collateral, to the extent there is any diminution in its cash collateral. Given these factors, and that Debtors' main clients will continue to do business with them, these findings clearly demonstrate that the Bank has not suffered any diminution of its security interest in the cash collateral. Bank has also failed to rebut this evidence, notwithstanding that its counsel argued strenuously that the Bank was not adequately protected, since arguments of counsel are not construed as evidence. Moreover, the challenged McTech transfers did not involve Debtors' assets. Accordingly, Debtors have carried their burden of demonstrating that Bank's interest in its cash collateral is adequately protected, and their motion for final authorization to use the cash collateral is granted, and Bank's objection is overruled. Judgment for Debtors.

ANALYSIS

While in this case the debtor had to prove there was adequate protection for cash collateral, the statutory scheme of § 361 indicates that adequate protection is intended to encompass a broad range of creditor interests and does not mandate an interpretation of the creditors' interest as the whole of the economic bargain. Although the concept of adequate protection is certainly intended to protect a creditor's interest in collateral, it is susceptible to differing applications over a wide range of fact situations. Debtors must establish adequate protection by a preponderance of the evidence in order to carry their burden of proof. Once the debtor carries its burden, then the burden shifts to the creditor to controvert the debtor's evidence.

Quicknotes

DEBTOR-IN-POSSESSION A Chapter 11 bankruptcy debtor who retains control of assets or property pursuant to a plan of reorganization.

In re Orexigen Therapeutics, Inc.

Creditor corporation (P) v. Debtor (D)

596 B.R. 9 (Bankr. D. Del. 2018)

NATURE OF CASE: Ruling on motion seeking to affect a setoff under § 553 of the Bankruptcy Code.

FACT SUMMARY: Debtor (D) is a biopharmaceutical company that contracted with McKesson Corporation (P) and its subsidiary McKesson Patient Relationship Solutions (MPRS) for distribution and services on a specific medication. When Debtor (D) filed for Chapter 11 bankruptcy, McKesson (P) owed Debtor (D) approximately $7,000,000, and Debtor (D) owed MPRS approximately $9,100,000. McKesson (P) sought to setoff its debt to Debtor (D) with the amount owed to MPRS.

RULE OF LAW

A corporation cannot affect a triangular setoff under § 553 of the Bankruptcy Code without strict mutuality.

FACTS: Debtor (D), Orexigen Therapeutics, Inc., is a biopharmaceutical company that manufactured an obesity treatment drug, Contrave®. Prior to filing its Chapter 11 bankruptcy petition, Debtor (D) entered into a distribution agreement with McKesson Corporation (P), where McKesson (P) agreed to purchase and distribute Contrave® to various pharmacies in exchange for certain rights, including a right to set off debts owed between Debtor (D) and its affiliates against debts owed by McKesson (P) and its affiliates. Additionally, Debtor (D) entered into a services agreement with MPRS, a wholly-owned subsidiary of McKesson (P), through which MPRS would administer Debtor's LoyaltyScript® program, which enabled patients to receive price discounts on Contrave® by paying retail pharmacies and patients. The services agreement with MPRS and the distribution agreement with McKesson (P) were wholly distinct. At time of petition, McKesson (P) owed Debtor (D) $6,932,816.40 under the distribution agreement, and Debtor owed MPRS approximately $9,100,000.

ISSUE: Can a corporation affect a triangular setoff under § 553 of the Bankruptcy Code without strict mutuality?

HOLDING AND DECISION: (Gross, J.) No. A corporation cannot affect a triangular setoff under § 553 of the Bankruptcy Code without strict mutuality. Setoff is a contractual right that allows entities owing each other money to apply their mutual debts against each other. Under the Bankruptcy Code's § 553(a), there is not a federal right to setoff, but the Code recognizes that parties may have setoff rights under state law. In order to prove a right to a § 553 setoff, the party seeking the setoff must acquire such right prepetition under nonbankruptcy law, and that party must meet the § 553(a) restriction that only allows a creditor to offset a "mutual debt." State and federal courts have found that a mutual debt is due to and from the same persons in the same capacity. Though McKesson (P) had a prepetition setoff right, it does not have a mutual debt under § 553(a). McKesson (P) and MPRS are legally distinct entities, despite their parent–subsidiary relationship, and therefore, the setoff sought by McKesson (P) is a triangular setoff, which is impermissible under § 553(a). Furthermore, McKesson's (P) argument that California law should apply is not relevant, because Congress recognized a distinct federal interest when it enacted § 553(a). Denied.

ANALYSIS

Creditors seek to benefit from setoffs because setoffs often allow the creditor to collect a greater amount than it would without the setoff. Section 506 of the Bankruptcy Code treats creditors with setoff claims as secured creditors for the amount subject to setoff. Without a setoff, the creditor's claim will likely not be secured, and the creditor may struggle to recover.

Quicknotes

SETOFF A creditor's equitable right to deduct a debt it owes to a debtor from a separate transaction.

SUBSIDIARY A company, a majority of whose shares are owned by another corporation and that is subject to that corporation's control.

In re Kmart Corp.

[Parties not identified.]

359 F.3d 866 (7th Cir. 2004)

NATURE OF CASE: Appeal from reversal of order authorizing payment of critical vendors in Chapter 11 reorganization.

FACT SUMMARY: Kmart Corporation argued that it should be allowed to pay all its critical vendors because doing so would provide a residual benefit to the remaining, unfavored creditors.

RULE OF LAW

A critical-vendors order may not be issued, providing preferential payments to one class of creditors, where there is no evidence in the record that there is a possibility that the class of disfavored creditors will benefit.

FACTS: Kmart Corporation, in Chapter 11 bankruptcy, sought permission to pay immediately, and in full, the prepetition claims of all "critical vendors." The bankruptcy court granted this request, without notifying any disfavored creditors, without receiving any pertinent evidence, and without making any finding of fact that disfavored creditors would gain or come out even. The bankruptcy court's order declared that the relief Kmart requested—open-ended permission to pay any debt to any vendor it deemed "critical" in the exercise of unilateral discretion, provided that the vendor agreed to furnish goods on "customary trade terms" for the next two years—was in the best interests of Kmart, its estate, and its creditors. The order did not explain why, nor did it contain any legal analysis, though it did cite § 105(a). Kmart used its authority to pay in full the prepetition debts to 2,330 suppliers, which collectively received about $300 million. This came from the $2 billion in new credit (debtor-in-possession or DIP financing) that the bankruptcy judge authorized, granting the lenders superpriority in postpetition assets and revenues. Another 2,000 or so vendors were not deemed "critical" and were not paid. They and 43,000 additional unsecured creditors eventually received about 10 cents on the dollar, mostly in stock of the reorganized Kmart. The district court reversed the order authorizing payment, and the court of appeals granted review.

ISSUE: May a critical-vendors order be issued, providing preferential payments to one class of creditors, where there is no evidence in the record that there is a possibility that the class of disfavored creditors will benefit?

HOLDING AND DECISION: (Easterbrook, J.) No. A critical-vendors order may not be issued, providing preferential payments to one class of creditors, where there is no evidence in the record that there is a possibility that the class of disfavored creditors will benefit. The theory behind a critical-vendors request is that that some suppliers may be unwilling to do business with a customer that is behind in payment, and, if it cannot obtain the merchandise that its own customers have come to expect, a firm such as Kmart may be unable to carry on, injuring all its creditors. Full payment to critical vendors thus could in principle make even the disfavored creditors better off: they may not be paid in full, but they will receive a greater portion of their claims than they would if the critical vendors cut off supplies and the business shut down. Putting the proposition in this way implies, however, that the debtor must prove, and not just allege, two things: that, but for immediate full payment, vendors would cease dealing; and that the business will gain enough from continued transactions with the favored vendors to provide some residual benefit to the remaining, disfavored creditors, or at least leave them no worse off. Here, neither of these things was proven, so the issue becomes whether the bankruptcy court had authority under the Code to prefer some vendors over others. While § 105(a) permits a bankruptcy court to "issue any order, process, or judgment that is necessary or appropriate to carry out the provisions of" the Code, this does not create discretion to set aside the Code's rules about priority and distribution. Therefore, the bankruptcy court may not authorize full payment of any unsecured debt unless all unsecured creditors in the class are paid in full. Also, a "doctrine of necessity," which permits departure from the Code, does not authorize overriding the Code's provisions. Arguably § 363(b)(1), when read broadly, may provide such authority. That provision permits the trustee, or debtor-in-possession, to use property of the estate other than in the ordinary course of administering the estate. Satisfaction of a prepetition debt to keep "critical" supplies flowing is a use of property other than in the ordinary course of administering an estate in bankruptcy. Nonetheless, it is prudent to read, and use, § 363(b)(1) to do the least damage possible to priorities established by contract and by other parts of the Code. The court here, however, need not decide whether § 363(b)(1) could support payment of some prepetition debts, because this particular order was unsound no matter how one reads § 363(b)(1). Again, as stated earlier, that is because there was no evidence that the disfavored creditor would be better off with reorganization than liquidation, for example, or that the purportedly critical vendors would in fact have ceased deliveries if the old debts were left unpaid during the bankruptcy proceedings. If vendors will deliver

Continued on next page.

against a promise of current payment, then reorganization can be achieved, and all unsecured creditors will obtain its benefit, without preferring any of the unsecured creditors. Some supposedly critical vendors will continue to do business with the debtor because they must. Also, Kmart could have paid cash or its equivalent. Some of the $2 billion line of credit could have been used to assure vendors that payment would be forthcoming for all postpetition transactions. The easiest way to do that would have been to put some of the $2 billion behind a standby letter of credit on which the bankruptcy judge could authorize unpaid vendors to draw. That would not have changed the terms on which Kmart and any of its vendors did business; it just would have demonstrated the certainty of payment. Yet the bankruptcy court did not explore the possibility of using a letter of credit to assure vendors of payment. The court did not find that any firm would have ceased doing business with Kmart if not paid for prepetition deliveries, and the scant record would not have supported such a finding had one been made. The court did not find that discrimination among unsecured creditors was the only way to facilitate reorganization. It did not find that the disfavored creditors were at least as well off as they would have been had the critical vendors order not been entered. Even if § 362(b)(1) allows critical vendors orders in principle, preferential payments to a class of creditors are proper only if the record shows the prospect of benefit to the other creditors. This record does not, so the critical vendors order cannot stand. Affirmed.

ANALYSIS

The 2005 Bankruptcy Act has significantly improved the position of trade vendors, regardless of whether they qualify for "critical vendor" status, by creating an administrative priority in favor of vendors for the value of all goods shipped to a debtor within 20 days of bankruptcy filing, § 503(b)(9). In addition, state reclamation rights under the Uniform Commercial Code (UCC) are preserved for goods shipped within 45 days of filing. Such an expansion of reclamation rights could significantly curtail any limitations on critical-vendor orders such as those imposed in this case.

Quicknotes

CHAPTER 11 BANKRUPTCY A legal proceeding whereby a debtor, who is unable to pay his or her debts as they become due, is relieved of the obligation to pay creditors through reorganization and payment from future income.

DEBTOR-IN-POSSESSION A Chapter 11 bankruptcy debtor who retains control of assets or property pursuant to a plan of reorganization.

LETTER OF CREDIT An agreement by a bank or other party that it will honor a customer's demand for payment upon the satisfaction of specified conditions.

UNILATERAL One-sided; involving only one party.

UNSECURED CREDITOR A creditor whose loan is not backed by specified collateral or a security agreement.

CHAPTER 19

Financing the Reorganization

Quick Reference Rules of Law

		PAGE
1.	*In re Devlin.* A debtor in a Chapter 11 bankruptcy will be granted authority to incur a secured debt with super priority status under Bankruptcy Code § 364(d)(1) where the debtor is unable to obtain unsecured or secured financing for purchases that are in the best interests of the debtor and its estate, notwithstanding that the debtor does not hold legal title to the property to be encumbered by the secured debt.	*116*
2.	*In re Colad Group, Inc.* (1) In a Chapter 11 bankruptcy, a first day motion for authority to obtain postpetition financing will be denied where the proposed interim order: fails to reflect any effort to limit the conditions of credit only to those that would be absolutely necessary to avoid immediate and irreparable harm; is overly complex; would change substantive and procedural rights, without allowing any reasonable opportunity for creditor objection; and violates criminal usury laws. (2) In a Chapter 11 bankruptcy, a motion to authorize a final debtor-in-possession lending facility will be denied where the proposed order would: sanction excessive and criminally usurious interest; authorize an inappropriate modification of statutory rights and obligations in bankruptcy; and include a finding of good faith that the parties had yet to establish on the record.	*118*
3.	*In re Michael Day Enterprises, Inc.* In a Chapter 11 bankruptcy, a motion for an interim order authorizing the obtaining of financing, and the use of cash collateral, will be granted to a debtor-in-possession on terms highly favorable to the postpetition lender where that lender is also the prepetition secured creditor with a secured interest in virtually all the debtor's assets.	*121*

In re Devlin

[Parties not identified.]

185 B.R. 376 (Bankr. M.D. Fla. 1995)

NATURE OF CASE: Motion for authority to incur a secured debt with super priority status under Bankruptcy Code § 364(d)(1).

FACT SUMMARY: Debtor, who operated a motel, sought authority to incur a secured debt with super priority under Bankruptcy Code § 364(d)(1) to replace motel's air conditioning system, hot water heaters, and boiler. Nat Max & Associates, the legal owner of the property, objected.

RULE OF LAW

A debtor in a Chapter 11 bankruptcy will be granted authority to incur a secured debt with super priority status under Bankruptcy Code § 364(d)(1) where the debtor is unable to obtain unsecured or secured financing for purchases that are in the best interests of the debtor and its estate, notwithstanding that the debtor does not hold legal title to the property to be encumbered by the secured debt.

FACTS: Debtor, a debtor in a Chapter 11 bankruptcy, operated a motel. The motel's antiquated air conditioning system, hot water heaters, and boiler needed replacement. Debtor did not have the cash to pay for the replacement equipment and related work, which would have cost around $124,000, and moved the bankruptcy court for authority to incur a secured debt with super priority status under Bankruptcy Code § 364(d)(1). Debtor's mother, Devlin, agreed to provide such financing contingent on her receiving first priority lien on the real property where the motel was located. Nat Max & Associates, the owner with legal title to the property, objected. Nat Max & Associates had contracted with Debtor to sell the property to him, and he, in turn, intended to sell the property to a third party. The motel was encumbered by a first priority mortgage lien in favor of the Resolution Trust Corporation (RTC) to secure a debt of approximately $2.3 million. There was a pending foreclosure by the RTC. Nat Max & Associates objected to the Debtor's selling the motel, and to Debtor's plan of reorganization. Nat Max & Associates also contended that the court did not have authority to encumber property for which the Debtor did not hold legal title. Under state law, the Debtor held equitable title in the property.

ISSUE: Will a debtor in a Chapter 11 bankruptcy be granted authority to incur a secured debt with super priority status under Bankruptcy Code § 364(d)(1) where the debtor is unable to obtain unsecured or secured financing for purchases that are in the best interests of the debtor and its estate, notwithstanding that the debtor does not hold legal title to the property to be encumbered by the secured debt?

HOLDING AND DECISION: (Funk, J.) Yes. A debtor in a Chapter 11 bankruptcy will be granted authority to incur a secured debt with super priority status under Bankruptcy Code § 364(d)(1) where the debtor is unable to obtain unsecured or secured financing for purchases that are in the best interests of the debtor and its estate, notwithstanding that the debtor does not hold legal title to the property to be encumbered by the secured debt. If Nat Max & Associates' objections are sustained, there is a substantial risk the Debtor's reorganization will fail and the case may convert to Chapter 7. In the event of a conversion, the prospects of a postpetition creditor being repaid in full are less than probable, even if such creditor were holding a Chapter 11 administrative expense claim superior to all others. The pending RTC foreclosure action would also foreclose any subordinate interests in the motel if the case were to convert to Chapter 7. Under these circumstances, the granting of a secured claim with super priority status is the only way the Debtor is likely to obtain financing. Moreover, the bankruptcy estate is comprised of all property interests of the Debtor, both legal and equitable. Bankruptcy Code § 364(d)(1) permits the court to authorize financing secured by a senior lien on any property of the estate if the Debtor is unable to obtain such credit otherwise. Here, it has been shown that Debtor would be unable to obtain the credit needed for the replacement equipment. Because the Debtor has an equitable interest in the property; the replacement equipment is necessary to preserve the value of the motel and maintain ongoing operations—which will inure to the benefit of all parties in interest, including Nat Max & Associates, regardless of whether the reorganization will succeed; and replacing the equipment is in the Debtor's and the estate's best interests, Debtor's motion is granted. Judgment for Debtor.

ANALYSIS

The Resolution Trust Corporation (RTC) did not object to Debtor's motion, presumably because its interests in the motel would remain adequately protected, even if its mortgage lien was subordinated to a lien in favor of Devlin for the cost of replacing the air conditioning system, boiler, and hot water heaters. The court in fact determined that RTC was adequately protected—as it is required to do under § 364 before granting a superseding lien—notwithstanding that Devlin would recover the full value of her loan from the proceeds of the sale of the motel before the

Continued on next page.

RTC received any repayment, because the increase in the value of the motel from the installation of the replacement equipment would be greater than the cost of that equipment installation.

Quicknotes

SUPERIOR LIEN A claim against certain property that takes priority over other liens.

In re Colad Group, Inc.

[Parties not identified.]

324 B.R. 208 (Bankr. W.D.N.Y. 2005)

NATURE OF CASE: In Chapter 11 bankruptcy first day motion for authority to obtain postpetition financing and subsequent motion for authorization of a final lending facility.

FACT SUMMARY: In its Chapter 11 bankruptcy, Colad Group, Inc. (Colad) made a first day motion for authority to obtain postpetition financing. The bankruptcy court rejected Colad's initial proposed postpetition financing order on the basis of several defects and issued a narrow interim lending order authorizing Colad to borrow funds on an emergency basis. Subsequently, Colad moved for an order authorizing a final lending facility with its principal secured creditor, Continental Plants Group, LLC (Continental).

RULE OF LAW

(1) In a Chapter 11 bankruptcy, a first day motion for authority to obtain postpetition financing will be denied where the proposed interim order: fails to reflect any effort to limit the conditions of credit only to those that would be absolutely necessary to avoid immediate and irreparable harm; is overly complex; would change substantive and procedural rights, without allowing any reasonable opportunity for creditor objection; and violates criminal usury laws.

(2) In a Chapter 11 bankruptcy, a motion to authorize a final debtor-in-possession lending facility will be denied where the proposed order would: sanction excessive and criminally usurious interest; authorize an inappropriate modification of statutory rights and obligations in bankruptcy; and include a finding of good faith that the parties had yet to establish on the record.

FACTS: After Colad Group, Inc. (Colad) filed for Chapter 11 bankruptcy protection, one of its first day motions was for authority to obtain postpetition financing from its principal secured creditor, Continental Plants Group, LLC (Continental). Continental had recently acquired its secured position, with the stated desire to affect a purchase of assets as a going concern under § 363 of the Bankruptcy Code. In fact, Colad had candidly indicated intent to liquidate, most likely through a sale of assets. Colad had pledged nearly all its assets as collateral to Continental to secure a prepetition credit facility. Continental and Colad proposed to link the postpetition financing facility to the prepetition revolver loan, so that proceeds of collateral would be applied first to the satisfaction of the balance due on the prepetition loan. Meanwhile, Continental would fund the Colad's postpetition activities through new advances under the postpetition facility. Under the proposed facility, postpetition advances would be secured by all Colad's assets, so that the obligation created by the facility would receive administrative and super priority status, as allowed under § 364(c). Colad represented that it could not operate without a postpetition line of credit and that it had no ability to obtain such credit from any source other than Continental. Because Colad intended to liquidate, any amounts it borrowed would be used to maintain operations as a going concern for the short term, until a sale could be completed. The proposed order would have approved an interim loan agreement with terms essentially identical to those contemplated for the final loan agreement. The proposed order was 26 pages long, and it referenced a 93-page loan agreement. The proposed order would change substantive and procedural rights, without allowing any reasonable opportunity for creditor objection. It included a grant of relief from the automatic stay in the event of default, limitations on Colad's right to propose a plan of reorganization, and a waiver of various claims that it might assert against Continental. It also purported to require, as a condition for interim funding, the disavowal and waiver of various "rights and remedies provided under the Bankruptcy Code, the Federal Rules of Civil Procedure, and the Bankruptcy Rules." Furthermore, it seemingly attempted to grant administrative priority to Continental's prepetition claims. Finally, it seemed to propose a rate of interest that violated the state's criminal 25 percent usury rate. The respective attorneys for Colad and Continental asserted that the proposed lending arrangement represented the best and only terms available to Colad. Finding several defects in the proposed financing arrangement, the court issued an interim financing order that simply authorized Colad to borrow funds needed to pay necessary expenditures. With respect to these advances, Continental received a super-priority administrative expense claim secured by a lien on all Colad's assets. After holding a hearing, of which other creditors received notice and attended, the court addressed Colad's motion to authorize a final debtor-in-possession lending facility. The Official Committee of Unsecured Creditors, appointed after the court's rulings on the first day motions, supported this motion. One creditor objected on the grounds that the proposed facility entailed excessive risk, and that creditor presented numerous objections to specific terms of the lending proposal. Under the

Continued on next page.

proposal, Colad sought to borrow no more than $494,000 over less than 90 days. However, with the proposed fees, Colad would actually receive operating funds of less than $381,000. As a consequence of the short term of the loan, the fees alone would represent charges equivalent to an interest rate in excess of 100 percent per annum—which was much higher than the state's criminal usury rate of 25 percent. Additionally, the proposed order would prohibit any surcharge of collateral under § 506(c). The proposed order would also change the procedural requirements for stay relief creating a default procedure, whereby the stay would automatically lift upon a failure by any interested party to demand a hearing within five business days following notice of an event of default. Finally, the proposed order included a finding that Continental was extending credit in good faith. The bankruptcy court detailed the defects of both the first day motion for interim financing and the motion for authorization of a final lending facility.

ISSUE:

(1) In a Chapter 11 bankruptcy, will a first day motion for authority to obtain postpetition financing be denied where the proposed interim order: fails to reflect any effort to limit the conditions of credit only to those that would be absolutely necessary to avoid immediate and irreparable harm; is overly complex; would change substantive and procedural rights, without allowing any reasonable opportunity for creditor objection; and violates criminal usury laws?

(2) In a Chapter 11 bankruptcy, will a motion to authorize a final debtor-in-possession lending facility be denied where the proposed order would: sanction excessive and criminally usurious interest; authorize an inappropriate modification of statutory rights and obligations in bankruptcy; and include a finding of good faith that the parties had yet to establish on the record?

HOLDING AND DECISION: (Bucki, J.)

(1) Yes. In a Chapter 11 bankruptcy, a first day motion for authority to obtain postpetition financing will be denied where the proposed interim order: fails to reflect any effort to limit the conditions of credit only to those that would be absolutely necessary to avoid immediate and irreparable harm; is overly complex; would change substantive and procedural rights, without allowing any reasonable opportunity for creditor objection; and violates criminal usury laws. Under Bankruptcy Rule 4001, a motion for authority to obtain credit must be treated as a contested matter, and notice must be given to the Official Committee of Unsecured Creditors, or if no committee has been appointed, then to the 20 largest unsecured creditors. In the context of first day motions, this notice requirement is problematic, as it may be impossible to provide timely notice where a debtor needs immediate financing. However, under Rule 4001(c)(2), a court may consider a first day motion to approve an emergency lending facility, but only if two conditions are satisfied: (1) any emergency authorization must be limited only "to the extent necessary to avoid immediate and irreparable harm;" and (2) the authorization may be effective only until a final hearing on appropriate notice to creditors as required under the Rules. Colad's representation that it could not operate without a postpetition line of credit and that it had no ability to obtain such credit from any source other than Continental justified an appropriate form of emergency lending until the scheduled hearing for final approval. However, the proposed order had four key defects. First, the proposed order would have approved an interim loan agreement with terms essentially identical to those contemplated for the final loan agreement, thus failing to reflect any effort to limit the conditions of credit only to those which would be absolutely necessary to avoid immediate and irreparable harm. Second, given the length of the proposed order and the lending agreement, the order was inappropriately complex, and thereby denied to the court a sufficient basis of confidence in the reasonableness of its terms. Such complexity is inappropriate for an emergency order since there is no benefit of opportunities for comment from creditors on notice; the court must view with skepticism the exigent submission of any such complex instrument. Third, the proposed order would change substantive and procedural rights, without allowing any reasonable opportunity for creditor objection. This included a grant of relief from the automatic stay in the event of default, limitations on Colad's right to propose a plan of reorganization, a waiver of various claims that Colad might assert against Continental and the disavowal and waiver of various rights and remedies under federal law. As part of a first day order, where unsecured creditors have had no opportunity to object, such terms are unacceptable. Fourth, the proposed financing would violate the state's criminal usury laws. Notwithstanding counsels' representations that the proposed lending arrangement represented the best and only terms available to Colad, these representations seemed disingenuous, especially in light of Continental's desire to affect a purchase of assets under § 363. With this objective, Continental would be obviously disinclined to compel a distressed liquidation of its position, and, as holder of a first lien in Colad's inventory and receivables, Continental was positioned to dictate terms. Consequently, the proposed loan did not represent terms negotiated in any form of open market, and, without the opportunity for unsecured creditors to object, the order cannot be granted in its present form. Motion denied; substitute interim financing order issued. [In fact, the resolution of the motion for interim financing confirmed the court's perception of disingenuousness: after the court refused to approve an order in the form that the debtor had first presented, the parties

Continued on next page.

negotiated an arrangement that the court could accept on an interim basis.]

(2) Yes. In a Chapter 11 bankruptcy, a motion to authorize a final debtor-in-possession lending facility will be denied where the proposed order would: sanction excessive and criminally usurious interest; authorize an inappropriate modification of statutory rights and obligations in bankruptcy; and include a finding of good faith that the parties had yet to establish on the record. First, as a consequence of the short term of the proposed loan, the proposed fees alone would represent charges equivalent to an interest rate in excess of 100 percent per annum—which is much higher than the state's criminal usury rate of 25 percent. Second, Colad and Continental may not implement a private agreement that effectively changes the bankruptcy law with regard to the statutory rights of third parties. The proposed agreement would do just that by prohibiting any surcharge on collateral under § 506(c), which would prejudice the rights of any trustee. That section permits a trustee to recover from property securing an allowed secured claim the reasonable, necessary costs and expenses of preserving, or disposing of, such property to the extent of any benefit to the holder of such claim. Continental and Colad, however, would either deny the means to pay such charges, or would impose such costs on funds available for distribution to unsecured creditors. There is no basis for allowing such disregard of § 506. The agreement would also affect the statutory rights of third parties by providing that the automatic stay would automatically lift upon a failure by any interested party to demand a hearing within five business days following notice of an event of default. While such a modification of statutory rights could be approved with the consent of Colad and unsecured creditors, a waiver of the controlling standard for a hearing on notice to any trustee that may hereafter be appointed cannot be sanctioned. Third, § 364(e) provides generally that a reversal or modification on appeal of an order authorizing secured debt "does not affect the validity of any debt so incurred, or any priority or lien so granted, to an entity that extended such credit in good faith. . . ." Accordingly, Colad has proposed an order that includes a finding that Continental is extending credit in good faith. At the hearing on this motion, the debtor offered only one witness and his statements about good faith were conclusory. Moreover, the order's other defects cause uncertainty about intent, particularly with respect to any attempt to discourage competitive bidding. Any finding of good faith is more appropriately made with the benefit of testimony and argument after a reversal or modification on appeal. While Colad might be able to establish good faith at a future hearing, at this time, however, there simply is not an adequate basis to reach any conclusion about Continental's good faith. For these reasons, the proposed order is denied, but without prejudice, and a proposed order that eliminates the defects detailed here may be approved in the future. The interim financing authorization is continued until further order. Motion denied.

ANALYSIS

Bankruptcy courts often approve the postpetition use of a revolving credit facility, such as the one proposed here by Continental and Colad, provided the financing arrangement does not also have other defects, such as the ones the court identified in this decision. From the lender's perspective, such an arrangement avoids the various legal problems of cross-collateralization. In a cross-collateralization arrangement, a lender advances new credit on condition that an enhanced set of collateral will secure both prepetition and postpetition loans. Instead, the revolver arrangement permits a satisfaction of the prepetition loan, so that an increasing percentage of the lender's total exposure will receive the security and benefits of the new postpetition credit facility.

Quicknotes

AUTOMATIC STAY Upon the filing of a bankruptcy petition, creditors are prohibited from extrajudicial collection efforts against the debtor or the debtor's property.

CROSS-COLLATERAL CLAUSE Provision contained in a contract pursuant to which both parties provide security that performance will be rendered or that payment will be made.

DEBTOR-IN-POSSESSION A Chapter 11 bankruptcy debtor who retains control of assets or property pursuant to a plan of reorganization.

In re Michael Day Enterprises, Inc.

[Parties not identified.]

2009 WL 7195491 (Bankr. N.D. Ohio 2009)

NATURE OF CASE: Chapter 11 emergency motion for interim and final orders authorizing the obtaining of financing, and the use of cash collateral.

FACT SUMMARY: The debtors-in-possession (Debtors) made an emergency motion for interim and final orders authorizing the obtaining of financing, and the use of cash collateral, attesting that they were unable to obtain sufficient levels of credit under §§ 364 and 503(b)(1) of the Bankruptcy Code to maintain and conduct their businesses, and that Key Bank National Association, which was the prepetition lender (Prepetition Lender) and letter of credit issuer (Prepetition LC Issuer), was willing to advance monies to the Debtors, and to consent to the use of cash collateral, upon the terms and conditions contained in the proposed order.

RULE OF LAW

In a Chapter 11 bankruptcy, a motion for an interim order authorizing the obtaining of financing, and the use of cash collateral, will be granted to a debtor-in-possession on terms highly favorable to the postpetition lender where that lender is also the prepetition secured creditor with a secured interest in virtually all the debtor's assets.

FACTS: The debtors-in-possession (DIP) (Debtors) in a Chapter 11 bankruptcy made an emergency motion for interim and final orders authorizing the obtaining of financing, and the use of cash collateral. Under the proposed order, Key Bank National Association (Key Bank), which was the prepetition lender (Prepetition Lender) and letter of credit issuer (Prepetition LC Issuer), was to be the postpetition lender (DIP Lender). Key Bank was willing to advance monies to the Debtors, and to consent to the use of cash collateral upon the terms and conditions contained in the proposed order. In support of their motion, the Debtors averred that they were unable to obtain sufficient levels of unsecured credit allowable as an administrative expense under § 503(b)(1) of the Bankruptcy Code to maintain and conduct their businesses, and that they were unable to obtain the necessary financing as unsecured credit allowable under § 364(a), (b), or (c)(1) or as secured credit pursuant to §§ 364(c)(2) and (3). They also averred that they were unable to procure the necessary financing on more favorable terms than those offered by the DIP Lender. The bankruptcy court found that Key Bank's conditions for advancing money to Debtors and allowing the use of cash collateral were made in good faith, in an arms' length, open and honest fashion. The court also found that it was in the best interests of the Debtors' creditors and estates that they be allowed to finance their operations under the terms and conditions set forth in the proposed order. Notice of the relief sought by the motion was given to a variety of parties in interest, including the U.S. Trustee and the 20 largest unsecured creditors. The Debtors stipulated that without the use of cash collateral, and the financing proposed by the motion, they would be unable to pay postpetition payroll, payroll taxes, trade vendors, suppliers, overhead, and other expenses necessary for the continued operation of their business and the management and preservation of their assets and properties. As of the date the motion was made, an official committee of unsecured creditors had not been appointed. The court addressed the motion for the interim order, which the court issued.

ISSUE: In a Chapter 11 bankruptcy, will a motion for an interim order authorizing the obtaining of financing, and the use of cash collateral, be granted to a debtor-in-possession on terms highly favorable to the postpetition lender where that lender is also the prepetition secured creditor with a secured interest in virtually all the debtor's assets?

HOLDING AND DECISION: (Shea-Stonum, J.) Yes. In a Chapter 11 bankruptcy, a motion for an interim order authorizing the obtaining of financing, and the use of cash collateral, will be granted to a debtor-in-possession on terms highly favorable to the postpetition lender where that lender is also the prepetition secured creditor with a secured interest in virtually all the debtor's assets. The Debtors are authorized to pay the prepetition lenders for prepetition obligations, and to pay or reimburse the lenders for all present and future costs and expenses, including, without limitation, all reasonable professional fees and reasonable legal expenses, paid or incurred by the lenders in connection with the financing. These costs and expenses will become part of the principal secured by the collateral. The DIP Lender is granted a super priority administrative claim in accordance with § 364(c)(1) over any-and-all administrative expenses or priority claims of any kind whether arising in these Chapter 11 cases or in any superseding Chapter 7 cases concerning the Debtors. As security for the prompt payment and performance of any and all obligations incurred by the Debtors to the lenders, the Debtors are authorized, and deemed to have granted to the lenders, effective as of the petition date, valid, binding, enforceable, and perfected first priority liens, mortgages and security interests, superior to the liens, mortgages,

Continued on next page.

security interests or other interests or rights of all other creditors of the Debtors' estates on property owned or leased by the Debtors, in and upon all of the collateral, both prepetition and postpetition. Debtors may seek at the final hearing to include as part of the postpetition collateral, to secure the postpetition obligations only, bankruptcy-related causes of action and recoveries. The liens, mortgages and security interests and super priority claims granted to the lenders are subject and subordinate to a carve-out consisting of: (a) up to $485,000 in the aggregate for the allowed fees and expenses of: Debtors' counsel (up to $350,000) and counsel or any profession hired by any committee (up to $35,000). However, no part of this carve-out may be used to litigate, object, contest, or challenge in any manner or raise any defenses to the lenders' debt or collateral position. Parties in interest, including a committee of creditors, has 55 days to challenge the Debtors' stipulation that all the lenders' security interests and other rights are invulnerable to legal attack. The time of payment of any-and-all postpetition obligations of the Debtors arising out of the credit facility may not be altered, extended, or impaired by any plan or plans of reorganization that may be accepted or confirmed by the court, or by any other court orders. This order will become permanent unless an objection is made in less than two weeks. Motion granted.

ANALYSIS

The key to understanding the result of this extraordinary debtor-in-possession (DIP) decision (which seems to invert the whole conception of reorganization and DIP control) is that the secured creditor through its control of the debtor's assets seems to have complete control of Chapter 11. It has been contended that this result happens in most—maybe virtually all—Chapter 11 cases. However, it seems that the leverage necessary to thwart the debtor with such a DIP order arises from a prepetition security interest covering most, if not all the debtor's assets. That is, the debtor is helpless to resist the severe DIP order because the secured party already controls most of the debtor's assets through its prepetition security interest. The debtor is thus at the mercy of the secured creditor, as are most of its other creditors.

Quicknotes

DEBTOR-IN-POSSESSION A Chapter 11 bankruptcy debtor who retains control of assets or property pursuant to a plan of reorganization.

CHAPTER 20

Avoiding Liens

Quick Reference Rules of Law

In re Diabetes America, Inc.

[Parties not identified.]

2012 WL 6694074 (Bankr. S.D. Tex. 2012)

NATURE OF CASE: Motion for summary judgment in Chapter 11 adversary proceeding.

FACT SUMMARY: The Chapter 11 plan agent (Plan Agent) for Diabetes America, Inc. (Debtor) contended that because Basile had not perfected his security interest in Debtor's assets—because he had not filed the financing statement in Debtor's state of incorporation—the security interest was avoidable under Bankruptcy Code § 544(a)(1).

RULE OF LAW

Where a secured creditor fails to perfect his security interest, and state law gives the debtor-in-possession in a Chapter 11 bankruptcy, or its plan agent, priority over the unperfected interest, the debtor-in-possession or the plan agent may avoid the unperfected interest under Bankruptcy Code § 544(a)(1).

FACTS: Diabetes America, Inc. (Debtor), which was incorporated in Delaware, filed for Chapter 11 bankruptcy protection. Soon after Debtor filed its petition, Basile filed a fully secured proof of claim in the amount of $161,402.39, which related to a security interest Basile received in essentially all of Debtor's assets in exchange for his lending Debtor $150,000. Basile filed a UCC-1 financing statement only in Texas. Texas law provides that while a debtor is located in a jurisdiction, the local law of that jurisdiction governs perfection, the effect of perfection or nonperfection, and the priority of a security interest in collateral. The Plan Agent, contending that Basile had failed to perfect his security interest—since Basile failed to file a financing statement in Delaware as required by Delaware law—and that the Plan Agent therefore had priority over Basile's unperfected security interest, sought to avoid Basile's interest using the strong-arm powers under § 544(a)(1) of the Bankruptcy Code. The Plan Agent moved for summary judgment.

ISSUE: Where a secured creditor fails to perfect his security interest, and state law gives the debtor-in-possession in a Chapter 11 bankruptcy, or its plan agent, priority over the unperfected interest, may the debtor-in-possession or the plan agent avoid the unperfected interest under Bankruptcy Code § 544(a)(1)?

HOLDING AND DECISION: (Isgur, J.) Yes. Where a secured creditor fails to perfect his security interest, and state law gives the debtor-in-possession in a Chapter 11 bankruptcy, or its plan agent, priority over the unperfected interest, the debtor-in-possession or the plan agent may avoid the unperfected interest under Bankruptcy Code § 544(a)(1). Under the Texas UCC, "[a] registered organization that is organized under the law of a state is located in that state." Because Debtor was organized in Delaware, for purposes of Texas law, it was located in Delaware, and, hence, Delaware law governed perfection. The Delaware UCC requires that a filing statement be filed in the office of the Delaware Secretary of State to properly perfect a security interest. Basile argues that there is an exception in Texas Business & Commerce Code § 9.301(3)(C), which provides, inter alia, that while certain tangible assets are located in a jurisdiction, the local law of that jurisdiction governs the effect of perfection or nonperfection and the priority of a nonpossessory security interest in the collateral. This provision does not provide the exception to the general rule that Basile seeks, since it governs the effect of perfection, nonperfection, or priority—it does not supplant the law governing perfection, nonperfection, or priority. Accordingly, Basile's security interest in the collateral was not perfected. The effect of this nonperfection is that Basile is an unsecured creditor. In Chapter 11, instead of the trustee, the debtor-in-possession (and here, the Plan Agent) has strong-arm powers. Under § 544(a)(1), the trustee (now the Plan Agent) is granted the powers and rights of a judgment lien creditor, as determined under state law. Here, both Texas and Delaware law give the Plan Agent priority over Basile's unperfected security interest. Because Basile is an unsecured creditor, and the Plan Agent has priority over that unsecured interest, the Plan Agent may use its strong-arm powers under § 544(a)(1) to avoid Basile's interest. Basile argues that the Plan Agent (as the successor to the Debtor's rights and agreements) is estopped from denying the secured nature of Basile's claim. This argument is rejected because § 544(a)(1) expressly forecloses these types of estoppel arguments. Even if estoppel were applicable, this would not help Basile, because the loan agreement between the parties cannot trump Texas law. Summary judgment is granted to the Plan Agent.

ANALYSIS

To give a trustee (or debtor-in-possession, or a plan agent) priority over an unsecured creditor, § 544(a)(1) uses a legal fiction, whereby the trustee hypothetically extends credit to the debtor at the time of the bankruptcy filing and, at that moment, obtains a judicial lien on all property in which the debtor has any interest that could be reached by a creditor. As this case demonstrates, the ultimate advantage of this status derives not from the Bankruptcy Code, but from the relevant state law defining creditor rights. Thus, the

Continued on next page.

strength of the trustee's strong-arm rights will correspond to the strength of a lien creditor's rights under state law.

Quicknotes

DEBTOR-IN-POSSESSION In a Chapter 11 proceeding, refers to a debtor who retains control of assets or property pursuant to a plan of reorganization.

SECURED CREDITOR A creditor, the repayment of whose loan is secured by collateral sufficient to repay the debt owed.

SECURITY INTEREST An interest in property that may be sold upon a default in payment of the debt.

PERFECT Execute; enforce; make marketable.

UNPERFECTED Not executed, completed, or finished; unmarketable.

In re Bowling

Mortgagor-debtor (P) v. Mortgagee-creditor (D)

314 B.R. 127 (Bankr. S.D. Ohio 2004)

NATURE OF CASE: Cross-motions for summary judgment in trustee's bankruptcy action to avoid a mortgage.

FACT SUMMARY: **The bankruptcy trustee for the Bowlings' (P) estate contended that a defectively executed mortgage (because a notary had not witnessed it) could be avoided under the trustee's strong-arm powers under § 544(a)(3) of the Bankruptcy Code.**

RULE OF LAW

A defectively executed mortgage can be avoided under a Chapter 7 trustee's strong-arm powers under § 544(a)(3) of the Bankruptcy Code.

FACTS: Mr. Bowling (P) was the sole owner of real estate. Although the deed conveying the property to Bowling (P) reflected that he was married, it did not include Mrs. Bowling (P) as a grantee. Subsequently, Mr. Bowling (P) executed a mortgage in favor of a mortgage company (predecessor to the Mortgage Registration System (MERS)) (D), conveying the property as security. On its face, the mortgage reflected that Mr. Bowling's (P) signature was notarized by Ms. Eisenhut, a notary. By her certificate, Eisenhut certified that Mr. Bowling (P) had executed the mortgage in her presence. The Bowlings (P) filed a Chapter 7 petition, and the trustee sought to avoid the mortgage on the ground that in fact Eisenhut was not present when Mr. Bowling (P) executed the mortgage. Mrs. Bowling (P) did not sign the promissory note or the mortgage. Mr. Bowling (P) testified that Eisenhut had not been present at the closing, and that in addition to himself and his wife, only another man had been present.

ISSUE: Can a defectively executed mortgage be avoided under a Chapter 7 trustee's strong-arm powers under § 544(a)(3) of the Bankruptcy Code?

HOLDING AND DECISION: (Aug, J.) Yes. A defectively executed mortgage can be avoided under a Chapter 7 trustee's strong-arm powers under § 544(a)(3) of the Bankruptcy Code. The trustee must show by clear and convincing evidence that the mortgage was not signed and notarized as purported. MERS (D) contests Mr. Bowling's (P) assertion that Eisenhut was not present when Mr. Bowling (P) signed the mortgage. However, MERS (D) has presented no evidence that Eisenhut was present. On the other hand, Mr. Bowling (P) testified that the refinancing was done at his home and that there was only one other person besides Mr. and Mrs. Bowling (P) present at the closing, that being a male. A refinancing is an extraordinary event for a consumer, so it would stick out in Mr. Bowling's (P) mind. In particular, it seems that Mr. Bowling (P) would remember whether the person coming to close the loan was male or female. Given that there is no per se state rule that Mr. Bowling's (P) testimony alone is insufficient to overcome the notary's certification, in the absence of MERS's (D) presentation of any evidence to the contrary, the trustee has met his burden and presented clear and convincing evidence that a notary was not present at the time Mr. Bowling (P) executed the mortgage. Summary judgment is granted.

ANALYSIS

The court also held that given that the trustee had avoided the mortgage pursuant to the trustee's strong-arm powers, MERS (D) would not be entitled to a replacement lien in the real estate pursuant to Code § 550. In reaching this conclusion, the court relied on the Sixth Circuit's determination that where the trustee has avoided a mortgage pursuant to its strong-arm powers, the mortgagee's interest is preserved and becomes a part of the bankruptcy estate without the need for the trustee to resort to the recovery process pursuant to § 550(a). Therefore, the court reasoned, the statutory provisions of § 550(e) providing for a replacement lien for the creditor are not triggered for the benefit of the mortgagee.

Quicknotes

CHAPTER 7 BANKRUPTCY A legal proceeding whereby a debtor, who is unable to pay his or her debts as they become due, is relieved of the obligation to pay creditors by liquidation and distribution of remaining assets.

MORTGAGEE Party to whom an interest in property is given in order to secure a loan.

MORTGAGOR Party who grants an interest in property in order to secure a loan.

STRONG-ARM CLAUSE A clause in the Bankruptcy Code that allows a bankruptcy trustee to avoid unperfected security interests when the bankruptcy case is filed.

In re TWA Inc. Post Confirmation Estate

Debtor (P) v. Federal agency (D)

312 B.R. 759 (Bankr. D. Del. 2004)

NATURE OF CASE: Motion for summary judgment in proceeding to reclassify a proof of claim, allegedly secured by a statutory lien, as an unsecured claim.

FACT SUMMARY: The postconfirmation bankruptcy estate of TWA Inc. (TWA) (P) contended that the U.S. Department of Agriculture's (USDA's) (D) proof of claim, allegedly secured by a statutory lien, should be reclassified as an unsecured claim because the USDA (D) had failed to record the lien with the Federal Aviation Administration (FAA).

RULE OF LAW

Where a statute requires that a statutory lien be recorded to render it valid against a bona fide purchaser, the lien is avoidable in a Chapter 11 bankruptcy proceeding if it has not been recorded pursuant to the statute.

FACTS: The U.S. Department of Agriculture (USDA) (D) conducted inspections on TWA Inc.'s (TWA) (P) airplanes for about nine months before TWA (P) and its subsidiaries filed for Chapter 11 bankruptcy protection. The USDA (D) filed a proof of claim for the amount owed for aircraft inspection services, reimbursable overtime inspections, and violations of animal welfare regulations. The proof of claim asserted that it was secured by a statutory lien pursuant to 21 U.S.C. § 136a, which authorizes the Secretary of Agriculture to collect fees sufficient to cover the inspection services of the type provided by the USDA (D). TWA's (P) postconfirmation estate argued that the proof of claim should be reclassified as unsecured, because, it claimed, USDA (D) had to record its statutory liens pursuant to the Federal Aviation Administration Act (Act) to render them unavoidable, and USDA (D) had not so recorded the liens. Act § 44107 (49 U.S.C. § 44107) provides for the establishment of a recording system to record conveyances (including liens) that affect an interest in U.S. civil aircraft. Act § 44108 (49 U.S.C. § 44108) gives a statutory lien only limited effect until it is recorded, so that until recorded it is valid only against the person making it, that person's successors, or a person having actual notice of it. TWA (P) moved for summary judgment.

ISSUE: Where a statute requires that a statutory lien be recorded to render it valid against a bona fide purchaser, is the lien avoidable in a Chapter 11 bankruptcy proceeding if it has not been recorded pursuant to the statute?

HOLDING AND DECISION: (Walsh, J.) Yes. Where a statute requires that a statutory lien be recorded to render it valid against a bona fide purchaser, the lien is avoidable in a Chapter 11 bankruptcy proceeding if it has not been recorded pursuant to the statute. Code § 545(2) permits a trustee or debtor-in-possession to avoid a statutory lien if it "is not perfected or enforceable at the time of the commencement of the case against a bona fide purchaser. . . ." This means that the trustee's or debtor-in-possession's power is that of a bona fide purchaser, which is generally understood to mean one who has purchased property for value without notice of any defects in the title of the seller. Because the USDA (D) had not recorded its lien, there was no public notice of it, and, hence, a bona fide purchaser would not have had notice of it. Therefore, the lien is avoidable. USDA (D) is incorrect that merely because its lien is set forth in the statute (21 U.S.C. § 136a), and the statute's plain words do not require USDA (D) to take any additional steps to prefect its lien or enforce its rights, the statutory lien was automatically perfected. It is also incorrect that neither 21 U.S.C. § 136a nor the Act requires that the USDA's (D) statutory liens be recorded in the FAA registry system to render them unavoidable. That is because Congress is presumed to have been aware of the Code at the time it enacted § 136a, and, since Congress did not provide a recording requirement in § 136a, it may be presumed that the lien was not meant to be enforceable against a bona fide purchaser. The intent of the Act, on the other hand, was to create a central clearinghouse for recording aircraft titles so that the public would have ready access to the claims against, or liens, or other legal interests in an aircraft. Therefore, liens, such as the one at issue, must be recorded to be valid against third parties. Because TWA's (P) estate does not fall within any of the three enumerated exceptions in Act § 44108, it is deemed a bona fide purchaser with power to avoid the lien. Finally, contrary to USDA's (D) assertion, giving effect to the Act's recordation requirement will not nullify the lien. The Act is not in direct conflict with § 136a, since § 136a does not address recordation or perfection. When a debtor fails to pay the inspection fees, a § 136a statutory lien is still created, albeit with limited application, until it is recorded under the Act. Summary judgment granted to TWA's (P) estate.

ANALYSIS

As this case demonstrates, the trustee or debtor-in-possession in a Chapter 11 case may take on the powers of a bona fide purchaser in the case of a statutory lien. This

Continued on next page.

power is applicable to liens that have a perfection requirement, but not where perfection arises automatically.

Quicknotes

DEBTOR-IN-POSSESSION A Chapter 11 bankruptcy debtor who retains control of assets or property pursuant to a plan of reorganization.

LIEN A claim against the property of another in order to secure the payment of a debt.

PERFECT Execute; enforce; to make marketable.

SUMMARY JUDGMENT Judgment rendered by a court in response to a motion made by one of the parties, claiming that the lack of a question of material fact in respect to an issue warrants disposition of the issue without consideration by the jury.

CHAPTER 21

Preferences I

Quick Reference Rules of Law

In re Pysz

Debtor (P) v. Lienholder (D)

2008 WL 2001753 (Bankr. D.N.H. 2008)

NATURE OF CASE: Motion for summary judgment in action to avoid a judicial lien as a preference.

FACT SUMMARY: The Debtor (P) sought to avoid as a preference the Defendant's (D) judicial lien that arose from a postjudgment attachment for unpaid professional services, claiming that the Debtor (P) had been insolvent at the time of the attachment and that the Defendant (D) would receive more with the judicial lien than he would without the lien, thus satisfying all the requirements for avoiding the lien as a preference.

RULE OF LAW

A judicial lien will be avoided as a preference under 11 U.S.C. § 547(b) where the debtor was insolvent at the time of the postjudgment attachment that was the basis for the lien, where the lienholder would receive more with the lien than he would without the lien, and where all other elements of § 547(b) are met.

FACTS: The Defendant (D) obtained a judgment for unpaid professional services against the Debtor (P), and then issued a writ of attachment on the Debtor's (P) property (Newport Property) on January 18, 2007, and recorded it the following day. The Debtor (P) filed for bankruptcy protection under Chapter 13 on April 5, 2007. The Debtor (P) listed the Newport Property's fair market value as $300,000, but the Defendant (D) offered a separate appraisal report that valued it at $443,000. Even using the Defendant's (D) appraised value for the Newton Property, along with some unscheduled property, the Debtor's (P) liabilities exceeded his assets. The Debtor (P) moved for summary judgment seeking to avoid the Defendant's (D) judicial lien as a preference under 11 U.S.C. § 547(b).

ISSUE: Will a judicial lien be avoided as a preference under 11 U.S.C. § 547(b) where the debtor was insolvent at the time of the postjudgment attachment that was the basis for the lien, where the lienholder would receive more with the lien than he would without the lien, and where all other elements of § 547(b) are met?

HOLDING AND DECISION: (Vaughn, J.) Yes. A judicial lien will be avoided as a preference under 11 U.S.C. § 547(b) where the debtor was insolvent at the time of the postjudgment attachment that was the basis for the lien, where the lienholder would receive more with the lien than he would without the lien, and where all other elements of § 547(b) are met. There is no issue that the obtainment of the attachment was a transfer of the Debtor's (P) interest in property, as required by 11 U.S.C. § 547(b). This section also sets forth five elements that must be met. It is clear from the record, without further discussion, that three of those elements are satisfied here. These are: the subject lien was for the benefit of a creditor; the subject lien was for or on account of an antecedent debt; and the attachment occurred during the 90-day preference period. The two other elements—whether the Debtor (P) was insolvent at the time of the attachment (§ 547(b)(3)) and whether the Defendant (D) would receive more with the lien than he would without the lien (§ 547(b)(5))—merit further discussion. As to the insolvency issue, the Defendant (D), as creditor, bears the burden of proving that the Debtor (P) was not insolvent, i.e., there is a presumption that the Debtor (P) was insolvent during the 90 days immediately preceding the date of the filing of the petition. Even reading the record most favorably to the Defendant (D) (using the Defendant's (D) higher appraised value for the Newton Property and adding some nonexempt property that had not been scheduled), it is clear the Debtor's (P) liabilities exceeded his assets when he filed his petition, so that there is no genuine issue regarding the Debtor's (P) insolvency during the preference period. Thus, the Defendant (D) failed to rebut the presumption of insolvency. As to the "receive more" element, there are three sub-elements that must be met, showing that the judicial lien would enable the creditor to receive more than such creditor would receive if: (1) the case was a liquidation case under Chapter 7; (2) the transfer had not been made; and (3) the creditor received payment of such debt to the extent provided by Chapter 13. Where, as here, the creditor is a general unsecured creditor absent the attachment, if the distribution in bankruptcy is less than 100 percent, any payment "on account" to the creditor during the preference period will enable that creditor to receive more than he would have received in liquidation had the payment not been made. Also, as a matter of law, whenever a general unsecured creditor obtains within the preference period a judicial lien against a debtor who cannot fully repay his unsecured creditors, he has received a preference. Finally, because the Debtor's (P) liabilities exceed his assets, under a hypothetical Chapter 7 liquidation analysis, the Debtor (P) would not be able to repay his general unsecured creditors 100 percent. Thus, since the Defendant (D) converted an otherwise unsecured claim to a secured one, the lien would enable the Defendant (D) to receive more than he would without the lien in a Chapter 7 case. For these reasons, the "receive more" element is satisfied, and, consequently, all

Continued on next page.

the elements of § 547(b) are met. Summary judgment is granted to the Debtor (P).

ANALYSIS

Section 547 serves two primary purposes. First, it fosters equality of distribution among creditors, which is one of the primary goals of the Bankruptcy Code. Second, it discourages "secret liens" upon the debtor's collateral that are not perfected until just before the debtor files for bankruptcy.

Quicknotes

ATTACHMENT The seizing of the property of one party in anticipation of, or in order to satisfy, a favorable judgment obtained by another party.

LIEN A claim against the property of another in order to secure the payment of a debt.

SUMMARY JUDGMENT Judgment rendered by a court in response to a motion made by one of the parties, claiming that the lack of a question of material fact in respect to an issue warrants disposition of the issue without consideration by the jury.

Chase Manhattan Mortgage Corp. v. Shapiro

Mortgagee (P) v. Trustee (D)

530 F.3d 458 (6th Cir. 2008)

NATURE OF CASE: Appeal in action to determine whether a refinanced mortgage may be avoided as a preferential transfer. [The procedural posture of the case is not presented in the casebook extract.]

FACT SUMMARY: The Trustee (D) of Lee's bankruptcy estate contended that a residential mortgage loan that Lee obtained in a refinance transaction from Chase Manhattan Mortgage Corporation (Chase) (P), which was both the holder of the original mortgage and the refinanced mortgage, should be avoided as a preferential transfer under Bankruptcy Code § 547 because Chase (P) had failed to perfect its interest in the new loan within the grace period under § 547(e) that would take the transfer in Lee's property out of being made on account of an antecedent debt.

RULE OF LAW

A refinanced mortgage lien does not fall within the grace period of Bankruptcy Code § 547(e) where it is not perfected within the grace period, even where the same mortgagee holds both the new mortgage and prior mortgage, and the discharge of the prior mortgage is not recorded until after the new mortgage is recorded.

FACTS: Lee refinanced his residential mortgage with Chase Manhattan Mortgage Corporation (Chase) (P), which was both the holder of the original mortgage and the refinanced mortgage. About six months later, Lee filed a voluntary Chapter 7 bankruptcy petition. Seventy-seven days before Lee filed his bankruptcy case, and 72 days after Chase (P) had distributed the funds that were used to discharge the original mortgage, the new mortgage was recorded in favor of Chase (P) to secure Lee's obligation to repay the new loan. The discharge of the old mortgage was then recorded. The Trustee (D) sought to avoid Chase's (P) new mortgage lien as a preferential transfer under Bankruptcy Code § 547. The court of appeals granted review in the case. [The procedural posture of the case is not presented in the casebook extract.]

ISSUE: Does a refinanced mortgage lien fall within the grace period of Bankruptcy Code § 547(e) where it is not perfected within the grace period, even where the same mortgagee holds both the new mortgage and prior mortgage, and the discharge of the prior mortgage is not recorded until after the new mortgage is recorded?

HOLDING AND DECISION: (Cole, J.) No. A refinanced mortgage lien does not fall within the grace period of Bankruptcy Code § 547(e) where it is not perfected within the grace period, even where the same mortgagee holds both the new mortgage and prior mortgage, and the discharge of the prior mortgage is not recorded until after the new mortgage is recorded. Under § 547(b)(2), a trustee must demonstrate that the transfer sought to be avoided as preferential was made "for or on account of an antecedent debt owed by the debtor before such transfer was made." A debt is antecedent if it is incurred before the transfer in question. Thus, in the context of a loan, the borrower incurs the debt at the time the lender disburses the loan proceeds. The advance of loan proceeds prior to recording the mortgage is thus subject to preferential transfer liability. Section 547(e) provides a 10-day grace period for lenders for perfecting a security interest. Provided the mortgage is recorded within the 10-day period, the mortgage debt will not be deemed antecedent. To fall within the grace period, the lender must perfect its security interest within the grace period. If perfection occurs more than ten days after the transfer takes effect, the transfer occurs at the time of the perfection, and the debt is considered antecedent. To determine when perfection has occurred, § 547(e)(1)(A) states that perfection has occurred "when a bona fide purchaser of [the Property] from the debtor against whom applicable law permits such transfer to be perfected cannot acquire an interest that is superior to the interest of the transferee." Here, the "applicable law" is state law, under which perfection occurs upon recording. It is clear Chase (P) recorded the new mortgage lien 72 days after it disbursed the loan proceeds to Lee; therefore, Chase (P) did not perfect its interest within the 10-day grace period. Accordingly, the transfer of Lee's property must be deemed to have been made on account of an antecedent debt. Moreover, it does not matter, as Chase (P) argues, that the discharge was recorded after the new mortgage was recorded, so that third parties were on notice of Chase's (P) secured interest in the property. The fact that third parties may have been on notice of Chase's (P) original mortgage is irrelevant to the requirements of § 547(e)(1)(A), which is not couched in terms of third-party notice. Accordingly, the transfer occurred when Chase (P) perfected its security interest—72 days after disbursing the loan proceeds—and cannot be deemed not to have been made on account of an antecedent debt. [The disposition of the case is not presented in the casebook extract.]

ANALYSIS

The Bankruptcy Abuse Prevention and Consumer Protection Act of 2005 (BAPCPA) increased the grace period

Continued on next page.

from 10 days to 30 days. Because the new mortgage was recorded by Chase (D) well outside even the new 30-day grace period, the result would be the same under either version of the law.

Quicknotes

ANTECEDENT DEBT For the purposes of bankruptcy law, refers to a debt incurred more than four months prior to the filing of a petition in bankruptcy, and which does not constitute a preferential transfer.

PERFECT Execute; enforce; make marketable.

PREFERENTIAL TRANSFER A transfer made by the insolvent debtor to a creditor prior to filing the bankruptcy petition, giving a priority to one creditor over others with respect to the debtor's assets.

In re Stewart

Trustee (P) v. Unsecured creditor (D)

274 B.R. 503 (Bankr. W.D. Ark. 2002)

NATURE OF CASE: Action under Chapter 13 alleging an avoidable preferential transfer.

FACT SUMMARY: Barry County Livestock Auction, Inc. (Barry County) (D) argued that the contemporaneous exchange for new value exception in Bankruptcy Code § 547(c)(1) was applicable. The exception would relieve Barry County (D) from preferential transfer liability for payments made by Stewart (Debtor) by cashier's checks for livestock purchased two weeks earlier where the cashier's checks were used after Stewart's personal checks made at the time of purchase were returned for insufficient funds.

RULE OF LAW

The contemporaneous exchange for new value exception in Bankruptcy Code § 547(c)(1) does not apply to a preferential transfer made by cashier's check for an antecedent debt where the cashier's check was used after a personal check made in payment of the debt was dishonored for lack of sufficient funds.

FACTS: Stewart (Debtor) purchased cattle from Barry County Livestock Auction, Inc. (Barry County) (D) and paid by personal checks, both of which were later returned for insufficient funds. Two weeks later, Stewart paid with cashier's checks the amount he owed Barry County (D). Within 90 days of the purchase, Stewart filed a Chapter 13 bankruptcy petition, and the Trustee (P) brought an action claiming that the payments to Barry County (D) were avoidable preferential transfers. The payments made with the cashier's checks enabled Barry County (D) to receive more than it would have received if the case had been a Chapter 7 case. It was also stipulated that at the time he made the payments, Stewart was insolvent. The court found that the Trustee (P) met her burden of proof under Bankruptcy Code § 547 as to the preferential transfer of the two cashier's checks, and Barry County (D) argued that the contemporaneous exchange for new value exception in § 547(c)(1) applied to relieve it of preferential transfer liability.

ISSUE: Does the contemporaneous exchange for new value exception in Bankruptcy Code § 547(c)(1) apply to a preferential transfer made by cashier's check for an antecedent debt where the cashier's check was used after a personal check made in payment of the debt was dishonored for lack of sufficient funds?

HOLDING AND DECISION: (Fussell, J.) No. The contemporaneous exchange for new value exception in Bankruptcy Code § 547(c)(1) does not apply to a preferential transfer made by cashier's check for an antecedent debt where the cashier's check was used after a personal check made in payment of the debt was dishonored for lack of sufficient funds. First, the debt here was an antecedent debt because it was incurred prior to the allegedly preferential transfer—all buyers at the auction were required to pay for their purchases on the date of sale. Therefore, the debts were incurred two weeks before the delivery of the cashier's checks. Here, too, Barry County (D) is a creditor. Because the Trustee (P) met her burden of proving preferential transfers, Barry County (D) may avoid preference liability only if it can prove that if falls within one of the exceptions set forth in § 547(c). To qualify for the contemporaneous exchange for new value exception under § 547(c)(1), a creditor must prove that an otherwise preferential transfer was (A) intended by the debtor and the creditor to be a contemporaneous exchange for new value given to the debtor; and (B) in fact a substantially contemporaneous exchange. "New value" is defined as "money or money's worth in goods, services, or new credit, or release by a transferee of property previously transferred to such transferee in a transaction that is neither void nor voidable by the debtor or the trustee under any applicable law, including proceeds of such property, but does not include an obligation substituted for an existing obligation." Here, if the transfer of the cattle did not occur until the cashier's checks were presented to Barry County (D), the transactions may have been contemporaneous exchanges for new value. If, on the other hand, the transfer of the cattle occurred on the day of the sale, two weeks before Stewart presented the cashier's checks to Barry County (D), the issue becomes whether the subsequent delivery of the cashier's checks to replace the insufficient funds checks constituted contemporaneous exchanges for new value. Under the Uniform Commercial Code, title to the cattle passed to Stewart on the day of the sales. Thus, if Stewart's personal checks cleared, a contemporaneous exchange for value would have occurred. But the bank's dishonor of the personal checks changed the nature of the transactions, so that they became credit transactions and created an antecedent debt. Any subsequent payment, no matter how quickly made, would satisfy that antecedent debt. Thus, the cashier's checks satisfied the antecedent debt, and were not contemporaneous exchanges for new value. Accordingly, Barry County (D) does not qualify for the contemporaneous exchange for new value exception.

Continued on next page.

ANALYSIS

The legislative history of Bankruptcy Code § 547(c)(1) specifically references transactions in which checks are involved, and indicates that, while ordinarily a check is a credit transaction, for purposes of the contemporaneous exchange for new value exception, a transfer involving a check is considered to be "intended to be contemporaneous," and if the check is presented for payment in the normal course of affairs, which the Uniform Commercial Code specifies as 30 days, that will amount to a transfer that is "in fact substantially contemporaneous."

Quicknotes

ANTECEDENT DEBT For the purposes of bankruptcy law, refers to a debt incurred more than four months prior to the filing of a petition in bankruptcy, and which does not constitute a preferential transfer.

PREFERENTIAL TRANSFER A transfer made by the insolvent debtor to a creditor prior to filing the bankruptcy petition, giving a priority to one creditor over others with respect to the debtor's assets.

In re Stewart *(cont'd)*

Trustee (P) v. Unsecured creditor (D)

274 B.R. 503 (Bankr. W.D. Ark. 2002)

NATURE OF CASE: Action under Chapter 13 alleging an avoidable preferential transfer.

FACT SUMMARY: Barry County Livestock Auction, Inc. (Barry County) (D) argued that the ordinary course of business exception in Bankruptcy Code § 547(c)(2) applied to relieve it from preferential transfer liability for payments made by Stewart (Debtor) by cashier's checks for livestock purchased two weeks earlier where the cashier's checks were used after Stewart's personal checks made at the time of purchase were returned for insufficient funds.

RULE OF LAW

The ordinary course of business exception in Bankruptcy Code § 547(c)(2) does not apply to a preferential transfer made by cashier's check for an antecedent debt where the cashier's check was used two weeks after a personal check made in payment of the debt was dishonored for lack of sufficient funds, and such payment is not typical in the industry.

FACTS: Stewart (Debtor) purchased cattle from Barry County Livestock Auction, Inc. (Barry County) (D) and paid by personal checks, both of which were later returned for insufficient funds. Two weeks later, Stewart paid with cashier's checks the amount he owed Barry County (D). Within 90 days of the purchase, Stewart filed a Chapter 13 bankruptcy petition, and the Trustee (P) brought an action claiming that the payments to Barry County (D) were avoidable preferential transfers. The payments made with the cashier's checks enabled Barry County (D) to receive more than it would have received if the case had been a Chapter 7 case. It was also stipulated that at the time he made the payments, Stewart was insolvent. The court found that the Trustee (P) met her burden of proof under Bankruptcy Code § 547 as to the preferential transfer of the two cashier's checks, and Barry County (D) argued that the contemporaneous exchange for new value exception in § 547(c)(1) applied to relieve it of preferential transfer liability.

ISSUE: Does the ordinary course of business exception in Bankruptcy Code § 547(c)(2) apply to a preferential transfer made by cashier's check for an antecedent debt where the cashier's check was used two weeks after a personal check made in payment of the debt was dishonored for lack of sufficient funds, and such payment is not typical in the industry?

HOLDING AND DECISION: (Fussell, J.) No. The ordinary course of business exception in Bankruptcy Code § 547(c)(2) does not apply to a preferential transfer made by cashier's check for an antecedent debt where the cashier's check was used two weeks after a personal check made in payment of the debt was dishonored for lack of sufficient funds, and such payment is not typical in the industry. To qualify for the ordinary course of business exception, a creditor must prove that the transfer was "(A) in payment of a debt incurred by the debtor in the ordinary course of business or financial affairs of the debtor and the transferee; (B) made in the ordinary course of business or financial affairs of the debtor and the transferee; and (C) made according to ordinary business terms." Stewart and Barry County (D) had ongoing business relationships for several years. In the course of their business relationship, Stewart purchased cattle from Barry County (D) and was required to pay for the cattle purchased the same day of the purchases. Because the payments were made to satisfy debts that Stewart incurred in the ordinary course of his business dealings with Barry County (D), the elements of subsection (c)(2)(A) are satisfied. The second factor deals with the way the parties actually conducted their business dealings. During the course of their several-year relationship, Stewart paid Barry County (D) by personal check at the time of sale. It was only right before and during the preference period that those personal checks were dishonored. Thus, the payments by personal checks made during the preference period that were dishonored by the bank when presented for payment, but later paid with cashier's checks, were not sufficiently consistent with the payments made during the prior 12 months. Therefore, Barry County (D) has failed to meet the elements of subsection (c)(2)(B). Finally, the general practice in the industry is that cattle purchases are always paid on the day of purchase. Again, because payment by cashier's check two weeks after the date of sale is not typical in the industry, Barry County (D) fails to meet the elements of subsection (c)(2)(C); and it does not qualify for the ordinary course of business exception. Thus, the payments made by cashier checks were preferential transfers that may be avoided under § 547. Judgment for Trustee (P).

ANALYSIS

After this case was decided, the Bankruptcy Code was amended in 2005 by the Bankruptcy Abuse Prevention and Consumer Protection Act (BAPCPA) as to what a creditor must show to have an otherwise avoidable transfer come within the § 547(c)(2) exception. While the first element remains the same (i.e., that the debt was incurred in

Continued on next page.

the debtor's ordinary course of business), the creditor only needs to prove either the second or the third element, not both. Since Barry County (D) failed to prove both these elements, the outcome in this case would have been the same even post-BAPCPA.

Quicknotes

ORDINARY COURSE OF BUSINESS The conducting of business in accordance with standard customs and practices.

PREFERENTIAL TRANSFER A transfer made by the insolvent debtor to a creditor prior to filing the bankruptcy petition, giving a priority to one creditor over others with respect to the debtor's assets.

In re QMECT, Inc.

Debtor (P) v. Junior secured creditor (D)

373 B.R. 100 (Bankr. N.D. Cal 2007)

NATURE OF CASE: Motions for reconsideration and summary judgment in adversary proceeding to avoid security interests as preferential transfers.

FACT SUMMARY: The Trustee (P) for the Debtor's (P) Chapter 11 bankruptcy estate contended that the security interests of its undersecured junior secured creditor, Burlingame (D), should be avoided as preferential transfers because its debt had not increased during the preference period. Burlingame (D) asserted that its debt, which it claimed should include the accrual of interest and late fees, had increased even more than the value of its collateral had increased during the preference period, so that it had a complete "improvement in position" defense under 11 U.S.C. § 547(c)(5) to its interest being avoided as preferences.

RULE OF LAW

For purposes of determining a secured creditor's "improvement in position" pursuant to 11 U.S.C. § 547(c)(5), interest, late charges, and other fees may be considered in arriving at a value of "debt."

FACTS: Burlingame (D), a junior creditor of the debtor, had a security interest in virtually all the Debtor's (P) assets, including accounts receivable and inventory. Burlingame (D) was undersecured throughout the Chapter 11 preference period, meaning the value of its collateral, taking account of the amount of the senior secured debt, was less than the amount of Burlingame's (D) debt. During this period, the Debtor's (P) accounts receivable and inventory increased by $156,939, and Burlingame's (D) security interest likewise automatically increased by this amount. The Trustee (P) sought to avoid Burlingame's (D) security interests as preferential transfers. Burlingame (D) asserted the "improvement in position" defense under 11 U.S.C. § 547(c)(5), which provides that transfers during the preference period are only avoidable to the extent that its undersecured position on the beginning of the preference period is greater than its undersecured position on the petition date. Burlingame (D) argued that its "position" had not "improved" because its debt had increased during the preference period, due to the accrual of interest and late fees, even more than the value of its collateral had increased—to $165,184. Burlingame (D) moved for summary judgment (as well as reconsideration). The bankruptcy court granted review.

ISSUE: For purposes of determining a secured creditor's "improvement in position" pursuant to 11 U.S.C. § 547(c)(5), may interest, late charges, and other fees be considered in arriving at a value of "debt?"

HOLDING AND DECISION: (Tchaikovsky, J.) Yes. For purposes of determining a secured creditor's "improvement in position" pursuant to 11 U.S.C. § 547(c)(5), interest, late charges, and other fees may be considered in arriving at a value of "debt." The Trustee (P) argued, on policy grounds, that under § 547(c)(5) the only changes in the "debt" during the preference period that should be considered are increases due to additional "advances" or decreases pursuant to additional "payments." However, there is no support for this position in the Code. Instead, the Trustee (P) notes that this position is supported by the fact that if the transfers attacked as preferences had been payments rather than transfers of security interests and Burlingame (D) were asserting a "new value" defense pursuant to 11 U.S.C. § 547(c)(3), increases due to interest, late charges, and attorneys' fees would not qualify as "new value." He also observes that 11 U.S.C. § 506(b) excludes postpetition interest and attorneys' fees from an undersecured creditor's secured claim. Section 547(c)(3) refers only to "debt," not to "advances" or "new value." Also, unless otherwise indicated, the definition of terms used in the Code are governed by state law, under which additional interest, late fees, and attorneys' fees incurred during the preference period are clearly considered part of "debt." Debt is defined as "liability on a claim," and "claim" is defined broadly enough to encompass interest, late fees, and attorney fees. Finally, 11 U.S.C. § 506(b) excludes only "postpetition" interest and attorneys' fees from an undersecured creditor's secured debt—not during the prepetition preference period—and therefore has no bearing on the creditor's "debt." For these reasons, Burlingame (D) has a complete defense. Motions for rehearing and summary judgment granted to Burlingame (D).

ANALYSIS

It should be noted that the Trustee (P) was able to establish all the elements of a preference claim, so that barring Burlingame's (D) "improvement in position" defense, its interests would have been avoidable. Burlingame (D) had contended that the Trustee (P) would be unable, as a matter of law, to establish the fifth element of a preference claim, i.e., that the transfers of security interests in the accounts receivable generated and inventory acquired during the preference period permitted it to receive more than if the transfers had not been made and the assets of the debtor had been liquidated in accordance with bankruptcy law. The court rejected this contention, reasoning that the "proceeds" of Burlingame's (D) security interest

Continued on next page.

did not include new accounts receivable although the "floating lien" contained in its security agreement did cause its security interest to attach to them. The court further reasoned that even if its construction of the term "proceeds" was incorrect, the result still had to be the same, since the transfer of a security interest in an account receivable created during the preference period is subject to avoidance as a preference even if the account receivable in question is the "proceeds" of inventory in existence prior to the beginning of the preference period. Thus, without the legal fiction a different asset is not really a different asset, but merely a change in description, the result is a potentially avoidable transfer.

Quicknotes

PREFERENCE A transfer made by the insolvent debtor to a creditor prior to filing the bankruptcy petition, giving a priority to one creditor over others in respect to the debtor's assets.

SECURED CREDITOR A creditor, the repayment of whose loan is secured by collateral sufficient to repay the debt owed.

SUMMARY JUDGMENT Judgment rendered by a court in response to a motion made by one of the parties, claiming that the lack of a question of material fact in respect to an issue warrants disposition of the issue without consideration by the jury.

CHAPTER 22

Preferences II

Quick Reference Rules of Law

In re Denochick

Guarantors (D) v. Trustee (P)

287 B.R. 632 (Bankr. W.D. Pa. 2003)

NATURE OF CASE: Appeal from judgment for trustee in adversary action to avoid a preference.

FACT SUMMARY: Guarantors (D) on Denochick's (debtor) debt consolidation loan argued that payments made by Denochick could not be recovered from them as a preference by the Bankruptcy trustee (P).

RULE OF LAW

A bankruptcy trustee can avoid as a preference, and recover from guarantors of a loan, debtor's payments on the loan.

FACTS: Guarantors (D) agreed to guarantee a debt consolidation loan from NBOC to Denochick (debtor). Denochick made $1,713.35 in loan payments to NBOC in the year prior to filing bankruptcy. The Guarantors (D) received none of this money, but the payments had the indirect effect of reducing their exposure on the guarantee they gave to NBOC. The Trustee (P) commenced an adversary action to avoid as a preference and recover from the Guarantors (D) the money Denochick paid to NBOC. The bankruptcy court concluded that the Guarantors (D) fell within the definition of "creditors" and that they had failed to establish the applicability of the "ordinary course of business" exception. Thus, the court concluded that the Trustee (P) could avoid the $1,713.35 and recover that amount from the Guarantors (D). The district court granted review.

ISSUE: Can a bankruptcy trustee avoid as a preference, and recover from guarantors of a loan, debtor's payments on the loan?

HOLDING AND DECISION: (Cindrich, J.) Yes. A bankruptcy trustee can avoid as a preference, and recover from guarantors of a loan, debtor's payments on the loan. The definition of a "creditor" under the bankruptcy code and state law is very broad and encompasses a guarantor of a debt. Thus, the Guarantors (D) were "creditors," even though their claim was derivative of NBOC's and was contingent upon Denochick's default. Denochick's payments to NBOC conferred a benefit upon the Guarantors (D), to the detriment of her other creditors. Affirmed.

ANALYSIS

This case illustrates the problem of the "indirect preference," which arises from Code § 547(b)(2). The Code thus helps the lender, but not the guarantor, even though the lender already received the payment that is being sought, via the preference, from the guarantor. Thus, there may be two or more persons potentially liable for a preferential transfer: the transferee and others who benefit indirectly from the transfer.

Quicknotes

PREFERENCE A transfer made by the insolvent debtor to a creditor prior to filing the bankruptcy petition, giving a priority to one creditor over others in respect to the debtor's assets.

PREFERENTIAL TRANSFER A transfer made by the insolvent debtor to a creditor prior to filing the bankruptcy petition, giving a priority to one creditor over others with respect to the debtor's assets.

Chase Manhattan Mortgage Corp. v. Shapiro *(cont'd)*

Mortgagee (P) v. Trustee (D)

530 F.3d 458 (6th Cir. 2008)

NATURE OF CASE: Appeal from reversal of order avoiding a refinanced mortgage as a preferential transfer.

FACT SUMMARY: [The Trustee (D) of Lee's bankruptcy estate contended that a residential mortgage loan that Lee obtained in a refinance transaction from Chase Manhattan Mortgage Corporation (Chase) (P), which was both the holder of the original mortgage and the refinanced mortgage, should be avoided as a preferential transfer under Bankruptcy Code § 547 because Chase (P) had failed to perfect its interest in the new loan within the grace period under § 547(e) that would take the transfer in Lee's property out of being made on account of an antecedent debt.] Chase (P) argued that it was not a "new creditor" for purposes of the earmarking doctrine, and that the doctrine applied to negate the "transfer of an interest of the debtor in property" requirement of § 547(b).

RULE OF LAW

The earmarking doctrine does not apply to a refinanced mortgage interest where the mortgagee holds both the old and new mortgages and where the mortgagee perfects late, so that the debtor's bankruptcy estate is diminished.

FACTS: [Lee refinanced his residential mortgage with Chase Manhattan Mortgage Corporation (Chase) (P), which was both the holder of the original mortgage and the refinanced mortgage. About six months later, Lee filed a voluntary Chapter 7 bankruptcy petition. Seventy-seven days before Lee filed his bankruptcy case, and 72 days after Chase (P) had distributed the funds that were used to discharge the original mortgage, the new mortgage was recorded in favor of Chase (P) to secure Lee's obligation to repay the new loan. The discharge of the old mortgage was then recorded. The Trustee (D) sought to avoid Chase's (P) new mortgage lien as a preferential transfer under Bankruptcy Code § 547.] As one of its defenses, Chase (P) argued that the earmarking doctrine should apply. The earmarking doctrine is a judicially created doctrine under which the "transfer of an interest of the debtor in property" requirement of § 547(b) is negated whenever a third party transfers property to a designated creditor of the debtor for the agreed-upon purpose of paying that creditor. The bankruptcy court ordered the avoidance of the new mortgage lien, the district court reversed, and the court of appeals granted review.

ISSUE: Does the earmarking doctrine apply to a refinanced mortgage interest where the mortgagee holds both the old and new mortgages and where the mortgagee perfects late, so that the debtor's bankruptcy estate is diminished?

HOLDING AND DECISION: (Cole, J.) No. The earmarking doctrine does not apply to a refinanced mortgage interest where the mortgagee holds both the old and new mortgages and where the mortgagee perfects late, so that the debtor's bankruptcy estate is diminished. The earmarking doctrine is an exception to the general rule that the use of borrowed funds to discharge a debt constitutes a transfer of property of the debtor. To satisfy the doctrine, the lender must show that the borrowed funds have been specifically earmarked by the lender for payment to a designated creditor, regardless of whether the funds pass through the debtor's hands in getting to the selected creditor. If the doctrine is satisfied, it will be deemed that a transfer of an interest of the debtor in property has not occurred, thus negating the threshold requirement for preference treatment. It has been held that, for the doctrine to apply, the agreement must be between a new creditor and the debtor for the payment of a specific antecedent debt; the agreement must be performed according to its terms; and the transaction may not diminish the debtor's estate. Because Chase (P) is not a "new creditor," it is precluded for that reason alone from invoking the earmarking doctrine. Even if it were a "new creditor," however, it would still not be able to use that doctrine as a defense. While a minority of courts characterize a refinancing transaction such as the one at issue here as a single unitary transaction, the majority find that a refinancing involves multiple transfers. The latter approach is the better one. A unitary-transaction theory ignores the Code's plain meaning because it ignores the definition of "transfer" set forth in § 101(54), as supplemented by § 547(e). Under this definition, it is clear Lee's refinancing transaction was comprised of two transfers by him—first, a transfer of the proceeds of the new loan to Chase (P) to pay off the original mortgage, and second, the grant of the new mortgage to Chase (P) to secure his obligation to repay the new loan. Moreover, to apply the earmarking doctrine to the transfer of a lien interest would extend the doctrine beyond its logical limits, which were intended to encompass transfers of funds. A debtor's grant of a mortgage lien in a refinancing transaction does not involve a transfer of "earmarked" property because the debtor is not serving as a conduit for the transfer of property from a third party. As here, the grant of a mortgage to the mortgagee is a transfer of a property interest owned and controlled by the debtor. In addition, the earmarking doctrine is inapplicable here because Chase's (P) perfection of the new mortgage resulted in diminution of Lee's bankruptcy estate. During the period from when the new loan was made and the original mort-

Continued on next page.

gage was discharged up until Chase's (P) recording of the new mortgage, Chase (P) did not hold a perfected lien interest. Thus, Chase's (P) subsequent perfection of the new mortgage diminished Lee's estate because the nonexempt equity in the property that otherwise would have been available for distribution to Lee's unsecured creditors became encumbered, and unavailable to unsecured creditors, by the new mortgage that Chase (P) received. Finally, applying principles of equity here, as Chase (P) requests—on the grounds that the refinancing lowered Lee's monthly mortgage payments, thus making more money available to him to pay his other creditors—is inappropriate. Even if Chase (P) is correct that equitable considerations would favor it, the bankruptcy courts have only those equitable powers that they are granted by the Bankruptcy Code. The courts cannot substitute their judgment for that of Congress, which in this case clearly indicated that the appropriate length of time between a creditor's transfer of value and perfection was 10 days (subsequently expanded to 30 days by the Bankruptcy Abuse Prevention and Consumer Protection Act (BAPCPA)). By giving effect to Congress's plain meaning, the courts foster predictability in the law of preferences. Also, it is not clear that equity should extend to Chase (P)—a sophisticated lender well-aware of the consequences of failing to perfect its security interest within the grace period afforded by § 547(e)(2). Chase (P) could easily have avoided the harsh results it brought on itself by recording the new mortgage within the grace period; there is no equitable ground here for protecting a late-perfecting secured creditor. Accordingly, the recording of the new mortgage was a preferential transfer under § 547(b). The decision of the district court is reversed, and the opinion of the bankruptcy court is affirmed.

DISSENT: (Merritt, J.) As opposed to the majority, which focuses only on the time of recording by Chase (P) of the new mortgage, the inquiry should be broadened to consider the purpose, consequences, details, and common sense of the complete financing transaction at issue, and whether anyone was misled or if any congressional policies were violated.

ANALYSIS

As the court here also indicated, it believed that applying the earmarking doctrine to insulate a late-perfecting secured creditor from preference liability would essentially write § 547(e) out of the Code and, in the process, defeat the policy the statute was intended to promote—the discouragement of secret liens, which that section's grace period (previously 10 days, now, post-BAPCPA, 30 days) was intended to inhibit. For these and other reasons, the court, in another case, also declined to apply the earmarking doctrine where the mortgagee failed to record an original mortgage within the grace period. See *Moyer v. RBC Mortgage Co (In re Maracle)*, 159 F. Appx. 692 (6th Cir. 2005).

Quicknotes

ANTECEDENT DEBT For the purposes of bankruptcy law, refers to a debt incurred more than four months prior to the filing of a petition in bankruptcy, and which does not constitute a preferential transfer.

EARMARKING DOCTRINE An equitable bankruptcy principle in which a new creditor makes a loan for the purpose of paying off a specified creditor of a debtor.

PERFECT Execute; enforce; to make marketable.

PREFERENTIAL TRANSFER A transfer made by the insolvent debtor to a creditor prior to filing the bankruptcy petition, giving a priority to one creditor over others with respect to the debtor's assets.

In re Hurt

Federal agency (P) v. Debtor (D)

579 B.R. 765 (Bankr. W.D. Va. 2017)

NATURE OF CASE: Decision on cross-motions for summary judgment.

FACT SUMMARY: Debtor Adam Hurt (D) obtained a loan from the United States Department of Housing and Urban Development (P) and later defaulted. In the 90 days prior to filing for Chapter 7 bankruptcy, the United States Department of the Treasury determined that Debtors (D) had overpaid on their taxes and were entitled to a refund. Debtors (D) sought to recover the tax refund that had been setoff prepetition.

RULE OF LAW

A debtor is not entitled to recover his or her tax refund under 11 U.S.C. §§ 542(a), 547(b), or 553(b) when it was used to setoff a mutual debt to the United States Department of the Treasury that arose during the 90-day prepetition period.

FACTS: In 2011, Debtor Adam Hurt (D) obtained a Title 1 Loan from the United States Department of Housing and Urban Development (HUD) (P). Debtor Adam Hurt (D) did not make payments and the loan fell into arrears with an outstanding balance of $19,653.38 as of January 30, 2017. Prior to February 23, 2017, joint debtors Adam and Jessica Hurt (D) filed their 2016 income tax return with the Internal Revenue Service and were entitled to a refund of $5,267.00. In 2016, HUD (P) had sent a Notice of Intent to Collect by Treasury Offset to Debtor Adam Hurt (D), who did not object. HUD (P) referred the notice to the United States Department of the Treasury (Treasury). On February 23, 2017, the Treasury processed HUD's (P) request and offset Debtors' (D) tax refund to satisfy a portion of their debt to HUD (P). On March 3, 2017, Debtors (D) filed a petition for Chapter 7 bankruptcy and listed their tax refund as exempt under Schedule C. Debtors (D) contend they are entitled to their tax refund under 11 U.S.C. §§ 542(a) and 547(b) and seek summary judgment, asking the court to find that they are eligible to recover their 2016 tax refund. HUD (P) contends that the setoff is not recoverable under 11 U.S.C. §§ 542(a), 547(b), or 553(b) and requests that the court enter summary judgment in its favor, dismiss the complaint, and allow it to retain Debtors' (D) 2016 tax refund.

ISSUE: Is a debtor entitled to recover his or her tax refund under 11 U.S.C. §§ 542(a), 547(b), or 553(b) when it was used to setoff a mutual debt to the United States Department of the Treasury that arose during the 90-day prepetition period?

HOLDING AND DECISION: (Black, J.) No. A debtor is not entitled to recover his or her tax refund under 11 U.S.C. §§ 542(a), 547(b), or 553(b) when it was used to setoff a mutual debt to the United States Department of the Treasury that arose during the 90-day prepetition period. First, § 547 is not applicable, because a setoff involves a refusal of the offsetting party to pay a mutual obligation rather than a transfer of debtors' property. Section 553 of the Bankruptcy Code does not create a right to setoff, but instead recognizes the right (established by nonbankruptcy law) of entities that owe each other money to apply their mutual debts against each other. Section 553(b) of the Bankruptcy Code provides a basis for recovering a prebankruptcy setoff when the creditor improves its position within 90 days of bankruptcy. On the first day of the 90-day prepetition period, the government did not owe Debtors (D) any money for their overpayment of 2016 taxes, while the Debtors (D) owed HUD (P), a federal government agency, $19,653.38 arising from their loan obligations. Accordingly, there were no mutual debts, because Debtors' (D) refund was only an expectancy that did not arise until December 31, 2016, the end of the tax year. As of December 31, 2016, the HUD (P) "insufficiency" was $14,286.38: the $19,653.38 owed by the Debtors (D), minus the $5,267.00 refund they were owed by the Treasury. Section 553(b) requires a comparison between the creditor's setoff position and the initial reference point, and it permits the trustee to recover any improvement in the creditor's position. Here, there was no change favorable to the creditor. [Debtor's (D) motion for summary judgment is denied, the adversary proceeding is dismissed, and HUD's (P) motion for summary judgment is granted.]

ANALYSIS

Though it is not stated in the casebook, the court in *Hurt* referenced *Comer v. United States Social Security Admin.*, 386 B.R. 607 (Bankr. W.D. Va. 2008), in which debtors also attempted to use § 547(b) to recover a prepetition setoff against a federal tax refund. In *Comer*, the court stated that § 547(b) requires a prepetition transfer of the debtor's interest in property, and that because the term "setoff" is not included in the definition of a transfer, debtors were not entitled to the prepetition setoff of their refund. Similarly, in *Lopes v. United States Department of Housing and Urban Development*, 211 B.R. 443 (D. R. I. 1997), the court found that questions regarding setoff are governed exclusively by § 553 of the Bankruptcy Code, not § 547.

Continued on next page.

Quicknotes

PREPETITION Before bankruptcy petition has been filed.

SETOFF A creditor's equitable right to deduct a debt it owes to a debtor from a separate transaction.

In re SI Restructuring, Inc.

Trustee (P) v. Insider creditors (D)

532 F.3d 355 (5th Cir. 2008)

NATURE OF CASE: Appeal from affirmance of order in adversary proceeding equitably subordinating secured claims.

FACT SUMMARY: The Wooleys (D), former officers and directors, and the largest shareholders, of Schlotzsky's, Inc. (Schlotzsky's), contended that their secured claims should not be equitably subordinated and converted to unsecured claims because their conduct with respect to loans they made to Schlotzsky's was either not inequitable or did not injure Schlotzsky's or its general creditors.

RULE OF LAW

A secured claim belonging to a corporate debtor's insider creditors will not be equitably subordinated where there is no showing either that the creditors' conduct was inequitable, or that there was injury to the debtor or its other creditors.

FACTS: The Wooleys (D), officers and directors, and the largest shareholders, of Schlotzsky's, Inc. (Schlotzsky's), to relieve a critical cash crunch faced by Schlotzsky's, made two loans to the corporation: one in April for $1 million and another in November for $2.5 million. Both loans were secured with Schlotzsky's royalty streams from franchisees, intellectual property rights, and other intangible property. Schlotzsky's and the Wooleys (D) were represented by separate legal counsel for the April loan negotiations, the loan terms were approved by the audit committee and Schlotzsky's board of directors as a related-party transaction, and the transaction was disclosed in the company's filings with the Securities Exchange Commission (SEC). Despite the April loan, the company still desperately needed capital, and efforts to obtain outside funding continued and were known to the board, and were addressed at an October board meeting. A bank finally agreed to permit the Wooleys (D) to personally borrow capital, which they in turn would be permitted to lend to Schlotzsky's. The bank formally approved the loan to the Wooleys (D) on November 10, and the board was notified on November 11 of a special meeting to be held on November 13 to approve the Wooleys' (D) loan to the company. Before the special meeting, the board members were provided with copies of the proposed promissory note and the security agreement along with e-mails from the company's counsel. When the loan was made, the Wooleys (D) had in place personal guarantees that guaranteed pre-existing Schlotzsky's debt. As part of the November loan package, the Wooleys (D) also secured this potential liability under the guarantees with the same collateral that secured the April and November loans. (The Wooleys' (D) potential obligation on the guaranty agreements was never triggered, however, because the company never defaulted on its principal obligation covered by the guarantees.) At the November 13 board meeting, conducted via telephone conference call, the board was told that without the infusion of additional funds, payroll could not be met and that the company would default on a payment to a secured creditor. All the noninterested directors in attendance approved the loan without objection, an independent audit committee also approved the loan, and the transaction was publicly disclosed in SEC filings. The proceeds of the loan were used to pay the unsecured creditors and keep the company in operation. Several months later, the Wooleys (D) were terminated as officers and resigned as directors. Shortly afterward, the company filed for Chapter 11 bankruptcy protection, and the Wooleys (D) filed secured claims relating to the April and November loans. The committee of unsecured creditors brought an adversary proceeding against the Wooleys (D), seeking to have their secured claims equitably subordinated and treated as unsecured claims. The bankruptcy court found that the Wooleys (D) had breached their fiduciary duties with respect to the November loan for several reasons: first, because they had presented the loan to the board as the only option to the company collapsing; second, because the loans were putatively meant to be temporary, until permanent financing could be obtained, so there was no reason to secure the loans; third, because the collateral was the company's "crown jewels," so the Wooleys (D) took as much as they could for themselves; and fourth, because by securing their pre-existing contingent liability on their personal guarantees with the revenue stream of the franchise company, the Wooleys' (D) effectively released themselves as guarantors on the debt at the expense of the corporation and its unsecured creditors. Notwithstanding these conclusions, the bankruptcy court failed to make specific findings that the Wooleys' (D) regarding the loans or their pre-existing contingent liability on the guarantees resulted in harm to the corporation or to the unsecured creditors. It nevertheless ordered the Wooleys' (D) secured claims equitably subordinated and, thus, converted to unsecured status. The district court affirmed, and the court of appeals granted review.

ISSUE: Will a secured claim belonging to a corporate debtor's insider creditors be equitably subordinated where there is no showing either that the creditors' conduct was

Continued on next page.

inequitable, or that there was injury to the debtor or its other creditors?

HOLDING AND DECISION: (Davis, J.) No. A secured claim belonging to a corporate debtor's insider creditors will not be equitably subordinated where there is no showing either that the creditors' conduct was inequitable, or that there was injury to the debtor or its other creditors. The law regarding when equitable subordination should be applied is not found in the Code, but in case law, which provides that the claimant must have engaged in inequitable conduct; the misconduct must have resulted in injury to the creditors of the debtor or conferred an unfair advantage on the claimant; equitable subordination of the claim must not be inconsistent with the provisions of the Code; and a claim should be subordinated only to the extent necessary to offset the harm that the debtor or its creditors have suffered as a result of the inequitable conduct. Here, the bankruptcy court made no findings of inequitable conduct by the Wooleys (D) with respect to the April loan, and with regard to the November transactions, even assuming that there was inequitable conduct and unfair advantage, the bankruptcy court made no finding of harm, and the record does not support a finding that either the debtor or the unsecured creditors were harmed by the November transaction. Given that the proceeds of the loan were used to pay unsecured creditors, it cannot be said that unsecured creditors as a class were harmed by the November transaction, even if some unsecured creditors benefited at the expense of other unsecured creditors. Therefore, the argument by the Trustee (P) that when the company secured the Wooleys' (D) loan with franchise assets, the assets available to the unsecured creditors were reduced, thus injuring them, must fail. As to the Wooleys' (D) securing their existing personal guarantees with the same collateral used for the loans, there was never any harm to the company because the Wooleys' (D) potential obligation on the guaranty agreements was never triggered because the company never defaulted on its principal obligation covered by the guarantees. Thus, they also did not gain any unfair advantage as to this transaction. Finally, although the Trustee (P) denies it, it seems that he also is claiming damages under a "deepening insolvency theory," defined as prolonging an insolvent corporation's life through bad debt, causing the dissipation of corporate assets. The Trustee's (P) expert used this theory in determining that the company lost $3.5 million as a result of the loans. However, the bankruptcy court rejected this expert's testimony because it recognized that the Wooleys (D) were "highly committed" to keeping the company going. Moreover, the deepening insolvency theory has been rejected by many courts as a measure of damages, and, even if it were an accepted theory, it would not be supported by the record here, since there was no evidence that the company was undercapitalized or insolvent. For all these reasons, neither of the Wooleys' (D) claims should have been subordinated. Reversed.

ANALYSIS

Many courts, e.g., the Delaware Court of Chancery—the nation's preeminent court for corporate law matters—reject the doctrine of deepening insolvency as an independent cause of action or as a theory of damages. These courts reason that even when a company is insolvent, its directors may, in the appropriate exercise of their business judgment, take action that might, if it does not pan out, result in the company losing value or going into insolvency. The fact that the residual claimants of the company at that time are creditors does not mean that the directors cannot choose to continue the firm's operations in the hope that they can improve the company's financial health so that the company's creditors get a greater recovery; by doing so, however, the directors do not guaranty success and do not breach their fiduciary duties.

Quicknotes

BREACH OF FIDUCIARY DUTY The failure of a fiduciary to observe the standard of care exercised by professionals of similar education and experience.

CHAPTER 11 REORGANIZATION A plan formulated pursuant to Chapter 11 of the Bankruptcy Code whereby a debtor, who is unable to pay his or her debts as they become due, is relieved of the obligation to pay creditors through reorganization and payment from future income.

COLLATERAL Property that secures the payment of a debt.

INSOLVENT One's liabilities exceed one's assets; inability to pay one's debts.

POSTPETITION After bankruptcy petition has been filed.

SECURED CLAIM A claim, the repayment of which is secured by collateral sufficient to repay the debt owed.

SECURED CREDITOR A creditor, the repayment of whose loan is secured by collateral sufficient to repay the debt owed.

UNDERCAPITALIZATION Refers to a business that does not have sufficient funds to operate.

UNSECURED CREDITOR A creditor whose loan is not backed by specified collateral or a security agreement.

CHAPTER 23

Fraudulent Conveyances I

Quick Reference Rules of Law

Twyne's Case

Creditor (P) v. Debtor and creditor (D)

3 Coke 806, 76 Eng. Rep. 809 (Star Chamber, 1601)

NATURE OF CASE: Action to recover debt by execution and sale.

FACT SUMMARY: Pierce (D) secretly executed a deed in trust to Twyne (D) of all his personal property to satisfy his debt.

RULE OF LAW

A transfer solely to defeat the rights of other creditors where possession remains in the debtor is fraudulent and void.

FACTS: Pierce (D) owed Twyne (D) £400 and Creditor (P) £200. Creditor (P) instituted suit on the debt and applied for a writ of execution. Pierce (D) secretly transferred all of his property to Twyne (D), although he retained possession of the property in trust. Creditor (P) obtained a judgment and levied on Pierce's (D) property, which was worth approximately £300. Twyne (D) prevented execution alleging that he owned the property. Creditor (P) brought suit alleging that the transfer was made solely to defraud him. Twyne (D) alleged that the transfer was genuine/bona fide and was made for good consideration, i.e., satisfaction of the £400 debt. The court found that a secret transfer of all Pierce's (D) property that was made pending the writ, the debtor retaining possession, bore all the indices of a fraud on creditors. The transfer was voided, and Creditor (P) was allowed to attach.

ISSUE: Is a secret transfer in trust, made solely to defeat the rights of other creditors, fraudulent?

HOLDING AND DECISION: (Sir Thomas Egerton, Lord Keeper of the Great Seal) Yes. A secret transfer in trust, made solely to defeat the rights of other creditors is fraudulent. To be deemed a nonfraudulent transfer, it must be for good consideration and bona fide. While good consideration is present herein, the court below believed that no bona fide transfer took place. This court concurs. Pierce (D) retained both possession and use of the property. Pierce (D) was to hold it until the debt to Twyne (D) was paid. The transfer was merely a device to prevent Creditor (P) from executing his judgment. A secret transfer where the debtor retains possession in trust is presumptively fraudulent when it involves all or substantially all the debtor's assets and other creditors exist. It is especially true when another creditor has instituted suit. Affirmed.

ANALYSIS

A transfer made without good consideration under similar circumstances as above is also deemed fraudulent. The presence of a trust is not required. The creditor may go after the transferee who has obtained possession of the debtor's property. If Twyne (D) had actually obtained possession and use of Pierce's property, Creditor (P) could not prevail unless he could establish that Twyne (D) was really holding the property in trust for Pierce (D). A debtor can favor any of his creditors by giving preference to their debt without being guilty of fraud.

Quicknotes

BONA FIDE In good faith.

FRAUD A false representation of facts with the intent that another will rely on the misrepresentation to his detriment.

LEVY The collection or assessment of a tax; the legal process pursuant to which property is seized and sold in order to satisfy a debt.

ACLI Government Securities, Inc. v. Rhoades

Creditor (P) v. Debtor (D)

653 F. Supp. 1388 (S.D.N.Y. 1987)

NATURE OF CASE: Action to set aside fraudulent conveyances.

FACT SUMMARY: Nine days after a jury verdict against him was rendered, and one day before judgment for $1.5 million was entered, Rhoades (D) conveyed his 60 percent interest in sixty-eight acres of New York property to his sister (D).

RULE OF LAW

A fraudulent conveyance is one made with actual intent to hinder, delay, or defraud present or future creditors or is one made without receipt of fair consideration and which has the effect of rendering the conveyor insolvent.

FACTS: ACLI Government Securities (ACLI) (P) won a $1.5 million jury verdict against Daniel Rhoades (D). Daniel (D) practiced law and commingled his finances with his sister Norma (D). Together, in 1959, they purchased sixty-eight acres in Putnam County, New York, as tenants-in-common, with Daniel (D) having a three-fifths interest and Norma (D) a two-fifths interest; the 1983 appraised value of the property was $325,000. The day before ACLI's (P) judgment was to be entered against Daniel (D), he conveyed his interest in the Putnam County property to Norma (D) for one dollar. Norma (D) testified that the conveyance by Daniel (D) was to repay her for a half-million dollars in treasury bonds she had entrusted to him but were never returned, but there was no other evidence that this was truly a debt between them. Daniel (D) owned only three other assets, which he asserted could be used to satisfy ACLI's (P) judgment against him: two relatively worthless properties and 425 acres of undeveloped land in South Carolina, which by appraisal was worth about $212,500.

ISSUE: Will a conveyance be set aside as fraudulent if the debtor actually intended to hinder, delay, or defraud his creditors or if it rendered the debtor insolvent and was made for inadequate consideration?

HOLDING AND DECISION: (Lasker, J.) Yes. A fraudulent conveyance is one made with actual intent to hinder, delay, or defraud present or future creditors or is one made without receipt of fair consideration and which has the effect of rendering the conveyor insolvent. ACLI (P) first contended that Daniel's (D) conveyance to Norma (D) was made without fair consideration and rendered Daniel (D) insolvent. ACLI (P), as creditor, had the burden of establishing that unfairness of consideration unless, as here, evidence was presented as to the nature and value of consideration having been within the transferee's control. The evidence presented by Daniel (D) did not establish that the Putnam property was transferred to satisfy an antecedent debt. The transaction between Daniel (D) and Norma (D) was closer to a bailment, the Rhoades's (D) personal and professional finances had been inextricably commingled, and the debt was not proportionate to Daniel's (D) interest in the property. Nor was Daniel's (D) interest in the South Carolina property sufficient to satisfy ACLI's (P) judgment; so the Putnam transfer rendered Daniel (D) insolvent. ACLI (P) also contended that Daniel (D) actually intended to defraud it by the Putnam conveyance. ACLI (P) bore the burden of proving this by clear and convincing circumstantial evidence including: (1) close relationship between the parties to the transaction; (2) secrecy and haste of sale; (3) inadequacy of consideration; (4) transferor's knowledge of creditor's claim and his inability to pay it. Here, Daniel (D) and Norma (D) were siblings who had practiced law together for forty years; the conveyance was in secret, contrary to court order one day prior to entry of judgment; only $1 was given for three-fifths interest in the Putnam property; and Daniel (D) knew he could not pay the judgment. Conveyance ordered set aside as fraudulent.

ANALYSIS

This case relies on New York's enactment of the Uniform Fraudulent Transfer Act (UFTA), which was promulgated in 1984 to replace the 1918 Uniform Fraudulent Conveyance Act (UFCA). Section 5(a) of UFTA carries over the UFCA provisions of "presumptive" or "constructive" fraud and allows an innocent conveyance by the debtor to be set aside if the exchange was for unfairly low consideration at a time when the debtor was insolvent. Sections 4(a)(1) and (2) provide "quasi-constructive" grounds for fraud where a debtor had guilty intent or was negligent in making the conveyance.

Quicknotes

CONVEYANCE The transfer of property, or title to property, from one party to another party.

Fed. Natl. Mortgage Assn. v. Olympia Mortgage Corp.

Mortgage-backed securities issuer (P) v. Mortgage corporation/insolvent transferor (D)

792 F. Supp. 2d 645 (E.D.N.Y. 2011)

NATURE OF CASE: Cross motions for summary judgment on crossclaims to recover on allegedly fraudulent transfers.

FACT SUMMARY: In an action initiated by Federal National Mortgage Association ("Fannie Mae") (P) against Olympia Mortgage Corp. (Olympia) (D), Olympia (D) cross-claimed against several individuals ("the Donner Relatives"), claiming that they received transfers from Olympia (D) that were constructively fraudulent under state law while Olympia (D) was insolvent, and sought money damages for the amounts of the transfers.

RULE OF LAW

(1) Where state law provides that if a conveyance is made without fair consideration and the transferor is a debtor who is insolvent or will be rendered insolvent by the transfer, the conveyance is deemed constructively fraudulent, money transfers by a corporation while it is insolvent to, and on behalf of, individuals who have performed no services for the corporation or provided it with any consideration will be deemed constructively fraudulent.

(2) To be liable for money damages for constructively fraudulent transfers, it is not required that the transferee or beneficiary of the transfers have participated in the underlying fraud.

FACTS: Federal National Mortgage Association ("Fannie Mae") (P) brought suit against Olympia Mortgage Corp. (Olympia) (D). As a result, Olympia (D) was placed in receivership. Olympia (D) cross-claimed against several individuals ("the Donner Relatives") who received transfers that Olympia (D) asserted were constructively fraudulent under state law. The Donner Relatives were family members of Donner, Olympia's (D) president and 32 percent shareholder. The transfers, which were made on behalf of the Donner Relatives in the form of wages, mortgage payments, and healthcare payments, were made after Olympia (D) was insolvent. However, none of the Donner Relatives performed services in exchange for the monies or benefits they received. Instead, they asserted that the transfers were part of Donner's compensation for the services that he provided as Olympia's (D) president. The only evidence in support of the Donner Relatives' assertion was Donner's affidavit, which asserted that his annual salary was significantly less than what it should have been and that the balance of the compensation he should have received was paid through the transfers to the Donner Relatives. While Donner received an annual salary for being Olympia's (D) president, he performed little work for the company, and he was not involved in its day-to-day operations. The Donner Relatives also argued that in addition to Donner's salary, the transfers in question also included shareholder profits disbursed to Donner, but they offered no evidence in support of this position. Olympia (D) sought money damages for the transfers. Olympia (D) and the Donner Relatives cross-moved for summary judgment.

ISSUE:

(1) Where state law provides that if a conveyance is made without fair consideration and the transferor is a debtor who is insolvent or will be rendered insolvent by the transfer, the conveyance is deemed constructively fraudulent, will money transfers by a corporation while it is insolvent to, and on behalf of, individuals who have performed no services for the corporation or provided it with any consideration be deemed constructively fraudulent?

(2) To be liable for money damages for constructively fraudulent transfers is it required that the transferee or beneficiary of the transfers have participated in the underlying fraud?

HOLDING AND DECISION: (Gershon, J.)

(1) Yes. Where state law provides that if a conveyance is made without fair consideration and the transferor is a debtor who is insolvent or will be rendered insolvent by the transfer, the conveyance is deemed constructively fraudulent, money transfers by a corporation while it is insolvent to, and on behalf of, individuals who have performed no services for the corporation or provided it with any consideration will be deemed constructively fraudulent. All the elements necessary for Olympia (D) to make out a case of constructive fraud are present and are proved by sufficient evidence. First, it is undisputed that the money transfers were made to, or on behalf of, the Donner Relatives. Second, these transfers occurred after Olympia (D) was insolvent. The Donner Relatives dispute that Olympia (D) was insolvent, or that the transfers contributed to its insolvency, but offer no evidence in support of their assertion. Moreover, the element of insolvency is presumed when a conveyance is made without fair consideration, and the burden of overcoming such presumption is on the transferee. Here, there was no fair consideration for the transfers, so the transferor's insolvency is presumed. As to the fair

Continued on next page.

consideration element, fraudulent intent is not required of the transferee. To be considered "fair consideration," a conveyance must satisfy an antecedent debt or constitute a present exchange, and the value of the consideration may not be disproportionately small when compared with the value of the conveyance. Here, the Donner Relatives provided no services for the transfers, nor did they provide any kind of consideration therefor. Donner's W-2s did not indicate that the transfers were part of his taxable compensation, thus contradicting his conclusory affidavit that the transfers were part of his salary. Moreover, W-2s improperly issued to some of the Donner Relatives also contradict the affidavit in this regard. Given that Donner spent little time at Olympia (D) and had no responsibilities there, and only highly conclusory evidence was presented in rebuttal, and given the uncontroverted W-2 evidence, no reasonable jury could conclude that the transfers to the Donner Relatives constituted salary payments to Donner. As to the argument that the transfers were a return on profits owed to Donner, no evidence supporting this assertion was presented, and, in any event, under state law a corporation may not pay dividends when the corporation is insolvent or would thereby be made insolvent. For these reasons, Olympia (D) has satisfied all the elements needed to prove that the transfers to the Donner Relatives were constructively fraudulent. Accordingly, the Donner Relatives' motion for summary judgment is denied, and Olympia's (D) motion for summary judgment is granted, as to this issue.

(2) No. To be liable for money damages for constructively fraudulent transfers, it is not required that the transferee or beneficiary of the transfers have participated in the underlying fraud. The Donner Relatives argue that they cannot be held liable for money damages for the transfers at issue because they did not participate in the underlying fraud. No precedent holds that a transferee or beneficiary of a fraudulent transfer had to have also been a participant in the underlying fraud. One need only be a transferee or beneficiary to be a participant in a fraudulent transfer; not either a transferee or beneficiary of a fraudulent conveyance and a participant in the underlying fraud. Thus, the Donner Relatives participated in the fraud as transferees or beneficiaries. Although state law protects the rights of certain transferees who paid "fair consideration" for assets without "knowledge of the fraud at the time of the purchase," that law is inapplicable here, since the Donner Relatives did not offer any fair consideration in exchange for the money transfers. Thus, the Donner Relatives are liable for the entire amount of the fraudulent transfers. Accordingly, the Donner Relatives' motion for summary judgment is denied, and Olympia's (D) motion for summary judgment is granted, as to this issue.

ANALYSIS

As this case indicates, a corporation may not declare or pay dividends while it is insolvent, or if it will be rendered insolvent thereby. This is because a corporation holds its assets in trust for the benefit of the corporation's creditors and cannot lawfully distribute its assets to shareholders to the prejudice of those creditors. An insolvent corporation cannot make distributions to shareholders, and such distributions are classic fraudulent conveyances prohibited by law.

Quicknotes

CONSTRUCTIVE FRAUD Breach of a duty at law or in equity that tends to deceive another to whom the duty is owed, resulting in damages.

FRAUDULENT CONVEYANCE Conveyances made with intent to defraud creditors; may be voidable.

In re Video Depot, Ltd.

Bankruptcy trustee (P) v. Creditor (D)

127 F.3d 1195 (9th Cir. 1997)

NATURE OF CASE: Appeal from district court decision affirming bankruptcy court's judgment for trustee plaintiff.

FACT SUMMARY: The owner of Video Depot used corporate funds to pay off his personal gambling debts; the Bankruptcy trustee (P) later sought to recover the funds.

RULE OF LAW

A trustee may not recover from a subsequent transferee if the subsequent transferee accepted the transfer for value, in good faith, and without knowledge of the transfer's voidability.

FACTS: The owner of Video Depot purchased a check in the company's name and used it to pay his personal gambling debt at the Las Vegas Hilton (Hilton) (D). Video Depot later filed for bankruptcy and the Trustee (P) filed suit against Hilton (D) to recover the proceeds of the check. The parties stipulated that the payment to Hilton (D) was a fraudulent transfer. The bankruptcy court determined, and the district court agreed, that Hilton (D) was the initial transferee. Hilton (D) claimed that it was a subsequent transferee and appealed.

ISSUE: May a trustee recover from a subsequent transferee if the subsequent transferee accepted the transfer for value, in good faith, and without knowledge of the transfer's voidability?

HOLDING AND DECISION: (Nelson, J.) No. A trustee may not recover from a subsequent transferee if the subsequent transferee accepted the transfer for value, in good faith, and without knowledge of the transfer's voidability. The bankruptcy courts are split as to whether the principal of a debtor corporation necessarily is the initial transferee of corporate funds used to satisfy a personal obligation. The owner's control over the business operations of Video Depot does not, in itself, compel a finding that the owner had dominion and control over the funds transferred from Video Depot to Hilton (D). The owner was a courier, not a transferee. The bankruptcy court had enough grounds to find that Hilton (D) was an initial transferee. Affirmed.

ANALYSIS

Hilton (D) also unsuccessfully argued on appeal that the check was really a loan to the owner. The only issue in this case was whether the owner was the initial transferee. Since the check was made out to Hilton (D), the court found that the Video Depot owner had not had dominion over the funds.

Quicknotes

CORPORATION A distinct legal entity characterized by continuous existence; free alienability of interests held therein; centralized management; and limited liability on the part of the shareholders of the corporation.

FRAUDULENT CONVEYANCE Conveyances made within one year of filing the bankruptcy petition with intent to defraud creditors and which may be voidable.

VOIDABLE TRANSFER Conveyances made within one year of filing the bankruptcy petition with the intent to defraud creditors.

CHAPTER 24

Fraudulent Conveyances II

Quick Reference Rules of Law

In re The Personal and Business Insurance Agency

[Parties not identified.]

334 F.3d 239 (3d Cir. 2003)

NATURE OF CASE: Appeal from affirmance of dismissal of a fraudulent conveyance claim.

FACT SUMMARY: The trustee (Trustee) in the Chapter 7 bankruptcy of The Personal & Business Insurance Agency (PBI) (Debtor) contended that even if the fraud of PBI's sole owner and CEO, Kesselring, was properly imputed to PBI prepetition, the fraud could not be imputed to the Trustee, who was bringing a fraudulent conveyance claim under § 548 of the Bankruptcy Code on behalf of innocent creditors, because the court had to consider his claim in light of a postpetition event, namely his appointment as Trustee in place of the "bad actor" Kesselring, in determining whether the transfers were fraudulent under § 548.

RULE OF LAW

A court may consider post-bankruptcy petition events, including the appointment of a trustee, in evaluating a fraudulent conveyance claim brought under § 548 of the Bankruptcy Code.

FACTS: The Personal & Business Insurance Agency (PBI) (Debtor), an insurance brokerage firm, was solely owned by Kesselring, who also served as its CEO. Kesselring started a fraudulent scheme whereby he made false applications for finance company loans in the name of actual PBI clients or fictitious entities, either forging the borrower's signature or signing as the borrower's agent/broker. He then submitted the applications to Premium Finance Specialists (PFS), a finance company, and obtained the loan proceeds. Rather than paying for insurance coverage with these funds, however, Kesselring pocketed the money. To avoid detection, Kesselring caused PBI to make payments on the fraudulent loans using PBI funds. PBI filed for Chapter 7 bankruptcy protection, and the Chapter 7 trustee (Trustee) sought to recover the funds Kesselring had transferred to PFS pursuant to his illegal scheme as fraudulent conveyances under Bankruptcy Code § 548 and state law. The bankruptcy court held that the transfers were not fraudulent because they were made in repayment of a debt owed to PFS. The district court agreed and rejected the Trustee's argument that Kesselring's fraudulent conduct could not be imputed to PSI and that the debt was Kesselring's alone. In rejecting the Trustee's argument, the district court reasoned that the fraud of an officer of a corporation is imputed to the corporation when the officer's fraudulent conduct is (1) in the course of his employment, and (2) for the benefit of the corporation, notwithstanding that the officer's conduct was unauthorized and effected for his own benefit but clothed with apparent authority of the corporation, or contrary to instructions. The underlying rationale is that a corporation can speak and act only through its agents and so must be accountable for any acts committed by one of its agents within his actual or apparent scope of authority and while transacting corporate business. There is an exception to this rule, known as the "adverse interest exception," which holds that fraudulent conduct will not be imputed if the officer's interests were adverse to the corporation. This exception applied here because Kesselring's illegal actions were only for his benefit not that of PBI. Nevertheless, there is an exception to this exception, known as the "sole actor" exception, which provides that if an agent is the sole representative of a principal, that agent's fraudulent conduct is imputable to the principal regardless of whether the agent's conduct is adverse to the principal's interests. The rationale for this rule is that the sole agent has no one to whom he can impart his knowledge, or from whom he can conceal it, and that the corporation must bear the responsibility for allowing the agent to act without accountability. The district court applied this sole actor exception since Kesselring was the sole representative of PBI in the scheme. Based on this determination, the district court concluded that the transfers of money from PBI to PFS were not constructively fraudulent because the corporation, through Kesselring's imputed conduct, received a reasonably equivalent value for them (the loan proceeds disbursed by PFS to PBI), and therefore the transfers were made in payment of an antecedent debt. The district court also found no actual fraud, since the "badges of fraud," in particular inadequate consideration, were absent. Accordingly, the district court affirmed the bankruptcy court's dismissal of the Trustee's claims. The court of appeals granted review.

ISSUE: May a court consider post-bankruptcy petition events, including the appointment of a trustee, in evaluating a fraudulent conveyance claim brought under § 548 of the Bankruptcy Code?

HOLDING AND DECISION: (Becker, J.) Yes. A court may consider post-bankruptcy petition events, including the appointment of a trustee, in evaluating a fraudulent conveyance claim brought under § 548 of the Bankruptcy Code. PFS's arguments hinge on there being antecedent debt. It incorrectly argues that PFS transferred the loan monies directly to PBI's general checking account, not to Kesselring, and therefore PBI was responsible for using the funds appropriately and for making repayment to

Continued on next page.

PFS. To the extent that PBI held the loan monies, it did so only as a conduit for Kesselring and exercised no control over them. Therefore, PBI's transitory possession of the loan funds did not create a debt owed to PFS. PFS also argues that under the sole actor exception, Kesselring's conduct and debt must be imputed to PBI, so that PBI had a debt to PFS. The Trustee, however, asserts that even if the debt may be imputed to PBI, it may not be imputed to the Trustee—the party bringing the claim. The Trustee argues that the court must consider his claim in light of a postpetition event, namely his appointment as Trustee in place of the "bad actor" Kesselring, in determining whether the transfers were fraudulent under § 548. Strong equitable arguments support the Trustee's position, and some courts have accordingly ruled that the defense of in pari delicto should not be applied when a bad actor has been removed and the defense is serving only to bar the claims of an innocent successor. Such equitable considerations apply in this case, since the Trustee comes to the court with clean hands, representing the interests of innocent creditors; and since if the doctrine of imputation were applied to bar PBI's recovery, this application would lead to an inequitable result, i.e., loss to innocent creditors. Neither state law nor § 548 bars the application of such equitable considerations. Accordingly, the court may consider the postpetition event of the Trustee's appointment. When this postpetition event is considered, for the purpose of affecting an equitable result, Kesselring's conduct should not be imputed to the Trustee. The concomitant removal of the taint of Kesselring's fraud from PBI means that the Trustee had no "antecedent debt," and consequently no value was received for the payments made by PBI to PFS. Vacated and remanded.

ANALYSIS

This case demonstrates not only the difficulty of pursuing a fraudulent conveyance claim against a solely owned corporation where its owner is the perpetrator of fraud, but also shows that the maxim, that a trustee standing in the shoes of the corporation takes no greater rights than the debtor, in some instances is too limited, and that, in situations such as the one presented in this case, the trustee's rights may expand beyond those the debtor would otherwise have under state law.

Quicknotes

ANTECEDENT DEBT For the purposes of bankruptcy law, refers to a debt incurred more than four months prior to the filing of a petition in bankruptcy, and which does not constitute a preferential transfer.

FRAUDULENT CONVEYANCE Conveyances made with intent to defraud creditors; may be voidable.

IN PARI DELICTO Doctrine that a court will not enforce an illegal contract in an action for losses incurred as a result of the breach of that contract; the parties are at equal fault or guilt.

In re Image Worldwide, Ltd.

Trustee (P) v. Creditor (D)

139 F.3d 574 (7th Cir. 1998)

NATURE OF CASE: Appeal from order granting trustee right to recover funds.

FACT SUMMARY: The bankruptcy Trustee (P) sought to avoid loan guarantees to a Corporate affiliate (D).

RULE OF LAW

Indirect benefits to a guarantor may be considered when determining whether a corporation receives reasonably equivalent value for a guarantee.

FACTS: Image Worldwide (IW) had guaranteed loans paid to an affiliate corporation, Image Marketing (IM) (D). When IW later filed for bankruptcy, the Trustee (P) alleged that the guarantees made IW insolvent and were fraudulent transfers because IW had not received reasonably equivalent value in exchange for its guarantees. When the court ruled in the Trustee's (P) favor, IM (D) appealed, claiming IW had received indirect benefits.

ISSUE: May indirect benefits to a guarantor be considered when determining whether a corporation receives reasonably equivalent value for a guarantee?

HOLDING AND DECISION: (Eschbach, J.) Yes. Indirect benefits to a guarantor may be considered when determining whether a corporation receives reasonably equivalent value for a guarantee. A bankruptcy trustee can avoid any transaction of the debtor that would be voidable by any actual unsecured creditor under state law. In this case, however, there were not two functioning corporations that benefited mutually from the loan. The bankruptcy court did not clearly err when it found that IW did not receive reasonably equivalent value for its guarantees. Affirmed.

ANALYSIS

Both corporations were owned by the same person. This case involved an involuntary Chapter 7 bankruptcy. The Trustee (P) had initially relied on the federal Uniform Fraudulent Transfer Act, but the one-year statute of limitations had run, so the court applied the strong-arm provision of the Bankruptcy Code.

Quicknotes

CHAPTER 7 BANKRUPTCY A legal proceeding whereby a debtor, who is unable to pay his or debts as they become due, is relieved of the obligation to pay creditors by liquidation and distribution of remaining assets.

CORPORATION A distinct legal entity characterized by continuous existence; free alienability of interests held therein; centralized management; and limited liability on the part of the shareholders of the corporation.

FRAUDULENT TRANSFER The conveyance of title to property with the intent to defraud creditors or with the intent to deceive others.

GUARANTOR A party who agrees to be liable for the debt or default of another.

INVOLUNTARY BANKRUPTCY Proceedings brought against a debtor by his creditors thereby forcing him into bankruptcy.

STRONG-ARM CLAUSE A clause in the Bankruptcy Code that allows a bankruptcy trustee to avoid unperfected security interests when the bankruptcy case is filed.

UNSECURED CREDITOR A creditor whose loan is not backed by specified collateral or a security agreement.

Paloian v. LaSalle Bank

Bankruptcy trustee (P) v. Investment pool trustee (D)

619 F.3d 688 (7th Cir. 2010)

NATURE OF CASE: Cross-appeals from judgments in adversary proceedings to determine whether a bankruptcy trustee could recover as fraudulent conveyances payments made to an investment pool trustee. [The complete procedural posture of the case is not presented in the casebook extract.]

FACT SUMMARY: Paloian (P), the bankruptcy trustee in Doctors Hospital of Hyde Park's (Hospital's) bankruptcy, sought to recover as fraudulent conveyances payments made to an investment pool trust, the trustee of which was LaSalle National Bank (LaSalle Bank) contending, inter alia, that an entity, MMA Funding, LLC, used in obtaining financing for the Hospital, had not been successfully set up as a "bankruptcy-remote vehicle," and that, therefore, payments to MMA Funding by the Hospital could be avoided as preferential transfers after Hospital became insolvent.

RULE OF LAW

To be a bankruptcy-remote vehicle, an entity must be separate from the debtor by buying assets, managing the assets in its own interest rather than the debtor's, and observing corporate formalities.

FACTS: Doctors Hospital of Hyde Park (Hospital), which was owned by Desnick, entered separate loan arrangements with Daiwa Healthco (Daiwa) and Nomura Asset Capital Corporation (Nomura). In March 1997, Daiwa extended a revolving $25 million line of credit to MMA Funding, LLC, which made the money available to the Hospital for operating expenses. The Hospital transferred all its current and future accounts receivable to MMA Funding, which gave Daiwa a security interest in them. The plan was to use MMA Funding as a "bankruptcy-remote vehicle" so that Daiwa could be assured of repayment even if the Hospital entered bankruptcy. The idea behind the bankruptcy-remote vehicle is that, if a debtor sells particular assets to a separate corporation, the lender can rely on those assets without the complications (such as preference-recovery actions) that attend bankruptcy. For the entity to be "bankruptcy-remote," it must be separate from the debtor. To be separate, it must buy assets, manage the assets in its own interest rather than the debtor's, and observe corporate formalities. MMA Funding was not independent of Desnick or the Hospital, as Desnick owned MMA Funding, and MMA Funding operated as if it were a department of the Hospital. It did not have an office, a phone number, a checking account, or stationery; all its letters were written on the Hospital's stationery. It did not prepare financial statements or file tax returns. It did not purchase the receivables for any price, and instead of buying the receivables at the outset, MMA Funding took a small cut of the proceeds every month to cover its miniscule costs of operation. The Hospital continued to carry the accounts receivable on its own books, as a corporate asset; it told other creditors that Daiwa had a security interest in the receivables. In August 1997, Nomura loaned $50 million to the Hospital through HPCH LLC, which owned the Hospital's building and land. As part of this transaction, the Hospital promised to pay HPCH additional rent. HPCH gave Nomura a security interest in the incremental rent, which was to be transferred to MMA Funding. This loan was securitized before the end of 1997, and the assets underlying the loan were transferred to an investment pool trust, of which LaSalle National Bank (LaSalle Bank) was the trustee. In 2000, Hospital filed for Chapter 11 bankruptcy protection. Paloian (P), the Chapter 11 trustee, sought to recover as fraudulent conveyances payments made by the Hospital to the trust. In multiple adversary proceedings, the bankruptcy court concluded the Hospital was insolvent no later than August 1997 and that the increased rental rate for the lease of the building and grounds was in reality debt service by the Hospital. The bankruptcy court concluded that the repayments on the Nomura loan were fraudulent conveyances, which had to be returned to the bankruptcy estate. The district court, which, like the bankruptcy court, determined MMA Funding was a bankruptcy-remote vehicle, affirmed. The court of appeals granted review and decided to remand as to the issue of insolvency. In addressing issues to be addressed on remand, the court of appeals set forth the requirements of a bankruptcy-remote vehicle.

ISSUE: To be a bankruptcy-remote vehicle, must an entity be separate from the debtor by buying assets, managing the assets in its own interest rather than the debtor's, and observing corporate formalities?

HOLDING AND DECISION: (Easterbrook, C.J.) Yes. To be a bankruptcy-remote vehicle, an entity must be separate from the debtor by buying assets, managing the assets in its own interest rather than the debtor's, and observing corporate formalities. A key issue on remand is whether Daiwa and Desnick succeeded in making MMA Funding a bankruptcy-remote vehicle. If they did not, and the Hospital went insolvent before the Hospital filed its bankruptcy petition, the payments routed through or for the account of MMA Funding potentially could be recaptured for the benefit of creditors in general. If they succeeded, however, and MMA Funding was a legitimate bankruptcy-remote vehicle, this would prevent recovery of

Continued on next page.

payments made on the Nomura loan from July 1998 forward. Here, based on the record, MMA Funding lacked the usual attributes of a bankruptcy-remote vehicle, as it was not independent of Desnick or the Hospital; it did not purchase the receivables on its own account; and it failed to observe any corporate formalities. In other words, the record as it stands shows that MMA Funding was nothing more than a shell. A trustee in bankruptcy can step into the shoes of any hypothetical lien creditor. Here, that means Paloian (P) can step into the shoes of a creditor ignorant of the contracts signed by the Hospital, Daiwa, Nomura, LaSalle Bank, and MMA Funding. If a hypothetical creditor could have obtained an interest in assets that the Hospital's books declared belonged to it, then a bankruptcy trustee can maintain an avoidance action. The bankruptcy court and district court reasoned that treating MMA Funding as a bankruptcy-remote vehicle allowed Daiwa and Nomura to charge lower rates of interest. While this is true, it overlooks the fact that, if some creditors are protected from preference-recovery actions and thus can charge lower interest, other creditors bear higher risk and must charge higher interest. The trustee must look out for the interests of these other creditors, who may not appreciate that they should have charged extra to offset the effects of a bankruptcy-remote vehicle that they could not easily know about. On remand, to overcome the conclusion that MMA Funding was not a legitimate bankruptcy-remote vehicle, LaSalle Bank could show that there was a bona fide sale of accounts receivable from the Hospital to MMA Funding in March 2007, and that MMA Funding was a genuine business entity, not just a name in the lending agreements. Alternatively, LaSalle Bank could contend that a hypothetical lien creditor must be charged with knowledge of those aspects of the earlier transactions that were matters of public record. Vacated and remanded.

ANALYSIS

The court's discussion of the requirements for a legitimate bankruptcy-remote vehicle highlights that debtors and creditors cannot evade bankruptcy law through clever choice of words, but must structure their transactions so their economic substance lies outside particular sections of the Bankruptcy Code. Thus, here, hypothetically, if Daiwa had loaned $25 million to Remote Vehicle, Inc., a corporation independent of Desnick and the Hospital, which then purchased the Hospital's accounts receivable for $22 million (using the proceeds of the loan) and stood to make a profit, or suffer a loss, depending on how much eventually came in, there would be little ground to treat Remote Vehicle's payments on the loan as preferential transfers by the Hospital. The transfer by the Hospital would have occurred with the initial sale of the receivables, and, if that sale predated the Hospital's insolvency (or the bankruptcy filing) by enough time, it would be outside the bankruptcy trustee's avoiding powers, even though particular payments occurred within the look-back periods (90 days or one year under § 547(b), two years under § 548(a)). Thus, under this scenario, the economic substance of the transaction would place Remote Vehicle outside the Bankruptcy Code's reach.

Quicknotes

CHAPTER 11 BANKRUPTCY A legal proceeding whereby a debtor, who is unable to pay his or her debts as they become due, is relieved of the obligation to pay creditors through reorganization and payment from future income.

PREFERENCE A transfer made by the insolvent debtor to a creditor prior to filing the bankruptcy petition, giving a priority to one creditor over others in respect to the debtor's assets.

Boyer v. Crown Stock Distribution, Inc.

Trustee (P) v. Dividend distribution vehicle (D)

587 F.3d 787 (7th Cir. 2009)

NATURE OF CASE: Cross-appeals from affirmance of judgment in Chapter 7 adversary proceeding seeking to recover the proceeds of a sale of a corporation as a fraudulent conveyance.

FACT SUMMARY: Boyer (Trustee) (P), the trustee in the Chapter 7 bankruptcy of "new" Crown Unlimited Machine, Inc. (New Crown), sought to recover as a fraudulent conveyance the money paid for the assets of "old" Crown Unlimited Machine, Inc. (Old Crown) (D), which was renamed Crown Stock Distribution, Inc., as well as a dividend the shareholders (D) of Old Crown (D) paid to themselves from the company's cash just prior to closing, on the theory that the sale was a leveraged buyout (LBO) that should have been recharacterized as a sale to Old Crown's shareholders (D), and that the Old Crown shareholders (D) had not given reasonably equivalent value in the transaction, which fatally depleted the corporation's assets.

RULE OF LAW

An asset sale of a corporation may be deemed a leveraged buyout (LBO) and the transaction recharacterized as a sale by the corporation's shareholders, so that the shareholders are liable for repayment of fraudulent conveyances in the form of payments received from the purchaser and of the corporation's cash distributed to the shareholders in the form of a dividend prior to closing, where the shareholders did not give reasonably equivalent value and the transaction fatally depleted the corporation's assets.

FACTS: Smith agreed to purchase the assets of "old" Crown Unlimited Machine, Inc. (Old Crown) (D) for $6 million. The new entity, also called Crown Unlimited Machine, Inc. (New Crown), paid $3.1 million in cash and provided a $2.9 million promissory note. The cash was borrowed, and the loan for the cash was secured by all of New Crown's assets. The note was also secured by all New Crown's assets, and under the agreement of sale, New Crown was required to pay $100,000 a year on the note. Smith contributed only $500 of his own money toward the purchase. Just prior to closing in January 2000, the Old Crown shareholders (D), members of the Stroup family, had Old Crown transfer $590,328 from its corporate bank account to a separate bank account so that it could be distributed to Old Crown's shareholders as a dividend. The dividend represented 50 percent of the company's profits for 1999. After closing, Old Crown (D) was renamed Crown Stock Distribution, Inc., and it distributed the $3.1 million of cash it received in the sale to the shareholders (D). It then ceased operating. New Crown filed for Chapter 7 bankruptcy protection in July 2003. Its assets were sold for $3.7 million, most of which went to paying the lender. Unsecured creditors were owed around $1.7 million. Boyer (Trustee) (P), the Chapter 7 trustee, brought an adversary proceeding on behalf of the unsecured creditors, seeking to recover as a fraudulent conveyance the amounts paid to Old Crown (D) and its shareholders (D), as well as the dividend paid to the shareholders (D) just prior to closing. The Trustee (P) asserted that the transaction should be recharacterized as a sale to the shareholders (D) through a leveraged buyout (LBO), and that the transaction was a fraudulent conveyance under the Uniform Fraudulent Transfer Act (UFTA) because Old Crown (D) had not given reasonably equivalent value in exchange for the cash and note it received, and left New Crown needing "life support" from its inception. The Trustee (P) asserted that the dividend the Old Crown shareholders (D) had paid to themselves was part of the transaction, which fatally depleted the corporation's assets. The bankruptcy court ruled that the $6 million that New Crown had paid or had obligated itself to pay for Old Crown's (D) assets had been paid without New Crown receiving a reasonably equivalent value in exchange, so that New Crown had embarked upon "a business . . . for which [its] remaining assets . . . were 'unreasonably small in relation to the business,'" in the language of the UFTA. Accordingly, the bankruptcy court awarded the Trustee (P) $3,295,000 (which included two payments of $100,000 made on the note) plus prejudgment interest. However, the bankruptcy court determined that the $590,328 dividend was legitimate, because it had been paid out of cash that belonged to Old Crown (D) rather than to New Crown. In so ruling, the court rejected the Trustee's (P) argument that the purchase of Old Crown's (D) assets had been an LBO that should have been "collapsed" and the sale thus recharacterized as a sale by the shareholders of Old Crown (D). The district judge affirmed, and Old Crown (D) and its shareholders (D) appealed. The Trustee (P) cross-appealed, seeking an additional $590,328. The court of appeals granted review.

ISSUE: May an asset sale of a corporation be deemed a leveraged buyout (LBO) and the transaction recharacterized as a sale by the corporation's shareholders, so that the shareholders are liable for repayment of fraudulent conveyances in the form of payments received from the purchaser and of the corporation's cash distributed to the shareholders in the form of a dividend prior to closing, where the shareholders did not give reasonably equivalent

Continued on next page.

value and the transaction fatally depleted the corporation's assets?

HOLDING AND DECISION: (Posner, J.) Yes. An asset sale of a corporation may be deemed a leveraged buyout (LBO) and the transaction recharacterized as a sale by the corporation's shareholders, so that the shareholders are liable for repayment of fraudulent conveyances in the form of payments received from the purchaser and of the corporation's cash distributed to the shareholders in the form of a dividend prior to closing, where the shareholders did not give reasonably equivalent value and the transaction fatally depleted the corporation's assets. The transaction at bar differs from a traditional LBO, in which the acquired corporation's stock is purchased from the shareholders. Here, and in a traditional LBO, the purchase is made with the proceeds of a loan secured by the corporation's own assets. If the acquired company goes broke after and because of the LBO, i.e., if the burden of debt created by the transaction was so heavy that the corporation had no reasonable prospect of surviving, the payment to the shareholders by the buyer of the corporation is deemed a fraudulent conveyance because in exchange for the money the shareholders received, they provided no value to the corporation but merely increased its debt and by doing so pushed it into insolvency. Under UFTA, there is not a requirement of fraudulent intent for there to be a fraudulent conveyance. A corporate transfer is thus "fraudulent" within the meaning of UFTA if the corporation did not receive "reasonably equivalent value" in return for the transfer and as a result was left with insufficient assets to have a reasonable chance of surviving indefinitely. Some LBOs can create value and are legitimate, and some LBOs are fraudulent conveyances. Here, the LBO was a fraudulent conveyance because it was highly likely to plunge the company into bankruptcy, given that it left the firm with so few assets. Whether it is called an LBO or not is not determinate. Rather, it is the economic substance of the transaction that is controlling. Thus, if the dividend was part and parcel of the transaction that fatally depleted New Crown's assets, it was part and parcel of a fraudulent conveyance. In any event, the overarching transaction can be called an LBO, notwithstanding its differences from a classic LBO. An LBO can take the form of an asset acquisition, where, as here, the substance of the sale is a change in ownership. Also, with a traditional LBO that acts as a fraudulent conveyance, the new entity does not survive for any length of time. Here, however, New Crown survived for over three years. Such length of staving off bankruptcy does not indicate the transaction was not a fraudulent conveyance LBO. A firm might be insolvent in the bankruptcy sense of negative net worth, where its liabilities exceeded its assets, yet it might continue operating as long as it is able to raise enough money to pay its debts as they became due, or even longer if its creditors are forbearing. By encumbering all the company's assets, the sale reduced its ability to borrow on favorable terms, as it could offer no collateral to lenders. By surrendering most of Old Crown's (D) cash (the cash that was paid as a dividend) and obligating itself to pay $100,000 a year under the note and $495,000 a year to service the $3.1 million bank loan, without receiving anything in return except Smith's $500, New Crown was forced to engage in continual borrowing during its remaining life, and on unfavorable terms. New Crown did not receive "reasonably equivalent value" in return for its payments and obligation, and, even if it was not actually insolvent from inception, as a result of the lack of equivalence it began life with "unreasonably small" assets, and bankruptcy was a consequence both likely and foreseeable. Regardless of whether subsequent events hastened New Crown's demise, whether a transfer was fraudulent when made depends on conditions that existed when it was made, not on what happened later to affect the timing of the company's collapse. The length of time between an LBO and a company's bankruptcy filing is relevant evidence, and the longer the interval, the less likely that the collapse was fated at the formation of the new company. Here, that interval was longer than in other cases, but there is no scenario under which New Crown could have survived indefinitely despite being cash starved as a result of the terms of the LBO that brought it into being. Notwithstanding mistakes that Smith may have made in running the company, every business makes mistakes, which is precisely why businesses need adequate capital to have a good chance of surviving. As for the "dividend," it was an integral part of the LBO. It was unreasonably high, given the company's cash needs, and drained it of its cash—all unbeknownst to the corporation's unsecured creditors. This indicates that the dividend was part of a fraudulent transfer rather than a normal distribution of previously earned profits; it was not an ordinary dividend but rather the withdrawal of an asset vital to the acquiring firm. These indications were sufficient to place a burden on the Old Crown shareholders (D) of producing evidence that it was a bona fide dividend, a burden they failed to carry. In sum, the transaction was a fraudulent conveyance. As to recovery, Bankruptcy Code § 550(b)(2) denies recovery of property that was transferred to "any immediate or mediate good faith transferee" of the initial transferee of a fraudulent transfer if the subsequent transferee took for value and "in good faith and without knowledge of the voidability of the transfer avoided." If the asset sale is recharacterized as a sale of Old Crown (D) by its shareholders (D) through an LBO, the shareholders (D) lose the protection of § 550(b) because they then are initial rather than subsequent transferees and the "dividend" becomes an adjustment in the purchase price. Even if the transaction is not collapsed, the shareholders (D) would not be protected by § 550(b) because the initial transferee of the $3.3 million was Old

Continued on next page.

Crown (D) and the second-stage transferees were the shareholders (D), but they gave no "value" in the transfer. The shareholders received their distributions of the transaction consideration merely by virtue of being shareholders of Old Crown (D), not because they gave anything of value for it. For these reasons, the Trustee (P) is entitled to the judgment awarded by the bankruptcy judge, plus the $590,328 dividend. The judgment of the district court is therefore affirmed in part and reversed in part (the part relating to the dividend), and the case remanded for further proceedings consistent with this opinion. Affirmed in part, reversed in part, and remanded.

ANALYSIS

Some courts have been reluctant to apply Uniform Fraudulent Transfer Act (UFTA) as written to leverage buyouts (LBOs), and sympathize with minority shareholders who have no power to prevent such deals. Some courts are also persuaded that LBOs are welfare-enhancing transactions because by making the managers owners (managers are often the buyers in an LBO) and thus fusing ownership with control, an LBO increases the managers' incentive to operate the corporation with a view to maximizing its value rather than their salaries and perks and may increase the mobility of capital. Judge Posner, however, explained that such beneficial effects usually occur in LBOs involving publicly held companies, where there is a separation of ownership from control, and the managers may use their control to manage the company in a way that will increase their personal wealth rather than maximize the profits of the corporation; the conflict of interest is eliminated by making the managers the owners. However, this rationale for an LBO was missing from this case because both Old Crown (D) and New Crown were closely held corporations.

Quicknotes

FRAUDULENT CONVEYANCE Conveyances made with intent to defraud creditors; may be voidable.

LEVERAGED BUY OUT A transaction whereby corporate outsiders purchase the outstanding shares of a publicly held corporation mostly with borrowed funds.

CHAPTER 25

Executory Contracts I

Quick Reference Rules of Law

In re Jamesway Corp.

Debtor (P) v. Landlord (D)

201 B.R. 73 (Bankr. S.D.N.Y. 1996)

NATURE OF CASE: Motion requesting an order declaring lease provisions unenforceable.

FACT SUMMARY: Jamesway (P), a debtor in bankruptcy, claimed that certain lease provisions limited his ability to realize the full economic value of the leases, and asked the court to find them void and unenforceable.

RULE OF LAW

Provisions restricting, conditioning, or prohibiting a debtor's right to assign a subject lease are invalid.

FACTS: Jamesway (P) operated a business in a mall and filed for relief under Chapter 11 of the Bankruptcy Code. Jamesway (P) alleged that lease provisions conditioning his right to assignment upon the payment of a portion of the profit limited his ability to realize the intrinsic value of the lease. Jamesway (P) requested an order declaring the profit sharing provisions of the leases unenforceable and asked the court for permission to assume and assign a lease over the landlord's (D) objection.

ISSUE: Are provisions restricting, conditioning, or prohibiting a debtor's right to assign a subject lease invalid?

HOLDING AND DECISION: (Garrity, J.) Yes. Provisions restricting, conditioning, or prohibiting a debtor's right to assign a subject lease are invalid. The statute must be read in light of the congressional policy favoring the assumption and assignment of unexpired leases as a means of assisting the debtor in its reorganization or liquidation efforts. Motion granted.

ANALYSIS

The Landlord's (D) proposed reading of the statute was held to be very narrow. The Landlord (D) claimed that the court did not have the power to nullify the lease provisions. The court ruled that all provisions of a contract were subject to court scrutiny regarding their anti-assignment effect.

Quicknotes

ASSIGNMENT A transaction in which a party conveys his or her entire interest in property to another.

ASSUMPTION Laying claim to or taking possession of.

CHAPTER 11 BANKRUPTCY A legal proceeding whereby a debtor, who is unable to pay his or her debts as they become due, is relieved of the obligation to pay creditors through reorganization and payment from future income.

LEASE An agreement or contract that creates a relationship between a landlord and tenant (real property) or lessor and lessee (real or personal property).

In re TSB, Inc.

[Parties not identified.]

302 B.R. 84 (Bankr. D. Idaho 2003)

NATURE OF CASE: Application for allowance of administrative expenses for rent during Chapter 11 and subsequent conversion to Chapter 7.

FACT SUMMARY: After TSB, Inc.'s (Debtor's) Chapter 11 bankruptcy was converted to a Chapter 7 bankruptcy, Knapp-Block 44, LLC (Lessor), the landlord of space leased by Debtor, applied for rent Lessor alleged accrued during both the Chapter 11 and Chapter 7 periods, including rent for a fraction of the space used post-rejection by the Chapter 7 trustee (Trustee) to store personal property the parties anticipated would be purchased by a third party that planned to acquire the lease.

RULE OF LAW

(1) Under Bankruptcy Code § 365(d)(3), a lessor of property leased to the debtor is entitled to the full amount owing under the lease during the first 60 days of a Chapter 11 case that is converted to a Chapter 7 case during that period.

(2) Under Bankruptcy Code § 365, a lessor of property leased to a debtor in a case that has been converted to a Chapter 7 case is entitled to the full amount owing under the lease for the time-period the Chapter 7 trustee is in possession of the property prior to rejection.

(3) Where a Chapter 7 trustee stores personal property during the post-rejection period on a fraction of real property previously leased by the debtor, the lessor's administrative expense for such use may be calculated under Bankruptcy Code § 503 by multiplying the base rental amount by the fraction of space used and multiplying the result by the time the property was stored.

FACTS: TSB, Inc. (Debtor), which ran a restaurant, filed for Chapter 11 bankruptcy protection on April 9, 2003. The bankruptcy was converted to a Chapter 7 bankruptcy on June 2, 2003. Prior to filing for bankruptcy, Debtor had leased space from Knapp-Block 44, LLC (Lessor) for $3,430.50 per month, and, during the Chapter 11 period, Debtor paid Lessor $6,100. On the conversion date, the Chapter 7 trustee (Trustee) took possession of the leased space. Around a week later, Lessor informed Trustee that it would be renting the space to City Grill. The Trustee removed some of the personal property of the estate located on the premises. He left the tables, chairs, and bar equipment on site (which remained there until September 19, 2003). The space occupied by the property was approximately 10 percent of the entire space. It was understood by the Trustee and the Lessor that City Grill would seek to purchase that personal property from the estate and would enter a lease with the Lessor. On June 16, 2003, Lessor surrendered the space, and City Grill commenced remodeling it. The Trustee did not assume the lease within 60 days of Debtor's filing its Chapter 11 bankruptcy. Lessor subsequently filed an application for an allowance of administrative expenses during the Chapter 11 and Chapter 7 periods.

ISSUE:

(1) Under Bankruptcy Code § 365(d)(3), is a lessor of property leased to the debtor entitled to the full amount owing under the lease during the first 60 days of a Chapter 11 case that is converted to a Chapter 7 case during that period?

(2) Under Bankruptcy Code § 365, is a lessor of property leased to a debtor in a case that has been converted to a Chapter 7 case entitled to the full amount owing under the lease for the time-period the Chapter 7 trustee is in possession of the property prior to rejection?

(3) Where a Chapter 7 trustee stores personal property during the post-rejection period on a fraction of real property previously leased by the debtor, may the lessor's administrative expense for such use be calculated under Bankruptcy Code § 503 by multiplying the base rental amount by the fraction of space used, and multiplying the result by the time the property was stored?

HOLDING AND DECISION: (Myers, J.)

(1) Yes. Under Bankruptcy Code § 365(d)(3), a lessor of property leased to the debtor is entitled to the full amount owing under the lease during the first 60 days of a Chapter 11 case that is converted to a Chapter 7 case during that period. Under Bankruptcy Code § 365(d)(3), Debtor was required to timely perform under the terms of its lease with the Lessor during the first 60 days of the Chapter 11 case, and Lessor was entitled to the full amount of rent for that period, including post-conversion. Here, the Chapter 11 case was converted after 54 days. Thus, two months of rent, or $6,861 was owed to Lessor. Because Debtor paid Lessor $6,100, the Lessor is entitled to the difference, i.e., $761, as an administrative expense.

(2) Yes. Under Bankruptcy Code § 365, a lessor of property leased to a debtor in a case that has been converted to a Chapter 7 case is entitled to the full amount owing under the lease for the time-period the Chapter 7 trustee is in possession of the property prior to rejection.

Continued on next page.

Under § 365(d)(4), a lease of nonresidential real property must be assumed within 60 days of the date of the order for relief or it will be deemed rejected. When Debtor's case was converted to Chapter 7, only 7 days of this period remained, since under § 348 conversion does not alter the order-of-relief date. Because the Trustee did not assume the lease, it was deemed rejected by operation of law on June 9, 2003. Under § 365(d)(3), Debtor was liable for the full rent for the pre-rejection period occupied by the Trustee post-conversion, i.e., one week. Thus, Lessor is entitled to an administrative expense for this period of the rent amount ($3,430.50 per month) for a quarter of the month (one week). This comes to $857.63.

(3) Yes. Where a Chapter 7 trustee stores personal property during the post-rejection period on a fraction of real property previously leased by the debtor, the lessor's administrative expense for such use may be calculated under Bankruptcy Code § 503 by multiplying the base rental amount by the fraction of space used and multiplying the result by the time the property was stored. As for the post-rejection period, the Trustee surrendered the space seven days after rejection, and stored property there for around 3 and 1/3 months. Although the Trustee did not "immediately surrender" the premises upon rejection as required by § 365(d)(4), other than storing the personal property there, the Trustee in no way interfered with the Lessor's total control over the premises. Thus, no administrative expense is owed under § 365 for this period. However, an administrative expense did accrue for this period under § 503(b)(1)(A) for the benefit conferred on the Debtor's estate for use of the real property during this time. The claim for this benefit can be characterized as a "use claim," since the estate received a tangible benefit for its use of the real property. Although the monthly rental amount may in some instances be used to calculate the amount of a use claim, the rental amount may not be used where doing so would be unreasonable. Here, it would be unreasonable to use the monthly base rent amount to measure the benefit conferred for the limited use of a portion of the premises for storage. Because the Lessor had almost absolute and uninterrupted enjoyment of, and control over, the space, and because the storage of the personal property on the premises did not interfere with Lessor or City Grill—which had complete access for remodeling—treating the situation as a "continued lease" of the entire premises at the pre-bankruptcy commercial rate would give Lessor a windfall and would be detrimental to the Debtor's estate. Under such circumstances, the amount of administrative expenses can be determined by determining either the benefit conferred by use of the premises or the reasonable worth of the premises used. Here, it would have cost $75 per month to store the personal property. Because the Trustee did not choose storage as an option, the worth of the premises used method may be applied. Under that method, the amount of total space used was 10 percent of the leased premises. Applying that to the base monthly rate yields $343.05 per month. Multiplying this by the period uses—3 and 1/3 months—results in approximately $1,145.00, which is the administrative expense allowed for this post-rejection period use. Lessor's application is granted to this extent plus the amounts granted for the pre-rejection period.

ANALYSIS

Segregating the claims between the time frames of Chapter 11 and Chapter 7, as the court did in this case, is important in converted Chapter 11 cases because § 726(b) gives higher priority in distribution to the Chapter 7 administrative expenses than to similar expenses incurred in the superseded Chapter 11 case.

Quicknotes

CHAPTER 7 BANKRUPTCY A legal proceeding whereby a debtor, who is unable to pay his or her debts as they become due, is relieved of the obligation to pay creditors by liquidation and distribution of remaining assets.

CHAPTER 11 BANKRUPTCY A legal proceeding whereby a debtor, who is unable to pay his or her debts as they become due, is relieved of the obligation to pay creditors through reorganization and payment from future income.

In re Taylor Investment Partners II, LLC

Franchisor (P) v. Debtor corporation (D)

553 B.R. 837 (Bankr N.D. Ga. 2015)

NATURE OF CASE: Hearing on Motion for Relief from Stay.

FACT SUMMARY: Debtor Taylor Investment Partners II (D) operated two franchises of Moe's Southwestern Grill, and one of the locations was placed into default after it failed to pass the Franchisor's (P) standards evaluations. Debtor (D) subsequently filed for Chapter 11 bankruptcy.

RULE OF LAW

11 U.S.C. § 365(c)'s restriction on a bankruptcy trustee's power to assume an executory contract applies to debtors in possession.

FACTS: Taylor Investment Partners II-Ansley, LLC and Taylor Investment Partners II-Suburban, LLC operate Moe's Southwestern Grill franchises in Atlanta and Decatur, Georgia, and pay common expenses to Taylor Investment Partners II (Debtor/Debtors) (D), which is also the franchisee of record. Franchisor Moe's (P) was entitled to terminate the franchise agreement in the event of Debtor's (D) repeated failure to meet certain franchise standards. Franchisor (P) alleged that Debtor (D) failed consecutive Restaurant Operations and Standards Evaluations (ROSE) and was placed in default. Debtor (D) failed a follow-up inspection before arbitration and a final inspection after arbitration. Accordingly, Franchisor (P) sent a termination notice regarding the Decatur franchise agreement and gave Debtor (D) six months to sell or vacate. Shortly before the termination deadline, Debtor (D) filed a Chapter 11 petition. Franchisor (P) filed a Motion for Relief from Stay, arguing that under 11 U.S.C. § 365(c), Debtors (D) may not assume the franchise agreements without Franchisor's (P) consent.

ISSUE: Does 11 U.S.C. § 365(c)'s restriction on a bankruptcy trustee's power to assume an executory contract apply to debtors in possession?

HOLDING AND DECISION: (Murphy, J.) Yes. 11 U.S.C. § 365(c)'s restriction on a trustee's power to assume an executory contract applies to debtors in possession. Section 365(c) restricts a trustee's power to assume an executory contract if, under applicable law, the other party to the contract would be excused from rendering performance to an entity other than the debtor. Franchisor (P) argues that because the applicable trademark law prevents Debtors (D) from assigning the franchise agreement without Franchisor's (P) consent, a trustee cannot assume the franchise agreement. Franchisor (P) also argues that because Debtors (D) are debtors-in-possession, they are subject to the same limitations of § 365(c) as a trustee and cannot assume the franchise agreement. There is a circuit court split regarding whether the restriction of § 365(c) applies to debtors-in-possession. The Third, Fourth, and Ninth Circuit Courts of Appeals agree with Franchisor's (P) interpretation, while the First Circuit Court of Appeals, in *Summit Inv. & Development Corp. v. Leroux*, 69 F.3d 608 (1st Cir. 1995), determined that § 365 (c) was not meant to apply unless the executory contract would *actually* be assumed, rather than hypothetically assumed. Franchisor (P) also points to the Eleventh Circuit Court of Appeals' ruling in *In re James Cable Partners, L.P.*, 27 F.3d 534 (11th Cir. 1994), which unequivocally holds that a debtor-in-possession is restricted by § 365(c). Because (1) Franchisor (P) would be excused under the Lanham Act from accepting performance from a party other than the Debtor (D) and (2) Franchisor (P) does not consent to Debtors' (D) assumption of the executory contract, Debtors (D) are barred from assuming the franchise agreement. Motion granted.

ANALYSIS

In *In re James Cable*, 27 F.3d 534 (11th Cir. 1994), James Cable Partners held a cable franchise agreement with the city of Jamestown, Tennessee, and filed a Chapter 11 petition. Under its Plan of Reorganization, James Cable Partners planned to assume the cable franchise, but Jamestown objected to the assumption. The Eleventh Circuit Court of Appeals acknowledged the circuit split regarding the "hypothetical" and "actual" tests but looked to the plain language of 11 U.S.C. § 365(c)(1). Under the plain language, because applicable law did not prohibit Jamestown from accepting performance from another entity as the Lanham Act did in *In re Taylor Investment Partners II, LLC*, § 365(c) did not bar James Cable from assuming the agreement.

Quicknotes

DEBTOR-IN-POSSESSION A Chapter 11 bankruptcy debtor who retains control of assets or property pursuant to a plan of reorganization.

FRANCHISE An agreement whereby one party (the franchisor) grants another (the franchisee) the right to market its product or service.

FRANCHISE AGREEMENT A contract pursuant to which a supplier of goods or services agrees to permit a re-seller

Continued on next page.

to sell the good or service or to otherwise conduct business on behalf of the franchise.

FRANCHISEE A party, whom a supplier of goods or services agrees to permit to sell the good or service or to otherwise conduct business on behalf of the franchise.

FRANCHISOR A supplier of goods or services, who agrees to permit a re-seller to sell the good or service or to otherwise conduct business on behalf of the franchise.

CHAPTER **26**

Executory Contracts II

Quick Reference Rules of Law

In re Riodizio, Inc.

Debtor (P) v. Creditor (D)

204 B.R. 417 (Bankr. S.D.N.Y. 1997)

NATURE OF CASE: Debtor's motion to reject stock option agreement.

FACT SUMMARY: When a Debtor (P) sought to reject a stock option agreement, the Creditor (D) claimed the contract was not executory.

RULE OF LAW

A contract is executory if each side must render performance, on account of an existing legal duty or to fulfill a condition, to obtain the benefit of the counterparty's performance.

FACTS: Riodizio (P) owned and operated a restaurant and had borrowed money from Riodizio Company, LLC (LLC) (D) in exchange for a stock option contract. When Riodizio (P) filed for Chapter 11 bankruptcy and sought to reject the agreement, LLC (D) claimed that the stock option contract was not executory and therefore could not be rejected by the trustee.

ISSUE: Is a contract executory if each side must render performance, on account of an existing legal duty or to fulfill a condition, to obtain the benefit of the counterparty's performance?

HOLDING AND DECISION: (Bernstein, J.) Yes. A contract is executory if each side must render performance, on account of an existing legal duty or to fulfill a condition, to obtain the benefit of the counterparty's performance. Here the contract is executory, and the court must decide whether its rejection will benefit the estate. Since the Debtor's (P) management has an interest in preventing the exercise of the option by LLC (D), the court will not defer to the business judgment of the debtor's management. Breaching the contract through rejection produces a minimal, adverse effect on the estate. Motion granted.

ANALYSIS

For a bankruptcy trustee to accept or reject a contract, the contract must be executory. Most courts apply the material breach test to determine whether a contract is executory. If both parties have material obligations to perform at the time of filing, the contract is executory.

Quicknotes

CHAPTER 11 BANKRUPTCY A legal proceeding whereby a debtor, who is unable to pay his or her debts as they become due, is relieved of the obligation to pay creditors through reorganization and payment from future income.

CONTRACT An agreement pursuant to which a party agrees to act, or to forbear from acting, in exchange for performance on the part of the other party.

EXECUTORY Something that has not been fully completed or performed.

OPTION CONTRACT A contract pursuant to which a seller agrees that property will be available for the buyer to purchase at a specified price and within a certain time period.

TRUSTEE A person who is entrusted to keep or administer something.

Sunbeam Products, Inc. v. Chicago American Mfg., LLC

Asset purchaser (P) v. Manufacturer (D)

686 F.3d 372 (7th Cir. 2012)

NATURE OF CASE: Appeal from decision in adversary action filed in involuntary bankruptcy case.

FACT SUMMARY: Chicago American Mfg., LLC (CAM) (D) manufactured box fans using Lakewood Engineering & Manufacturing Co.'s (Lakewood's) patents and trademarks as provided by contract. When Lakewood was forced into involuntary bankruptcy, Sunbeam Products, Inc., dba Jarden Consumer Solutions (Jarden) (P), bought the assets, including the patents and trademarks. Jarden (P) did not want CAM (D) to continue the manufacture or sale of box fans, so the trustee rejected the executory portion of the contract. CAM (D) wanted to continue using Lakewood's intellectual property.

RULE OF LAW

Bankruptcy trustee's rejection of a contract pursuant to 11 U.S.C. § 365(a) does not avoid contractual obligations to intellectual property licensees.

FACTS: Lakewood manufactured box fans covered by its patents and trademarks. Lakewood, losing money, contracted its manufacturing to Chicago American Mfg., LLC (CAM) (D), which would practice Lakewood's patents and put Lakewood's trademarks on each box fan. Lakewood would take orders from retailers, buy the fans from CAM (D), and CAM (D) would ship to the retailers. Given Lakewood's financial difficulties, CAM (D) and Lakewood contracted for CAM (D) directly to sell the 2009 line of box fans if Lakewood did not pay for the manufactured fans. A few months into the contract, Lakewood creditors filed a petition for involuntary bankruptcy, a trustee was appointed, and the trustee decided to sell the business. Jarden (P) did not want the manufactured Lakewood fans or for CAM (D) to sell those fans in competition with Jarden's (P) fans. The Lakewood trustee rejected the executory portion of the contract pursuant to 11 U.S.C. § 365 (a). CAM (D) continued to manufacture and sell Lakewood fans, so Jarden (P) filed the adversary action. The trial judge determined the CAM contract was ambiguous, relied on extrinsic evidence, and found CAM (D) was entitled to make sufficient fans for the 2009 season and sell them bearing Lakewood trademarks. Jarden (P) appealed.

ISSUE: Does the bankruptcy trustee's rejection of a contract pursuant to 11 U.S.C. § 365(a) void contractual obligations to intellectual property licensees?

HOLDING AND DECISION: (Easterbrook, J.) No. Bankruptcy trustee's rejection of a contract pursuant to 11 U.S.C. § 365(a) does not avoid contractual obligations to intellectual property licensees. *Lubrizol Enterprises, Inc. v. Richmond Metal Finishers, Inc.*, 756 F.2d 1043 (4th Cir. 1985) held that an intellectual property licensee loses the ability to use the licensed property when the license is rejected in bankruptcy. Three years after *Lubrizol*, Congress added § 365(n) to the Bankruptcy Code, which now allowed licensees to continue using the intellectual property under certain conditions after rejection. 11 U.S.C. § 101(35A) defines "intellectual property" to include patents, copyrights, and trade secrets, but it is silent as to trademarks. The trial judge did not address the effect of the contract's rejection on the Lakewood trademarks, but permitted the continued use on "equitable grounds." The Bankruptcy Code cannot be overturned on grounds of equity. The trial judge's basis for the decision is untenable, but that may not demand reversal. The issue is whether *Lubrizol* correctly understood the consequences of contract rejection. The issue has not arisen in any other court of appeals. Section 365(g) states rejection is a breach of the contract. Outside of bankruptcy, Lakewood could not terminate the license by failing to perform its obligations. *Lubrizol* confuses rejection with avoidance and is not persuasive. Rejection is not the same as a bankruptcy trustee's avoiding power, such as the ability to avoid payments exceeding the value of goods. Here, the trustee did not employ an avoiding power and cannot use § 365(a) as a method of rescission. The contract rejection did not abrogate CAM's (D) contractual rights to continue manufacturing box fans and affixing Lakewood marks. Affirmed.

ANALYSIS

A non-executory contract cannot be rejected, and, therefore, the debtor may be forced to perform. This has led many courts to focus on whether the contract at issue is executory or non-executory in attempt to provide equity to the debtor (permitting rejection) or the other contracting party (forced performance of the debtor). The Bankruptcy Code's silence on issues such as trademarks adds to the confusion. A bankruptcy trustee is left to determine the appropriate assertion of an avoidance power versus rejection when a property right is at issue.

Quicknotes

EXTRINSIC EVIDENCE Evidence that is not contained within the text of a document or contract, but which is

Continued on next page.

derived from the parties' statements or the circumstances under which the agreement was made.

INTELLECTUAL PROPERTY A body of law pertaining to the ownership of rights in intangible products of the human intellect.

In re Ortiz

Debtor boxer (P) v. Claimant promoter (D)

400 B.R. 755 (C.D. Cal. 2009)

NATURE OF CASE: Appeal from adversary action in Chapter 7 bankruptcy.

FACT SUMMARY: Ortiz (P) filed Chapter 7 bankruptcy and the trustee rejected the contract between Ortiz (P) and his promoter, Top Rock (D). Ortiz (P) wanted his obligations, including an exclusivity provision, terminated and Top Rock (D) wanted to enforce Ortiz's (P) obligations through injunctive relief.

RULE OF LAW

Rejection of a contract does not terminate the non-debtor's rights under the contract, but the court must determine whether a right to an equitable remedy is a "claim" that survives bankruptcy or is dischargeable.

FACTS: Ortiz (P), a professional boxer, contracted with Top Rank (D), a boxing promoter, in a five-year promotional agreement in which Ortiz (P) would fight in a minimum number of bouts promoted by Top Rank (D) and Top Rank would pay a minimum purse per bout. Further, Ortiz (P) would not fight in any televised bout promoted by another promoter for 90 days prior to or after a televised fight promoted by Top Rank (D). Three years into the contract, Ortiz (P) filed a voluntary Chapter 7 bankruptcy petition and the bankruptcy trustee did not assume the Top Rank (D) contract within 60 days. Ortiz (P) filed an adversary action against Top Rock (D) seeking declaratory and injunctive relief with attorneys' fees and costs. Ortiz (P) asked the court to declare his obligations pursuant to the contract terminated because the agreement was rejected. He also sought to enjoin Top Rock (D) from interfering with his negotiations with third-party promoters. The bankruptcy court found in Ortiz's (P) favor, holding the trustee's rejection of the contract terminated Ortiz's obligations and limited Top Rock's (D) rights to seeking monetary damages against the bankruptcy estate. The court also found the exclusivity provision in the contract was unenforceable in Nevada law as an unreasonable non-competition agreement. [Top Rank (D) appealed].

ISSUE: Does rejection of a contract terminate the non-debtor's rights under the contract, including a right to equitable relief?

HOLDING AND DECISION: (Morrow, J.) No. Rejection of a contract does not terminate the non-debtor's rights under the contract, but the court must determine whether a right to an equitable remedy is a "claim" that survives bankruptcy or is dischargeable. The bankruptcy court decision was error. The parties agree the trustee rejected the executory contract at issue but disagree about the consequences of that rejection. Top Rank (D) argues the rejection is a prepetition breach of the contract and does not affect the parties' rights and obligations to the contract. It claims it can seek monetary damages against the estate and request injunctive relief enforcing the exclusivity provision. Ortiz (P) and the bankruptcy court determined the rejection terminated Top Rock's (D) rights to equitable relief. The court must look elsewhere other than § 365 to determine whether non-monetary relief arising from an executory contract can be asserted against the debtor post-bankruptcy. The issue is whether the equitable remedy sought constitutes a "claim" that is dischargeable in bankruptcy. In pertinent part, the Bankruptcy Act defines "claim" as a right to an equitable remedy for breach of performance if the breach gives rise to a right to payment. 11 U.S.C. § 101(5)(B). An injunction gives rise to a right to payment, and therefore discharged, if monetary damages are an alternative relief. The bankruptcy court must look to the availability of equitable relief under state law. [If the exclusivity provision is permitted under Nevada law, the bankruptcy court would have to determine if damages were an alternative remedy thus making Top Rock's (D) requested relief a "claim" and dischargeable.] Reversed and remanded.

ANALYSIS

Section 365 does confer power to debtors to terminate contract obligations, but other provisions in the Bankruptcy Code limit the debtor's power to terminate the non-debtor's rights to relief. The federal bankruptcy court must consider the relevant state law statutes to determine the availability of a claim that survives the bankruptcy petition filing.

Quicknotes

EQUITABLE REMEDY A remedy that is based upon principles of fairness as opposed to rules of law; a remedy involving specific performance rather than money damages.

EXECUTORY CONTRACT A contract in which performance of an obligation has yet to be rendered.

CHAPTER 27

Negotiating the Plan

Quick Reference Rules of Law

In re Puff

[Parties not identified.]

2011 WL 2604759 (Bankr. N.D. Iowa, 2011)

NATURE OF CASE: Objections to Debtor's Third Amended Disclosure Statement in Chapter 11 bankruptcy case.

FACT SUMMARY: Two creditors object to Debtor's proposed Disclosure Statement as providing inaccurate and insufficient information to permit the claim holders to make an informed decision to accept or reject the proposed plan.

RULE OF LAW

The Disclosure Statement must provide enough information that a reasonable claim holder can make an informed decision to accept or reject the proposed plan, but it does not need to resolve all issues of feasibility at the disclosure stage.

FACTS: Wells Fargo Financial Leasing (WFFL) and Farmers Savings Bank (FSB) were Debtor's secured creditors objecting to Debtor's Third Amended Disclosure Statement. WFFL and FSB objected on the basis that Debtor significantly undervalued real property on which WFFL and FSB would hold security interests. That would result in the secured debt, which is paid at nearly full rate, being much lower than unsecured debt, which would be paid at one cent on the dollar. They also argued WFFL had "true leases" while Debtor claimed they were secured claims. If the obligations are true leases, then the proposed plan is not feasible. The court held an evidentiary hearing and took the matter under advisement. In posthearing briefs, WFFL and FSB included a new argument that the objections should be disclosed so the unsecured creditors would have sufficient information to vote on accepting or rejecting the plan. They also asked the court to find their valuations of the real property accurate.

ISSUE: Must the Disclosure Statement resolve all issues of feasibility at the disclosure stage?

HOLDING AND DECISION: (Collins, J.) No. The Disclosure Statement must provide enough information that a reasonable claim holder can make an informed decision to accept or reject the proposed plan, but it does not need to resolve all issues of feasibility at the disclosure stage. Section 1125(b) of the Bankruptcy Code provides the requirements for and adequacy of disclosure statements. The statements must contain "adequate information," which is further defined to permit a hypothetical reasonable investor typical of a claim holder to make an informed judgment about the plan. A "hypothetical reasonable investor" is expected to have the ability to obtain information from sources other than the disclosure. Case law has developed a list of 19 factors that meet the statutory requirement of disclosure of adequate information. Not all factors are necessary for each case. The disclosure hearing should not become the confirmation hearing; internal inconsistencies in the disclosure statement could inform the claim holders to vote no to the plan. It is clear from the arguments that WFFL and FSB have information from sources other than the disclosure. The additional information sought in the form of objections to the plan will not aid them in voting to accept or reject the plan. They argue the plan is not feasible, but this stage of the case is not appropriate to make that determination. The other interested parties have not sought additional information, but WFFL and FSB argue the competing valuations and the dispute over true leases versus secured interests would be useful in helping the general unsecured creditors make a decision on the plan. It is appropriate for Debtor to disclose the competing specific values on each parcel of property and disclose Debtor intends to treat the obligations as secured claims rather than true leases. The Disclosure Statement also should state if WFFL claims are "true leases," then that will affect the feasibility and ultimate payout. The Disclosure Statement is approved except as specifically set forth here.

ANALYSIS

The Disclosure Statement is the first move in projecting a reorganization and payment plan for a debtor's secured and unsecured creditors. Overvaluing assets and income could lead to an easy acceptance of the plan but ultimate disappointment when the plan fails. Undervaluing assets and income could encourage a creditor to settle for far less than a claim's value. A comprehensive Disclosure Statement provides debtor information that creditors should add to their own information and research to make independent calculations about true values.

Quicknotes

LEASE An agreement or contract that creates a relationship between a landlord and tenant (real property) or lessor and lessee (real or personal property).

SECURED CLAIM A claim, the repayment of which is secured by collateral sufficient to repay the debt owed.

In re Ultra Petroleum Corporation

Creditors (P) v. Debtor (D)

943 F.3d 758 (5th Cir. 2019)

NATURE OF CASE: Petition for rehearing regarding bankruptcy plan.

FACT SUMMARY: Debtor Ultra Petroleum Corporation (D) filed for Chapter 11 bankruptcy after the price of oil plummeted. Over the course of the bankruptcy proceedings, however, the price of oil rose and Debtor (D) became solvent again. Creditors who had claims under a Note Agreement and a Revolving Credit Facility (P), which had been issued prior to bankruptcy, argued that they were entitled to (1) the outstanding principal, prepetition interest, and postpetition interest that they were entitled to under the Bankruptcy Code and (2) additional postpetition interest that was disallowed under the Bankruptcy Code.

RULE OF LAW

When a company that filed for Chapter 11 bankruptcy later becomes solvent, its creditors are not impaired by a reorganization plan that paid them everything they were allowed under the Bankruptcy Code but did not include unmatured interest that is disallowed by the Bankruptcy Code.

FACTS: Debtor Ultra Petroleum Corporation (Petroleum) (D) is an oil and gas holding company with oil exploration and production subsidiaries. One of its subsidiaries, Ultra Resources (Resources), issued $1.46 billion of unsecured notes between 2008 and 2010, and borrowed another $999 million under a Revolving Credit Facility to finance its operations. Petroleum (D) and another subsidiary, UP Energy Corporation (Energy), guaranteed both debt obligations. In 2014, crude oil cost over $100 a barrel, but a year and a half later, a barrel cost less than $30. Petroleum (D) and its subsidiaries accumulated substantial debt and filed for Chapter 11 bankruptcy in April of 2016. Over the course of the bankruptcy proceedings, oil prices rose again, to close to $80 per barrel, which made Petroleum (D) and its subsidiaries solvent again. Accordingly, Petroleum (D) proposed a reorganization plan that was designed to compensate its creditors in full. Under the reorganization plan, creditors with claims under the Note Agreement and Revolving Credit Facility (Class 4 Creditors) (P) would be paid the outstanding principal on their obligations, prepetition interest, and postpetition interest. Under 11 U.S.C. § 1126(f), the Class 4 Creditors (P) were unimpaired and thus could not object to the plan. Nevertheless, the Class 4 Creditors (P) did object, arguing that their claims *were* impaired and that they were entitled to additional postpetition interest at contractual default rates and an additional $186 million in postpetition interest. Both parties agreed that the bankruptcy court could resolve the dispute by deeming the Class 4 Creditors (P) unimpaired and requiring Petroleum (D) to set aside $400 million to compensate the Class 4 Creditors (P) if necessary. The bankruptcy court agreed and confirmed the plan.

ISSUE: When a company that filed for Chapter 11 bankruptcy later becomes solvent, are its creditors impaired by a reorganization plan that paid them everything they were allowed under the Bankruptcy Code but did not include unmatured interest that is disallowed by the Bankruptcy Code?

HOLDING AND DECISION: (Oldham, J.) No. When a company that filed for Chapter 11 bankruptcy later becomes solvent, its creditors are not impaired by a reorganization plan that paid them everything they were allowed under the Bankruptcy Code but did not include unmatured interest that is disallowed by the Bankruptcy Code. Section 1124(1) of the Bankruptcy Code provides that a class of claims is not impaired if the reorganization plan "leaves unaltered the legal, equitable, and contractual rights to which such claim" entitles the holder. Section 502(b)(2) of the Bankruptcy Code also states that the court should disallow a claim that seeks unmatured interest. Debtors (D) argue that creditors are entitled to postpetition interest at the "legal rate," which is the federal judgment rate under 28 U.S.C. § 1961, instead of the rates set by the contract. The bankruptcy court determined that if a plan does not provide a creditor with everything it would receive under state law, then it remains impaired even if the Code disallows something provided by state law outside of bankruptcy. In order to be impaired by a plan, a creditor's legal, equitable, or contractual rights must have been altered by it. Incorporation of the Bankruptcy Code's disallowance provisions is insufficient to deem a creditor impaired. Accordingly, the Class 4 Creditors (P) are not impaired. Reversed in part, vacated in part, and remanded for further proceedings.

ANALYSIS

The Fifth Circuit Court of Appeals issued a previous ruling regarding Ultra Petroleum in January of 2019, in the case *Ultra Petroleum Corp v. Ad Hoc Committee of Unsecured Creditors*, 2019 WL 237365 (5th Cir. 2019). In the prior opinion, the Fifth Circuit similarly determined that the alteration of a claim by the Bankruptcy Code does not render the claim impaired under 11 U.S.C. § 1124(1). However, the

Continued on next page.

prior opinion also suggested that an appropriate postpetition interest rate could be set by statute or a bankruptcy court, which was withdrawn in *In re Ultra Petroleum.*

In re Mangia Pizza Investments

Debtor (P) v. Cloud Cap (D)

480 B.R. 669 (Bankr. W.D. Tex. 2012)

NATURE OF CASE: Confirmation stage of Chapter 11 bankruptcy case.

FACT SUMMARY: Mangia Pizza Investments (Mangia) (P) filed Chapter 11 bankruptcy and one claimant filed a competing disclosure statement. That statement created a new class of claims, which Mangia (P) argued was artificial.

RULE OF LAW

A class of claims is impaired only if the plan itself alters the claimant's legal, equitable, and contractual rights.

FACTS: Mangia Pizza Investments (Mangia) (P) filed Chapter 11 bankruptcy and its Disclosure Statement. Cloud Cap (D) purchased another claimant's claim, destroyed exclusivity, and filed its competing Disclosure Statement with much more information about the pizza industry and a potential business plan for Mangia (P). It also created an additional class of claimant for HEB Grocery Company's (HEB) (D) secured claim under a rejected lease. HEB (D) had held Mangia's (P) cash deposit in escrow, earning interest, predating the bankruptcy filing, but the Cloud Cap (D) plan did not provide an offset for this money, nor did it provide for payment as of the Effective Date. Cloud Cap (D) planned for payment to HEB (D) 30 days later, which created an impairment of HEB's (D) right to payment in full of its secured claim as of the Effective Date. The court permitted both disclosure plans sent to voters for approval or rejection. The parties agreed the court could consider confirmation of each plan with Mangia (P) presenting first and Cloud Cap (D) second.

ISSUE: Is a class of claims impaired only if the plan itself alters the claimant's legal, equitable, and contractual rights?

HOLDING AND DECISION: (Gargotta, J.) Yes. A class of claims is impaired only if the plan itself alters the claimant's legal, equitable, and contractual rights. Cloud Cap's plan provides payment to HEB (D) within 30 days from the Membership Purchase Agreement and operations of the reorganized Mangia (P). It does not recognize the existing deposit or that HEB (D) would be paid in full as of the Effective Date. Mangia (P) defaulted prior to the bankruptcy petition, so HEB's (D) rights to the deposit plus accrued interest vested at that time. The only reason HEB (D) did not get the money was due to the automatic stay. Cloud Cap (D) is creating impairment with delaying payment 30 days, but it is an artificial impairment because HEB (D) is entitled to the money at the Effective Date. The only true impairment here is created by the automatic stay provisions of the Bankruptcy Code, not treatment under the Plan. HEB (D) does not have an impaired claim and it is not a voting class. [No decision on which plan was confirmed is in the excerpt].

ANALYSIS

Only those creditors with impaired claims can vote to approve or reject a debtor's plan for reorganization and payment. The Bankruptcy Code does not define "impairment" so the courts are left to determine whether a claimant's claim is sufficiently legally or economically impaired such that the creditor's vote on the plan is permitted.

Quicknotes

AUTOMATIC STAY Upon the filing of a bankruptcy petition, creditors are prohibited from extrajudicial collection efforts against the debtor or the debtor's property.

IMPAIRMENT The weakening or diminishing in power of a right.

In re Bernhard Steiner Pianos USA, Inc.

Unsecured creditors (P) v. Piano-maker debtor (D)

292 B.R. 109 (Bankr. N.D. Tex. 2002)

NATURE OF CASE: Classification objection to a reorganization plan in bankruptcy case.

FACT SUMMARY: The Kahn family made and sold pianos for generations and wanted to reorganize its U.S.-based piano company to repay creditors in full and be profitable once again.

RULE OF LAW

Substantially similar claims should be placed in the same class except for good business reasons that cannot include gerrymandering.

FACTS: Kahn Pianos Group owned Bernhard Steiner Pianos based in South Africa. Ivan Kahn (Kahn) was a fourth-generation piano maker when he moved his family to the United States and began operating Bernhard Steiner Pianos USA, Inc. (Debtor) (P). Debtor (P) sold new pianos, consignment pianos, and repaired pianos. Bad business decisions, the September 11 terrorist attacks, and a struggling economy hit the piano business hard. Debtor (P) filed a bankruptcy case on March 14, 2002, and remained open during the action. Objecting Creditors—the floor plan lenders who had not received payment on sale of new pianos—repossessed their collateral, so Debtor (P) entered into third-party agreements to sell new pianos and split the profits. Debtor (P) needed to repair its reputation in the consignment industry, however, to become a profitable business again. Debtor (P)'s reorganization plan included repayment in full of the Class 4 consignment claims over a period of 10 months beginning on the effective date. Class 6, the Objecting Creditors, would receive a portion of excess cash flow but would not receive scheduled full repayment until after the Class 4 claims were paid. The Class 6 claimants objected to the separate classification and argued the Class 4 and Class 6 claims should be combined.

ISSUE: Should substantially similar claims be placed in the same class except for good business reasons that cannot include gerrymandering?

HOLDING AND DECISION: (Hale, J.) Yes. Substantially similar claims should be placed in the same class except for good business reasons that cannot include gerrymandering. Some plans provide for separate classes to gerrymander an affirmative vote for the reorganization plan. Debtor (P) has good business reasons for separating the Class 4 and Class 6 claims although each are unsecured creditor claims. Kahn testified the damage to the reputation in the consignment industry affected whether pianos would be consigned to Debtor (P) or competitors. Quick repayment in full of the Class 4 claims would repair Debtor's (P) reputation and restore trust for future consignors. Debtor's (P) reorganization plan and full repayment of its creditors hinged on recovering consignment business. The plan treats the consignment class and the general unsecured class differently and there is no evidence it does so for gerrymandering purposes. Objections overruled.

ANALYSIS

Creditors with similar claims typically get placed in the same class so they get repaid the same percentage on the same schedule. If the debtor can articulate a good business reason why a similar claim should be paid on a different schedule, then the courts can consider the factual basis for the classification and weigh the legal equity of creating the different classes.

Quicknotes

COLLATERAL Property that secures the payment of a debt.

CONSIGNMENT An agreement whereby one party is to deliver goods to another party who will pay the first party for those goods that the second party sells and will return any of the items that he does not sell.

CHAPTER 28

Confirming the Plan

Quick Reference Rules of Law

In re Abengoa Bioenergy Biomass of Kansas, LLC

Affiliate creditors (P) v. Debtor (D)

2018 WL 812941 (Bankr. D. Kan. 2018)

NATURE OF CASE: Bankruptcy court ruling on objection to Chapter 11 plan.

FACT SUMMARY: Debtor Abengoa Bioenergy Biomass of Kansas (ABBK) (D) operated a demonstration plant that was used to showcase the capabilities of its upstream corporate parents. The plant encountered operational and equipment problems that prevented it from becoming commercially viable. A creditor filed an involuntary Chapter 7 petition against ABBK (D), which ABBK (D) converted into Chapter 11. ABBK's (D) Chapter 11 plan placed third-party trade creditors in Class 2 and ABBK's sibling affiliates (P) as Class 3. Class 2 creditors were impaired but received pro rata pay, while Class 3 creditors were impaired and would receive nothing. The affiliates (P) objected to the plan's confirmation.

RULE OF LAW

A Chapter 11 plan may separately classify the claims of a debtor's affiliates below nonaffiliate general unsecured creditors.

FACTS: Debtor Abengoa Bioenergy Biomass of Kansas (ABBK) (D) is wholly owned by Abengoa Bioenergy Hybrid of Kansas (ABHK). ABHK and several sibling affiliates (Abengoa affiliates) have an upstream American corporate parent, Abengoa Bioenergy US Holding, LLC (ABUSH). In late 2015, ABBK's (D) Spanish parent company, Abengoa, S.A. (Abengoa) filed for restructuring in Spain. Abengoa's foreign proceeding was recognized in the United States with a Chapter 15 filing in Delaware. In early 2016, ABUSH, ABBK (D), and ABBK's sibling affiliates filed for Chapter 11 in Missouri (Missouri Debtors, collectively), in cases that began as voluntary petitions. After the combined bankruptcy plan for the Missouri Debtors was confirmed, their estates were consolidated. Additionally, some Abengoa subsidiaries and affiliates filed voluntary Chapter 11 cases in Delaware in late March and early April of 2016. On March 23, 2016, several mechanic's lien creditors filed an involuntary Chapter 7 petition against ABBK (D). ABBK (D) converted the case into Chapter 11 and sought transfer of the venue to Delaware, which the court denied. ABBK (D) subsequently sold its principal asset—a Kansas ethanol and cogeneration plant that had been built as a demonstration project for its upstream corporate parents—for $48.5 million. Because of operational and equipment problems, the plant had never approached commercial viability as a result. On April 14, 2017, after the Delaware case was complete and those debtors' claims against ABBK (D) had been released, ABBK (D) filed its plan and disclosure statement. The plan placed unsecured third-party trade creditors in Class 2, relegated unsecured intercompany claims from other Abengoa entities (P) to Class 3, and placed equity interests in Class 4. Classes 2, 3, and 4 were impaired, and Classes 3 and 4 would not receive a distribution. Only Class 2 claims were entitled to vote on the plan. The unsecured creditors accepted the plan by a wide margin. As of 2015, ABBK (D) was wholly dependent upon its affiliates and Abengoa to fund its operation. ABBK (D) operated with its affiliates in an integrated manner, sharing legal, IT, management, and other services, and relying upon its affiliates to supply its biomass. ABBK (D) also relied upon its affiliates to source funding from Abengoa's "central treasury" in Spain, which would be passed to ABBK (D) through the affiliate's accounts.

ISSUE: May a Chapter 11 plan separately classify the claims of a debtor's affiliates below nonaffiliate general unsecured creditors?

HOLDING AND DECISION: (Nugent, J.) Yes. A Chapter 11 plan may separately classify the claims of a debtor's affiliates below nonaffiliate general unsecured creditors. ABBK's (D) Executive Vice President, Mr. Santos, argued that the affiliates' (P) claims were different because the affiliates (P) had inside knowledge that the other third-party creditors did not. Additionally, Santos argued that none of the affiliates expected to be paid. The affiliates (P) clearly knew of ABBK's (D) condition when the debts were incurred, understood ABBK's (D) dependence upon them, and knew that ABBK was a demonstration project that was not a revenue-producing entity. The affiliates (P) had access to financial information regarding ABBK (D) and participated in board meetings regarding ABBK's (D) condition, which gave it an advantage over nonaffiliates. Bankruptcy Code § 1129(a)(7)(A)(ii), the "best interest of creditors" requirement, provides that with respect to each nonaccepting impaired class of claims under the plan, as of the effect date of the plan, each claim holder will receive or retain property that is at least as valuable as the amount that the holder would receive or retain if the debtor were liquidated under Chapter 7. The Abengoa affiliates (P) assert that liquidation analysis submitted by ABBK (D) demonstrates that the affiliated intercompany claims would receive substantially more in a Chapter 7 liquidation than under ABBK's (D) plan. Taking into account the potential claims against insiders and subordinations, and disallowed claims under § 502(d), rational speculation would include the likelihood that a Chapter 7 trustee would question paying claims from

Continued on next page.

four affiliated companies who shared information, management, and objectives. Because it is a fact that ABBK (D), the Delaware debtors, and the Missouri debtors had a shared intention to subordinate their claims, the Code honors that agreement under § 510(a). Abengoa affiliates (P) clearly understood, when they extended credit to ABBK (D), that trade creditors would be paid first. Therefore, ABBK's (D) plan satisfies the best interests of the creditors test. Objection to confirmation overruled; plan confirmed.

ANALYSIS

Following the bankruptcy court's affirmation of the Chapter 11 plan in *In re Abengoa Bioenergy*, the plaintiffs appealed to the district court, which dismissed the appeal. The plaintiffs subsequently appealed to the Tenth Circuit Court of Appeals, asking the court to find that equitable mootness, the doctrine that permits bankruptcy appeals to be dismissed when confirmed plans have been substantially completed, did not apply. The Tenth Circuit similarly dismissed the plaintiffs' appeal, finding that a Chapter 11 liquidation appeal should be treated the same as a reorganization plan with regard to equitable mootness.

Quicknotes

LIQUIDATION The reduction to cash of all assets for distribution to creditors.

UNSECURED CREDITOR A creditor whose loan is not backed by specified collateral or a security agreement.

In re Cheerview Enterprises, Inc.

Creditors (P) v. Debtor (D)

586 B.R. 881 (Bankr. E.D. Mich. 2018)

NATURE OF CASE: Bankruptcy court ruling on objections to reorganization plan.

FACT SUMMARY: Mohamad Berro purchased all of a gas station and convenience store's (Cheerview) (D) stock and became its sole owner. Berro operated the gas station as an unsuccessful absentee owner until he was no longer able to make payments to its creditors (P). The creditors (P) initiated foreclosure proceedings, and Cheerview (D) filed for Chapter 11. Cheerview's (D) Chapter 11 reorganization plan stated that Berro intended to reopen the gas station with a new oil supplier.

RULE OF LAW

A Chapter 11 reorganization plan is not feasible if it relies upon unrealistic sales estimates.

FACTS: Cheerview Enterprises (Cheerview) (D) owned a gas station and convenience store. In 2015, Mohamad Berro (Berro), a 26-year-old oil change business owner, purchased stock in Cheerview (D) and became the sole owner of the gas station and convenience store. Berro formed Mikey's Fuel Mart, Inc. (Mikey's) to operate the gas station and convenience store. Berro continued working full-time at his oil change business and was an absentee owner of Mikey's, visiting the property approximately once a month. Berro kept the Cheerview employees, but after some time, discovered that at least one of the employees was stealing from the business. Upon discovering the theft, he fired the employees and filed a police report. However, Berro continued losing money on Mikey's and was unable to make payments to its creditors. Berro shut down the operation of Mikey's in 2017, and secured creditors began foreclosure proceedings on their mortgages. The value of the property was far less than the mortgages on it. Cheerview (D) filed for Chapter 11 bankruptcy and had not transacted any business since. However, its Third Amended Disclosure Statement and Plan stated that Cheerview (D) intends to reopen the gas station, Cheerview (D) has entered a special transaction, subject to court approval, stating that it believes the gas station can become profitable. On April 13, 2018, Cheerview (D) entered into a series of agreements with RPF Oil Company (RPF), through which RPF will provide gas to Cheerview (D) and pay a 4% commission on any gas that Cheerview (D) sells. Under the projections, the net revenue would be double the net revenue of Mikey's and would be used to pay Cheerview's (D) creditors. Cheerview's (D) largest secured creditor, Stockbridge (P), and largest unsecured creditor, U.S. Oil (P), each filed objections to Cheerview's (D) third amended combined disclosure statement and reorganization plan; Stockbridge (P) also filed a motion for relief from the automatic stay.

ISSUE: Is a Chapter 11 reorganization plan feasible if it relies upon unrealistic sales estimates?

HOLDING AND DECISION: (Shefferly, J.) No. A Chapter 11 reorganization plan is not feasible if it relies upon unrealistic sales estimates. Stockbridge (P) and U.S. Oil (P) argue that the plan does not meet the feasibility requirement of § 1129(a)(11), because confirmation of the plan will not likely be followed by the debtor's liquidation or need for further financial reorganization. The feasibility requirement is designed to protect creditors against unrealistic reorganization plans with little or no chance of success. In order to meet the feasibility test, the debtor has the burden of proving by a preponderance of the evidence that the plan is not likely to fail. The plan must include a realistic, workable framework that is based in objective fact. The proposed payments to creditors under the plan are entirely dependent on the RPF Agreements. The RPF Agreements require Cheerview (D) to sell a minimum of 70,000 gallons of gas per month, which Berro, his partner Ouza, and a Sales Manager from RPF agree is reasonable. However, Stockbridge (P) and U.S. Oil (P) correctly state that there is no evidence in the record that the gas station has ever come close to 70,000 gallons of gas per month for even a single month; Mikey's averaged 35,000 gallons of gas per month with 51,392 gallons in its highest month. Relevant testimony demonstrated that an area competitor sets the lowest prices, which countered Cheerview's (D) assertion that it could undercut the competition in order to meet its sales requirements. Even Cheerview's (D) own projections planned for only 54,000 gallons of gas a month for the entire duration of the plan, which would put Cheerview (D) immediately into default under the RPF Agreements and allow RPF to terminate the contract. Berro and Ouza's projections were similarly unrealistic in their line-item projections, which did not include any annual increases in payroll over the plan, and proposed that Berro, Ouza, and one full-time employee would be able to cover the gas station's 24/7 hours for the entire plan period. Berro and Ouza were unable to explain the inconsistencies in their plan, and clearly lacked familiarity regarding its details. Because Cheerview (D) has failed to show at least some evidence of objective facts indicating that all plan payments will likely be made, Cheerview (D) did not meet its burden to prove that the

Continued on next page.

plan is feasible. Plan not confirmed. Motion for Stay Relief granted.

ANALYSIS

In *Tennessee Pub. Co. v. American Nat. Bank*, 299 U.S. 18 (1936), the United States Supreme Court stated that the District Court is "not bound to clog its docket with visionary or impractical schemes for resuscitation" with regard to reorganization plans. Though a debtor does not need to show that a plan is guaranteed to succeed, different courts often have varying requirements on the likelihood of success. A debtor's historical performance is often the key component of this analysis.

Quicknotes

CHAPTER 11 REORGANIZATION A plan formulated pursuant to Chapter 11 of the Bankruptcy Code whereby a debtor, who is unable to pay his or her debts as they become due, is relieved of the obligation to pay creditors through reorganization and payment from future income.

DEFAULT Failure to carry out a legal obligation.

FEASIBILITY Capable of being completed, executed, or accomplished with reasonable assurance of success.

PREPONDERANCE OF THE EVIDENCE A standard of proof requiring the trier of fact to determine whether the fact sought to be established is more probable than not.

In re Aurora Memory Care, LLC

Creditor (P) v. Debtor (D)

589 B.R. 631 (Bankr. N.D. Ill. 2018)

NATURE OF CASE: Bankruptcy court ruling on reorganization plan following § 1112(b) motion from creditor.

FACT SUMMARY: Aurora Memory Care (AMC) (D) is a healthcare facility that defaulted on a $6.5 million loan to the Bank (P) and filed for Chapter 11. An investment fund associated with AMC (D) and other properties owned by the same individual were operated as an investment vehicle for foreign nationals to obtain citizenship. However, the financing for AMC's (D) reorganization plan relied solely upon a nonbinding letter of intent.

RULE OF LAW

A Chapter 11 reorganization plan that is challenged under § 1112(b) is not plausible without a firm commitment of financing.

FACTS: Aurora Memory Care (AMC) (D) operates a health care facility in Aurora, Illinois. Taher Kameli, a Chicago immigration lawyer, is AMC's (D) 100% owner. Kameli also operates other health care facilities in Florida and Illinois, and established investment funds in connection with his facilities. Kameli has used these investment funds as vehicles for foreign nationals interested in obtaining U.S. citizenship through the EB-5 Program, which extends citizenship to immigrants who invest in designated U.S. businesses that create a certain number of jobs. The Securities and Exchange Commmission had previously brought a civil enforcement action against Kameli because of his scheme. Furthermore, Kameli defaulted on a $6.5 million loan from the Bank (P), and the Bank (P) filed an action in Illinois state court to foreclose upon the mortgage. Shortly thereafter, AMC (D) filed for Chapter 11, but failed to file the monthly operating reports that Chapter 11 requires under § 1106(a)(1) and 704(a)(8).

ISSUE: Is a Chapter 11 reorganization plan that is challenged under § 1112(b) plausible without a firm commitment of financing?

HOLDING AND DECISION: (Goldgar, J.) No. A Chapter 11 reorganization plan that is challenged under § 1112(b) is not plausible without a firm commitment of financing. AMC's (D) reorganization plan entails refinancing its $8.4 million debt to the bank, but it does not have any financing available and has no prospect of obtaining any. AMC's (D) only evidence of financing was a letter of intent stating it had discussed the possibility of a loan with T2 Investments, but the letter was not binding. The Bank (P) demonstrated that AMC (D) has no reasonable likelihood of success confirming a reorganization plan, because its plan to obtain financing was not a firm commitment and could not demonstrate anything beyond a hope to obtain funding. Motion granted.

ANALYSIS

In granting the Bank's (P) motion, the bankruptcy court converted AMC's case to Chapter 7. The court noted that the AMC (D) facility could still have significant equity with which to pay unsecured creditors, which justified conversion to Chapter 7. Furthermore, the court stated that conversion would allow the Chapter 7 trustee to investigate whether sale of the facility would produce adequate dividend for AMC's (D) unsecured creditors and believed the delay of conversion would be minimal.

Quicknotes

CHAPTER 7 BANKRUPTCY A legal proceeding whereby a debtor, who is unable to pay his or her debts as they become due, is relieved of the obligation to pay creditors by liquidation and distribution of his remaining assets.

CHAPTER 11 BANKRUPTCY A legal proceeding whereby a debtor, who is unable to pay his or her debts as they become due, is relieved of the obligation to pay creditors through reorganization and payment from future income.

CHAPTER 11 REORGANIZATION A plan formulated pursuant to Chapter 11 of the Bankruptcy Code whereby a debtor, who is unable to pay his or her debts as they become due, is relieved of the obligation to pay creditors through reorganization and payment from future income.

LETTER OF INTENT A written draft embodying the proposed intent of the parties and that is not enforceable or binding.

CHAPTER 29

Cramming Down Unsecured Creditors

Quick Reference Rules of Law

In re Deming Hospitality, LLC

Creditor (P) v. Debtor (D)

2013 WL 1397458 (Bankr. D.N.M. 2013)

NATURE OF CASE: Hearing on creditor's objection to debtor's reorganization plan.

FACT SUMMARY: Debtor Deming Hospitality (D) filed a reorganization plan that provided unsecured creditors with 75 percent payment of their claims, while the next class, which included the United States Small Business Administration (SBA) (P), received payment of only 1.6 percent of its deficiency claim. SBA (P) objected to the plan, arguing that it was facially unconfirmable.

RULE OF LAW

A reorganization plan that proposes a gross disparity between the proposed dividend to a nonpriority unsecured creditor and the proposed dividend to another creditor is not facially unconfirmable.

FACTS: Debtor Deming Hospitality (D) filed a reorganization plan that provided for eight classes of claims, four of which were secured. Class 5 contained Choice Hotels, the debtor's (D) franchisor; Class 6 contained unsecured creditors to be paid at 75 percent within 30 days; and Class 7 contained the United States Small Business Administration (SBA) (P), which was to be paid $25,000 on its $1.5 million deficiency claim (about 1.67%). SBA (P) argued that the plan was facially unconfirmable under § 1129(b)(1)'s prohibition against unfair discrimination.

ISSUE: Is a reorganization plan that proposes a gross disparity between the proposed dividend to a nonpriority unsecured creditor and the proposed dividend to another creditor facially unconfirmable?

HOLDING AND DECISION: (Thuma, J.) No. A reorganization plan that proposes a gross disparity between the proposed dividend to a nonpriority unsecured creditor and the proposed dividend to another creditor is not facially unconfirmable. The Tenth Circuit Court of Appeals has not established what unfair discrimination means under § 1129(b)(1), and different lower courts have varying definitions and tests, none of which are helpful or tailored enough to be adopted. In *In re Crawford*, 324 F.3d 359 (7th Cir. 2003), the Seventh Circuit Court of Appeals was reluctant to establish a concrete test of fair treatment and stated that bankruptcy judges should seek a result that is reasonable in light of the purposes of Chapter 13. Accordingly, the only helpful general rules are that the burden on the plan proponent to justify disparate treatment will be heavy (1) if the disparate treatment is "grossly disproportionate," and (2) if a plan is feasible and could be confirmed without materially disparate treatment. Otherwise, determining whether discriminatory treatment is "unfair" is left up to the court's discretion. Here, there is a gross disparity between the proposed dividend to nonpriority unsecured creditors and the proposed dividend to SBA (P), and it may be possible to draft a plan that would not discriminate against the SBA (P). Accordingly, while the current plan is not facially unconfirmable, the debtor (D) will carry a heavy burden to justify SBA's (P) disparate treatment.

ANALYSIS

Though it was not stated in the casebook, the court did disapprove Debtor's (D) Disclosure Statement, which proposed that existing equity holders would invest new capital of $150,000 in exchange for retention of their equity. This was an attempt to comply with the "new value" exception to the absolute priority rule, as established in *Bank of America Nat'l Trust and Sav. Ass'n. v. 203 North LaSalle Street Partnership*, 526 U.S. 434 (1999). The *LaSalle* court established that "plans providing junior interest holders with exclusive opportunities free from competition and without benefit of market valuation fall within the prohibition of § 1129(b)(2)(B)(ii)." 526 U.S. at 457. Because the SBA (P) planned to object to the plan and debtors (D) did not comply with the mandated market testing, this portion of the plan could not be confirmed.

Quicknotes

UNSECURED CREDITOR A creditor whose loan is not backed by specified collateral or a security agreement.

Bank of America Nat'l Trust & Sav. Ass'n v. 203 North LaSalle Street Partnership

Creditor (P) v. Debtor (D)

526 U.S. 434 (1999)

NATURE OF CASE: Review of approval of bankruptcy reorganization plan.

FACT SUMMARY: When the old equity holders in 203 North LaSalle Street Partnership (D) contributed new equity in exchange for ownership interests in the reorganized entity, Bank of America (P), the major senior creditor, objected.

RULE OF LAW

Plans providing junior interest holders with exclusive opportunities free from competition and without benefit of market valuation are prohibited under the Bankruptcy Code.

FACTS: 203 North LaSalle Street Partnership (203 North LaSalle) (D), an Illinois real estate limited partnership, was in Chapter 11 bankruptcy. Bank of America (P), the major senior creditor, objected to its reorganization plan because a group of old equity holders were to receive ownership interests in the reorganized entity and that opportunity had been given exclusively to the old equity holders without consideration of alternatives. Confirmation of the plan on a consensual basis was effectively blocked. 203 North LaSalle (D) proceeded to have the plan approved under the judicial cramdown process. To succeed under § 1129(b), the plan must be found to be fair and equitable, that is, the holder of any junior claim or interest should not receive or retain under the plan on account of such junior claim or interest any property. The plan was approved, and the appeals court affirmed. Bank of America (P) appealed, claiming that the plan was unfair, because the exclusive opportunity offered the old equity holders was property of some value that was obtained at no cost. The United States Supreme Court granted certiorari.

ISSUE: Are plans providing junior interest holders with exclusive opportunities free from competition and without benefit of market valuation prohibited under the Bankruptcy Code?

HOLDING AND DECISION: (Souter, J.) Yes. Plans providing junior interest holders with exclusive opportunities free from competition and without benefit of market valuation are prohibited under the Bankruptcy Code. The plan is unfair in that it vests equity in the reorganized business in 203 North LaSalle's (D) partners, without offering the opportunity to anyone else to compete for that equity. This opportunity should be treated as an item of property in its own right. Some form of market valuation should be applied to test the adequacy of the old equity holders' proposed contribution. Reversed and remanded.

CONCURRENCE: (Thomas, J.) I agree that the reorganization plan should not be confirmed. The analysis of the statute should begin with the text itself and not with external sources. The relevant Code provision does not expressly authorize prepetition equity holders to receive or retain property in a reorganized entity in exchange for new capital. The court's unnecessary speculation only thickens the fog.

DISSENT: (Stevens, J.) The Court should now definitely resolve the issue whether § 1129(b)(2)(B)(ii) preserved or repealed the new value component of the absolute priority rule. If the debtor's plan would be entitled to approval if it had been submitted by a third party, it should not be disqualified simply because it did not include a unique provision that would not be required in an offer made by another party.

ANALYSIS

There is a split on the application of the absolute priority rule. The Seventh and Ninth Circuits have supported confirmation of such plans. The Second and Fourth Circuits have disapproved of similar plans. The Supreme Court did not resolve the issue in this case since it found that the statute would not be satisfied by either reading.

Quicknotes

CHAPTER 11 BANKRUPTCY A legal proceeding whereby a debtor, who is unable to pay his or her debts as they become due, is relieved of the obligation to pay creditors through reorganization and payment from future income.

CHAPTER 11 REORGANIZATION A plan formulated pursuant to Chapter 11 of the Bankruptcy Code whereby a debtor, who is unable to pay his or her debts as they become due, is relieved of the obligation to pay creditors through reorganization and payment from future income.

CRAMDOWN Refers to a court's confirmation of a reorganization plan in a bankruptcy proceeding despite the opposition of creditors.

Continued on next page.

EQUITY Fairness; justice; the determination of a matter consistent with principles of fairness and not in strict compliance with rules of law.

SECURED CREDITOR A creditor, the repayment of whose loan is secured by collateral sufficient to repay the debt owed.

In re Red Mountain Machinery Co.

Debtor (P) v. Bank creditor (D)

448 B.R. 1 (Bankr. D. Ariz. 2011)

NATURE OF CASE: Confirmation hearing in Chapter 11 bankruptcy case.

FACT SUMMARY: **Red Mountain Machinery Co. (Debtor) (P) filed a Chapter 11 petition. The First Amended Plan of Reorganization included new value contributions of the Debtor's equity owners, the Cowings. Comerica Bank (D), the lender creditor, argued the new value was insufficient and objected to the plan of reorganization.**

RULE OF LAW

Prior equity owners may receive equity interests in the debtor on account of new value contribution so long as the prior equity did not retain the exclusive right to contribute the new value.

FACTS: Owen and Linda Cowing formed Red Mountain Machinery Co. (Debtor) (P), an Arizona-based company, in 1986. The couple is no longer married but they retain equity ownership of Debtor (P) and co-manage the business. The business model is purchase and rent used, large earth moving equipment, and to maintain reliable maintenance. By 2001, Debtor (P) had annual gross revenues in excess of $43 million, but the economic downturn resulted in a decline to $10 million. Comerica Bank (D) financed Debtor (P) with a revolving line of credit, which in 2009 was at approximately $33 million. The Cowings attempted to negotiate forbearance agreements and workouts, but then Owen Cowing was diagnosed with leukemia. The Cowings turned over negotiations to Debtor's (P) CFO, Darren Dierich. Dierich repeatedly advised workouts were not available and Comerica (D) was demanding preparation for liquidation. The Cowings learned Comerica Bank (D) secretly was negotiating with Dierich to sell Debtor (P) assets to Dierich's business, which would compete with Debtor (P). The Cowings confronted Comerica Bank (D) with information about the secret dealings and Comerica Bank (D) refused to fund payroll or pay trade vendors. Debtor (P) filed its Chapter 11 petition on August 11, 2009. Debtor (P) also filed an adversary action against Comerica Bank (D) based on the secret negotiations. Comerica Bank (D) does not deny the alleged facts but claims no harm occurred because Debtor (P) learned of the dealings prior to the sale to Dierich. In the First Amended Plan of Reorganization, the Cowings are scheduled to contribute $480,000 cash on the effective date when their equity ownership is extinguished. In exchange, they will receive 100 percent of the equity of the reorganized debtor. Also, the Cowings will fund a $1.25 million exit loan facility. Comerica Bank (D) objected to and rejected the plan.

ISSUE: May prior equity owners receive equity interests in the debtor on account of new value contribution so long as the prior equity did not retain the exclusive right to contribute the new value?

HOLDING AND DECISION: (Haines, J.) Yes. Prior equity owners may receive equity interests in the debtor on account of new value contribution so long as the prior equity did not retain the exclusive right to contribute the new value. The Ninth Circuit held in *Bonner Mall*, 513 U.S. 18, 29 (1994), this was a logical corollary of the absolute priority rule. Comerica Bank (D) claims the plan violates the absolute priority rule and its new value corollary. Congress codified what the rule "includes" in § 1129(b)(2)(B)(ii) but this clearly was not the entirety of the rule. The Supreme Court has addressed the absolute priority rule, but expressly declined to vacation the Ninth Circuit holding and did not overrule the new value corollary. It did not define "on account of" but did hold that requirement cannot be satisfied of old equity controls the exclusive right to propose a plan. Determination of new equity interests "on account of" prior equity versus new value contribution is a fact question, not a legal one. If a proposed plan with new value contribution provides new value that is (1) new, (2) substantial, (3) money or money's worth, (4) necessary for a successful reorganization, and (5) reasonably equivalent to the value or interest received. Comerica Bank (D) did not dispute Debtor's (P) expert testimony that the value was new, money or money's worth. Comerica Bank (D) argues the new value contribution of $480,000 is not sufficient, but there is no support for that argument. It is sufficient and more than reasonably equivalent. The fifth new value requirement is the most conceptually difficult because the equity interests may retain value due to retention of control of an insolvent enterprise, but it has never indicated how the amount of that value is to be determined. Old equity cannot retain its interest only for control even if the entity is insolvent, but the bankruptcy court must determine whether the retained value exceeds the new value contribution without benefit of any legal, accounting, or economic analysis or methodology. In *Bank of America Nat'l Trust & Sav. Ass'n v. 203 North LaSalle*, 526 U.S. 434 (1999), the court pinpointed the value to be in the exclusive right to propose a reorganization plan. There then is the right to reject the "no value"

Continued on next page.

analysis when exclusivity has expired, and no option value exists. [The court disallowed key elements of Debtor's (P) CFO because he was not an expert]. No expert opinion evidence exists here to conclude otherwise, so the balance sheet approach is sufficient to confirm the plan. Debtor (P) will be insolvent on a balance sheet basis, so there is no value to its equity interests. Thus, the new value contribution of $480,000 or $1.2 million exceeds the value of the equity interests the Cowings will receive under the plan. The First Amended Plan satisfies the requirements of § 1129(a) and (b), Comerica Bank's (D) objections are overruled, and the plan must be confirmed.

ANALYSIS

Any individual or entity can propose a reorganization plan after the exclusivity period expires. That can aid the court in determining value of the equity interests and new value contributions. Another aid is an auction during which old equity and other parties can bid on the new equity. The absolute priority rule is violated if only old equity can bid, so value determination fairly relies on competition among creditors.

CHAPTER 30

Cramming Down Secured Creditors

Quick Reference Rules of Law

		PAGE
1.	*In re Buena Vista Oceanside, LLC.* The bankruptcy court may make its own determination of property value and is not bound by valuation opinions or expert reports.	*196*
2.	*In re Exide Technologies.* No one valuation method for a company's enterprise value provides greater instruction to the court over another.	*197*
3.	*In the Matter of Texas Grand Prairie Hotel Realty, LLC,* The common cramdown rate methodology comes from a United States Supreme Court fractured plurality decision in *Till v. SCS Credit Corp.*, 541 U.S. 465, 479 (2004), addressing Chapter 13 cases, but frequently applied in Chapter 11 cases.	*199*

In re Buena Vista Oceanside, LLC

Hotel owners (P) v. Bank lender creditor (D)

479 B.R. 342 (Bankr. W.D. Pa. 2012)

NATURE OF CASE: Motion for valuation of secured claim and avoidance of lien in Chapter 11 bankruptcy case.

FACT SUMMARY: Buena Vista Oceanside, LLC (Debtor) (P) owns and operates the Buena Vista Hotel (Buena Vista) and the Courtyard Villa Hotel (Courtyard) (collectively, the "Properties"). Optimum Bank (Optimum) (D) loaned Debtor (P) financing secured by a first priority mortgage lien on the Properties. Debtor (P) and Optimum (D) disagree on the value of the Properties and, thus, the value of Optimum's (D) secured claim.

RULE OF LAW

The bankruptcy court may make its own determination of property value and is not bound by valuation opinions or expert reports.

FACTS: Buena Vista Oceanside, LLC (Debtor) (P) owns and operates the Properties and borrowed $4,368,000 from Optimum Bank (Optimum) (D). The loan was secured by a first priority mortgage lien on the Properties. [Debtor filed a Chapter 11 bankruptcy petition]. The parties disagreed on the valuation of the Properties and the value of Optimum's (D) secured claim. Debtor's (P) expert appraisers Jesse Vance (Vance) and Ronald Ames (Ames) opined the Buena Vista had a market value of $750,000 and Courtyard of $1,425,000 with a combined value of $1,690,000. Optimum (D) retained Lawrence Pendleton (Pendleton) as its expert appraiser who determined the collective market value was $3,375,000. The parties agreed the Cost Approach was not an appropriate valuation method in this case, so all experts used the Sales Comparison Approach and the Income Capitalization Approach.

ISSUE: May the bankruptcy court make its own determination of property value or is it bound by valuation opinions or expert reports?

HOLDING AND DECISION: (Fitzgerald, J.) Bankruptcy court may make its own determination of property value and is not bound by valuation opinions or expert reports. Here, the court will use the Income Capitalization Approach with pieces of each expert's report. First, deferred maintenance costs should be deducted from the value of the Properties. Next, the court will determine the value by beginning with the Potential Gross Income (PGI) for each property at full occupancy. The number is determined by selection an Average Daily Rate (ADR) attainable by the hotel. After determination of PGI, the Net Operating Income (NOI) is established by deducting operating expenses. NOI is then divided by the selected Capitalization Rate, which evaluates the reasonableness of estimated income and expenses given the current and future market. Pendleton based his ADR by evaluating Buena Vista's slightly higher than average rental rates and choosing a lower "rack rate." Ames opined the "rack rate" is 10-20 percent higher than actual rents received, so the Court will deduct 15 percent from Pendleton's rates and determine Buena Vista's PGI at $568.046.50. Pendleton and Ames looked to area average occupancy rates while Vance used Buena Vista's actual occupancy rates. Buena Vista was closed for several months, however, so the market data approach is more accurate. The Court will use a 65 percent occupancy rate; using the selected ADR, the projected room revenue is $369,230.23. The court considers market data and the expert's opinions in establishing 60 percent to be deducted as operating expenses. That established the NOI at $147,692.09. As for the Capitalization Rate, Ames was highly optimistic at 10 percent while Pendleton selected 11 percent based on market ranges. Vance used a vastly different six percent rate, which was based on comparable sales rather than national and local market trends. The court will apply the 11 percent rate and deduct deferred maintenance. That final value of the Buena Vista is $1,217,655.36. [The court completed the same analysis for the Courtyard]. The combined value of the Properties is $2,238,182.63. Optimum's (D) secured claim is $2,238,182.63 and unsecured claim is $2,739,802.07.

ANALYSIS

Claim valuation can be quite difficult in areas of the country where property values and market trends fluctuate wildly. The courts essentially have to predict the future when determining the present-day value of properties. Highly qualified expert opinions can differ significantly even while using accepted valuation methods. Creditors can be served best by looking at past performance to indicate future performance.

In re Exide Technologies

Battery manufacturer (P) v. Creditors (D

303 B.R. 48 (Bankr. D. Del. 2003)

NATURE OF CASE: Confirmation for Fourth Amended Joint Plan of Reorganization in Chapter 11 bankruptcy case.

FACT SUMMARY: Exide Technologies (Debtor) (P) requested confirmation of its Fourth Amended Joint Plan of Reorganization under Chapter 11 of the Bankruptcy Code (the "Plan"). Several parties, including the Official Committee of Unsecured Creditors (the "Creditors Committee"), filed objections. Debtor (P) submitted its expert's report on valuation and creditors submitted their experts' reports.

RULE OF LAW

No one valuation method for a company's enterprise value provides greater instruction to the court over another.

FACTS: Exide Technologies (Debtor) (P) manufactures and supplies lead acid batteries. In 2000, it acquired another manufacturer. The acquisition required prepetition financing, which was approved in a final order on the Debtor-in-Possession Credit Agreement. After investigation, the Creditors Committee determined it had causes of action against the prepetition lenders and filed an adversary action. The Voting Report shows the prepetition lenders overwhelmingly voted in favor of the Plan while the unsecured creditors overwhelmingly voted against it. The objections to the Plan include an objection the plan proposals are for the self-interest of the Prepetition Lenders who will receive excess of full value of their claims. The Debtor (P) and the Creditors Committee (D) each offered experts to opine on the Debtor's enterprise value. Arthur B. Newman (Newman), Debtor's (P) expert, valued the company between $950 million and $1.050 billion. William Q. Derrough (Derrough), the Creditors Committee expert, valued the company between $1.478 billion and $1.711 billion. The parties also disagree about the "hurdle amount." Newman conducted a private equity process in which he solicited bids from prospective buyers and no party was interested in increasing a $950 million low bid. The Creditors Committee used a straightforward application of the three standard valuation methodologies: (1) comparable company analysis; (2) comparable transaction analysis; and (3) discounted cash flow. Debtor (P) argues the Creditors Committee (D) has overvalued the company and the Plan offered is fair and reasonable to unsecured creditors. The Creditors Committee (D) argues Debtor (P) undervalued the company and will overpay the Prepetition Lenders.

ISSUE: Does one valuation method for a company's enterprise value provide greater instruction to the court over another?

HOLDING AND DECISION: (Carey, J.) No. No one valuation method for a company's enterprise value provides greater instruction to the court over another. The key components of a comparable company analysis include the debtor's EBITDA (i.e., earnings before interest, taxes, depreciation, and amortization) and an appropriate multiple. The multiple is determined by comparing the enterprise value of a comparable publicly traded company (although Debtor (P) has been delisted by the New York Stock Exchange) to the trailing twelve months EBITDA. The experts arrived at similar multiples, but Newman reduced his because he believed the Debtor's (P) industrial division should be given less weight. The present analysis requires a consideration of the benefit of the Debtor's (P) restructuring and whether giving common stock to the Prepetition Lenders results in greater than 100 percent of the value of their claims. The court will look at projected, rather than historic, EBITDAR (i.e., earnings before interest, taxes, depreciation, amortization, and restructuring charges). The appropriate multiple lies between Newman's original multiple of 7.2 and Derrough's multiple of 7.7. The comparable transaction analysis requires an analysis of recent merger and acquisition transactions in the relevant industry. For the reasons set forth in analyzing the comparable company, the trailing twelve months ending December 31, 2003, will be used with a 6.4 EBITDA multiple. The Discounted Cash Flow (DCF) analysis adds together (1) the present value of the company's projected distributable cash flow and (2) the present value of the company's terminal value. The parties dispute the discount rate and the multiple to calculate terminal value. Both experts relied on the weighted average cost of capital (WACC) while Derrough used capital asset pricing model (CAPM) and Newman noted CAPM can be inaccurate when applied to a not-publicly-traded company. Newman, therefore, used information showing the rate of return on equity a prospective purchaser would demand. Newman uses too many subjective adjustments, so the court will rely on Derrough's more straightforward analysis of DCF. Debtor (P) argues Derrough relies too strongly on his DCF given the uncertainty of the company's ability to meet long-range projections, but the court finds it is appropriate to consider DCF when determining value. After consideration of the valuation methods, the Debtor's en-

Continued on next page.

terprise value is in the range of $1.4 billion to $1.6 billion. [The court upheld other objections to the Plan.] The Debtor's (P) Plan cannot be confirmed.

ANALYSIS

A court may not lend greater credence to any one valuation method, but the facts of the case and the subjective factors considered in the analysis of a particular valuation method may persuade the court of its greater or lesser value. In *Exide Technologies*, the court specifically noted it would not follow one expert's opinion on valuation because too many subjective adjustments had been made. While factual circumstances may require subjective adjustments, a straight-forward approach to the valuations process may not be as flashy but will prevail in the end.

Quicknotes

DEBTOR-IN-POSSESSION A Chapter 11 bankruptcy debtor who retains control of assets or property pursuant to a plan of reorganization.

In the Matter of Texas Grand Prairie Hotel Realty, LLC

Debtor hotelier (P) v. Lender (D)

710 F.3d 324 (5th Cir. 2013)

NATURE OF CASE: Appeal from confirmation of a Chapter 11 cramdown plan.

FACT SUMMARY: Texas Grand Prairie Hotel Realty, LLC (Debtor) (P) had a loan with Wells Fargo Bank National Association (Wells Fargo) (D) and then had to file a Chapter 11 petition when the hotels suffered serious downturns. Debtor (P) filed a plan for reorganization that included a forced loan from Wells Fargo (D) at prime-plus interest. Wells Fargo (D) objected to the proposed plan on the grounds the interest should be much higher.

RULE OF LAW

The common cramdown rate methodology comes from a United States Supreme Court fractured plurality decision in *Till v. SCS Credit Corp.*, 541 U.S. 465, 479 (2004), addressing Chapter 13 cases, but frequently applied in Chapter 11 cases.

FACTS: Texas Grand Prairie Hotel Realty, LLC (Debtor) (P) obtained $49,000,000 in financing from Morgan Stanley Mortgage Capital, Inc. in 2007 to acquire and renovate four hotel properties. Wells Fargo Bank National Association (Wells Fargo) (D) acquired the loan and accepted a security interest in all four properties plus other Debtor (P) assets. In 2009 the hotels suffered, and Debtor (P) filed a Chapter 11 petition. Wells Fargo (D) rejected the proposed plan of reorganization and Debtor (P) sought to cram down the plan under 11 U.S.C. § 1129(b). The cramdown forced loan was the secured claim at $39,080,000 paid over a term of 10 years at 5 percent interest, which was prime plus 1.75 percent. At the evidentiary hearing, Debtor's (P) expert, Louis Robichaux (Robichaux), testified in support of the 5 percent cramdown while Wells Fargo's (D) expert, Richard Ferrell (Ferrell), testified the rate had to be at least 8.8 percent. [The bankruptcy court confirmed the plan at the 5 percent cramdown rate and Wells Fargo (D) appeals.]

ISSUE: Does the common cramdown rate methodology come from a United States Supreme Court fractured plurality decision in *Till v. SCS Credit Corp.*, 541 U.S. 465, 479 (2004)?

HOLDING AND DECISION: (Higginbotham, J.) Yes. The common cramdown rate methodology comes from a United States Supreme Court fractured plurality decision in *Till v. SCS Credit Corp.*, 541 U.S. 465, 479 (2004), addressing Chapter 13 cases, but frequently applied in Chapter 11 cases. Wells Fargo (D) argues the trial court erred in setting a 5 percent cramdown rate. It further argues the court must review de novo the methodology for calculating the § 1129(b) cramdown rate, suggesting *Till* is controlling. *Till*, however, is not controlling precedent here because it involved Chapter 13 petition and this is a Chapter 11 plan. The review of the methodology and the rate will be for clear error. The parties agree the *Till* plurality's method applies, but disagree on the approach that method requires. The *Till* plurality held bankruptcy courts should take the national prime rate and add a supplemental risk adjustment of 1-3 percent. Scalia's dissent warned this approach would "systematically undercompensate" creditors. The plurality observed this methodology likely could apply in Chapter 11 cases, but in footnote 14 noted the existence of "efficient markets" for exit financing and suggested a "market rate" approach might be more suitable. The vast majority of bankruptcy courts have ignored Justice Scalia's warning and applied *Till* to Chapter 11 cases. Here, Robichaux used a holistic approach to evaluate Debtor's (P) business and a straightforward application of the *Till* plurality approach. He began with prime rate plus 3.25 percent, looked at the general health of Debtor's (P) business, and determined Debtor's proposed cramdown rate was tight but feasible, so a 1.75 percent risk adjustment was appropriate. Ferrell concluded there was no equivalent market for the forced loan contemplated under the cramdown plan, so he took the weighted average of multi-tiered exit financing packages. This methodology yielded a market rate of 9.3 percent. He made adjustments up and down for other factors and finalized at 8.8 percent. The bankruptcy court found Robichaux's determination rested on an uncontroversial application of *Till* formula while Ferrell's rested on the oft-rejected comparable loans analysis. Wells Fargo does not attempt to predicate Ferrell's finding on the *Till* footnote 14. The bankruptcy court did not err here even if footnote 14 did not have persuasive value. "Efficient markets" exist only if there is a loan with a similar term, size, and collateral comparable to the forced loan. Ferrell himself acknowledged that is not the case. The trial court arrived at the 5 percent cramdown rate by a straightforward application of the *Till* prime-plus approach. While this is not the only or even the optimal, method in a Chapter 11 cramdown case, it is not clear error. Affirmed.

ANALYSIS

Courts may not be required to follow *Till v. SCS Credit Corp.* as precedent, but it has persuasive value to the vast majority of bankruptcy courts determining appropriate

Continued on next page.

cramdown rates on forced loans. As noted in *Texas Grand Prairie Hotel Realty*, critics of the "efficient markets" approach argue the market is no less illusory for Chapter 11 forced loans than for Chapter 13. With the comparable information so difficult to gather, the prime-plus methodology, however flawed, appears here to stay.

Quicknotes

CRAMDOWN Refers to a court's confirmation of a reorganization plan in a bankruptcy proceeding despite the opposition of creditors.

CHAPTER 31

Sales and Beyond I

Quick Reference Rules of Law

In re Chrysler LLC

Claimants (P) v. Debtor (D)

576 F.3d 108 (2d Cir. 2009)

NATURE OF CASE: Appeal of bankruptcy court order authorizing the sale of substantially all of debtor's assets.

FACT SUMMARY: Chrysler LLC (Chrysler) (D) filed for an asset-sale transaction under 11 U.S.C. § 363, where substantially all its assets were transferred into "New Chrysler." Pensioners (P), who hold secured claims, appealed the approval of the sale, arguing that it was a *sub rosa* plan, impermissible under § 363(b).

RULE OF LAW

A bankruptcy court did not abuse its discretion in approving an 11 U.S.C. § 363(b) asset-sale transaction that transformed the debtor into a new entity.

FACTS: Chrysler LLC (Chrysler) (D) and its related companies filed a prepackaged bankruptcy petition under Chapter 11, following months of significant losses, a bailout from the United States government, an unsuccessful search for a merger partner, and an unsuccessful search for additional bailout funds for a standalone restructuring. Eventually, Chrysler (D) agreed to an asset-sale transaction pursuant to 11 U.S.C. § 363, which was approved and detailed in a Master Transaction Agreement (the Agreement). Under the Agreement, substantially all of Chrysler's assets would be transferred to New CarCo Acquisition LLC (New Chrysler), in exchange for New Chrysler's assumption of certain liabilities and $2 billion in cash. Fiat S.p.A. agreed to provide New Chrysler with fuel-efficient vehicle platforms, access to its global distribution system, and experienced management. The Indiana State Police Pension Trust, Indiana State Teachers Retirement Fund, and the Indiana Major Moves Construction Fund (Pensioners, collectively) (P), secured claim holders, challenged the Sale Order on grounds that the sale of Chrysler's auto manufacturing assets so closely approximate a final plan of reorganization that it is an impermissible *sub rosa* plan under § 363(b). Pensioners (P) argue that the sale is a "sale" in name only. Pensioners (P) argue that because New Chrysler will be the same as the old Chrysler in essentially every respect, including retention of the same employees and manufacture of the same vehicles, the substance of the transaction is instead a reorganization.

ISSUE: Did a bankruptcy court abuse its discretion in allowing an § 363(b) asset-sale transaction that transformed the debtor into a new entity?

HOLDING AND DECISION: (Jacobs, C.J.) No. A bankruptcy court did not abuse its discretion in approving an 11 U.S.C. § 363(b) asset-sale transaction that transformed the debtor into a new entity. Under § 363(b) of the Bankruptcy Code, a Chapter 11 debtor-in-possession is permitted to use, sell, or lease real estate property outside of the ordinary course of business, provided the movant provide notice and a hearing. Typically, courts approve § 363(b) sales to preserve wasting assets, which could include a disappearing business opportunity or depreciating assets. The term "*sub rosa*" is used to describe transactions that treat the requirements of the Bankruptcy Code as something to be evaded or subverted. Pensioners (P) argue that the sale of Chrysler (D) is *sub rosa* because it gives value to unsecured creditors without paying off secured debt in full, and without complying with the procedural requirements of Chapter 11. Pensioners (P) argue that the sale fails to satisfy the discretionary, multifarious test from *Holders v. Lionel Corp*, 722 F.2d 1063, 1071 (2d Cir. 1983), which requires a "good business reason" for a § 363(b) transaction and provided a nonexhaustive list of possible factors. The bankruptcy judge found good business reasons for the sale, because the only possible alternative was an immediate liquidation that would yield far less for both the state and the Pensioners (P)—the sale would yield $2 billion, while an immediate liquidation would yield between $0 and $800 million. Chrysler's transaction with Fiat was the only available offer following a worldwide search, and with its factories shuttered, Chrysler was losing going concern value of $100 million each day. Similarly, Pensioners' (P) claims that New Chrysler would be the same as the old Chrysler were exaggerated, because New Chrysler would also make newer, smaller vehicles using its new Fiat technology under a new CEO and would have access to a new European market. Accordingly, the bankruptcy court did not abuse its discretion in approving the sale. Sale order affirmed.

ANALYSIS

The *Lionel* court's "good business reason" factors included: the proportionate value of the asset to the estate as a whole; the amount of elapsed time since filing; the likelihood that a plan of reorganization will be proposed and confirmed in the near future; the effect of the proposed disposition on future plans of reorganization; the proceeds to be obtained from the disposition vis-à-vis any appraisals of the property; which of the alternatives of use, sale, or lease the proposal envisions; and the most important factor: whether the asset is increasing or decreasing in value. *Holders v. Lionel Corp*, 722 F.2d 1063, 1071 (2d Cir. 1983).

Continued on next page.

Quicknotes

ASSET An item of real or personal property that is owned and has tangible value.

CHAPTER 11 BANKRUPTCY A legal proceeding whereby a debtor, who is unable to pay his or her debts as they become due, is relieved of the obligation to pay creditors through reorganization and payment from future income.

DEBTOR-IN-POSSESSION A Chapter 11 bankruptcy debtor who retains control of assets or property pursuant to a plan of reorganization.

LIQUIDATION The reduction to cash of all assets for distribution to creditors.

SECURED CLAIM A claim, the repayment of which is *secured* by collateral sufficient to repay the debt owed.

SUB ROSA Secret; confidential.

UNSECURED CREDITOR A creditor whose loan is not backed by specified collateral or a security agreement.

Czyzewski v. Jevic Holding Corp.

Creditors (P) v. Debtor (D)

137 S. Ct. 973 (2017)

NATURE OF CASE: Appeal from bankruptcy court ruling allowing dismissal of a Chapter 11 petition in favor of a settlement agreement.

FACT SUMMARY: Jevic Transportation Corporation (Jevic) (D) filed for Chapter 11 bankruptcy. Shortly thereafter, Jevic (D) was sued in bankruptcy court by its truckdrivers (P) for failing to provide them with statutorily required notice before they were terminated. The bankruptcy court granted summary judgment in favor of the truckdrivers (P). Part of the judgment included an $8.3 million priority wage claim, which was entitled to payment ahead of general unsecured claims. Additionally, a committee representing Jevic's (D) unsecured creditors sued its parent company, Sun Capital Partners (Sun), and CIT Group for fraudulent conveyance. The fraudulent conveyance case settled, and a settlement agreement was approved by the bankruptcy court that dismissed the Chapter 11 case and allowed Jevic's (D) remaining assets to be used in part to pay low-priority general unsecured creditors without distributing anything to the truckdrivers (P). The truckdrivers (P) appealed the bankruptcy court's approval of the settlement agreement.

RULE OF LAW

A bankruptcy court cannot approve a structured dismissal that provides for distributions that do not follow ordinary priority rules without the affected creditors' consent.

FACTS: In 2006, Sun Capital Partners (Sun), a private equity firm, acquired Jevic Transportation Corporation (Jevic) (D) with borrowed money in a leveraged buyout. Two years later, Jevic (D) filed for Chapter 11 bankruptcy, owing over $53 million to senior secured creditors Sun and CIT Group (CIT) and over $20 million to tax and general unsecured creditors at the time of filing. Prior to filing for bankruptcy, Jevic (D) halted almost all operations and told its truckdrivers (P) that they would be fired. A group of former Jevic truckdrivers (P) filed suit in bankruptcy court against Jevic (D), claiming that Jevic (D) had violated the federal Worker Adjustment and Retraining Notification (WARN) Acts by not providing 60-days' notice before the truckdrivers' (P) termination. The bankruptcy court granted summary judgment in favor of the truckdrivers (P), leaving them with a judgment that the truckdrivers (P) allege is worth $12.4 million, $8.3 million of which is a priority wage claim under 11 U.S.C. § 507(a)(4) and is entitled to payment ahead of general unsecured claims. Additionally, the bankruptcy court authorized a committee representing Jevic's (D) unsecured creditors to sue Sun and CIT for saddling Jevic (D) with unserviceable debts (fraudulent conveyance). The bankruptcy court and the parties acknowledged that proceeds of any suit would return to the bankruptcy estate instead of going to the unsecured creditors directly. Sun, CIT, and Jevic (D) reached a settlement agreement which provided that (1) the bankruptcy court would dismiss the fraudulent conveyance action with prejudice; (2) CIT would deposit $2 million into an account for the Jevic (D) committee's legal fees; (3) Sun would assign its lien on Jevic's (D) remaining assets—$1.7 million—to a trust to pay taxes and administrative expenses, and would distribute the remainder on a pro rata basis to low-priority general unsecured creditors but would not distribute anything to the truckdrivers (P); and (4) Jevic's (D) Chapter 11 bankruptcy would be dismissed. Sun insisted on excluding the truckdrivers (P) from the distribution, despite the exclusion being contrary to ordinary priority rules, because the truckdrivers (P) had a separate pending WARN suit against Sun directly, which Sun did not want to help finance. The truckdrivers (P) and the Chapter 11 trustee objected to the bankruptcy court's approval of the settlement agreement, arguing that the settlement distribution plan violated the Bankruptcy Code's priority scheme by skipping petitioners with mid-level priority claims and instead distributing money to low-priority general unsecured creditors. The bankruptcy court agreed that ordinary priority rules had not been followed but held that the failure to follow ordinary priority rules did not bar approval because the proposed payments would occur pursuant to a structured dismissal of a Chapter 11 petition rather than the approval of a Chapter 11 plan. The bankruptcy court predicted that without the settlement and dismissal, there was no realistic prospect of a meaningful distribution for anyone other than the secured creditors. The Third Circuit Court of Appeals affirmed the District Court, finding that structured dismissals do not always need to respect priority. The United States Supreme Court granted the truckdrivers' (P) petition for writ of certiorari.

ISSUE: Can a bankruptcy court approve a structured dismissal that provides for distributions that do not follow ordinary priority rules without the affected creditors' consent?

HOLDING AND DECISION: (Breyer, J.) No. A bankruptcy court cannot approve a structured dismissal that provides for distributions that do not follow ordinary priority rules without the affected creditors' consent. The

Continued on next page.

Bankruptcy Code's priority system is a basic underpinning of business bankruptcy law and is fundamental to the operation of the Bankruptcy Code. While the Bankruptcy Code does give a bankruptcy court the power to dismiss a Chapter 11 case, the word "dismiss" does not indicate anything about the power to make nonconsensual priority-violating distributions of estate value, nor does any other relevant part of the Bankruptcy Code. Similarly, while § 349(b) of the Bankruptcy Code says that a bankruptcy judge may make other orders for cause, that provision appears designed to allow the court to protect rights acquired in reliance of the bankruptcy case. There is no significant offsetting bankruptcy-related justification for the violation of ordinary priority rules in this case: the structured dismissal in the case at bar did not preserve the debtor as a going concern, make disfavored creditors better off, promote the possibility of a confirmable plan, restore the *status quo ante*, or protect reliance interests. Here, the bankruptcy court cannot deviate from the Bankruptcy Code's specified priority rules, even if the bankruptcy court sincerely believes that creditors would be better off. Reversed and remanded.

ANALYSIS

The Court's holding in *Czyzewski* was narrow, focusing specifically on priority requirements in structured dismissals. The Court left open the possibility of bankruptcy courts approving plans that circumvent ordinary priority rules in circumstances outside of structured dismissals, including distributions that occur after a sale, as was the case in *In re Chrysler*, 576 F.3d 108 (2d Cir. 2009).

Quicknotes

BANKRUPTCY ESTATE Created by the filing of a petition in bankruptcy and includes all legal and equitable interests of the debtor in property as of that time.

FRAUDULENT CONVEYANCE Conveyances made with intent to defraud creditors; may be voidable.

GOING CONCERN A commercial enterprise operating with the expectation of continued operation.

SECURED CREDITOR A creditor, the repayment of whose loan is secured by collateral sufficient to repay the debt owed.

UNSECURED CREDITOR A creditor whose loan is not backed by specified collateral or a security agreement.

In re Bridge Associates of SOHO, Inc.

Tenants (P) v. Debtor (D)

589 B.R. 512 (Bankr. E.D.N.Y. 2018)

NATURE OF CASE: Bankruptcy court ruling on Debtor's (D) motion to sell an occupied residential building.

FACT SUMMARY: Debtor (D) owned an occupied residential loft building that it attempted to sell at an auction. The building was covered by New York City's Loft Law, which prohibits a building owner from collecting rent if the building owner has not complied with certain Loft Law requirements and/or is not on track to come into compliance. Debtor (D) argued that because its tenants (P) did not pay rent, they were not entitled to a possessory right, and the building could be sold "free and clear" at auction.

RULE OF LAW

Tenants covered by New York City's Loft Law are entitled to possessory rights that cannot be disturbed by § 363 of the Bankruptcy Code, even if they do not pay rent due to the building owner's failure to comply with the Loft Law.

FACTS: Debtor Bridge Associates of Soho (D) sought to sell an occupied residential loft building it owned in the SOHO district of New York City. Debtor (D) sought to sell the building free and clear of any liens, claims, or encumbrances, including the current occupants' possessory rights. Debtor (D) proposed an auction sale of the building, with a reserve price of $12.5 million, which Debtor (D) stated was sufficient to ensure payment of secured claims. Debtor (D) argued it could sell the building unencumbered because the building's occupants (P) were holdover tenants who had not paid rent in decades and therefore did not have a possessory interest in the property. Three groups objected to the sale: (1) the building's occupants (P), arguing that they were protected by Article 7-C of the New York Multiple Dwelling Law (Loft Law); (2) the New York City Loft Board (Board), on the basis that the Debtor (D) should not be permitted to use the Bankruptcy Code to strip the building of otherwise valid and controlling statutory regulations; and (3) the Debtor's (D) senior secured creditors, tax lienholders, who both objected and sought relief from the stay in order to complete a foreclosure sale of the building. The Loft Law was enacted to ensure that when New York City buildings were converted from commercial to residential, the new space conformed with statutory, regulatory, and code requirements for residential occupancy. The building was covered by the Loft Law after it was converted into an interim multiple dwelling and registered with the Board in 1991. The building was acquired by the Debtor (D) in 2002. All parties agree that the Debtor (D) does not have, and has never had, a certificate of occupancy for residential use, nor is Debtor (D) prepared to bring the building into compliance.

ISSUE: Are tenants covered by New York City's Loft Law entitled to possessory rights that cannot be disturbed by § 363 of the Bankruptcy Code, even if they do not pay rent due to the building owner's failure to comply with the Loft Law?

HOLDING AND DECISION: (Grossman, J.) Yes. Tenants covered by New York City's Loft Law are entitled to possessory rights that cannot be disturbed by § 363 of the Bankruptcy Code, even if they do not pay rent due to the building owner's failure to comply with the Loft Law. Under §§ 301 and 302 of the Multiple Dwelling Law, a property owner may not collect rent on a building that is occupied without a certificate of occupancy for residential use. However, the Loft Law permits an owner to collect rent without a certificate of occupancy, provided the building complies with the rules and regulations of the Loft Law that are necessary to move the building towards legal compliance. The tenants (P) argued that their continued occupancy rights are conditioned only upon the requirement that the unit they occupy is their primary residence. The Debtor (D) argued that because the building's tenants did not pay rent, they had no possessory rights to occupy the premises, even if the primary residence requirement was met. The tenants' (P) argument is correct: the discussion of rent in § 286 assumes that the owner is permitted to collect rent. Furthermore, the New York Court of Appeals in *Chazon LLC v. Maugenest*, 19 N.Y.3d 410 (2012), determined that statutory tenants covered by the Loft Law could not be evicted based on nonpayment of rent when the building owner was not in compliance with the Loft Law. Debtor's (D) argument that a "free and clear" sale under § 363(f) can cut off the tenant's statutory rights of possession is similarly incorrect: the rights of possession conferred by § 286 of the Multiple Dwelling Law cannot be stripped without satisfaction of the requirements of § 363(f)(1) or (4). Accordingly, the tenants (P) have possessory rights granted to them under the Loft Law, which cannot be disturbed under § 363 of the bankruptcy code. Debtor's (D) motion is denied.

ANALYSIS

New York City's Loft Law was expanded in 2010 and again in 2019. Previously, the Loft Law covered only certain parts of Manhattan, including the SOHO building discussed in

Continued on next page.

Bridge Associates. However, the 2010 amendment expanded coverage to include loft buildings in Brooklyn and Long Island, and protected tenants who lived in lofts prior to 2009. The 2019 amendment permitted tenants who moved into lofts in 2015 and 2016 to petition the city to bring their loft buildings into compliance. Critics of the Loft Law argue that residential conversion of loft spaces, especially in historically industrial areas of Brooklyn, will discourage local manufacturing and encourage further residential development.

Quicknotes

CLAIM The demand for a right to payment or equitable relief; the fact or facts giving rise to such demand.

ENCUMBRANCE An interest in property that operates as a claim or lien against its title potentially making it unmarketable.

HOLDOVER TENANT A tenant who remains in possession of the property after the expiration of a lease.

LIEN A claim against the property of another in order to secure the payment of a debt.

POSSESSORY INTEREST The right to possess particular real property to the exclusion of others.

POSSESSORY RIGHT The right to possess particular real property to the exclusion of others.

SECURED CREDITOR A creditor, the repayment of whose loan is secured by collateral sufficient to repay the debt owed.

In re Chrysler LLC *(cont'd)*

Claimants (P) v. Debtor (D)

576 F.3d 108 (2d Cir. 2009)

NATURE OF CASE: Appeal of bankruptcy court order authorizing the sale of substantially all debtor's assets.

FACT SUMMARY: Chrysler LLC (Chrysler) (D) filed for an asset-sale transaction under 11 U.S.C. § 363, where substantially all its assets were transferred into "New Chrysler." Pensioners (P), who hold secured claims, appealed approval of the sale, arguing that they had not consented to the release of their assets in the sale.

RULE OF LAW

Under 11 U.S.C. § 363(f), a collateral trustee can act on behalf of all credit holders and consent to the § 363(b) sale of assets free and clear of any interest.

FACTS: Chrysler LLC (Chrysler) (D) and its related companies filed a prepackaged bankruptcy petition under Chapter 11, following months of significant losses, a bailout from the United States government, an unsuccessful search for a merger partner, and an unsuccessful search for additional bailout funds for a standalone restructuring. Eventually, Chrysler (D) agreed to an asset-sale transaction pursuant to 11 U.S.C. § 363, which was approved and detailed in a Master Transaction Agreement (Agreement). Under the Agreement, substantially all Chrysler's assets would be transferred to New CarCo Acquisition LLC (New Chrysler), in exchange for New Chrysler's assumption of certain liabilities and $2 billion in cash. Fiat S.p.A. agreed to provide New Chrysler with fuel-efficient vehicle platforms, access to its global distribution system, and experienced management. The Indiana State Police Pension Trust, Indiana State Teachers Retirement Fund, and the Indiana Major Moves Construction Fund (Pensioners, collectively) (P), secured claim holders, challenged the Sale Order, arguing that they had not consented to the release of their own sold assets. Pensioners (P) stated that a subclause in one of their loan agreements required them to provide Chrysler (D) with consent before selling collateral assets. The bankruptcy court ruled that while the Pensioners (P) themselves did not consent to the release of their assets, that consent was validly provided by the collateral trustee, who was authorized to act on behalf of all first-lien credit holders. Pensioners (P), who hold secured claims, appealed approval of the sale, arguing that they had not consented to the release of their assets in the sale.

ISSUE: Under 11 U.S.C. § 363(f), can a collateral trustee act on behalf of all credit holders and consent to the § 363(b) sale of assets free and clear of any interest?

HOLDING AND DECISION: (Jacobs, C.J.) Yes. Under 11 U.S.C. § 363(f), a collateral trustee can act on behalf of all credit holders and consent to the § 363(b) sale of assets free and clear of any interest. Section 363(f) states that assets sold pursuant to § 363(b) may be sold "free and clear of any interest" in the assets if the entity holding the interest consents to the sale. The contractual clause in question states that if the requested amendment would result in the release of all, or substantially all, of the collateral property, then the amendment of the loan documents themselves requires written consent of all lenders. However, the § 363(b) sale did not entail amendment of the loan document. Rather, the sale was affected by implementing the clear consent terms of the loan agreement. Pensioners' (P) argument that the majority lenders were intimidated or coerced into approving the sale is similarly meritless, as no evidence in the record supports a finding of coercion. Sale order affirmed.

ANALYSIS

Following the decision in *In re Chrysler LLC*, the Pensioners (P) continued to argue in public that the decision to affirm the sale was a clear violation of the Fifth Amendment and bankruptcy law. However, defenders of the bankruptcy court's decision argued that the pension funds had lost less than one percent of their assets in the Chrysler sale, and expressed concern at the larger economic ramifications if Chrysler had been permitted to fail.

Quicknotes

ASSET An item of real or personal property that is owned and has tangible value.

COERCION The overcoming of a person's free will as a result of threats, promises, or undue influence.

COLLATERAL Property that secures the payment of a debt.

SECURED CLAIM A claim, the repayment of which is secured by collateral sufficient to repay the debt owed.

CHAPTER 32

Sales and Beyond II

Quick Reference Rules of Law

In re Texas Rangers Baseball Partners

Baseball franchise (P) v. Lenders (D)

431 B.R. 706 (Bankr. N.D. Tex. 2010)

NATURE OF CASE: Reconsideration of order in Chapter 11 bankruptcy action.

FACT SUMMARY: Debtor (P) sought to sell its assets but needed to market-test its prepetition sale price through approved bidding procedures. Lenders (D) objected to the bidding procedures.

RULE OF LAW

The court may direct the bidding process for a Section 363 sale or for a trustee sale to ensure the highest value is achieved for debtor.

FACTS: Debtor (P) entered into an asset purchase agreement ("APA") with Express wherein Express would purchase Debtor's (P) assets, including the Texas Rangers. Debtor (P) then filed a Chapter 11 bankruptcy petition and sought to implement the APA in the reorganization plan ("the Plan"). The Rangers Equity Owners ("Snyder") had to approve the Plan. Snyder negotiated with other potential bidders, Debtor (P), and Express to agree on bidding procedures to market-test the APA. After hearing, comment review, and arguments, the court completed Approved Procedures implemented in its Procedures Order. The Lender Parties (D) filed a joint motion for the court to reconsider its Procedures Orders.

ISSUE: May the court direct the bidding process for a Section 363 sale or for a trustee sale to ensure the highest value is achieved for debtor?

HOLDING AND DECISION: (Lynn, J.) Yes. The court may direct the bidding process for a Section 363 sale or for a trustee sale to ensure the highest value is achieved for debtor. The parties have not contested the court's authority to draft and adopt the bidding procedures, but it is worth noting the court is authorized in §§ 363(b)(1) and 102(1). The court exercised its authority on the belief the asset purchase agreement (APA) was under severe time constraints. The Lenders (D) seek to wait until the confirmation hearing and would accept the loss of Express as a purchaser. The court prefers to have appropriate bidding procedures in place to timely market-test the APA. Lenders (D) and Snyder argue there is insufficient time for potential bidders to obtain financing and complete due diligence. The three-week period is short, but two or more bidders have prequalified with BOC [the Commissioner of Baseball] and all parties agree to act promptly. The potential bidders have had access to information for due diligence and necessarily are wealthy. Next, the Lenders (D) argue the stalking horse provisions for Express are overly generous. If the APA is not consummated, Express may assert an unsecured claim against Debtor (P) because the APA was prepetition. The alternative provided is a $10,000,000 breakup fee [although the Lenders (D) argue the breakup fee is $1,500,000] and 125 percent of Express's actual costs and damages. The court erred in establishing the 125 percent because it encourages Express to up excessive costs. The court also did not intend for the breakup fee to extend past the $15,000,000 overbid protection provided for in the Approved Procedures. Thus, the Approved Procedures must be modified such that Express elects to rely on 125 percent or the breakup fee, and, in no event will the fee exceed $13,000,000. The court presumes Debtor (P) will act in good faith in evaluating potential bids or the court will intervene to further protect the interests of Lenders (D) and other creditors. If no other bidder appears at the auction, Debtor (P) will have to prove the Approved Procedures were an effective market test. Debtor (P) could argue, although the court does not now find, that the instant motion and hearing chilled potential bidding during the first of the three-week process and the motion pointed out weaknesses in the Approved Procedures. Should even one bidder appear to compete, the court will assume the market-test was fair. [Granted in part; denied in part].

ANALYSIS

The "stalking horse" bidder is a predetermined bidder, typically selected by the debtor, to set the pace of the bidding and the presumptive purchase price. A "breakup fee" negotiation is standard to protect the stalking horse bidder from significant financial outlay to attorneys, financial planners, and other advisors only to have the deal rejected during reorganization. It also is common to have bidders prequalified although such a tight timetable as in *Texas Rangers* is somewhat unusual.

Quicknotes

GOOD FAITH An honest intention to abstain from taking advantage of another.

MARKET VALUE The price of particular property or goods that a buyer would offer and a seller accept in the open market, following full disclosure.

In re Fisker Automotive Holdings, Inc.

Debtors (P) v. Unsecured creditors (D)

510 B.R. 55 (Bankr. D. Del. 2014)

NATURE OF CASE: Hearing on sale motion and bidding procedures motion in Chapter 11 bankruptcy case.

FACT SUMMARY: Fisker Automotive Holdings, Inc. (Debtors) (P) manufactured hybrid electric cars but suffered a series of setbacks that resulted in a need to sell substantially all the assets. Hybrid Tech Holdings, LLC (Hybrid) wanted to enter into an asset purchase agreement with Debtors (P) for private sale or at least wanted to credit bid at an auction. The Committee of Unsecured Creditors (Committee) (D) wanted to cap or eliminate the credit bid.

RULE OF LAW

A court may limit a credit bid for cause.

FACTS: Fisker Automotive Holdings, Inc. (Debtors) (P) had a goal to manufacture hybrid electric vehicles, but experienced a recall of the third-party supplier batteries, a loss of inventory during a hurricane, and loss of the United States Department of Energy (DOE) lending facility. Debtors (P) intended a private sale to Hybrid Tech Holdings, LLC (Hybrid) and then manage the estates through the Chapter 11 liquidation plan. Hybrid purchased DOE's outstanding principal for $25 million and became Debtors' (P) senior secured lender. Hybrid wanted to enter into an asset purchase agreement (APA) and acquire substantially all Debtors' (P) assets for $75 million in the form of a credit bid. Debtors (P) filed a Sale Motion to proceed with the private sale. The Committee of Unsecured Creditors (Committee) (D) opposes the motion and seeks an auction as set forth in the Bidding Procedures Motion. The alternative to the private sale is an auction with Wanxiang America Corporation (Wanxiang). The parties limited the issues to Hybrid's ability to credit bid as proposed.

ISSUE: May a court limit a credit bid for cause?

HOLDING AND DECISION: (Gross, J.) Yes. A court may limit a credit bid for cause. Wanxiang will not participate if Hybrid is entitled to credit bid more than $25 million. Hybrid argues it should be able to credit bid at $75 million. If Hybrid's credit bid is eliminated or capped, Wanxiang is prepared to increase its bid at auction. Hybrid paid $25 million for its claim and is entitled to credit bid. The question becomes at what amount. Section 363(k) permit a court to authorize an asset sale for cause because the right to credit bid is not absolute. Here, there is not just the risk of chilling bidding but the loss of the auction altogether if Hybrid's credit bid is not capped. Debtors (P) filed these cases just three business days before the Thanksgiving holiday and insisted on confirmation hearings right after the New Year. Hybrid claimed a "drop dead" date of January 3, 2014, but it is January 17 and Hybrid still works to acquire Debtors' (P) assets. The rush to purchase is troublesome and appears to short-circuit the bankruptcy process. Further, Hybrid's claim is a hybrid, and it is not known how much of the claim is secured. A lienholder may not bid its lien when the amount is uncertain. The Court will limit for cause Hybrid's credit bid to $25 million. [Order on motions is not included].

ANALYSIS

Hybrid appealed but the bankruptcy order was affirmed. The appellate court also noted Hybrid's many "emergency motions" that had no true emergency basis and appeared only to pressure the sale. The court prohibited Hybrid from filing further motions related to the credit bid.

In re DBSD North America, Inc.

Debtor (P) v. Creditor class (D)

634 F.3d 79 (2d Cir. 2011)

NATURE OF CASE: Consolidated appeals from bankruptcy plans of reorganization.

FACT SUMMARY: DBSD North America, Inc. and its subsidiaries (collectively, "Debtor") (P) submitted a plan of reorganization ("the Plan") for confirmation. The Plan was confirmed over the objections of Dish Network Corporation (DISH) (D).

RULE OF LAW

The court can designate a vote on plan confirmation if it is found to have been made in bad faith.

FACTS: DBSD North America, Inc. and its subsidiaries (collectively, "Debtor") (P) used satellites and land-based transmission towers to develop a mobile communications network, but it amassed significant debt. It filed a voluntary petition for bankruptcy and proposed a plan of reorganization. Claims against Debtor (P) included the First Lien Debt of a $40 million revolving credit facility with a first-priority security interest and a Second Lien Debt of $650 million with a second-priority security interest that had grown to $740 million by the time of filing. Dish Network Corporation (DISH) (D), in the same industry and part-owner of a competing company, purchased all the First Lien Debt at full face value for strategic purposes and in exchange for an agreement with the sellers that they would make objections to the Plan that DISH (D) could adopt after the sale. In court and in internal documents, DISH (D) admitted it made the purchase to control the bankruptcy process of this asset and potentially to obtain a blocking position in the Second Lien Debt. DISH (D) voted against confirmation of the Plan, asserted the Plan was not feasible under 11 U.S.C. § 1129(a)(11), and argued the Plan did not comply with 11 U.S.C. § 1129(b)(2)(A) to permit a cram down. Debtor (P) moved for the court to find DISH's (D) rejection was not in good faith. The bankruptcy court granted the motion, designated (i.e., disregarded) DISH's (D) vote, and disregarded the entirety of the First Lien Debt class to determine the Plan's acceptance. The bankruptcy court confirmed the Plan, the district court affirmed, and these consolidated appeals followed.

ISSUE: May the court designate a vote on plan confirmation if it is found to have been made in bad faith?

HOLDING AND DECISION: (Lynch, J.) Yes. The court can designate a vote on plan confirmation if it is found to have been made in bad faith. Claim holders must approve a plan of reorganization to confirm it. The bankruptcy court can designate any votes made "not in good faith" pursuant to 11 U.S.C. § 1126(e). The Bankruptcy Code provides no guidance for what constitutes a bad faith vote and voters are permitted to have "ulterior motives." What type of motive triggers § 1126(e) designation is a question of law reviewed de novo and whether DISH (D) had such a voting motive is a question of fact. *Texas Hotel Securities Corp. v. Waco Development Co.*, 87 F.2d 395 (5th Cir. 1936), triggered Congress to create the "good faith" rule. The most famous case demonstrating bad faith ulterior motives, and the case upon which the bankruptcy court here heavily relied, is *In re Allegheny Intl., Inc.*, 118 B.R. 282, 289-90 (Bankr. W.D. Pa. 1990). In this case, the party bought a blocking position in several classes and then sought to defeat the plan and take control of the debtor through approval of its own plan. Here, DISH (D) bought a blocking position not with the intention to maximize its debt return but to control the bankruptcy process for its competitor, Debtor (P). This conclusion is supported by DISH's (D) own admissions, internal communications, and attempt to propose its own plan. The Loan Syndications and Trading Association (LSTA) filed amicus curiae in support of strategic transactions that benefit all parties to bankruptcy estates. DISH (D), however, cannot use its purchased votes to secure an advantage in pursuing its strategic transaction. Determination of the proper designation of a vote is a fact-intensive inquiry and this court finds no error in the decision to designate DISH's (D) vote as cast in bad faith. DISH's (D) next argument is that the bankruptcy court erred in disregarding the entire First Lien Debt class, but common sense dictated that decision even if it is not explicitly required by the Bankruptcy Code. [Affirmed; the court found the Plan feasible].

ANALYSIS

A showing of bad faith or improper ulterior motives is fact-intensive because parties may have a variety of strategic but proper reasons for voting to confirm or reject a plan for reorganization. A party's benefit from the vote is not an automatic basis for disregarding that vote; in fact, many parties will vote in the way that benefits them the most because they are seeking to maximize the recovery from the bankruptcy reorganization process.

Continued on next page.

Quicknotes

CRAMDOWN Refers to a court's confirmation of a reorganization plan in a bankruptcy proceeding despite the opposition of creditors.

GOOD FAITH An honest intention to abstain from taking advantage of another.

CHAPTER 33

Governance in Chapter 11

Quick Reference Rules of Law

In re Marvel Entertainment Group, Inc.

Debtor (P) v. Senior creditor (D)

209 B.R. 832 (D. Del. 1997)

NATURE OF CASE: Appeal from bankruptcy injunction order in Chapter 11 adversary cases.

FACT SUMMARY: Bondholders sought to replace the board of directors but were faced with the automatic stay prohibiting such action.

RULE OF LAW

The automatic stay provisions of the Bankruptcy Code are not implicated by the exercise of shareholders' corporate governance rights.

FACTS: Ronald O. Perelman owns Marvel Holdings, Inc., Marvel [Parent] Holdings, Inc., and Marvel III Holdings, Inc. (collectively, the "Marvel Holding Companies"). The Marvel Holding Companies own or control 80 percent of Marvel Entertainment Group, Inc. (Marvel) common stock. In 1993 and 1994, the Marvel Holding Companies issued bonds and raised $894 million. The bonds were secured by 80 percent of Marvel stock and 100 percent of the stock of Marvel Holdings, Inc. and Marvel [Parent] Holdings, Inc. An indenture trustee, LaSalle, acts for the bondholders. In 1996, Marvel and its subsidiaries (collectively, "Debtors") and Marvel Holding Companies filed Chapter 11 bankruptcy petitions and LaSalle filed several proofs of claims so the bondholders could recover against Marvel if Marvel is liable for the Marvel Holding Companies' debt. After evidentiary hearings, the bankruptcy court lifted the stay in the Marvel Holding Companies cases so LaSalle and the bondholders could foreclose on and vote the pledged shares. LaSalle and the Bondholders Committee then informed Debtors of their intent to replace Marvel's board of directors. Debtors then instituted an adversary proceeding to enjoin the replacement of Marvel's board. Chase Manhattan Bank (Chase) (D), agent for the senior secured lenders, filed a similar adversary proceeding seeking similar relief. The court determined § 362(a)(3) prohibited the board replacement until relief from the automatic stay was first sought and granted. LaSalle, the Bondholders Committee, and Chase (D) moved for relief from the automatic stay.

ISSUE: Are the automatic stay provisions of the Bankruptcy Code implicated by the exercise of shareholders' corporate governance rights?

HOLDING AND DECISION: (McKelvie, J.) No. The automatic stay provisions of the Bankruptcy Code are not implicated by the exercise of shareholders' corporate governance rights. Shareholders have the right to elect a new board of directors during reorganization unless circumstances demonstrate "clear abuse." Debtors (P) argue the bondholders are not acting as shareholders here, but as creditors. The bondholders, however, acquired shareholder rights in Marvel by exercising creditor remedies after relief from the automatic stay in the *Marvel Holdings Companies* case. Chase (D) argues Marvel is insolvent and the automatic stay applies, but the court has never found Marvel insolvent. The bondholders may vote the pledged shares. [Injunction vacated.]

ANALYSIS

The shareholders in *Marvel* were not Marvel creditors, so they had the right to control the Debtor-in-Possession. *Johns-Manville Corp. v. Equity Security Holders Committee*, 801 F.2d 60 (2d Cir. 1986), held the shareholders could not replace the board if the purpose only was to improve a bargaining position in Chapter 11 negotiations and the entity was insolvent. That behavior constituted "clear abuse" of the system.

Quicknotes

AUTOMATIC STAY Upon the filing of a voluntary bankruptcy petition, creditors are prohibited from attempting to recover payment from the debtor or his property.

DEBTOR-IN-POSSESSION A Chapter 11 bankruptcy debtor who retains control of assets or property pursuant to a plan of reorganization.

In re Blue Stone Real Estate, Constr. & Dev. Corp.

Debtor (P) v. Trustee (D)

392 B.R. 897 (Bankr. M.D. Fla. 2008)

NATURE OF CASE: Expedited hearing request in Chapter 11 bankruptcy case.

FACT SUMMARY: Blue Stone Real Estate, Constr. & Dev. Corp. (Debtor) (P) filed a motion to appoint its own Chief Restructuring Officer to oversee the corporation during the bankruptcy proceedings. The United States Trustee (Trustee) (D) objected on the grounds a "disinterested" trustee should be appointed.

RULE OF LAW

A Chapter 11 debtor-in-possession retains ability to elect a private trustee, subject to judicial approval, to manage corporate governance issues.

FACTS: James W. DeMaria (DeMaria), principal of Blue Stone Real Estate, Constr. & Dev. Corp. (Debtor) (P), allegedly failed to provide complete and truthful testimony, documentation, and information about property transfers. Due to DeMaria's refusal to cooperate, the creditors' meeting did not take place. The Trustee (D) moved the court to appoint a Chapter 11 trustee pursuant to § 1104(a)(1). Debtor (P) sought to retain Steven S. Oscher, CPA (Oscher) and Oscher Consulting, P.A. as the Chief Restructuring Officer (CRO) to review Debtors' (P) books and records, inventory assets, negotiate with potential purchasers, and oversee the liquidation of Debtors' (P) assets. Trustee (D) objected on the grounds a "disinterested" trustee should be appointed and DeMaria would control Oscher. Debtor (P) moved for an expedited hearing.

ISSUE: Does a Chapter 11 debtor-in-possession retain ability to elect a private trustee, subject to judicial approval, to manage corporate governance issues?

HOLDING AND DECISION: (McEwen, J.) Yes. A Chapter 11 debtor-in-possession retains ability to elect a private trustee, subject to judicial approval, to manage corporate governance issues. DeMaria selected Oscher and the evidence indicates Oscher is independent, disinterested, and only met DeMaria just prior to the proceedings. No party could articulate a credible difference in the skill set between Oscher and a Chapter 11 trustee. Trustee (D) argued section 1107(a) limits the functions of a CRO compared to a Chapter 11 trustee, but that is a misreading of the statute. The Court can require the CRO perform the duties set forth in subsections (a)(2), (3), and (4). Here, Oscher is required to undertake the duties in (a)(2) and (3) and may, but need not, undertake those in (a)(4). The allegations that Oscher cannot perform the same as a Chapter 11 trustee border on the frivolous. Trustee (D) also argues the court cannot order conditions or limitations under § 1107(a) that would leave Debtors (P) without boards of directors. The Bankruptcy Code is replete with express requirements of and limitations on business operations of a debtor-in-possession. The plain meaning of § 1107(a) permits the court to alter the boards and management. Further, the court can impose requirements that will alleviate any concern, however unfounded, that Oscher is operating other than as an independent professional with absolute control over Debtors (P). Trustee (D) next argues the appointment of a CRO is a disguised attempt for Debtors (P) to invade the province of the Trustee (D). Essentially, Trustee (D) asserts that a motion for appointment of a Chapter 11 trustee freezes a debtor-in-possession from changing management even if such a change would obviate the need for the trustee. This is a disappointing argument because it appears nothing more than Trustee (D) protecting its "turf." The appointment of a Chapter 11 trustee is an "extraordinary remedy" and nothing in the Bankruptcy Code prohibits a change in management just because a motion to appoint a trustee is filed. The court must examine the integrity of the new management and this court has done so. The reality is that the Trustee's (D) motion triggered Debtors' (P) voluntary response to cure the very allegations of mismanagement that Trustee (D) alleges. Debtors' (P) proposed immediate change in management would cure these ills, but Trustee (D) seeks the usual elements of due process, such as discovery and trial, which would be time-consuming. Debtors' (P) expedited hearing request on the CRO motion provides immediate relief. CRO Motion is granted; Debtors (P) are authorized to retain Oscher as CRO pursuant to §§ 327(a) and 105(a) rather than § 363.

ANALYSIS

The Bankruptcy Code authorizes appointment of a trustee through the United States Trustee, but it also permits the election of a private trustee nominated by current management or control of a Chapter 11 debtor-in-possession. The private trustee must be disinterested, and the court reviews compensation so concerns about cronyism should be addressed.

Quicknotes

DEBTOR-IN-POSSESSION A Chapter 11 bankruptcy debtor who retains control of assets or property pursuant to a plan of reorganization.

In re Hawker Beechcraft, Inc.

[Parties not identified.]

479 B.R. 308 (Bankr. S.D.N.Y. 2012)

NATURE OF CASE: Motion to approve key employee incentive plan in Chapter 11 bankruptcy case.

FACT SUMMARY: Debtors filed the key employee incentive plan for court approval.

RULE OF LAW

A debtor's key employee incentive plan must incentivize insiders to meet challenging targets rather than provide payment merely for staying with the company during the bankruptcy process.

FACTS: Debtors manufacture and service Hawker and Beechcraft-branded aircraft. Prior to filing the Chapter 11 petitions, Debtors entered into a Restructuring Support Agreement with the majority of the creditors (the "Standalone Transaction") with deadlines to accomplish certain tasks. Simultaneously, the Debtors pursued a Third-Party Transaction for sale of the assets. Debtors received a Superior Proposal that would provide $1.79 billion in cash but required a 45-day exclusive access period. Debtors filed the Superior Exclusivity Motion, which was granted over objection. Debtors then filed the key employee incentive plan (KEIP) and noninsider key employee retention plan (KERP). Debtors identified eight "insiders" denominated as the Senior Leadership Team (SLT). SLT members received bonuses based on targets identified in the Standalone Transaction or the Third-Party Transaction and continued employment on the date bonuses were due. The Standalone Transaction bonus was based on timing of the consummation of the transaction and financial performance. The deadlines can be extended at Debtors' discretion. The Third-Party Transaction bonus is based on the purchase price and closing date. At the evidentiary hearing, the court approved the KERP but took the KEIP under advisement.

ISSUE: Must a debtor's key employee incentive plan incentivize insiders to meet challenging targets?

HOLDING AND DECISION: (Bernstein, J.) Yes. A debtor's key employee incentive plan must incentivize insiders to meet challenging targets rather than provide payment merely for staying with the company during the bankruptcy process. Section 503(c)(1) of the Bankruptcy Code governs insider retention plans, which essentially reward employees for staying with the debtor. Congress enacted the subsection with the 2005 BAPCPA amendments to address the concern that insiders frequently were being paid simply to report to work during the bankruptcy process. A key employee retention plan (KERP) must satisfy the rigorous requirements of § 503(c)(1). A key employee incentive plan (KEIP) must only comply with 11 U.S.C. § 503(c)(3), which is a "facts and circumstances" standard. A KEIP cannot be a retention plan but must incentivize insiders to meet challenges. Here, the Senior Leadership Team (SLT) must meet minimally challenging targets, at least one of which is almost certain to occur. The SLT members must be employed as of the date the bonuses are paid, which appears to be a retention bonus. Further, the SLT can seek an extension of deadlines at the discretion of Debtors. Finally, Debtors' CEO testified the purpose of the bonus structure was to discourage the SLT from seeking other employment opportunities. Here, the targets at the higher end of the KEIP are a challenge, but the lower end targets do not meet the minimum threshold for approval. The motion is denied without prejudice.

ANALYSIS

Many companies attempt to structure insider bonus payments as part of the reorganization process. The bonus payments encourage key employees to stay with a company that is saddled with so much debt that it filed a Chapter 11 petition. Congress fought against the outsized bonus payments being handed to executives merely for continuing to perform in the manner that brought the company to the bankruptcy process. The resulting requirements of 11 U.S.C. § 503(c) are exceptionally difficult to meet, but creative drafting can provide the payments sought.

Quicknotes

CHAPTER 11 BANKRUPTCY A legal proceeding whereby a debtor, who is unable to pay his or her debts as they become due, is relieved of the obligation to pay creditors through reorganization and payment from future income.

CHAPTER 34

Practicing in Chapter 11

Quick Reference Rules of Law

		PAGE
1.	*In re Lee.* A single attorney or law firm will be disqualified from representing two or more Chapter 11 debtors when the lawyer has failed to disclose a retainer or the existence of parallel employment applications or when the joint representation gives rise to an actual conflict of interest.	*220*
2.	*In re SONICblue, Inc.* (1) Where debtor's counsel has failed to disclose a material conflict of interest, it is in the creditors' best interest to disqualify counsel and to have counsel replaced by a Chapter 11 trustee. (2) Conversion of a Chapter 11 case to a Chapter 7 case is not preferable to appointing a Chapter 11 trustee, and in the creditors' best interest, where the committee of unsecured creditors and its counsel may not be fulfilling their duties to the creditor class.	*221*
3.	*In re Hungry Horse.* A bankruptcy court is not prevented from approving a fee defense provision in a retention agreement as a "reasonable term and condition" under Bankruptcy Code § 328(a).	*224*
4.	*In re Energy Partners, Ltd.* An application for employment of a professional under Bankruptcy Code § 328 will not be granted where the record supporting such employment is comprised primarily of conclusory statements; the proposed compensation is unreasonable; and the proposed employment is not in the best interests of the estate.	*225*

In re Lee

Law firm applicant (P) v. Bankruptcy court (D)

94 B.R. 172 (Bankr. C.D. Cal. 1989)

NATURE OF CASE: Parallel employment applications for appointment as counsel for two Chapter 11 debtors.

FACT SUMMARY: The law firm Lee, Scott & Young sought appointment as counsel for both Seoul Corporation and Lee (P), who was one of Seoul's shareholders, but the law firm's application failed to disclose its retainer with Lee (P).

RULE OF LAW

A single attorney or law firm will be disqualified from representing two or more Chapter 11 debtors when the lawyer has failed to disclose a retainer or the existence of parallel employment applications or when the joint representation gives rise to an actual conflict of interest.

FACTS: Seoul Corporation, a seller of general merchandise and wholesale costume jewelry, filed for Chapter 11 bankruptcy. One week later, its sole shareholders, including Lee (P), also filed for Chapter 11 protection. The schedules of both debtors revealed that there was a substantial overlap of creditors for the individuals and for the corporation. Both Seoul Corporation and Lee (P) filed employment applications for the appointment of the law firm Lee, Scott & Young as counsel for the debtors. However, the applications failed to disclose that the firm had received a $2,500 retainer from Lee (P) (but not from Seoul Corporation) and that there were parallel applications. The firm's declaration to the court represented that it did not represent any adverse interests to the bankruptcy estates. When the court discovered the parallel applications, it issued an order to show cause why the law firm should not be disqualified in both cases for failure to disclose them.

ISSUE: Will an attorney or law firm be disqualified from representing two or more Chapter 11 debtors when it has failed to disclose a retainer or the existence of parallel employment applications or when the joint representation gives rise to an actual conflict of interest?

HOLDING AND DECISION: (Bufford, J.) Yes. An attorney or law firm will be disqualified from representing two Chapter 11 debtors when it has failed to disclose a retainer or the existence of parallel employment applications or when the joint representation gives rise to an actual conflict of interest. There is a presumption that for two or more related bankruptcy cases it is improper to appoint a single trustee, creditor's committee, or the same counsel for trustees, creditor's committee, or debtors in possession when: (1) creditors of the debtors have dealt with such debtors as an economic unit; (2) there is a substantial overlap of creditors; (3) the affairs of the debtors are substantially entangled; (4) assets have been transferred from one debtor to another in non-arm's length transactions; or (5) the corporate veil of one of the debtors should be pierced. Here Lee, Scott & Young did not disclose its retainer with Lee (P) or its parallel employment applications, both in violation of Bankruptcy Rule 2014(a). Further, Seoul Corporation and Lee (P) have joint liability on many of the debts owing by the respective estates, and thus the interests of Seoul Corporation and Lee (P) were in actual conflict. Bankruptcy Code § 327(a) prohibits an attorney from representing a debtor if he is not disinterested or holds an interest adverse to the bankruptcy estate. Therefore, on any of these three grounds, the law firm may be disqualified from representing either Seoul Corporation or Lee (P) or both. [Because such nondisclosures and conflicts are common in the district, the court will only disqualify the firm from representing Lee (P) and will grant the employment application with regard to Seoul Corporation; the standards set forth in the opinion will be applied prospectively.]

ANALYSIS

This case demonstrates one influential bankruptcy judge's attempt to enunciate ethical standards governing the appointment of counsel who attempt to represent Chapter 11 debtors with relating estates. Because bankruptcy counsel can serve only with court approval under Bankruptcy Code § 327(a), and the counsel's fees must be approved by the court under §§ 328(a) and 329(b), the court exercises final supervision over the debtor's choice of counsel.

Quicknotes

CONFLICT OF INTEREST Refers to ethical problems that arise, or may be anticipated to arise, between an attorney and his client if the interests of the attorney, another client, or a third-party conflict with those of the present client.

RETAINER Fee paid upon employing an attorney in advance of services rendered; sometimes paid to prevent employment by adversary.

TRUSTEE A person who is entrusted to keep or administer property for the benefit of another.

In re SONICblue Inc.

Trustee and creditors (P) v. Debtor's counsel (D)

2007 WL 926871 (Bankr. N.D. Cal. 2007)

NATURE OF CASE: Motions for disqualification of debtors' counsel and disgorgement of attorneys' fees; appointment of a Chapter 11 trustee; and conversion of the debtors' case to Chapter 7.

FACT SUMMARY: Counsel for SONICblue Inc. and its subsidiaries (the "debtors") in their Chapter 11 bankruptcy was Pillsbury Winthrop Shaw Pittman LLC (PWSP) (D). PWSP (D) had issued a prepetition opinion letter, several years before the bankruptcy, assuring payment to certain of the debtors' senior bondholders who effectively controlled the creditors' committee in the debtors' bankruptcy. After the opinion letter came to light when the senior bondholders demanded indemnification from PWSP (D), and only after PWSP (D) failed to disclose the conflict in its initial disclosures, the United States Trustee moved to disqualify PWSP (D) and to appoint a Chapter 11 trustee. Because of PWSP's (D) conflict of interest, which had not been timely disclosed, a claims trader that acquired claims against the estate moved to convert the case to Chapter 7.

RULE OF LAW

(1) Where debtor's counsel has failed to disclose a material conflict of interest, it is in the creditors' best interest to disqualify counsel and to have counsel replaced by a Chapter 11 trustee.

(2) Conversion of a Chapter 11 case to a Chapter 7 case is not preferable to appointing a Chapter 11 trustee, and in the creditors' best interest, where the committee of unsecured creditors and its counsel may not be fulfilling their duties to the creditor class.

FACTS: In 2001, SONICBlue Inc. formed S3 Graphics Co., Ltd., a joint venture with VIA Technologies, Inc. (VIA), and contributed certain intellectual property assets to the joint venture. In April 2002, SONICblue raised financing in a private placement issuance of $75 million in 7 percent senior secured subordinated convertible debentures. Three institutional bondholders acquired the senior debentures at a discount for $62.5 million. The indenture provided for the subordination of the senior debentures to certain obligations to VIA. In its capacity as counsel to SONICblue, Pillsbury Winthrop Shaw Pittman LLC (PWSP) (D) issued to the senior bondholders a written opinion as to the enforceability of the debentures. The opinion indicated the debentures were enforceable against SONICblue, but, most likely as the result of a scrivener's error, the opinion failed to indicate that enforceability would be limited by bankruptcy or similar circumstances. In October 2002, SONICblue retained PWSP (D) as bankruptcy counsel in the Chapter 11 bankruptcy that SONICblue and its subsidiaries (the "debtors") had filed, and in April 2003, PWSP (D) filed an employment application accompanied by a verified statement pursuant to Bankruptcy Rule 2014, which failed to disclose PWSP's (D) potential conflict of interest resulting from the issuance of the opinion letter to the senior bondholders one year earlier. PWSP (D) was appointed debtors' counsel. Smith, the company's chief financial officer (CFO), was appointed responsible individual. PWSP (D) diligently filed supplemental disclosures between May 2003 and June 2006, none of which mentioned the opinion letter. In addition, the Office of the United States Trustee appointed an Official Committee of Unsecured Creditors in March 2003, and the court authorized the employment of Bender of the law firm Levene, Neale, Bender, Rankin & Brill LLP (LNBRB) as the committee's counsel. The committee was dominated by the three senior bondholders. The debtors anticipated exhausting their cash reserves, and the cases became Chapter 11 liquidating cases. The debtors held nearly $80 million in funds for distribution and anticipated receiving an additional $6 million from preference settlements. Secured claims were paid in full from the proceeds of sale and a distribution of 33 percent to unsecured creditors was anticipated. After most of the assets were liquidated, PWSP (D), along with LNBRB, engaged in prosecuting avoidance actions and objections to claims. In doing so, PWSP (D) discovered that the bondholders may have received post-petition interest on their unsecured claim, contravening the prohibition in 11 U.S.C. § 502(b)(2)—which meant that SONICblue could challenge the bondholders' claim. In response, the bondholders asserted that they had relied on the opinion letter, which they interpreted as assuring that their claims were allowable in a subsequent bankruptcy case, and in September 2006 sought indemnification from PWSP (D) for any losses resulting from SONICblue's challenge to their claim—which could amount to $43 million. PWSP (P) turned the handling of the objection to the claim over to Bender, and informed him of the indemnification demand, but still did not disclose to the court the senior bondholders' claim or the opinion letter on which it was based. It was not until March 2007, after the United States Trustee (P) had filed motions both to appoint a trustee and to disqualify PWSP (D), as well as for disgorgement of attorneys' fees, that PWSP (D) finally provided a disclosure and detailed explanation of PWSP's (D) conflict of interest with the senior bondholders. In addition to the Trustee's

Continued on next page.

(P) motions, a claims trader, SB Claims LLC (SBClaims), moved to convert the case to a Chapter 7 case.

ISSUE:

(1) Where debtor's counsel has failed to disclose a material conflict of interest, is it in the creditors' best interest to disqualify counsel and to have counsel replaced by a Chapter 11 trustee?

(2) Is conversion of a Chapter 11 case to a Chapter 7 case preferable to appointing a Chapter 11 trustee and in the creditors' best interest, where the committee of unsecured creditors and its counsel may not be fulfilling their duties to the creditor class?

HOLDING AND DECISION: (Morgan, J.)

(1) Yes. Where debtor's counsel has failed to disclose a material conflict of interest, it is in the creditors' best interest to disqualify counsel and to have counsel replaced by a Chapter 11 trustee. Under § 327(a), a debtor-in-possession may employ attorneys that do not hold an interest adverse to the estate and that are disinterested persons, and, therefore, to serve as debtor's counsel, counsel must be free of all conflicting interests that might impair the impartiality and neutral judgment that they are expected to exercise. To disqualify PWSP (D) and to have a Chapter 11 trustee appointed, the Trustee (P) need only prevail either under § 1104(a)(1) and show cause, or under § 1104(a)(2), and show that the requested action is in the creditors' best interest; the Trustee (P) does not have to prevail under both. A review of the facts clearly demonstrates that PWPS (D) knew it had a continuing duty to update its Rule 2014 disclosures upon learning of any undisclosed connections or conflicts, that as of August 2006 it knew it had a disabling conflict of interest because it immediately sought the aid of LNBRB in attempt to resolve the conflict, and that in the face of its duties it nonetheless failed to apprise the court of these facts. Its attempt to characterize its failings as mere oversight is highly unpersuasive, especially since it made ongoing supplemental disclosures. These facts also demonstrate the need for a strong, independent, neutral trustee to restore creditor confidence. Since the creditors also have their doubts about Smith as responsible individual—since he does not report to a board, his duties are only part time, and he had been named as a defendant in a breach of fiduciary duty action in regard to the issuance of the senior debentures—the appointment of a trustee will allay these concerns as well. For these reasons, appointment of a trustee is warranted. Motion as to this issue granted.

(2) No. Conversion of a Chapter 11 case to a Chapter 7 case is not preferable to appointing a Chapter 11 trustee, and in the creditors' best interest, where the committee of unsecured creditors and its counsel may not be fulfilling their duties to the creditor class. The main reason to convert to Chapter 7 would be to remove the influence of the creditors' committee from the case, since there seems to be at least the appearance of impropriety by the committee and LNBRB. The bondholders appear to have used their position on the committee to insert themselves into the settlement negotiations without revealing a hidden agenda, so that they may have breached their fiduciary duties to the unsecured creditor body. It also appears that LNBRB may have failed to fulfill its role as a watchdog on behalf of the unsecured creditors. When the conflict arose between PWSP (D) and the senior bondholders, LNBRB accepted responsibility for prosecuting the objections to the bondholders' claims without considering its own connections to the bondholders and the fact, or at least appearance, that it might also be conflicted. Professionals retained by an official committee of unsecured creditors owe fiduciary duties to the committee and the entire creditor class. Therefore, SBClaims' concerns about the committee and its counsel are substantial. Because of these troubling improprieties, having an active trustee who will formulate an independent strategy and direct its own counsel is critical. Additionally, by having the case remain in Chapter 11, the United States Trustee's (P) application for an order approving either the appointment or the election of a trustee would have to include a disclosure of all proposed trustee's connections to the debtor, creditors, and other parties in interest; there is no similar disclosure requirement in Chapter 7. For these reasons case will not be converted to a Chapter 7 case. Motion as to this issue denied.

ANALYSIS

At some point in its opinion, the court noted that there were serious allegations that the case was being run by and for the benefit of counsel. PWSP's (D) actions, as well as those of LNBRB, which seemed to be self-interested acts aimed at protecting referral sources and revenue, are the kind of conduct that the Bankruptcy Reform Act of 1978 intended to put an end to. The legislative history of that Act decried the "opprobrious" bankruptcy ring and cronyism that the "protective atmosphere surrounding the close-knit referral circle" of attorneys in this case seems to manifest.

Quicknotes

CHAPTER 7 BANKRUPTCY A legal proceeding whereby a debtor, who is unable to pay his or her debts as they become due, is relieved of the obligation to pay creditors by liquidation and distribution of remaining assets.

CHAPTER 11 BANKRUPTCY A legal proceeding whereby a debtor, who is unable to pay his or her debts as they

Continued on next page.

become due, is relieved of the obligation to pay creditors through reorganization and payment from future income.

CONFLICT OF INTEREST Refers to ethical problems that arise, or may be anticipated to arise, between an attorney and the client if the interests of the attorney, another client, or a third-party conflict with those of the present client.

In re Hungry Horse

Unsecured Creditors (P) v. Debtor (D)

574 B.R. 740 (Bankr. D.N.M. 2017)

NATURE OF CASE: Bankruptcy court ruling on objection to engagement agreement.

FACT SUMMARY: Debtor Hungry Horse (D) sought approval of an engagement agreement that required Debtor (D) to pay legal fees for all services, including legal fees for defense of objections to its fees.

RULE OF LAW

A bankruptcy court is not prevented from approving a fee defense provision in a retention agreement as a "reasonable term and condition" under Bankruptcy Code § 328(a).

FACTS: Debtor Hungry Horse (D), an LLC that engaged in oilfield services, filed for Chapter 11 bankruptcy. Hungry Horse (D) sought approval of an engagement agreement with a new law firm under Bankruptcy Code § 328(a) after a substitution of counsel. The agreement required Hungry Horse (D) to pay all reasonable legal fees incurred in (1) obtaining court approval of employment and fee applications including dealing with objections to applications; (2) dealing with any objections to court approval; and (3) collecting and/or obtaining approval of its fees and costs by the bankruptcy or any other court. The Unsecured Creditors (P) objected to the engagement agreement.

ISSUE: Is a bankruptcy court prevented from approving a fee defense provision in a retention agreement as a "reasonable term and condition" under Bankruptcy Code § 328(a)?

HOLDING AND DECISION: (Thuma, J.) No. A bankruptcy court is not prevented from approving a fee defense provision in a retention agreement as a "reasonable term and condition" under Bankruptcy Code § 328(a). Unsecured Creditors (P) argued that the Supreme Court's decision in *Baker Botts LLP v. ASARCO LLC*, 135 S. Ct. 2158 (2015), barred the proposed fee defense provision. In *ASARCO*, the Supreme Court reversed the bankruptcy court's award of $5.2 million of legal fees for a law firm to defend a fee application. The Supreme Court stated that each litigant must pay his own attorney's fees unless otherwise required by statute, which is commonly referred to as the American Rule. The Court concluded that attorney's fees did not qualify under relevant statute: in this case, § 330(a)(1)'s reasonable compensation provision, because a law firm that spends time litigating a fee application against a bankruptcy estate administrator is not performing loyal and disinterested service in the interest of a client. Debtor Hungry Horse (D) instead asks the fee defense provision to be approved under § 328(a), which provides that the trustee may employ a professional on any reasonable terms, including on a retainer, hourly, fixed fee, or contingent basis, and that the court may allow different compensation if the terms and conditions proved to be improvident. If employment terms and conditions are approved by a bankruptcy court under § 328(a), then the professional's compensation is governed by those terms rather than the "reasonable compensation for services rendered" language from § 330(a)(1)(A). *ASARCO* does not state that a fee defense provision can never be a "reasonable term" under § 328(a), and the Bankruptcy Code does not require an employment term to benefit the estate in order to be reasonable. Furthermore, requiring estate counsel to pay for the defense of its own fees would likely substantially reduce the net compensation in a bankruptcy case. Accordingly, the contract exception to the American Rule remains viable in bankruptcy cases. A properly drafted fee defense could constitute a "reasonable term" under § 328(a), as long as the provision (1) is agreed to by the bankruptcy estate; (2) allows the bankruptcy court to review and approve the reasonableness of any fee defense fees sought; (3) provides that the estate will also agree to a similar provision for committee counsel; and (4) provides that no fees will be allowed for unsuccessful fee defense work.

ANALYSIS

In *Baker Botts LLP v. ASARCO LLC*, 135 S. Ct. 2158 (2015), the debtor was represented by two law firms who together sought $120 million for their work on the bankruptcy proceeding, in addition to the $5.2 million that was rejected by the United States Supreme Court. In its opinion in *ASARCO*, the Court provided the Equal Access to Justice Act (Act) as an example of when departure from the American Rule is warranted. Section 2412(d)(1)(A) of the Act provides that a prevailing party, other than the United States, will be awarded fees and other expenses incurred by that party in any civil action brought by or against the United States, with exception of tort cases. This Act allows individuals, small businesses, and public interest groups to receive representation in cases against the federal government.

Quicknotes

AMERICAN RULE The rule that attorney's fees are not recoverable, unless expressly provided by law or pursuant to a contract.

In re Energy Partners, Ltd.

[Parties not identified.]

409 B.R. 211 (Bankr. S.D. Tex. 2009)

NATURE OF CASE: Applications in Chapter 11 bankruptcy to hire investment banking firms for, inter alia, their valuation services.

FACT SUMMARY: In the Chapter 11 bankruptcy of Energy Partners, Ltd. (Debtor), the Official Committee of Unsecured Noteholders (the Unsecured Noteholders' Committee) and the Official Committee of Equity Security Holders (the Equity Holders' Committee), dissatisfied with prior valuations of Debtor, filed separate applications to hire separate investment banking firms to perform independent valuations of Debtor. Bank of America, N.A., as agent for itself and on behalf of the Prepetition Secured Lenders, (the Agent) objected, contending that (1) the proposed fees for the investment banks were too high; (2) the proposed fees were nonrefundable; (3) the proposed fees were to be paid from the Debtor's cash collateral on which the Agent had a lien; and (4) the amount of cash collateral that would have to be used to pay the fees would violate the limitations set forth in the budget for paying consultants.

RULE OF LAW

An application for employment of a professional under Bankruptcy Code § 328 will not be granted where the record supporting such employment is comprised primarily of conclusory statements; the proposed compensation is unreasonable; and the proposed employment is not in the best interests of the estate.

FACTS: Energy Partners, Ltd. (Debtor), a publicly held entity in the oil and gas industry, filed a voluntary Chapter 11 petition. Shortly thereafter, Debtor applied to hire Parkman Whaling, LLC as its financial advisor. The bankruptcy court granted the application, approving $75,000 in monthly fees and expenses. The court then established a procedure for professionals retained by the estate to seek interim compensation on monthly basis. The court also issued a cash collateral order, which contained a budget (Budget) that had to be complied with. For example, the budget for consultants, including investment banks, for an 18-day period was $84,000. Parkman Whaling provided a valuation of Debtor, valuing its common shares (i.e., its equity) at no (zero) value, but valuing the common shares of a reorganized Debtor (New EPL) at $499 million. Birch Run Capital, LLC (Birch Run), which owned stock in Debtor, objected to Debtor's initial disclosures, in particular objecting to Parkman Whaling's valuation as too low and outdated. Birch Run commissioned its own valuation, which placed the value of Debtor's equity at over $212 million. The U.S. Trustee (UST) appointed an Official Committee of Unsecured Noteholders (the Unsecured Noteholders' Committee) and an Official Committee of Equity Security Holders (the Equity Holders' Committee). The Equity Holders' Committee then filed an application to hire Tudor Pickering Holt & Co. Securities, Inc. (Tudor Pickering), an investment banking firm. Under this Tudor Pickering Application, the proposed fee terms were: (a) a nonrefundable advisory fee of $500,000.00; (b) a nonrefundable expert witness fee of $25,000.00 per day, payable each day that a Tudor Pickering employee was requested, and made available, for the purpose of deposition or testimony; (c) a nonrefundable extended assignment fee of $100,000.00 per month; and (d) any out-of-pocket expenses. The Unsecured Noteholders' Committee then filed a similar application, proposing similar financial terms, to hire the investment banking firm Houlihan Lokey. Both investment firms were to provide the committees with valuation services, among other services. The aggregate fees would be around $1 million. Bank of America, N.A., as agent for itself and on behalf of the Prepetition Secured Lenders, (the Agent) objected, contending that (1) the proposed fees for the investment banks were too high; (2) the proposed fees were nonrefundable; (3) the proposed fees were to be paid from the Debtor's cash collateral on which the Agent had a lien; and (4) the amount of cash collateral that would have to be used to pay the fees would violate the limitations set forth in the Budget for paying consultants. The committee of unsecured creditors also objected on the grounds that the proposed fees were too high and nonrefundable. At a hearing held by the court, in support of the Houlihan Lokey application, testimony was presented that the fee arrangements had been vigorously negotiated between the Unsecured Noteholders' Committee and Houlihan Lokey. There was also testimony that the Unsecured Noteholders' Committee (which believed there was no equity in Debtor) wanted to obtain an appraisal that would rebut the anticipated valuation that Tudor Pickering would produce. In support of the Tudor Pickering application, the Equity Holders' Committee (which believed there was equity in Debtor) presented evidence that it picked Tudor Pickering because of that firm's "attractive fee level" and its "concentration in oil and gas." There was testimony that the Equity Holders' Committee was not satisfied to use the higher valuation from Birch Run because Birch Run was not an oil and gas "expert" or "in the business of valuation," and the Equity Holders' Committee wanted a defensible valuation from a reputable

Continued on next page.

valuation firm. There was also evidence that the terms in the engagement letter were typical in the industry and the proposed fees were even lower than some of the other fee arrangements that Tudor Pickering had negotiated in similar situations.

ISSUE: Will an application for employment of a professional under Bankruptcy Code § 328 be granted where the record supporting such employment is comprised primarily of conclusory statements; the proposed compensation is unreasonable; and the proposed employment is not in the best interests of the estate?

HOLDING AND DECISION: (Bohm, J.) No. An application for employment of a professional under Bankruptcy Code § 328 will not be granted where the record supporting such employment is comprised primarily of conclusory statements; the proposed compensation is unreasonable; and the proposed employment is not in the best interests of the estate. Under § 328, the proponents of the application have the burden of proving by a preponderance of the evidence that the proposed professional should be hired. Once an application is approved, a court may not alter the employment terms except under exceptional circumstances. Therefore, in exercising its gatekeeping function, the court must be presented with a strong record supporting employment. Here, the proponents of the applications have failed to provide such a record. Some factors to be considered when determining whether to approve employment include: (1) whether terms of an engagement agreement reflect normal business terms in the marketplace; (2) the relationship between the debtor and the professionals, i.e., whether the parties involved are sophisticated business entities with equal bargaining power who engaged in an arms-length negotiation; and (3) whether the retention, as proposed, is in the best interests of the estate. The record does not address these factors, except in the most conclusory fashion. Here, Parkman Whaling was willing to provide the same services that Houlihan Lokey and Tudor Pickering would provide, but for much less, and there was virtually no evidence that the committees in the case at bar could not have obtained comparable services without paying the excessive fees demanded by Houlihan Lokey and Tudor Pickering. Insufficient evidence was adduced that these proposed professionals should be treated so much more favorably than Parkman Whaling, or that their services would in any way be superior to those provided by Parkman Whaling. Even if it is true the compensation they seek is standard in the industry, that by itself does not render that level of compensation reasonable under § 328. Instead, specific evidence of reasonableness must be adduced. For example, the proponents needed—but failed—to adduce testimony about the specific compensation earned by investment bankers in engagements similar in size and circumstance to the engagement proposed in this case. Here, the only evidence of reasonableness was that Parkman Whaling was willing to work for significantly less than either of the proposed professionals, even though its services were comparable to those of the proposed investment banking firms. Thus, this factor weighs against approval. Second, testimony that negotiations between the proponents and the investment bankers were "robust" or "vigorous" is extremely generalized and too conclusory. More specific testimony was needed. For example, evidence should have been presented as to who conducted the negotiations for the proponent? Who conducted the negotiations for the investment banker? Where did the negotiations take place? How long did the negotiations occur? Were proposals and counterproposals made and, if so, were they reduced to writing? Given the dearth of specific evidence as to whether the negotiations were at arm's length, the factor also weighs against approval. Third, the proposed retention of Houlihan Lokey and Tudor Pickering is not in the best interest of the estate, as it has not been demonstrated that they would provide a tangible, identifiable, and material benefit to the estate. "These professionals may not just simply appear at the hearing, give conclusory testimony, and then expect to walk out of the courtroom with nonrefundable checks aggregating $1 million." Further, because the funds that would be used to pay these two investment banking firms constitute the Debtor's cash collateral, it must be determined whether allowing such use of these funds is in the best interests of the Debtor's estate. However, the record is insufficient as to this factor, as none of the witnesses gave any testimony that demonstrated how the Debtor's estate would benefit from the immediate reduction of $1 million in cash collateral. Accordingly, this factor also weighs against approval. Another consideration is that Tudor Pickering has also requested a $25,000.00 per day witness fee, to be earned regardless of how long a witness is working on behalf of the estate on any given day. "In these dire financial times, a request to be paid a $25,000.00 per day witness fee out of the coffers of a publicly traded company in bankruptcy is not only excessive, but unconscionable. . . ." Assuming an eight-hour workday, this is an hourly rate of $3,125—and such a rate is per se unreasonable; "[n]o witness is worth such an absurd amount regardless of the dollars at stake in the case." Finally, the investment banking firms are not entitled to "appearance fees" for merely showing up. While some of the world's top athletes, for example, command such fees, their appearance guarantees a financial benefit at any event where they appear. Here, the investment banking firms not only do not guarantee success; they do not even guarantee they will work a minimum number of hours in order to try to achieve success. For all these reasons, both applications are denied. Judgment for the Agent.

ANALYSIS

Section 328 was added to the Bankruptcy Code in 1978, prior to which time some professionals refused to work for bankruptcy estates because their compensation could po-

Continued on next page.

tentially be changed by a bankruptcy judge after the professionals had completed the work. Now, however, § 328 protects professionals from such uncertainties by allowing them to obtain prior approval of their compensation plan from the bankruptcy court. Once a bankruptcy court approves a professional's compensation under § 328, only extremely limited circumstances warrant altering that compensation. It should also be noted that § 328 is not itself a separate source of employment approval. If the terms and conditions of employment are not reasonable under § 328, the bankruptcy judge may exercise his discretion—as happened in this case—and deny the employment under § 1103(a).

Quicknotes

RETAINER FEES Compensation paid in advance for professional services.

CHAPTER 35

The Discharge of Future Claims

Quick Reference Rules of Law

Kane v. Johns-Manville Corp.

Claimants (P) v. Debtor (D)

843 F.2d 636 (2d Cir. 1988)

NATURE OF CASE: Appeal challenging the legality of a Chapter 11 reorganization plan.

FACT SUMMARY: Kane (P), representing a group of asbestos claimants (collectively referred to as "Kane (P)"), challenged the Chapter 11 reorganization plan submitted by Johns-Manville Corp. (D) and confirmed by the bankruptcy court on several grounds, including that the plan submitted and approved failed to comply with the requirements of 11 U.S.C. § 1129(a) and (b).

RULE OF LAW

Corporations faced with "mass tort" litigation may attempt to resolve liability through a Chapter 11 reorganization plan so long as the plan is submitted in good faith in attempt to accomplish a successful reorganization of the corporation and creditors are at least assured of receiving what they would have received had the corporation undergone a liquidation pursuant to Chapter 7 of the Bankruptcy Code.

FACTS: Johns-Manville Corp. (D), a major manufacturer of products containing asbestos, was faced with an estimated $2 billion liability associated with present and anticipated asbestos-related disease claims. To attempt to address such claims, it filed a voluntary petition in bankruptcy under Chapter 11. A legal representative was appointed to represent the interests of those who were termed "future asbestos health claimants." A plan was ultimately submitted whereby a trust was created out of which all present and future claimants would be paid. The trust was funded by insurance proceeds, cash, notes, receivables, long-term notes, and 20 percent of Johns-Manville's (D) profits, until all claims were paid. Through a multimedia notice campaign, potential asbestos claimants were notified of the plan and given the opportunity to vote on the plan by submitting a combined "proof of loss and voting" form. For voting purposes, each claim was valued at one dollar. Roughly 96 percent of those submitting forms approved the plan. The plan included injunction against bringing suit directly against Johns-Manville (D) or its insurers, provided for a procedure whereby a claimant could proceed against the Trust, and its terms applied to all claimants, present and future. Kane (P), representing a group of present asbestos claimants, challenged the plan, contending it discharged the rights of future claimants who did not technically have a dischargeable claim under Chapter 11. Kane (P) further argued that notice of the plan was inadequate, that the voting procedures utilized violated the Bankruptcy Code, and that the plan failed to conform with the requirements of 11 U.S.C. § 1129(a) and (b). The plan was confirmed despite these objections, and the district court affirmed. Kane (P) appealed.

ISSUE: Can a corporation faced with "mass tort" litigation attempt to resolve its liability through a Chapter 11 reorganization plan if the plan is submitted in good faith in attempt to accomplish a successful reorganization of the corporation and assures creditors of receiving at least as much as they would have received under a Chapter 7 liquidation of the corporation?

HOLDING AND DECISION: (Newman, J.) Yes. Corporations faced with "mass tort" litigation may attempt to resolve liability through a Chapter 11 reorganization plan so long as the plan is submitted in good faith in attempt to accomplish a successful reorganization of the plan, and creditors are at least assured under the plan of receiving what they would have received had the corporation undergone a Chapter 7 liquidation. This is what is required under 11 U.S.C. § 1129(a) and (b). The court first found that Kane (P) lacked standing to assess claims on behalf of any future third-party claimants because as a present claimant his interests were potentially opposed to those claimants because those claimants were already represented by the legal representative in these hearings and because the legal representative had expressly stated on appeal that he did not wish Kane (P) to assert the future claimants' rights. The court also rejected any challenge by Kane (P) as to the voting procedures employed, determining that any error in voting procedures constituted harmless error, and that any of the procedures claimed to be required by Kane (P) under the Bankruptcy Code would have resulted in no changes in the ultimate vote. The court was within its discretion in determining that the plan as submitted by Johns-Manville (D) was a good-faith attempt to accomplish a successful reorganization while keeping the best interests of all the creditors in mind. The court accepted the figures submitted by Johns-Manville (D) that the claimants would receive 100 percent payment on their claims, considerably higher than if there was Chapter 7 liquidation, and its acceptance of those findings was not clearly erroneous. The long-arm funding techniques employed by the Trust assure the continued payment of claims, while the injunction allows Johns-Manville (D) its best attempt to successfully reorganize, without the yoke of the continuing asbestos-disease litigation. The court's finding that the reorganization plan offers reasonable assurance of success is not clearly erroneous. Affirmed.

Continued on next page.

ANALYSIS

Even though there are a great many problems associated with employing a bankruptcy solution to mass tort litigation, it continues to be a primary response to such litigation. Such an approach has been utilized in the pharmaceutical context. In *In re A.H. Robbins,* 880 F.2d 769 (4th Cir. 1989), A.H. Robbins utilized the bankruptcy courts to resolve its liability arising out of the manufacture of the Dalkon Shield intrauterine device. It is interesting to note that one of Kane's (P) claims in the present litigation proved to be true: Shortly after the plan's inception, the Trust began to run out of money.

Quicknotes

CHAPTER 11 REORGANIZATION A plan formulated pursuant to Chapter 11 of the Bankruptcy Code whereby a debtor, who is unable to pay his or her debts as they become due, is relieved of the obligation to pay creditors through reorganization and payment from future income.

INJUNCTION A court order requiring a person to do, or prohibiting that person from doing, a specific act.

TRUST The holding of property by one party for the benefit of another.

Signature Combs, Inc. v. United States

Owner of polluted land (P) v. Federal government (D)

253 F. Supp. 2d 1028 (W.D. Tenn. 2003)

NATURE OF CASE: Motion for judgment on the pleadings in action to recover environmental response costs under the Comprehensive Environmental Response, Compensation and Liability Act, 42 U.S.C.S. § 9601 et seq.

FACT SUMMARY: Signature Combs, Inc. (P) sought to recover environmental response costs under the Comprehensive Environmental Response, Compensation and Liability Act, 42 U.S.C.S. § 9601 et seq. from Mason and Dixon Lines, Inc. (MDL) (D). MDL asserted that Plaintiffs' (P) claims against it were discharged pursuant to MDL's (D) Chapter 11 bankruptcy reorganization.

RULE OF LAW

Post-reorganization environmental claims brought against a debtor under the Comprehensive Environmental Response, Compensation and Liability Act have not been previously discharged in Chapter 11 where the Environmental Protection Agency could not have fairly contemplated the debtor's potential liability prior to its reorganization.

FACTS: Two Superfund sites contaminated with hazardous waste were cleaned up by the Environmental Protection Agency (EPA) and its state counterpart. Under the Comprehensive Environmental Response, Compensation and Liability Act (CERCLA), 42 U.S.C.S. § 9601 et seq., the government obtained reimbursement for the cleanup costs, known as response costs, from Signature Combs, Inc. (P). The Plaintiffs (P) then sought reimbursement of some of these costs from Mason and Dixon Lines, Inc. (MDL) (D), which defended by asserting that Plaintiffs' (P) claims against it were discharged pursuant to MDL's (D) Chapter 11 bankruptcy reorganization, which became final 12 years before Plaintiffs (P) instituted their action. MDL (D) contended that its liability to Plaintiffs (P) depended on whether it was potentially liable to the United States (D), and that such liability had been discharged. MDL (D) moved for judgment on the pleadings.

ISSUE: Have post-reorganization environmental claims brought against a debtor under the Comprehensive Environmental Response, Compensation and Liability Act (CERCLA) been previously discharged in Chapter 11 where the Environmental Protection Agency (EPA) could not have fairly contemplated the debtor's potential liability prior to its reorganization?

HOLDING AND DECISION: (Donald, J.) No. Post-reorganization environmental claims brought against a debtor under the Comprehensive Environmental Response, Compensation and Liability Act (CERCLA) have not been previously discharged in Chapter 11 where the Environmental Protection Agency (EPA) could not have fairly contemplated the debtor's potential liability prior to its reorganization. The issue here—when a party's contingent CERCLA liability may be discharged through bankruptcy—is an issue of first impression for this court, but other courts that have considered this issue are split on the standards to apply in determining the issue. Some courts take a "right to payment" approach, which discharge a claim only when all four elements of a CERCLA claim existed prior to bankruptcy. This approach has been criticized for failing to address bankruptcy law and policy and for undermining the fresh start policy because the debtor cannot receive a fresh start from its CERCLA liabilities stemming from prebankruptcy conduct if any of the four elements (some of which are not in the debtor's control) have not been met. Another criticism is that under bankruptcy law, a claim is defined more broadly than under CERCLA, so that nonbankruptcy law should not control what constitutes a claim. Further, this approach might encourage some creditors to delay cleanup until after the close of bankruptcy proceedings, thereby increasing the response costs. Another approach, known as the "underlying act approach," discharge is possible provided the underlying polluting act occurred prior to the debtor's bankruptcy. This means that even if the EPA does not yet know of a potential CERCLA claim against the debtor, the debtor's liability is discharged so long as the debtor's conduct relating to the contamination concluded prior to its bankruptcy petition. This approach favors bankruptcy law (unlike the "right to payment" approach) but has been criticized as unfair to creditors because it would allow a polluting party to undergo bankruptcy proceedings and receive a discharge from any liabilities before the EPA or any other creditor ever has a reason to know about the debtor's polluting acts. This approach would enable the circumvention of CERCLA's goal of making polluters accountable for their actions. Moreover, this approach could cause the EPA to divert its energies from cleaning up sites to determining a debtor's potential status as a responsible party and might risk violating the EPA's or other creditors' right to reasonable notice prior to the discharge of a claim. A third approach, known as the "debtor-creditor relationship" approach provides that CERCLA liability is discharged if the creditor and debtor began a relationship before the debtor filed for bankruptcy, so long as the underlying act occurred before the bankruptcy petition was filed. Because some of the courts that have used this

Continued on next page.

approach have defined "relationship" very broadly, this approach has been criticized as becoming the equivalent of the "underlying acts" approach. Still, a fourth approach, known as the "fair contemplation" or "foreseeability" approach, posits that a contingent CERCLA claim arises prepetition only if it is "based upon prepetition conduct that can fairly be contemplated by the parties at the time of the debtors' bankruptcy." Under such an approach, a claim accrues when the potential CERCLA claimant, at the time of bankruptcy, "could have ascertained through the exercise of reasonable diligence that it had a claim" against the debtor. This standard allows a claim to accrue earlier than the right to payment standard because the potential claimant need not incur response costs (the fourth CERCLA element) for a contingent claim to arise under this standard. At the same time, the standard requires more awareness of a potential CERCLA claim by a potential creditor than do the underlying act or debtor-creditor relationship standards, both of which allow claims to accrue even if the potential creditor had no idea that it might have a CERCLA claim against the debtor. Thus, the "fair contemplation" approach attempts to reconcile the goals of both the bankruptcy courts and CERCLA, something the Supreme Court has directed to be reconciled whenever possible. It attempts to accommodate both the fresh start goal of bankruptcy and the speedy cleanup and polluter accountability CERCLA goals, and, unlike the other approaches, it does not violate notice requirements because creditors must be aware of potential claims against debtors before such claims can be discharged. Finally, it might also encourage bankruptcy goals in addition to the fresh start objective. One such goal is to provide creditors with the maximum recovery on their claims. The fair contemplation approach may support this goal because "including uncertain future CERCLA claims in the bankruptcy plan may entail added transaction costs that place an additional drain on the debtor company and actually diminish the creditors' recovery." By using the fair contemplation standard, these added costs can be diminished or eliminated. Since the fresh start goal may not be appropriate for a corporation seeking reorganization, the fair contemplation standard further supports bankruptcy goals in the context of CERCLA claims. For all these reasons, the fair contemplation approach is the appropriate approach for determining whether MDL's (D) liability had been discharged. Nothing in the record indicates that at the time of reorganization order the EPA fairly contemplated or had reason to foresee MDL's (D) potential liability to it for the contaminated sites. Therefore, based on the evidence presented in the pleadings, it cannot be said that the EPA had a contingent claim against MDL (D) at the time MDL (D) discharged its "claims" in its bankruptcy reorganization. Motion dismissed.

ANALYSIS

One criticism of the fair contemplation approach is that in situations where the debtor itself does not know of its potential Comprehensive Environmental Response, Compensation and Liability Act (CERCLA) liability until well after the close of its bankruptcy proceedings, because its liability stems from the wrongful conduct of a third party, applying a fair contemplation standard requiring contemplation by the EPA of the debtor's potential liability makes it highly unlikely that the debtor will ever be able to discharge its contingent CERCLA liabilities through bankruptcy.

Quicknotes

COMPREHENSIVE ENVIRONMENTAL RESPONSE, COMPENSATION AND LIABILITY ACT (CERCLA) Enacted to fill gaps in environmental clean-up efforts left by Resource Conservation and Recovery Act of 1976; permits both the government and private plaintiffs to recover clean-up costs.

CHAPTER 11 REORGANIZATION A plan formulated pursuant to Chapter 11 of the Bankruptcy Code whereby a debtor, who is unable to pay his or her debts as they become due, is relieved of the obligation to pay creditors through reorganization and payment from future income.

In re Motors Liquidation Co.

Creditors (P) v. Debtor (D)

829 F.3d 135 (2d Cir. 2016)

NATURE OF CASE: Appeal from bankruptcy court decision.

FACT SUMMARY: "Old" General Motors (Old GM) was sold to "New" General Motors (New GM) (D) in an 11 U.S.C. § 363 sale. As part of the sale, Old GM became a debtor-in-possession, was acquired by New GM (D), and later liquidated and disbanded. New GM was able to continue operating, free and clear of Old GM's liabilities, with exception of 15 categories of liabilities, including liability for accidents that occurred after the sale closed. Three years after Old GM filed its liquidation plan, there was a massive recall on GM vehicles due to a defect in the ignition switch that would prevent the vehicle airbags from deploying. A report indicated that Old GM engineers were aware of the issue and had remedied it in a way that was designed to conceal detection. Plaintiffs (P) sued New GM (D) in bankruptcy court, seeking compensation for losses due to the ignition switch defect. The bankruptcy court found that New GM (D) could not be sued.

RULE OF LAW

(1) A successor corporation that is "free and clear" of the prior corporation's liabilities is shielded from claims arising out of a defect that occurred prior to the sale.

(2) Potential claimants' procedural due process rights are violated when they are not provided direct mail notice of potential claims when the debtor corporation is aware of the defect giving rise to those claims.

FACTS: "Old" General Motors (Old GM) received billions of dollars of TARP [Troubled Asset Relief Program] funds from the United States government in 2008 and 2009. However, it was nonetheless unable to save itself from bankruptcy. Old GM petitioned for Chapter 11 bankruptcy while also filing a motion to sell itself to Vehicle Acquisition Holdings LLC/NGMCO, Inc (New GM) (D). This created a 11 U.S.C. § 363 sale rather than a traditional Chapter 11 reorganization. In a § 363 sale, a debtor sells its primary assets to a successor corporation, which immediately takes over the business. Under the proposal, Old GM would become a debtor-in-possession under the Bankruptcy Code and would be acquired by New GM (D). New GM (D) would also acquire substantially all Old GM's business and could immediately begin operating, free and clear of Old GM's debts. Old GM would continue existing for a period of time as a separate entity with $1.175 billion in cash, interests in the Saturn brand, and certain real and personal property. Additionally, Old GM would receive consideration from New GM (D), including a promise to repay [U.S.] Treasury and Canadian government loans and a 10 percent stake in New GM (D). Later, Old GM would liquidate and disband, renaming itself "Motors Liquidation Company" and arranging a traditional bankruptcy liquidation plan that addressed the payment of its remaining liabilities. After Old GM provided public notice of the proposed sale order, the bankruptcy court received and heard over 850 objections to the order over the course of three days. The bankruptcy court then approved the § 363 sale and issued the Sale Order, effecting the final sale agreement between Old GM and New GM (D). As part of the sale agreement, New GM (D) assumed 15 categories of liabilities, including liability for accidents that occurred after the sale closing date. New GM (D) also agreed to make repairs pursuant to express warranties issued in connection with the sale of GM cars and assumed liability for Lemon Law claims. New GM (D) was otherwise free and clear of Old GM's liabilities. In 2011, Old GM filed its liquidation plan, under which it would establish GUC Trust, which existed to hold certain assets, including New GM stock and other financial instruments, and then Old GM would dissolve. Creditors with unsecured claims against Old GM would receive New GM (D) securities and units of GUC Trust on a pro rata basis in satisfaction of their claims. As of March 14, 2014, GUC Trust had distributed roughly 90 percent of its New GM (D) securities and nearly 32 million units of GUC Trust. Accordingly, the bankruptcy was approaching an end. However, on February 7, 2014, New GM (D) informed the National Highway Traffic Safety Administration (NHTSA) that it would be recalling, among other vehicles, the 2005 Chevrolet Cobalt due to a defect in the ignition switch that could prevent the airbags from deploying. An investigative report regarding the defect suggested that knowledge of the defect was widespread and downplayed by Old GM since the 1990s due to Old GM's dysfunctional corporate culture. The report found that as early as August 2001, Old GM engineers understood that turning off the ignition would also prevent the airbags from deploying. In late 2005 through 2006, Old GM's legal team became aware of fatalities resulting from airbag nondeployments. Around April 2006, Old GM engineers changed the design of the ignition switch without changing the part number in order to conceal that a change had been made. On April 21, 2014, plaintiffs (P) initiated an adversary proceeding against New GM (D) in bankruptcy court, asserting economic losses arising from the ignition switch defect. New GM (D)

Continued on next page.

moved to enforce the sale order and enjoin the ignition switch defect claims. The bankruptcy court granted New GM's (D) motion on the basis that New GM (D) could not be sued, because the claims should have been brought against Old GM.

ISSUE:

(1) Is a successor corporation that is "free and clear" of the prior corporation's liabilities shielded from claims arising out of a defect that occurred prior to the sale?

(2) Are potential claimants' procedural due process rights violated when they are not provided direct mail notice of potential claims when the debtor corporation is aware of the defect giving rise to those claims?

HOLDING AND DECISION: (Chin, J.)

(1) Yes. A successor corporation that is "free and clear" of the prior corporation's liabilities is shielded from claims arising out of a defect that occurred prior to the sale. The Sale Order transferred assets from Old GM to New GM (D), free and clear of liens or other interests, including rights or claims based on any successor or transferee liability. While 11 U.S.C. § 363 permits the sale to be free and clear of interests, it does not define exactly what constitutes an interest or the extent to which claims may qualify as interests. Courts analyze interests on a case-by-case basis. Successor liability claims are interests when they flow from a debtor's ownership of transferred assets, but they must also qualify as claims under Chapter 11. In order to qualify, a claim must arise from a right to payment that arose before the filing of the petition or resulted from pre-petition conduct fairly giving rise to the claim, *and* there must be some contact or relationship between the debtor and the claimant such that the claimant is identifiable. The preclosing accident claims are clearly within the scope of the Sale Order, because the accidents occurred preclosing and directly involve Old GM. Second, the economic loss claims were contingent: though the claims were not revealed until five years after the defect was discovered, the defect existed prior to closing and fairly gave rise to the claims. The bankruptcy court's holding that New GM (D) is not liable for Old GM's defect is affirmed.

(2) Yes. Potential claimants' procedural due process rights are violated when they are not provided direct mail notice of potential claims when the debtor corporation is aware of the defect giving rise to those claims. Plaintiffs (P) contend that enforcing the Sale Order and barring their claims would violate procedural due process. Procedural due process was violated because the Plaintiffs (P) were not provided with direct mail notice of the ignition switch issues, when Old GM knew or reasonably should have known about the ignition switch defect prior to bankruptcy. Because the Sale Order would violate procedural due process, the bankruptcy court erred in granting New GM's (D) motion to enforce the Sale Order to enjoin the ignition switch defect claims. Reversed.

ANALYSIS

Steven Groman, the lead plaintiff in *In re Motors Liquidation Co.*, claimed that his Chevrolet SUV shut off four times, two of which occurred when Groman was driving on the expressway and lost control of his power brakes and steering. In 2014, GM established a $625 million settlement fund to pay for 124 deaths and 275 injuries resulting from the defect, followed by an additional $275 million in 2015 and $120 million in 2020.

Quicknotes

DEBTOR-IN-POSSESSION A Chapter 11 bankruptcy debtor who retains control of assets or property pursuant to a plan of reorganization.

LEMON LAW State consumer protection statutes that outline remedies for purchasers of defective automobiles.

LIQUIDATION The reduction to cash of all assets for distribution to creditors.

PROCEDURAL DUE PROCESS The constitutional mandate that if the state or federal government acts so as to deny a citizen of a life, liberty, or property interest, the individual is first entitled to notice and the right to be heard.

In re Bernhard Steiner Pianos USA, Inc.

Objecting creditors (P) v. Debtor (D)

292 B.R. 109 (Bankr. N.D. Tex. 2002)

NATURE OF CASE: Objection to provision in confirmed Chapter 11 plan permitting a temporary stay against claims brought against third-party guarantors.

FACT SUMMARY: Creditors (P) objected to provisions in a modified Chapter 11 plan of reorganization permitting a temporary stay against claims brought against third-party guarantors to the extent those provisions acted as a release of their claims against Kahn, the Debtor's (D) principal.

RULE OF LAW

A Chapter 11 plan of reorganization may be confirmed where it provides a temporary injunction against enforcement of claims against a third-party guarantor where the third party enjoys an identity of interest with the debtor such that the claims against the third party are essentially claims against the debtor, and where the third-party claims would have an adverse effect on the debtor's ability to accomplish reorganization.

FACTS: Creditors (P) objected to modified paragraph 10.03 of the Debtor's (D) plan of reorganization. That paragraph provided that while no guarantors of the Debtor's (D) debt were released by the plan, the exclusive remedy for payment of any debt so long as the plan was not in default was the plan itself. It provided that "to the extent necessary, any applicable statute of limitations against collection from any third party (e.g., guarantor) is specifically tolled from the period of time from the bankruptcy petition date until the date upon which the debtor fails to cure any written notice of default as set forth in the plan." The creditors (P) objected to these provisions to the extent they acted as a release of their claims against Kahn, the Debtor's (D) principal. The confirmation order provided a ten-day cure period and relief from modified paragraph 10.03 upon "changed circumstances."

ISSUE: May a Chapter 11 plan of reorganization be confirmed where it provides a temporary injunction against enforcement of claims against a third-party guarantor where the third party enjoys an identity of interest with the debtor such that the claims against the third party are essentially claims against the debtor, and where the third-party claims would have an adverse effect on the debtor's ability to accomplish reorganization?

HOLDING AND DECISION: (Hale, J.) Yes. A Chapter 11 plan of reorganization may be confirmed where it provides a temporary injunction against enforcement of claims against a third-party guarantor where the third party enjoys an identity of interest with the debtor such that the claims against the third party are essentially claims against the debtor, and where the third-party claims would have an adverse effect on the debtor's ability to accomplish reorganization. Generally, a plan of reorganization cannot be confirmed if the plan purports to release guarantors of the debtor's debts and a creditor objects to the release. Here, paragraph 10.3 specifically states that guarantors are not discharged or released from any liability under the plan. Therefore, on its face, the plan does not purport to grant a release for third parties, such as Kahn. Further, nothing in paragraph 10.3 affects Kahn's ultimate liability under any guaranty agreement. Instead, it merely controls the timing of when a claim, if any, against Kahn, can be brought. And, under the plan the temporary stay could lift upon uncured default under the plan or upon a change in circumstances for Kahn. If the objecting creditors (P) are not paid under the plan, they may pursue their guarantor, Kahn. If his circumstances improve, or if the situation warrants, the objecting creditors (P) can seek relief from the stay imposed by the plan. Post-confirmation permanent injunctions that effectively release a nondebtor from liability are prohibited. However, temporary injunctions may be proper under unusual circumstances. These circumstances include (1) when the nondebtor and debtor enjoy such an identity of interest that the suit against the nondebtor is essentially a suit against the debtor, and (2) when the third-party action will have an adverse impact on the debtor's ability to accomplish reorganization. Here, those circumstances have been met, because Debtor's (D) success or failure depends primarily on Kahn, who, for practical purposes, can be deemed to be the Debtor (D). The Debtor (D) will survive and creditors will be paid only if Kahn is allowed to conduct the Debtor's (D) business without distraction. Thus, suit against Kahn is tantamount to suit against the Debtor (D), and pursuit of such suit would have an adverse impact on Debtor's (D) successful reorganization. Here, too, paragraph 10.03 has the effect of a temporary injunction, and the Debtor (D) must meet the burden of obtaining an injunction. Here, the Debtor (D) has met that burden. It has shown that it can likely reorganize successfully, but that it will suffer irreparable harm, i.e., will not successfully reorganize, if the objecting creditors are permitted to pursue their individual guaranty claims against Kahn. This would harm not only the Debtor (D) but also its other creditors. On the other hand, the objecting creditors would merely not be repaid as quickly as they would like. They are free to pursue Kahn on his

Continued on next page.

guaranties in the event Debtor (D) defaults on its plan payments and the default is not cured within 10 days. At that time, they need only to obtain an order lifting the "stay" and allowing them to proceed against Kahn directly. Thus, the harm to Debtor (D) far outweighs the harm to the objecting creditors (P). Finally, granting a temporary injunction in this case would not be against public policy. The plan, as modified, is approved.

ANALYSIS

By essentially giving the Debtor (D) and Kahn time to affect the reorganization plan, the court's decision in this case is in line with the ultimate purpose of Chapter 11: to give businesses in financial difficulties an opportunity to reorganize their business affairs, provide repayment to their creditors, and emerge from their bankruptcy case in a financially sound manner.

Quicknotes

CHAPTER 11 REORGANIZATION A plan formulated pursuant to Chapter 11 of the Bankruptcy Code whereby a debtor, who is unable to pay his or her debts as they become due, is relieved of the obligation to pay creditors through reorganization and payment from future income.

GUARANTOR A party who agrees to be liable for the debt or default of another.

INJUNCTION A court order requiring a person to do, or prohibiting that person from doing, a specific act.

CHAPTER 36

Beyond Chapter 11

Quick Reference Rules of Law

C&C Investment Properties, LLC v. Trustmark National Bank

Real estate investor (P) v. Bank (D)

838 F.3d 655 (5th Cir. 2016)

NATURE OF CASE: Appeal from district court's grant of defendant's motion for summary judgment.

FACT SUMMARY: C&C Investment Properties (C&C) (P) used promissory notes to purchase foreclosed properties from Heritage Banking Group (Heritage). C&C intended to rent and flip the properties. C&C (P) alleged that the purchases of the properties were covered by a side agreement that stated that C&C (P) would pay Heritage amounts equal to what Heritage had paid for the properties at foreclosure, and that Heritage would refinance the properties after C&C's (P) renovations were complete. The agreement was not formalized. C&C (P) stopped making payments on the loans, allegedly due to Heritage's noncompliance with the agreement, and defaulted. Heritage foreclosed on the properties and C&C (P) filed suit for breach of contract and fraudulent inducement. Heritage was later declared insolvent, and the Federal Deposit Insurance Corporation (FDIC) was appointed as Heritage's receiver. The FDIC entered into an agreement to transfer Heritage's assets and liabilities to Trustmark National Bank (Trustmark) (D). The FDIC was dismissed from the C&C (P) lawsuit and Trustmark (D) was added as a defendant. Trustmark (D) was granted summary judgment under a 12 U.S.C. § 1823(e) defense; C&C (P) appealed.

RULE OF LAW

A financial institution does not waive its right to assert a 12 U.S.C. § 1823(e) defense by purchasing the assets at issue from a separate institution or by waiting to assert the defense until after its answer.

FACTS: C&C Investment Properties (C&C) (P) was established in 2004 to buy, rent, and flip real estate. C&C (P) used promissory notes to finance the purchase of several foreclosed properties from Heritage Banking Group (Heritage) between 2006 and 2009. The properties were secured by deeds of trust encumbering the properties and were personally guaranteed by Glen and Charlotte Collins, the owners of C&C (P). According to the Collinses, the purchases were covered by a side agreement, which allegedly stated that C&C (P) would pay Heritage amounts equal to what Heritage paid for the properties at foreclosure, and Heritage would later refinance the properties to account for their value after renovation. C&C (P) stopped making payments on the loans after Heritage allegedly did not comply with the side agreement. C&C (P) defaulted on the notes and guarantees, and Heritage foreclosed on the properties. Glen Collins and C&C (P) sued Heritage for breach of contract and fraudulent inducement. While the suit was pending, Heritage was declared insolvent. The Federal Deposit Insurance Corporation (FDIC) was appointed as Heritage's receiver, and the FDIC entered into a Purchase and Assumption Agreement (the Agreement) with Trustmark National Bank (Trustmark) (D). Under the Agreement, the FDIC transferred Heritage's assets and liabilities, including the C&C (P) notes and guaranties, to Trustmark (D). After the FDIC was substituted for Heritage as the defendant in the breach of contract and fraudulent inducement case, it moved to dismiss the case. However, prior to the court's ruling on the motion, Glen Collins and C&C (P) obtained leave to amend and added Trustmark (D) as a defendant. The FDIC was subsequently dismissed as a defendant. Once added as a party, Trustmark (D) pleaded 12 U.S.C. § 1823(e) as a defense and filed counterclaims against C&C (P) and the Collinses (borrowers, collectively) for the amount still owed on the notes and sought reimbursement for its costs and expenses related to collection and enforcement of the loans. Trustmark (D) subsequently filed a motion for summary judgment, arguing that the claims against it were based on an unwritten side agreement between C&C (P) and the Collinses, which is impermissible under § 1823(e). The borrowers (P) objected on the basis that Trustmark (D) waived the defense either affirmatively or by its failure to timely act. The district court granted Trustmark's (D) motion for summary judgment, and the borrowers (P) appealed.

ISSUE: Does a financial institution waive its right to assert a 12 U.S.C. § 1823(e) defense by purchasing the assets at issue from a separate institution or by waiting to assert the defense until after its answer?

HOLDING AND DECISION: (Costa, J.) No. A financial institution does not waive its right to assert a 12 U.S.C. § 1823(e) defense by purchasing the assets at issue from a separate institution or by waiting to assert the defense until after its answer. Under the *D'Oench, Duhme* doctrine, established by *D'Oench, Duhme & Co v. FDIC*, 315 U.S. 447, 459–60 (1942), and codified at 12 U.S.C. § 1823(e), borrowers are prevented from relying upon oral agreements with a failed bank to defend against collection efforts of a federal receiver. The purpose of the rule is to allow bank examiners to rely upon a bank's records in evaluating the value of its assets, and to ensure mature consideration of unusual loan transactions and prevent fraudulent insertion of new terms by collusion of bank employees if a bank appears headed for failure. Section

Continued on next page.

1823(e) provides that any "agreement which tends to diminish or defeat the interest of the [FDIC] in any asset acquired by it under this section" will not be valid against the FDIC unless it is (1) in writing; (2) contemporaneously executed by the depository institution and the person claiming an adverse interest; (3) approved by the board of directors of the depository institution and reflected in the minutes of the board; and (4) continuously, from the time of its execution, an official record of the depository institution. These protections have been extended to private parties that purchase assets of insolvent banks from the FDIC, such as Trustmark (D). The borrowers (P) do not dispute the general principles of § 1823(e) or their applicability to the case, but rather, the borrowers (P) argue that Trustmark (D) waived the defense both substantively and by failing to assert the defense earlier in the suit. These waiver agreements are unsuccessful, as is the borrowers' (P) agreement regarding a dispute of material fact regarding the agreement. The borrowers (P) argued that the agreement had been in writing in some form, but they presented insufficient evidence with which a jury could conclude that all four conditions of § 1823(e) were met, because it was not signed, approved by the Board of Directors, or continuously kept as an official record. Affirmed.

ANALYSIS

The *D'Oench Duhme* doctrine operates similarly to the Statute of Frauds in contract cases, serving to protect financial institutions and the FDIC from potentially unscrupulous practices of failed banks. In order to invoke the *D'Oench Duhme* doctrine, the party seeking to invoke the doctrine must (1) be a regulatory agency or an assignee who purchased a failed bank's debts; (2) be confronting a claim or defense from the borrower that is based on an agreement that is functionally "secret"; (3) the "secret" agreement is either unwritten or fails to meet the four requirements of § 1823(e); and (4) enforcement of the agreement would cause a fundamental diminishment in the agency's interest in the debt.

Quicknotes

COLLUSION An agreement between two or more parties to engage in unlawful conduct or in other activities with an unlawful goal, typically involving fraud.

DEED OF TRUST A legal document that acts as a mortgage, placing a security interest in the deeded property with a trustee to insure the payment of a debt.

FEDERAL DEPOSIT INSURANCE CORPORATION (FDIC) Federal agency (established by the Federal Deposit Insurance Act) that insures deposits in certain banks up to the statutorily prescribed amounts.

In re City of Detroit, Michigan

[Parties not identified.]

504 B.R. 97 (Bankr. E.D. Mich. 2013)

NATURE OF CASE: Objection to the constitutionality of Chapter 9 as applied to a municipal debtor, and objection to the municipality's eligibility for Chapter 9 protection.

FACT SUMMARY: After the City of Detroit, Michigan (the City), sought Chapter 9 protection, objectors contended that permitting the City to seek such bankruptcy relief without explicitly providing for the protection of accrued pension benefits would violate the Tenth Amendment of the United States Constitution, and that, in any event, the City was ineligible to be a Chapter 9 debtor because, inter alia, it did not meet Chapter 9's insolvency requirement.

RULE OF LAW

(1) Permitting a municipality to seek Chapter 9 bankruptcy relief without explicitly providing for the protection of accrued pension benefits does not violate the Tenth Amendment of the U.S. Constitution where the state's constitution does not prohibit impairment of such debt in bankruptcy.

(2) A municipality satisfies Bankruptcy Code § 109(c)'s insolvency requirement for Chapter 9 eligibility where it meets the definition of insolvency in § 101(32)(C) because it is unable to fund essential government services, i.e., because it is service delivery insolvent.

FACTS: For decades, the City of Detroit, Michigan (the City) experienced dwindling population, employment, and revenues, which led to decaying infrastructure, outdated equipment, excessive borrowing, mounting crime rates, spreading blight, and a deteriorating quality of life. The City was unable to provide its residents with the basic police, fire, and emergency medical services that its residents needed for their basic health and safety. Accordingly, the City filed for Chapter 9 bankruptcy protection. The state's constitution permitted municipalities to file for bankruptcy, and it also expressly provided pension rights could not be "impaired or diminished." Its Contracts Clause also provided generally that laws "impairing" contract rights were prohibited. Objectors contended that permitting the City to seek bankruptcy relief without explicitly providing for the protection of accrued pension benefits would violate the Tenth Amendment of the U.S. Constitution, and that, in any event, the City was ineligible to be a Chapter 9 debtor because, inter alia, it did not meet Chapter 9's insolvency requirement under § 109(c).

ISSUE:

(1) Does permitting a municipality to seek Chapter 9 bankruptcy relief without explicitly providing for the protection of accrued pension benefits violate the Tenth Amendment of the U.S. Constitution where the state's constitution does not prohibit impairment of such debt in bankruptcy?

(2) Does a municipality satisfy Bankruptcy Code § 109(c)'s insolvency requirement for Chapter 9 eligibility where it meets the definition of insolvency in § 101(32)(C) because it is unable to fund essential government services, i.e., because it is service delivery insolvent?

HOLDING AND DECISION: (Rhodes, J.)

(1) No. Permitting a municipality to seek Chapter 9 bankruptcy relief without explicitly providing for the protection of accrued pension benefits does not violate the Tenth Amendment of the U.S. Constitution where the state's constitution does not prohibit impairment of such debt in bankruptcy. Although it would violate both the state and U.S. constitutions for the state to adjust the City's pension debts, as that would violate the prohibitions on impairing contracts in both constitutions, as well as the state constitution's prohibition on impairing pension-related contractual obligations, the bankruptcy court is not prohibited from making such adjustments. That is because the Bankruptcy Clause in the federal constitution authorizes Congress to make laws that can impair contracts, since impairing contracts is an inherent function of bankruptcy. Moreover, pension debts are not distinguished in bankruptcy from any other types of debt. Thus, there is nothing constraining the bankruptcy court from adjusting the City's pension debts for Tenth Amendment and sovereignty purposes. Further, contrary to the objectors' argument, the Michigan Constitution does not afford greater protection to pension debt than to other types of contract debt merely by providing that pension debt may not be "impaired or diminished" but providing that other contract debt may not be "impaired." While protecting pension contracts as contracts that the state may not impair, the Michigan Constitution fails to protect pensions from impairment in bankruptcy. Accordingly, the City's pension debts are subject to impairment in this case. Before such debts are impaired, however, the City's plan will have to meet the requirements of § 943(b) and the other applicable provisions of the Bankruptcy Code, and before confirming

Continued on next page.

such a plan, the court will have to carefully weigh the interests of the City and all its creditor. Objection overruled as to this issue.

(2) Yes. A municipality satisfies Bankruptcy Code § 109(c)'s insolvency requirement for Chapter 9 eligibility where it meets the definition of insolvency in § 101(32)(C) because it is unable to fund essential government services, i.e., because it is service delivery insolvent. The record shows that the City was broke. As of May 2013, the City stopped paying its trade creditors to avoid running out of cash, and but for these and other deferments, the City would have completely run out of cash by the end of 2013. In addition to this cash insolvency, the City was in a state of "service delivery insolvency" by July 2013, meaning that it was unable to provide essential services to its citizens, such as adequate policing, to provide for their health, welfare, and safety. Such service delivery insolvency, as well as budgetary insolvency (longer-term budget imbalances), inform the assessment of the relative degree and likely duration of cash insolvency under § 101(32)(C). Here, the degree of service delivery insolvency is striking and of the greatest concern. Objection overruled as to this issue.

ANALYSIS

As the court here notes, the Michigan Constitution, while explicitly giving accrued pension benefits the status of contractual obligations, failed to give pensions protection from impairment in bankruptcy. It could have done so in several ways. It could have simply prohibited Michigan municipalities from filing bankruptcy; it could have created a property interest that bankruptcy would be required to respect under *Butner v. United States,* 440 U.S. 48 (1979), which held that property issues in bankruptcy are determined according to state law; it could have established some sort of a secured interest in the municipality's property; or it could even have explicitly required the state to guaranty pension benefits. Because it did none of those, however, the City's pension debts were subject to impairment in Chapter 9.

Quicknotes

CHAPTER 9 BANKRUPTCY A legal proceeding whereby a municipality seeks debt adjustment.

TENTH AMENDMENT The Tenth Amendment to the United States Constitution reserves those powers therein, not expressly delegated to the federal government or prohibited to the states, to the states or to the people.

NML Capital, Ltd. v. Republic of Argentina

Bondholder (P) v. Sovereign nation (D)

699 F.3d 246 (2d Cir. 2012)

NATURE OF CASE: Appeal from permanent injunctions requiring nation to make payments on defaulted debt.

FACT SUMMARY: In 2001, Argentina (D) defaulted on a bond offering that contained an equal treatment provision, and it restructured its debt in 2005 and 2010. Argentina (D) contended that the equal treatment provision did not prohibit it from discriminating against the defaulted bonds in favor of other unsubordinated, foreign bonds issued in connection with the restructurings.

RULE OF LAW

A sovereign nation that has issued bonds, which are subject to a provision that the bonds will be unsubordinated and that the nation's payment obligations on the bonds will be at least equal with its other debt obligations, may be required, after default and restructuring of its debt, to make payments on the bonds that are comparable to payments on its restructured debt.

FACTS: Argentina (D) issued bonds pursuant to a Fiscal Agency Agreement (FAA Bonds), which contained a pari passu clause that provided that: "[t]he Securities will constitute . . . direct, unconditional, unsecured and unsubordinated obligations of the Republic and shall at all times rank pari passu without any preference among themselves. The payment obligations of the Republic under the Securities shall at all times rank at least equally with all its other present and future unsecured and unsubordinated External Indebtedness. . . ." The second sentence of this clause is an equal treatment provision ("Equal Treatment Provision"). The FAA was governed by New York law, and jurisdiction lay in New York City. In 2001, Argentina (D) defaulted on these FAA Bonds, and in 2005 and 2010, Argentina (D) offered holders of the FAA Bonds new exchange bonds (the "Exchange Bonds"). Argentina (D) continued to make payments to holders of those Exchange Bonds while failing to make any payments to persons who still held the defaulted FAA Bonds. After Argentina (D) defaulted, it placed a "temporary" moratorium on principal and interest payments on more than $80 billion of its public external debt including the FAA Bonds, and made no principal or interest payments on the defaulted debt. To induce holders of defaulted debt to accept restructured debt, whereby investors would exchange their defaulted bonds for new unsecured and unsubordinated external debt at a rate of 25 to 29 cents on the dollar, Argentina (D) warned the bondholders that defaulted bonds eligible for exchange that were not tendered could remain in default indefinitely. Holdout bondholders (P) who did not participate in the exchange (91 percent of bondholders did participate) filed suit in New York federal district court for breach of contract and for payment on their debt, estimating that, collectively, their unpaid principal and prejudgment interest amounted to approximately $1.33 billion. An important new feature of the Exchange Bonds was that they included "collective action" clauses, which permit Argentina (D) to amend the terms of the bonds and to bind dissenting bondholders if a sufficient number of bondholders (66 2/3 percent to 75 percent of the aggregate principal amount of a given series) agree, thus circumventing holdout litigation such as that initiated by the holdout bondholders (P). Argentina (D) made all payments due on the debt it restructured in 2005 and 2010. The district court granted injunctive relief, ordering Argentina (D) to specifically perform its obligations under the Equal Treatment Provision. In particular, whenever Argentina (D) paid any amount due under the terms of the exchange bonds, it had to concurrently or in advance pay the holdout bondholders (P) the same fraction of the amount due to them (the "Ratable Payment"). Argentina (D) appealed arguing, inter alia, that the pari passu clause is a boilerplate provision that, in the sovereign context, provides protection from legal subordination or other discriminatory legal ranking by preventing the creation of legal priorities by the sovereign in favor of creditors holding particular classes of debt. Argentina (D) also contended that the district court injunctions would deprive it of its property, and, therefore, violated the Foreign Sovereign Immunities Act (FSIA). The court of appeals granted review.

ISSUE: May a sovereign nation that has issued bonds, which are subject to a provision that the bonds will be unsubordinated and that the nation's payment obligations on the bonds will be at least equal with its other debt obligations, be required, after default and restructuring of its debt, to make payments on the bonds that are comparable to payments on its restructured debt?

HOLDING AND DECISION: (Parker, J.) Yes. A sovereign nation that has issued bonds, which are subject to a provision that the bonds will be unsubordinated and that the nation's payment obligations on the bonds will be at least equal with its other debt obligations, may be required, after default and restructuring of its debt, to make payments on the bonds that are comparable to payments on its restructured debt. Contrary to Argentina's (D) contention, the pari passu clause does not have the settled meaning that Argentina (D) would give it. Instead, Argentina's (D) interpretation of the pari passu clause is neither

Continued on next page.

well settled nor uniformly acted upon. Thus, the real issue is what constitutes subordination under the clause. Argentina (D) maintains that subordination means legal, formal subordination, and argues that none occurred here because "any claims that may arise from the Republic's restructured debt have no priority in any court of law over claims arising out of the Republic's unrestructured debt." The holdout bondholders (P), on the other hand, argue that there was "de facto" subordination because Argentina (D) reduced the rank of their bonds to a permanent nonperforming status by passing legislation barring payments on them while continuing to pay on the restructured debt and by repeatedly asserting that it had no intention of making payments on the defaulted bonds. Given the structure of the clause, Argentina's (D) argument is unpersuasive. The first sentence prohibits Argentina (D), as bond issuer, from formally subordinating the bonds by issuing superior debt. The second, "equal treatment" sentence prohibits Argentina, as bond payor, from paying on other bonds without paying on the FAA Bonds. Thus, the two sentences of the clause protect against different forms of discrimination: the issuance of other superior debt (first sentence) and the giving of priority to other payment obligations (second sentence). Accordingly, Argentina (D) has violated the clause. Injunctive relief is warranted for this violation because money damages would not be an effective remedy, given that Argentina (D) has shown that it will simply refuse to pay any judgments by closing the doors of its courts to judgment creditors, and through its continual disregard for the rights of its FAA creditors and the judgments of U.S. courts to whose jurisdiction it has submitted. Additionally, compliance with the injunctions would not deprive Argentina (D) of control over any of its property, and, therefore, the injunctions do not operate as attachments of foreign property prohibited by the FSIA. Instead, by directing Argentina (D) to comply with its contractual obligations, the injunctions affect Argentina's (D) property only incidentally to the extent that they prohibit Argentina (D) from transferring money to some bondholders and not others. Finally, the injunctions will not have the practical effect of enabling "a single creditor to thwart the implementation of an internationally supported restructuring plan," as the United States contends in an amicus brief. It is up to the sovereign—not any "single creditor"—whether it will repudiate that creditor's debt in a manner that violates a pari passu clause. In any event, it is highly unlikely that in the future sovereigns will find themselves in Argentina's (D) predicament since the majority of bond issuances since 2005 are protected by collective action clauses or are not governed by U.S. law. Affirmed.

ANALYSIS

The practical significance of an equal ranking obligation, such as the one at issue in this case, is readily apparent in the event of the bankruptcy or insolvency of a corporate debtor. In a corporate bankruptcy, holders of senior obligations have a priority claim over the debtor's assets. In the case of sovereign borrowers, like Argentina (D) here, however, the impact of the clause is less clear because creditors cannot force them into bankruptcy-like proceedings, and no comparable asset distribution plan applies. Thus, in the event of a debt crisis, sovereigns wishing to honor some portion of their defaulted debt must negotiate with individual creditors or groups of creditors to effectuate restructurings. Typically, these proceedings leave in their wake so-called "holdout" creditors who refuse to restructure, opting instead to seek judgments against the sovereign. In this case, that is what happened, as the bondholders (P) who brought the action were the "holdouts."

Quicknotes

BREACH OF CONTRACT Unlawful failure by a party to perform its obligations pursuant to contract.

SUBORDINATION The placement of a party's rights or claims in lower priority to the rights and claims of others.

In re Alpha Natural Resources, Inc.

Union (P) v. Debtor (D)

552 B.R. 312 (Bankr. E.D. Va. 2016)

NATURE OF CASE: Bankruptcy court ruling on debtors' motion for entry of order.

FACT SUMMARY: Debtors, Alpha Natural Resources (D), filed for Chapter 11 bankruptcy after losing millions of dollars when demand for coal significantly decreased, causing prices to drop dramatically. Debtors (D) sought the bankruptcy court's authorization of a going-concern sale to a Stalking Horse Bidder, however, the Stalking Horse Bidder refused to assume any of Debtor's (D) retirement obligations to its union employees. Debtors (D) and the Stalking Horse Bidder sought a Rejection Motion under Bankruptcy Code § 1113 and § 1114 that would permit the going-concern sale to proceed, free of Debtors' (D) retirement obligations.

RULE OF LAW

A bankruptcy court can grant a Rejection Motion under Bankruptcy Code §§ 1113 and 1114, allowing a debtor to reject certain collective bargaining agreements in order to proceed with a going-concern sale.

FACTS: Debtors, Alpha Natural Resources (D), produce and sell metallurgic and steam coal. In 2010, price of and demand for coal began to fall; between 2011 and 2015, the price of metallurgic coal fell 72 percent, and the price of steam coal fell 44 percent. By 2016, Debtors (D) incurred a net book loss of $126 million with cash burn of over $10 million per week. Debtors (D) petitioned for Chapter 11 bankruptcy. Under Debtors' (D) collective bargaining agreements (CBAs) with the United Mine Workers of America (UMWA) (P), Debtors (D) were required to make payments to four different union funds for the benefit of retired union employees. Debtors (D) filed a motion with the bankruptcy court seeking authorization of a going-concern sale of substantially all Debtors' (D) core, revenue-generating assets under § 363 of the Bankruptcy Code (Code), including substantially all Debtors' (D) coal-mining-related complexes. The Debtors' (D) prepetition lenders agreed to serve as a Stalking Horse Bidder, credit bidding $500 million for the Debtors' (D) core assets. Per the asset purchase agreement, the Stalking Horse Bidder would receive the core assets free and clear of liens, claims, and encumbrances. However, the Stalking Horse Bidder refused to assume any of Debtors' (D) liabilities under the Coal Industry Retiree Health Benefit Act of 1992 (Coal Act) or its retirement obligations to UMWA (P) Funds. The Stalking Horse Bidder filed a Rejection Motion in bankruptcy court, refusing to close the sale unless it can receive the core assets free and clear of Debtors' (D) obligations under its CBAs. Each of the CBAs subject to the Rejection Motion contains a successorship clause that would bind a subsequent purchaser to the Debtors' (D) business operations. The successorship provisions need to be waived by the UMWA (P) or rejected by the Debtors in order to consummate the sale to the Stalking Horse Bidder. Debtors (D) and UMWA (P) attempted to negotiate modifications to the CBAs that would permit Debtors (D) to outright reject the agreements, and exchanged proposals leading up to the hearing date. UMWA (P) also initiated negotiations directly with the Stalking Horse Bidder.

ISSUE: Can a bankruptcy court grant a Rejection Motion under §§ 1113 and 1114, allowing a debtor to reject certain collective bargaining agreements, in order to proceed with a going-concern sale?

HOLDING AND DECISION: (Huennekens, J.) Yes. A bankruptcy court can grant a Rejection Motion under Bankruptcy Code §§ 1113 and 1114, allowing a debtor to reject certain collective bargaining agreements, in order to proceed with a going-concern sale. Both §§ 1113 and 1114 are applicable to the Debtors (D), despite the Stalking Horse Bidder's (P) objection. Under § 1113(b)(1)(A), a debtor's proposal must be "necessary to permit the reorganization of the debtor," and § 1114(g)(3) requires the court to find that modification is necessary to permit the reorganization of the debtor in order to grant relief. Courts have found that the "necessary" standard is satisfied when a debtor proves that modification or rejection is necessary to achieve a sale under § 363 of the Bankruptcy Code. The UMWA (P) argues that elimination of the CBAs is unnecessary because UMWA (P)-operated mine complexes are still cash flow positive. This argument is not persuasive: Debtors (D) operate a single, fully integrated enterprise instead of a confederation of individual mines, so mine-by-mine analysis is not appropriate. A going-concern sale is not possible without elimination of the CBA, and Debtors (D) have met their burden of proving that rejection of the CBAs and modification of the retiree benefits are necessary. There is no indication of any other parties who are willing to assume the CBAs, and Debtors (D) must control their cash bleed in order to have any hope of avoiding liquidation. Accordingly, the balance of equities weighs in favor of the Debtors (D). Rejection Motion granted.

Continued on next page.

ANALYSIS

Bankruptcy Code § 1113 governs rejection of a collective bargaining agreement, while § 1114 governs modification of retiree benefits. Union disputes can often complicate reorganizations, as was the case in the bankruptcy of Hostess Brands. Faced with an inability to successfully negotiate with its bakers' union, Hostess Brands ended up closing completely instead of reorganizing.

Quicknotes

COLLECTIVE BARGAINING Negotiations between an employer and representative of organized employees that are mediated by a specified third party.

GOING CONCERN A commercial enterprise operating with the expectation of continued operation.

CHAPTER 37

Domestic Jurisdiction

Quick Reference Rules of Law

In re Dow Corning Corp.

Claimants (P) v. Debtor (D)

86 F.3d 482 (6th Cir. 1996)

NATURE OF CASE: Appeal from denial of transfer motions.

FACT SUMMARY: The district court claimed it lacked subject matter jurisdiction over claims that were not related to Dow Corning's bankruptcy proceedings.

RULE OF LAW

Bankruptcy jurisdiction exists so long as it is possible that a proceeding may impact on the debtor's rights, liabilities, options, or freedom of action.

FACTS: Dow Corning Corp. was the predominant producer of silicone gel breast implants and supplied silicone raw materials to other manufacturers. Dow Corning and other manufacturers and suppliers of silicone gel-filled implants were codefendants in a large number of personal injury lawsuits. Dow Corning filed for Chapter 11 bankruptcy. When claimants moved to transfer claims for compensatory and punitive damages to the federal district court, sitting as a bankruptcy court, the court ruled it did not have subject matter jurisdiction. An appeal followed.

ISSUE: Does bankruptcy jurisdiction exist so long as it is possible that a proceeding may impact on the debtor's rights, liabilities, options, or freedom of action?

HOLDING AND DECISION: (Martin, J.) Yes. Bankruptcy jurisdiction exists so long as it is possible that a proceeding may impact on the debtor's rights, liabilities, options, or freedom of action. The usual test to determine whether a civil proceeding is related to bankruptcy is whether the outcome of that proceeding could conceivably have any effect on the estate being administered in bankruptcy. In addition to the claims asserted by personal injury claimants, Dow Chemical and Corning Incorporated have asserted crossclaims on each other, and that will also have effect on the bankruptcy estate. Claims for indemnification and contribution obviously would affect the size of the estate, as well. Section 1334 (b) jurisdiction exists over breast implant claims pending against Dow Corning and one or both of its parents. The district court is in a better position to make abstention determinations. Reversed and remanded.

ANALYSIS

The district court later abstained. The case was returned to same court in 1997. The court then issued a writ of mandamus.

Quicknotes

COMPENSATORY DAMAGES Measure of damages necessary to compensate victim for actual injuries suffered.

CONTRIBUTION The right of a person or party who has compensated a victim for injury to seek reimbursement from others who are equally responsible for the injury in proportional amounts.

INDEMNIFICATION Reimbursement for losses sustained or security against anticipated loss or damages.

PERSONAL INJURY Harm to an individual's person or body.

PUNITIVE DAMAGES Damages exceeding the actual injury suffered for the purposes of punishment, deterrence, and comfort to plaintiff.

SUBJECT MATTER JURISDICTION A court's ability to adjudicate a specific category of cases based on the subject matter of the dispute.

Stern v. Marshall

Executor of decedent's wife's estate (D) v. Executor of decedent's son's estate (P)

564 U.S. 462 (2011)

NATURE OF CASE: Appeal from court of appeals decision holding that the district court should have given preclusive effect to a state court's prior decision instead of treating as proposed rather than final a bankruptcy court's judgment in favor of a debtor on the debtor's compulsory counterclaim of tortious interference with a gift expectancy.

FACT SUMMARY: Vickie (D), a debtor in bankruptcy and the wife of decedent J. Howard Marshall II (J. Marshall), contended that the bankruptcy court had constitutional as well as statutory authority to render judgment on her compulsory counterclaim against Pierce (P), J. Marshall's son, for tortious interference with a gift she expected from J. Marshall of half his property.

RULE OF LAW

A bankruptcy court does not have constitutional authority to enter judgment on a state common-law compulsory counterclaim, notwithstanding that it has statutory authority to do so.

FACTS: Vickie (D), also known to the public as Anna Nicole Smith, was the wife of J. Howard Marshall II (J. Marshall), one of the wealthiest men in Texas. J. Marshall did not include Vickie (D) in his will. Before J. Howard died, Vickie (D) filed suit in Texas probate court, asserting that Pierce (P), J. Howard's son, fraudulently induced J. Howard to sign a living trust that did not include her, even though J. Howard intended to give her half of his property. After J. Howard died, Vickie (D) filed for bankruptcy in federal bankruptcy court in California. Pierce (P) filed a complaint in that bankruptcy proceeding, contending that Vickie (D) had defamed him by inducing her lawyers to tell members of the press that he had engaged in fraud to gain control of his father's assets, and seeking a declaration that the defamation claim was not dischargeable. Pierce (P) subsequently filed a proof of claim for the defamation action, seeking to recover damages for his suit from Vickie's (D) bankruptcy estate. Vickie (D) defended by asserting truth, and she also filed a counterclaim for tortious interference with the gift she expected from J. Howard. The bankruptcy court granted Vickie (D) summary judgment on Pierce's (P) defamation claim, and then, after trial, the court issued a judgment on Vickie's (D) counterclaim in her favor, awarding her over $400 million in compensatory damages and $25 million in punitive damages. Pierce (P) argued that the bankruptcy court lacked jurisdiction over Vickie's (D) counterclaim, on the grounds that the counterclaim was not a "core proceeding" under § 157(b)(2)(C) of the Bankruptcy Code (Code). The bankruptcy court determined that Vickie's (D) claim was a core proceeding and that, therefore, it had the power to enter judgment on the counterclaim under § 157(b)(1). The district court concluded Vickie's (D) claim was not "core" and it would be unconstitutional to hold any-and-all counterclaims are core. However, the district court determined that it was required to treat the bankruptcy court's judgment as proposed, rather than final. Accordingly, after conducting independent review of the record, the court concluded that that Vickie's (D) counterclaim was meritorious, and it awarded her approximately $44 million for each type of damages, notwithstanding that by this time the Texas probate court, after a jury trial, had entered judgment in favor of Pierce (P). The court of appeals reversed on the ground that Vickie's (D) counterclaim did not meet the requirements for being a core proceeding, so that the district court should have afforded preclusive effect to the Texas probate court's factual and legal determinations, as that court's judgment was the earliest final judgment entered on the matters relevant to the counterclaim. The United States Supreme Court granted certiorari.

ISSUE: Does a bankruptcy court have constitutional authority to enter judgment on a state common-law compulsory counterclaim, notwithstanding that it has statutory authority to do so?

HOLDING AND DECISION: (Roberts, C.J.) No. A bankruptcy court does not have constitutional authority to enter judgment on a state common-law compulsory counterclaim, notwithstanding that it has statutory authority to do so. Congress in § 157(a) of the Code has divided bankruptcy proceedings into three categories: those that arise under title 11; those that arise in a title 11 case; and those that are related to a case under title 11. District courts may refer any or all such proceedings to the bankruptcy judges of their district, which is how the bankruptcy court in this case came to preside over Vickie's (D) bankruptcy proceedings. District courts also may withdraw a case or proceeding referred to the bankruptcy court "for cause shown." The manner, in which a bankruptcy judge may act on a referred matter depends on the type of proceeding involved. As § 157(b)(1) indicates, bankruptcy judges may hear and enter final judgments in "all core proceedings arising under title 11 or arising in a case under title 11. Core proceedings include, but are not limited to, counterclaims by a debtor's estate against persons filing claims against the estate. If a proceeding is not core, the bankrupt-

Continued on next page.

cy court must refer the case to the district court for a final entry of judgment after de novo review of any matter, to which a party objects. Designating all counterclaims as core proceedings raises serious constitutional concerns. Here, the canon of construction that requires that federal statutes be construed so as to avoid serious doubt of their constitutionality, i.e., the canon of avoidance, cannot be used to bypass the constitutional issue presented by § 157(b)(2)(C). However, that provision authorizes the bankruptcy court to enter a final judgment on her tortious interference counterclaim. In the alternative, Pierce (P) argues that the bankruptcy court lacked jurisdiction to resolve Vickie's (D) counterclaim because his defamation claim is a "personal injury tort" that the bankruptcy court lacked jurisdiction to hear under § 157(b)(5). The issue of what constitutes a "personal injury tort" need not be reached because Vickie (D) is correct that § 157(b)(5) is not jurisdictional, and Pierce (P) consented to the bankruptcy court's resolution of the defamation claim. Thus, although § 157 allowed the bankruptcy court to enter final judgment on Vickie's (D) counterclaim, Article III of the Constitution does not. Article III is "an inseparable element of the constitutional system of checks and balances" that "both defines the power and protects the independence of the Judicial Branch." Article III protects liberty not only through its role in implementing the separation of powers, but also by specifying the defining characteristics of Article III judges to protect the integrity of judicial decisionmaking. Article III could neither serve its purpose in the system of checks and balances nor preserve the integrity of judicial decision-making if the other branches could confer the government's judicial power on entities outside Article III. In *Northern Pipeline Constr. Co. v. Marathon Pipe Line Co.*, 458 U.S. 50 (1982), there was also an Article III challenge to a bankruptcy court's resolution of a debtor's suit. In that case, the Court considered whether bankruptcy judges serving under the Bankruptcy Act of 1978 (1978 Act)—who also lacked the tenure and salary guarantees of Article III—could "constitutionally be vested with jurisdiction to decide [a] state-law contract claim" against an entity that was not otherwise part of the bankruptcy proceedings. The plurality in *Northern Pipeline* recognized that there was a category of cases involving "public rights" that Congress could constitutionally assign to "legislative" courts for resolution. A full majority of the Court, while not agreeing on the scope of that exception, concluded that the doctrine did not encompass adjudication of the state law claim at issue in that case, and rejected the debtor's argument that the bankruptcy court's exercise of jurisdiction was constitutional because the bankruptcy judge was acting merely as an adjunct of the district court or court of appeals. After the decision in *Northern Pipeline*, Congress revised the statutes governing bankruptcy jurisdiction and bankruptcy judges in amendments it enacted in 1984. With respect to the "core" proceedings listed in § 157(b)(2), however, the bankruptcy courts under the 1984 Act exercise the same powers they wielded under the 1978 Act. The authority exercised by the newly constituted courts over a counterclaim such as Vickie's (D) exceeds the bounds of Article III. It is clear here the bankruptcy court exercised the "judicial power" of the United States in purporting to resolve and enter final judgment on a state common-law claim, just as the court did in *Northern Pipeline*. There is no "public right" that excuses the failure to comply with Article III in doing so. Vickie's (D) counterclaim does not fall within the public rights exception, however defined. The Court has long recognized that in general, Congress may not "withdraw from judicial cognizance any matter which, from its nature, is the subject of a suit at the common law, or in equity, or admiralty." *Murray's Lessee v. Hoboken Land & Improvement Co.*, 59 U.S. 272 (1856). The Court has also recognized that "[a]t the same time there are matters, involving public rights, . . . which are susceptible of judicial determination, but which [C]ongress may or may not bring within the cognizance of the courts of the United States, as it may deem proper." Several previous decisions have contrasted cases within the reach of the public rights exception—those arising "between the Government and persons subject to its authority in connection with the performance of the constitutional functions of the executive or legislative departments"—and those that are instead matters "of private right, that is, of the liability of one individual to another under the law as defined." Shortly after *Northern Pipeline*, the Court rejected the limitation of the public rights exception to actions involving the government as a party. The Court has continued, however, to limit the exception to cases in which the claim at issue derives from a federal regulatory scheme, or in which resolution of the claim by an expert government agency is deemed essential to a limited regulatory objective within the agency's authority. In other words, it is still the case that what makes a right "public" rather than private is that the right is integrally related to particular action of the federal government. In *Granfinanciera, S.A. v. Nordberg*, 492 U.S. 33 (1989), the most recent case considering the public rights exception, the Court rejected a bankruptcy trustee's argument that a fraudulent conveyance action filed on behalf of a bankruptcy estate against a noncreditor in a bankruptcy proceeding fell within the exception. Vickie's (D) counterclaim is similar to fraudulent conveyance claim at issue in *Granfinanciera*. It is not a matter that can be pursued only by grace of the other branches; it does not flow from a federal statutory scheme; and it is not "completely dependent upon" adjudication of a claim created by federal law. Instead, it is a claim made under state common law between two private parties; it involves the most prototypical exercise of judicial power: the entry of a final, binding judgment by a court with broad substantive jurisdiction, on a common-law cause of action, when the action neither derives from nor depends upon any agency regulatory regime. If such an exercise of

Continued on next page.

judicial power may nonetheless be taken from the Article III Judiciary simply by deeming it part of some amorphous "public right," then Article III would be transformed from the guardian of individual liberty and separation of powers "into mere wishful thinking." The fact that Pierce (P) filed a proof of claim in the bankruptcy proceedings does not change this analysis. Such filing did not give the bankruptcy court the constitutional authority to adjudicate Vickie's (D) counterclaim. Initially, Pierce's (P) defamation claim does not affect the nature of Vickie's (D) tortious interference counterclaim as one at common law that simply attempts to augment the bankruptcy estate—the type of claim that, under *Northern Pipeline* and *Granfinanciera*, must be decided by an Article III court. The cases on which Vickie (D) relies, *Katchen v. Landy*, 382 U.S. 323 (1966) and *Langenkamp v. Culp*, 498 U.S. 42 (1990), are inapposite. *Katchen* permitted a bankruptcy referee to exercise jurisdiction over a trustee's voidable preference claim against a creditor only where there was no question that the referee was required to decide whether there had been a voidable preference in determining whether and to what extent to allow the creditor's claim. The *Katchen* Court expressly noted that it did not intimate any opinion concerning whether the bankruptcy referee would have had "summary jurisdiction to adjudicate a demand by the bankruptcy trustee for affirmative relief, all of the substantial factual and legal bases for which had not been disposed of in passing on objections to the creditor's proof of claim." *Langenkamp* is to the same effect. In that case, the Court explained that a preferential transfer claim can be heard in bankruptcy when the allegedly favored creditor has filed a claim, because then the ensuing preference action by the trustee becomes integral to the restructuring of the debtor-creditor relationship. If, in contrast, the creditor has not filed a proof of claim, the trustee's preference action does not become part of the claims-allowance process subject to resolution by the bankruptcy court. In this case, by contrast, the bankruptcy court—in order to resolve Vickie's (D) counterclaim—was required to and did make several factual and legal determinations that were not "disposed of in passing on objections" to Pierce's (P) proof of claim. There was never any reason to believe that the process of adjudicating Pierce's (P) proof of claim would necessarily resolve Vickie's (D) counterclaim, notwithstanding some slight overlap between the two claims. The bankruptcy court could not rule in Vickie's (D) favor without ruling on questions of state law and the elements of her cause of action. In both *Katchen* and *Langenkamp*, moreover, the trustee bringing the preference action was asserting a right of recovery created by federal bankruptcy law. Vickie's (D) claim is instead a state tort action that exists without regard to any bankruptcy proceeding. In sum, Congress may not bypass Article III simply because a proceeding may have some bearing on a bankruptcy case; the question is whether the action at issue stems from the bankruptcy itself or would necessarily be resolved in the claims allowance process. Moreover, contrary to Vickie's (D) argument, the bankruptcy courts under the 1984 Act are not mere "adjuncts" of the district courts. The new bankruptcy courts, like the courts considered in *Northern Pipeline*, do not "ma[k]e only specialized, narrowly confined factual determinations regarding a particularized area of law" or engage in "statutorily channeled fact-finding functions." A bankruptcy court is not like an adjunct agency that possesses only a limited power to issue compensation orders that can be enforced only by order of the district court. Instead, a bankruptcy court resolving a counterclaim under § 157(b)(2)(C) has the power to enter "appropriate orders and judgments"—including final judgments—subject to review only if a party chooses to appeal. Such a court is an adjunct of no one. Finally, Vickie (D) predicts that restrictions on a bankruptcy court's ability to hear and finally resolve compulsory counterclaims will create significant delays and impose additional costs on the bankruptcy process. It goes without saying that the fact that a given law or procedure is efficient, convenient, and useful in facilitating functions of government, standing alone, will not save it if it is contrary to the Constitution. In addition, the Court is not convinced that the practical consequences of such limitations are as significant as Vickie (D) suggests. The framework Congress adopted in the 1984 Act already contemplates that certain state law matters in bankruptcy cases will be resolved by state courts and district courts, Thus, the removal of counterclaims such as Vickie's (D) from core bankruptcy jurisdiction will not meaningfully change the division of labor in the statute. Affirmed.

CONCURRENCE: (Scalia, J.) Simply put, a matter of public rights must at a minimum arise between the government and others, and there is no reason to have the numerous factors listed by the majority as part of Article III jurisprudence. Those factors have nothing to do with the text or tradition of Article III. For example, Article III gives no indication that state-law claims have preferential entitlement to an Article III judge, and it does not make pertinent the extent to which the area of the law is "particularized." The multiple factors relied on seem to have entered Article III jurisprudence almost randomly. The single test should be that an Article III judge is required in all federal adjudications, unless there is a firmly established historical practice to the contrary. Based on such a test, an Article III judge is not required for territorial courts, courts-martial, or true "public rights" cases. Regardless, whether historical practice permits non-Article III judges to render opinions on claims against the bankruptcy estate, Vickie (D) points to no historical practice that authorizes a non-Article III judge to adjudicate a counterclaim of the sort at issue, here.

Continued on next page.

DISSENT: (Breyer, J.) The majority errs in concluding that § 157(b)(2)(C) is inconsistent with Article III. In part, the majority's error stems from the way in which it interprets, or at least emphasizes, certain precedents. The majority overstates the current relevance of statements made in *Murray's Lessee*, and it overstates the importance of an analysis that did not command a Court majority in *Northern Pipeline*, and which was later disavowed. The majority also understates a watershed opinion widely thought to demonstrate the constitutional basis for the current authority of administrative agencies to adjudicate private disputes, namely, *Crowell v. Benson*, 285 U.S. 22 (1932). Finally, the majority fails to follow the analysis recently used to evaluate claims that a congressional delegation of adjudicatory authority violates separation-of-powers principles derived from Article III. These cases are *Thomas v. Union Carbide Agricultural Products Co.*, 473 U.S. 568 (1985), and *Commodity Futures Trading Commn. v. Schor*, 478 U.S. 833 (1986). As to *Murray's Lessee*, the majority relies on language from that case that is essentially dictum. More importantly, it is the case's distinction between "public rights" and "private rights" that has had the more lasting impact. Courts have seized on that distinction when upholding non-Article III adjudication, not when striking it down. The one exception is *Northern Pipeline*, where the Court struck down the Bankruptcy Act of 1978. In that case, however, there was no majority, and only a plurality, not a majority, read the statement roughly in the way the majority currently reads it. *Crowell* clarified the scope of the dictum in *Murray's Lessee*. In *Crowell*, Congress's delegation of primary fact-finding authority to an agency was upheld. The majority's reading of *Crowell* greatly limits it. *Crowell* has been hailed as the premier case validating administrative adjudication, but the majority distinguishes *Crowell* as a case in which the Court upheld the delegation of adjudicatory authority to an administrative agency simply because the agency's power to make the "specialized, narrowly confined factual determinations" at issue arising in a "particularized area of law," made the agency a district court adjunct. If *Crowell's* holding is truly as narrow as the majority suggests, Congress's delegation to various agencies of authority to adjudicate disputes among private parties—a question long deemed settled—would have to be revisited. In addition, instead of leaning so heavily on the approach taken by the plurality in *Northern Pipeline*, a better approach would be to look to the Court's more recent Article III cases *Thomas* and *Schor*. Not only did these cases command a majority, they also took a more pragmatic, flexible approach to the constitutional question. They sought to determine whether, in the particular instance, the challenged delegation of adjudicatory authority posed a genuine and serious threat that one branch of government sought to aggrandize its own constitutionally delegated authority by encroaching upon a field of authority that the Constitution assigns exclusively to another branch. To reach a determination of that issue, the Court in those cases looked at several factors, including: (1) the nature of the claim to be adjudicated; (2) the nature of the non-Article III tribunal; (3) the extent to which Article III courts exercise control over the proceeding; (4) the presence or absence of the parties' consent; and (5) the nature and importance of the legislative purpose served by the grant of adjudicatory authority to a tribunal with judges who lack Article III's tenure and compensation protections. The majority should have done so here, as well. Instead of applying a formalistic approach, it should have applied the bending, flexible approach taken by *Thomas* and *Schor*. Applying *Schor's* approach here leads to the conclusion that a grant of authority to a bankruptcy court to adjudicate compulsory counterclaims does not violate any constitutional separation-of-powers principle related to Article III. First, although the nature of the counterclaim—a state common-law claim—supports a finding of unconstitutionality, the significance of this factor is mitigated here by the fact that bankruptcy courts often decide claims that similarly resemble various common-law actions. Second, the nature of the tribunal here supports constitutionality, as the bankruptcy court is made up of judges who enjoy considerable protection from improper political influence—they are appointed and removed by the courts of appeals, and their salaries are paid by the Judiciary. Third, the control exercised by Article III judges over bankruptcy proceedings argues in favor of constitutionality. Article III judges control and supervise the bankruptcy court's determinations—at least to the same degree that Article III judges supervised the agency's determinations in *Crowell*, if not more so. Fourth, the fact that the parties have consented to bankruptcy court jurisdiction argues in favor of constitutionality, and strongly so. Here, Pierce (P) brought his claim voluntarily, and he likely had an alternative forum to the bankruptcy court in which to pursue his claim. This type of consent argues strongly in favor of using ordinary bankruptcy court proceedings. The Court's precedent, including *Northern Pipeline*, has recognized that even when private rights are at issue, non-Article III adjudication may be appropriate when both parties consent. Fifth, the nature and importance of the legislative purpose served by the grant of adjudicatory authority to bankruptcy courts argues strongly in favor of constitutionality. Congress's delegation of adjudicatory powers over counterclaims asserted against bankruptcy claimants constitutes an important means of securing a constitutionally authorized end, i.e., the establishment of uniform bankruptcy laws and to restructure debtor-creditor relations. To be effective, a single tribunal must have broad authority to restructure those relations, "having jurisdiction of the parties to controversies brought before them," "decid[ing] all matters in dispute," and "decree[ing] complete relief." When a creditor files a proof of claim in the bankruptcy court, he subjects himself to the court's equitable power and agrees to the court's resolution of his claim. When the

Continued on next page.

bankruptcy estate has a related claim against that creditor, that counterclaim may offset the creditor's claim, or even yield additional damages that augment the estate and may be distributed to the other creditors. A bankruptcy court's resolution of such a claim plays a critical role in Congress's constitutionally based effort to create an efficient, effective federal bankruptcy system. The Court should defer to Congress's determination in this area, as it is devoid of any legislative or executive motive, intent, purpose, or desire to encroach upon areas that Article III reserves to judges to whom it grants tenure and compensation protections. Taking all these factors together, the magnitude of any intrusion on the Judicial Branch would be minimal. Finally, contrary to the majority's prediction, its decision will have a great impact, as a typical bankruptcy case may give rise to counterclaims that would now have to be separately adjudicated. Such a "constitutionally required game of jurisdictional ping-pong between courts" would lead to inefficiency, increased cost, delay, and needless additional suffering among those faced with bankruptcy.

ANALYSIS

It can be argued that *Stern* has altered the key function of the bankruptcy courts by not allowing the fiduciaries who are vested with maximizing recoveries from creditors to utilize the expedited processes within the bankruptcy court system. What a trustee or other fiduciary is left with is utilizing state court processes, which in many jurisdictions are backlogged for years. Moreover, busy district courts may not readily undertake to initially adjudicate matters that prior to *Stern* would have been adjudicated by the bankruptcy courts. If the district courts wait to review bankruptcy court reports and conclusions on such matters, more delay will be engendered. Even more delay will arise if the district courts' decisions are appealed to the courts of appeals, rather than the bankruptcy appellate panels (BAPs), which have no authority to review district decisions. As the dissent observes, such changes would not facilitate an expedited resolution for debtor/creditor relations in the bankruptcy process, and, instead, likely will cause some bankruptcy cases to take considerably longer than they would have prior to the Supreme Court's decision in this case.

Quicknotes

COMPULSORY COUNTERCLAIM An independent cause of action brought by a defendant to a lawsuit that arises out of the same transaction or occurrence that is the subject matter of the plaintiff's claim.

DE NOVO The review of a lower court decision by an appellate court, which is hearing the case as if it had not been previously heard and as if no judgment had been rendered.

DICTUM Statement by a judge in a legal opinion that is not necessary for the resolution of the action.

In re United States Lines, Inc.

Debtor (P) v. Insurers (D)

197 F.3d 631 (2d Cir. 1999)

NATURE OF CASE: Interlocutory appeal.

FACT SUMMARY: When former employees filed claims for asbestos-related injuries sustained while they worked on United States Lines (USL) ships, USL (P) filed for bankruptcy and sought to recover insurance proceeds.

RULE OF LAW

Where a bankruptcy claim directly affects a core bankruptcy function, it is a core proceeding.

FACTS: The United States Lines (USL) (P) and United States Lines (S.A.) Inc. Reorganization Trust sued in bankruptcy court seeking a declaratory judgment to establish their rights under several insurance contracts. USL (P) also sought punitive damages for creation of an insurance maze. The bankruptcy court held that the action was within its core jurisdiction and denied the insurance companies' (D) motion to compel arbitration. The district court reversed, ruling that the insurance contract disputes were not core proceedings. The district court ordered arbitration to proceed and certified its order for interlocutory appeal.

ISSUE: Where a bankruptcy claim directly affects a core bankruptcy function, is it a core proceeding?

HOLDING AND DECISION: (Walker, J.) Yes. Where a bankruptcy claim directly affects a core bankruptcy function, it is a core proceeding. The impact that these contracts have on other core bankruptcy functions render them core, notwithstanding the fact that claims are on prepetition contracts. The bankruptcy court has core jurisdiction over claims arising from a contract formed postpetition. There are circumstances in which a bankruptcy court may stay arbitration, and in this case the bankruptcy court was correct that it had discretion to do so. Reversed and remanded.

CONCURRENCE: (Newman, J.) The efficient functioning of the bankruptcy system would be better served by a bright-line rule that treats as core-proceeding all suits alleging postpetition breaches of prepetition contracts.

CONCURRENCE: (Calabresi, J.) I would be inclined to follow a case-by-case approach.

ANALYSIS

The claims by employees were complicated by a pay-first provision in the insurance contracts. The insurer's liability was not triggered until the insured paid the claim of the personal injury victim. All the insurance contracts had been issued prior to bankruptcy.

Quicknotes

ARBITRATION An agreement to have a dispute heard and decided by a neutral third party, rather than through legal proceedings.

CHAPTER 11 REORGANIZATION A plan formulated pursuant to Chapter 11 of the Bankruptcy Code whereby a debtor who is unable to pay his or her debts as they become due is relieved of the obligation to pay creditors through reorganization and payment from future income.

DECLARATORY JUDGMENT An adjudication by the courts that grants not relief but is binding over the legal status of the parties involved in the dispute.

INTERLOCUTORY APPEAL The appeal of an issue that does not resolve the disposition of the case but is essential to a determination of the parties' legal rights.

CHAPTER 38

Transnational Bankruptcies

Quick Reference Rules of Law

In re McLean Industries, Inc.

Shipping company debtor (P) v. Creditor (D)

68 B.R. 690 (Bankr. S.D.N.Y. 1986)

NATURE OF CASE: Petition for preliminary injunction and contempt citation in Chapter 11 bankruptcy.

FACT SUMMARY: A foreign corporation with a subsidiary having a U.S. office contended it was not subject to U.S. jurisdiction for purposes of a Chapter 11 proceeding.

RULE OF LAW

A foreign corporation with a subsidiary having a U.S. office may be subject to U.S. jurisdiction for purposes of a Chapter 11 proceeding.

FACTS: United States Lines, Inc. (P), a shipping company, filed for bankruptcy under Chapter 11. One creditor was GAC Marine Fuels, Ltd. (GAC) (D), a British corporation with offices around the world. A wholly owned subsidiary of GAC (D) had an office in New Jersey, at which it solicited business for GAC (D). After U.S. Lines (P) filed for bankruptcy, GAC (D) obtained an order in Hong Kong attaching a ship owned by U.S. Lines (P), which brought a petition in bankruptcy court seeking a contempt citation and an injunction. GAC (D) contended it was not subject to U.S. jurisdiction.

ISSUE: May a foreign corporation with a subsidiary having a U.S. office be subject to U.S. jurisdiction for purposes of a Chapter 11 proceeding?

HOLDING AND DECISION: (Buschman, J.) Yes. A foreign corporation with a subsidiary having a U.S. office may be subject to U.S. jurisdiction for purposes of a Chapter 11 proceeding. The law as it relates to personal jurisdiction in bankruptcy is governed by standard due process considerations. A foreign entity will be subject to U.S. jurisdiction if it transacts business in the United States and if either the cause of action arose out of U.S. business or the entity's contacts are so continuous as to provide general personal jurisdiction. If an entity's contracts are through a subsidiary, jurisdiction will be afforded if the subsidiary's acts are for the benefit of the parent. Here, it appears that the subsidiary's New Jersey office made seven to fifteen transactions per month on account of GAC (D), and this is sufficient to confer general personal jurisdiction. Petition granted.

ANALYSIS

The jurisdictional analysis here was identical to the analysis underlying state "long-arm" jurisdictional statutes. Arguments have been made that the U.S. government has such a strong interest in its bankruptcy proceedings that its jurisdiction should have a broader reach than such state laws. The court here declined to rule on this issue, finding it unnecessary.

Quicknotes

CHAPTER 11 BANKRUPTCY A legal proceeding whereby a debtor, who is unable to pay his or her debts as they become due, is relieved of the obligation to pay creditors through reorganization and payment from future income.

JURISDICTION The authority of a court to hear and declare judgment in respect to a particular matter.

LONG-ARM STATUTE A state statute conferring personal jurisdiction to state courts over a defendant not residing in the state, when the cause of action arises as a result of activities conducted within the state or affecting state residents.

SUBSIDIARY A company, a majority of whose shares are owned by another corporation and which is subject to that corporation's control.

In re Ascot Fund Ltd.

Shareholder (P) v. Debtor (D)

603 B.R. 271 (Bankr. S.D.N.Y. 2019)

NATURE OF CASE: Bankruptcy court ruling on shareholder's objection to recognition of foreign main proceeding in the Cayman Islands.

FACT SUMMARY: Debtor Ascot Fund Ltd. (Ascot Fund) (D) is an investment fund organized under Cayman Islands law, which invested substantially all its assets in what later turned out to be a Ponzi scheme. All the assets that Ascot Fund (D) invested were lost, however, as part of a settlement from litigation surrounding the Ponzi scheme, Ascot Fund (D) received substantial assets to distribute to its shareholders. A Joint Official Liquidator for Ascot Fund (D) filed for recognition of Ascot Fund's (D) Cayman Islands liquidation as a foreign main proceeding.

RULE OF LAW

A United States bankruptcy court should recognize a proceeding in the Cayman Islands as a foreign main proceeding under Chapter 15 when the debtor is registered and headquartered in the Cayman Islands, even if the debtor invested substantially all its assets in a New York–affiliated partnership.

FACTS: Debtor Ascot Fund Ltd. (Ascot Fund) (D), is an investment fund organized under Cayman Islands law. Ascot Fund (D) invested substantially all its assets into Ascot Partners LP (Ascot Partners), which invested substantially all its assets with Bernard L. Madoff Investment Securities, LLC (BLMIS). BLMIS was the vehicle for a massive Ponzi scheme, and all direct and indirect investors of BLMIS lost their investments. As part of a settlement between BLMIS and Ascot Partners, among other entities, Ascot Partners was provided with tens of millions of dollars to distribute to its investors, including Ascot Fund (D) shareholders. Ascot Fund (D) filed for liquidation in the Cayman Islands, and one of its Joint Official Liquidators (JOLs), Michael Penner (Petitioner), filed under Chapter 15 of the Bankruptcy Code seeking recognition of the Cayman Proceeding as a foreign main proceeding. An Ascot Fund investor (P) objected on the grounds that Ascot Fund's center of main interests (COMI) is not in the Cayman Islands. The objecting shareholder (P) expressed concern that the distribution methodology adopted by the Ascot Fund Board would be less favorable than a New York court's methodology.

ISSUE: Should a United States bankruptcy court recognize a proceeding in the Cayman Islands as a foreign main proceeding under Chapter 15 when the debtor is registered and headquartered in the Cayman Islands, even if the debtor invested substantially all its assets in a New York–affiliated partnership?

HOLDING AND DECISION: (Bernstein, J.) Yes. A United States bankruptcy court should recognize a proceeding in the Cayman Islands as a foreign main proceeding under Chapter 15 when the debtor is registered and headquartered in the Cayman Islands, even if the debtor invested substantially all its assets in a New York–affiliated partnership. Section 1517(a) of the Bankruptcy Code requires the following for recognition of a foreign proceeding: (1) the foreign proceeding is a foreign main proceeding or foreign nonmain proceeding under § 1502; (2) the foreign representative applying for recognition is a person or body; and (3) the petition meets the requirements of § 1515. The objector (P) challenges only Ascot Fund's (D) inability to fulfill the first factor, as the second and third are clearly met. In order to recognize the Cayman Proceeding as a foreign main proceeding, its COMI must lie in the Cayman Islands. Under § 1516(c), the location of a debtor's main office is presumed to be its center of main interests (COMI). Ascot Fund's (D) registered address has been located in the Cayman Islands since its formation, so the Cayman Islands is presumed to be its COMI. Furthermore, Ascot Fund's (D) Board members all resided or were based in the Cayman Islands, as was its sole voting shareholder. The objector (P) argues that the Isle of Man may be Ascot Fund's (D) COMI, because Ascot Fund (D) employed an administrative services corporation that was based out of the Isle of Man, and the Isle of Man was where Ascot Fund's (D) register of shareholders was located. The objector (D) also argued that New York may be Ascot Fund's (D) COMI, because it has participated in liquidation activities in New York. Ascot Fund (D) has not engaged in the investment business since the BLMIS Ponzi scheme came to light, and its only significant activity since has been participation in New York litigation. However, the New York litigation does not define Ascot Fund's (D) COMI or imply that it is a silent partner in the New York litigation, as was suggested by the objector (P). Furthermore, there is no evidence that the COMI has been manipulated as Ascot Fund's (D) principal place of business, as was the case in *SPhinX, Ltd.*, 351 B.R. 103 (Bankr. S.D.N.Y. 2006). Even though Ascot Fund's (D) only significant asset is its limited partnership interest in Ascot Partners, a New York partnership, and Ascot Partners' customer claim in the BLMIS liquidation, this fact alone is not enough to outweigh the evidence that Ascot Fund's (D) COMI, based on the fund documents, was the Cayman

Continued on next page.

Islands. Objection overruled; Cayman Islands recognized as foreign main proceeding.

ANALYSIS

Bernard Madoff, the head of Bernard L. Madoff Investment Securities, LLC (BLMIS), was arrested in 2008 and sentenced to 150 years in prison after pleading guilty to 11 federal felonies, including securities fraud, investment adviser fraud, mail fraud, wire fraud, three counts of money laundering, false statements, perjury, false filings with the U.S. Securities and Exchange Commission, and theft from an employee benefit plan. It was estimated that Madoff defrauded over 4,800 clients of as much as $65 billion. Madoff used the funds from the Ponzi scheme's new clients to pay old clients their anticipated returns. By 2018, Irving Picard, BLMIS's trustee, had managed to recover $13.3 billion for investors by suing investors who withdrew more money from the scheme than they had initially put in, even though many believed they were merely taking legitimately earned profits. Madoff died in April 2021.

Quicknotes

LIQUIDATION The reduction to cash of all assets for distribution to creditors.

PONZI SCHEME An investment arrangement in which returns to investors are financed through the acquisition of new investors, rather than on the success of an underlying business venture.

In re Vitro S.A.B. de C.V.

[Parties not identified.]

701 F.3d 1031 (5th Cir. 2012)

NATURE OF CASE: Appeal from judgment denying enforcement of a foreign reorganization plan.

FACT SUMMARY: Vitro S.A.B. de C.V. (Vitro), a Mexican company, along with one of its largest third-party creditors, contended that the U.S. bankruptcy court erred as a matter of law in denying enforcement of Vitro's Mexican reorganization plan on the grounds that the plan would extinguish the obligations of subsidiary nondebtor guarantors.

RULE OF LAW

Absent exceptional circumstances, a bankruptcy court does not err as a matter of law in refusing to enforce a foreign reorganization because the plan extinguishes the guaranty obligations of nondebtor parties.

FACTS: Between 2003 and 2007, Vitro S.A.B. de C.V. (Vitro), a Mexican company, borrowed a total of approximately $1.216 billion, predominately from United States investors. Vitro's indebtedness was evidenced by three series of unsecured notes (collectively, the "Old Notes"). Payment in full of the Old Notes was guaranteed by substantially all of Vitro's subsidiaries (the "Guarantors"). The guaranties provided that the Guarantors' obligation would not be released, discharged, or otherwise affected by any settlement or release as result of any insolvency, reorganization, or bankruptcy proceeding affecting Vitro. The guaranties further provided they were to be governed and construed under New York law and included the Guarantors' consent to litigate any disputes in New York state courts. In late 2008, Vitro started experiencing serious financial problems, and, in early 2009, it stopped making scheduled interest payments on the Old Notes. Thereafter, it restructured its debt, primarily by reshuffling intercompany debt between itself and its subsidiaries. Prior to the restructuring, the subsidiaries owed Vitro around $1.2 billion. After the restructuring, Vitro owed the subsidiaries around $1.5 billion. Vitro did not disclose these transactions to the Old Notes holders. Only in October of 2010, approximately 300 days after completing the transactions with its subsidiaries, did Vitro disclose the existence of the subsidiary creditors. This took the transactions outside Mexico's 270-day "suspicion period," during which such transactions would be subject to additional scrutiny as fraudulent conveyances before a business enters bankruptcy. After negotiations with its noninsider creditors failed, Vitro initiated a voluntary reorganization "concurso" proceeding in Mexico. In April 2011, Vitro was declared in bankruptcy under Mexican law. The reorganization plan proposed for Vitro would extinguish the Old Notes, and the Guarantors' obligations would be discharged. Additionally, Vitro would issue new notes payable in 2019 (New 2019 Notes) with a total principal amount of $814,650,000. Principal payments on these New 2019 Notes would not be made during the first four years. In Mexico, plan approval requires over 50 percent creditor approval. However, insider creditors may participate in the approval. Vitro's restructuring obtained over 50 percent approval when its insider subsidiary creditors were included; but would not have obtained such approval if the vote of only noninsider creditors counted. The concurso plan approval was appealed within the Mexican judicial system. Pending the appeal, Vitro filed in the United States for Chapter 15 bankruptcy enforcement of the reorganization plan. The bankruptcy court denied the requested enforcement under Bankruptcy Code §§ 1507, 1521, and 1506 because approval of the plan would extinguish claims held by the objecting creditors against the subsidiary Guarantors. Vitro and one of its largest third-party creditors appealed directly to the court of appeals, which granted review.

ISSUE: Absent exceptional circumstances, does a bankruptcy court err as a matter of law in refusing to enforce a foreign reorganization because the plan extinguishes the guaranty obligations of nondebtor parties?

HOLDING AND DECISION: (King, J.) No. Absent exceptional circumstances, a bankruptcy court does not err as a matter of law in refusing to enforce a foreign reorganization because the plan extinguishes the guaranty obligations of debtor parties. Comity—the recognition by one nation of another nation's legislative, executive, or judicial acts—is a central impetus of Chapter 15, but such concern is not unbridled, and whether any relief under Chapter 15 will be granted is a separate question from whether a foreign proceeding will be recognized. In considering whether to grant relief, it is not necessary that the result achieved in the foreign bankruptcy proceeding be identical to that which would be had in the United States. This case gives rise to two questions of first impression: (1) whether a foreign representative may independently seek relief under either §§ 1521 or 1507, and whether a court may itself determine under which of Chapter 15's provision such relief would fall. The answer to these questions is that a court confronted by this situation should first consider the specific relief enumerated under §§ 1521(a) and (b). If the relief is not explicitly provided for there, a court should then consider whether the requested relief falls more gen-

Continued on next page.

erally under § 1521(a)'s grant of any appropriate relief, which is relief previously available under Chapter 15's predecessor, § 304. Only if a court determines the requested relief was not formerly available under § 304 should the court consider whether relief would be appropriate as "additional assistance" under § 1507. However, under § 1522, relief under § 1521 may be granted only if the interests of the creditors and other interested entities, including the debtor, are sufficiently protected. Applying this analytic framework here, the bankruptcy court did not err in denying relief. First, §§ 1521(a)(1)-(7) and (b) do not provide for discharging obligations held by nondebtor guarantors. The grant in § 1521(a) of "any appropriate relief" also does not provide the necessary relief because precedent has interpreted the Bankruptcy Code to foreclose such a release, and because when such relief has been granted, it has been granted under § 1507, not § 1521. Even if the relief sought were theoretically available under § 1521, the facts of this case run afoul of the limitations in § 1522. Finally, although the relief requested might theoretically be available under § 1507 generally, since that section provides for "additional assistance" to facilitate relief not otherwise available in the United States, Vitro has not demonstrated exceptional circumstances comparable to those that would make possible such a release in the United States, as contemplated by § 1507(b)(4), which requires a bankruptcy court to consider whether the requested relief is comparable to that available under the Bankruptcy Code. While a nonconsensual, nondebtor discharge is not available in this circuit, it could be available in other circuits upon a showing of exception circumstances. Vitro, however, has failed to make such a showing. To the contrary, the evidence shows that equity retained substantial value; that creditors did not receive a distribution close to what they were originally owed; that the affected creditors did not consent to the plan, but were grouped together into a class with insider voters who only existed by virtue of Vitro reshuffling its financial obligations between it and its subsidiaries; that a majority of the impacted group of creditors did not vote in favor of the plan; and that nonconsenting creditors were not given an alternative to recover what they were owed in full. Further, allowing Vitro to use approval by a majority of insider creditors to support enforcement would amount to letting one discrepancy between U.S. law and Mexican law make up for another (the discharge of nondebtor guarantors). Accordingly, Vitro has failed to show that the relief requested under the concurso plan is substantially in accordance with the circumstances that would warrant such relief in the United States. Looked at under a deferential standard of review, the bankruptcy court's decision in this case was reasonable. Finally, because relief is not warranted under §§ 1507 or 1521, there is no need to reach the question of whether the concurso plan would be manifestly contrary to a fundamental public policy of the United States, and thereby violate § 1506. Affirmed.

ANALYSIS

Chapter 15 was enacted in 2005 to implement the Model Law on Cross-Border Insolvency ("Model Law") formulated by the United Nations Commission on International Trade Law (UNCITRAL), and replaced former Bankruptcy Code § 304. It was intended to provide effective mechanisms for dealing with cases of cross-border insolvency, as well as to be the exclusive door to ancillary assistance to foreign proceedings, thus concentrating control of these questions in one court. It was also intended to increase legal certainty, promote fairness and efficiency, protect and maximize value, and facilitate the rescue of financially troubled businesses. It was enacted in response to international trade and the growth of multinational enterprise, as well as the increased incidence of multinational financial failure.

Quicknotes

COMITY A rule pursuant to which courts in one state give deference to the statutes and judicial decisions of the court of another state.

McGrath v. Riddell

[Parties not identified.]

House of Lords, UKHL 21 (2008)

NATURE OF CASE: Appeal from English lower court judgments denying a request to remit assets of Australian companies to Australian liquidators for distribution.

FACT SUMMARY: An Australian court requested that the English assets of four Australian companies in liquidation be remitted to Australian liquidators for distribution in accordance with Australian insolvency law.

RULE OF LAW

English courts have the authority to remit assets of an entity of a relevant country to liquidators in that country to be distributed in accordance with the insolvency laws of that country, even where doing so will favor some creditors at the expense of others.

FACTS: Four Australian insurance companies were in liquidation in Australia. Some of their assets—mostly reinsurance claims on policies taken out in London—were situated in England. Provisional liquidators were appointed in England to protect these assets. In Australia, liquidators were also appointed. As part of the liquidation process, an Australian court made a request to the appropriate English court requesting that the English provisional liquidators be directed, after payment of their expenses, to remit the assets to the Australian liquidators for distribution. The Australian court made its request pursuant to section 426(4) of England's Insolvency Act 1986, which provides that: "The courts having jurisdiction in relation to insolvency law in any part of the United Kingdom shall assist the courts having the corresponding jurisdiction in . . . any relevant country." The English Secretary of State has the power to designate a country as "relevant" and has so designated Australia. Section 426(5) provides that the court to which a request is made under § 426(4) has the authority "to apply, in relation to any matters specified in the request, the insolvency law which is applicable by either court in relation to comparable matters falling within its jurisdiction." The alternative to granting the Australian court's request was a separate liquidation and distribution of the English assets in accordance with the Insolvency Act. The outcome under each scenario would be different for different classes of creditors. The lower court denied the request, on the grounds the distribution in Australia would not be pari passu, but would give preference to some creditors (the policy holders) at the expense of other creditors (the rest of the creditors). The Court of Appeal affirmed, and the House of Lords granted review.

ISSUE: Do English courts have the authority to remit assets of an entity of a relevant country to liquidators in that country to be distributed in accordance with the insolvency laws of that country, even where doing so will favor some creditors at the expense of others?

HOLDING AND DECISION: Yes. English courts have the authority to remit assets of an entity of a relevant country to liquidators in that country to be distributed in accordance with the insolvency laws of that country, even where doing so will favor some creditors at the expense of others.

OPINION: (Lord Hoffmann) The courts' authority derives from case law principles, and is reinforced by Insolvency Law § 462. Prior to that statute's enactment, case law provided for international cooperation in corporate insolvency based on principles of private international law and comity, and that bankruptcy should be unitary and universal. This principle holds that the unitary bankruptcy proceeding in the court of the bankrupt's country receives international recognition and applies to all the bankrupt's assets. In the United States, this aspirational principle is known as "modified universalism." Full universalism is achieved only by treaty. The judicial practice that developed around this principle in ancillary cases was to limit the powers and duties of liquidators to collecting the English assets and settling a list of the creditors who sent in proofs. The English liquidators were given the authority to remit the English assets to the liquidators in the relevant country. Some courts denied such authority where distribution would not be made in accordance with English law, reasoning that they did not have jurisdiction to do otherwise because creditors in an English liquidation (principal or ancillary) cannot be deprived of their statutory rights under English law. However, once it is accepted that the court has the authority to direct an English ancillary liquidator to remit the assets for distribution by the principal liquidator, it logically follows that those assets do not have to be distributed according to English law to endow the court with jurisdiction to order the remittal in the first place. As a practical matter, most countries have their own lists of preferential creditors that differ from those of England. Thus, the court has jurisdiction at common law to direct the remittal. The court is not, under § 462, applying Australian law to the distribution, but ordering the remittal under English law for distribution in Australia, in accord with that country's laws. The decision the English court is making is that there is a foreign jurisdiction more appropriate than England for dealing with the liquidation. The court is not deciding a choice of law question. Here, apply-

Continued on next page.

ing these principles of universalism, it would not offend any principles of justice for the assets to be remitted to Australia. The Australian court's request should have been granted. Appeal allowed (Reversed).

ANALYSIS

The United States has not been designated a "relevant country" by England's Secretary of State for purposes of § 462. Thus, if a U.S. bankruptcy trustee or court made a request similar to one made by the Australian court in this case, Lord Scott would not have permitted remittal—but it seems that a majority of the other Lords would have.

Quicknotes

COMITY A rule pursuant to which courts in one state give deference to the statutes and judicial decisions of the court of another state.

COMMON LAW A body of law developed through the judicial decisions of the courts as opposed to the legislative process.

Glossary

Common Latin Words and Phrases Encountered in the Law

A FORTIORI: Because one fact exists or has been proven, therefore a second fact that is related to the first fact must also exist.

A PRIORI: From the cause to the effect. A term of logic used to denote that when one generally accepted truth is shown to be a cause, another particular effect must necessarily follow.

AB INITIO: From the beginning; a condition that has existed throughout, as in a marriage that was void ab initio.

ACTUS REUS: The wrongful act; in criminal law, such action sufficient to trigger criminal liability.

AD VALOREM: According to value; an ad valorem tax is imposed upon an item located within the taxing jurisdiction calculated by the value of such item.

AMICUS CURIAE: Friend of the court. Its most common usage takes the form of an amicus curiae brief, filed by a person who is not a party to an action but is nonetheless allowed to offer an argument supporting his legal interests.

ARGUENDO: In arguing. A statement, possibly hypothetical, made for the purpose of argument is one made arguendo.

BILL QUIA TIMET: A bill to quiet title (establish ownership) to real property.

BONA FIDE: True, honest, or genuine. May refer to a person's legal position based on good faith or lacking notice of fraud (such as a bona fide purchaser for value) or to the authenticity of a particular document (such as a bona fide last will and testament).

CAUSA MORTIS: With approaching death in mind. A gift causa mortis is a gift given by a party who feels certain that death is imminent.

CAVEAT EMPTOR: Let the buyer beware. This maxim is reflected in the rule of law that a buyer purchases at his own risk because it is his responsibility to examine, judge, test, and otherwise inspect what he is buying.

CERTIORARI: A writ of review. Petitions for review of a case by the United States Supreme Court are most often done by means of a writ of certiorari.

CONTRA: On the other hand. Opposite. Contrary to.

CORAM NOBIS: Before us; writs of error directed to the court that originally rendered the judgment.

CORAM VOBIS: Before you; writs of error directed by an appellate court to a lower court to correct a factual error.

CORPUS DELICTI: The body of the crime; the requisite elements of a crime amounting to objective proof that a crime has been committed.

CUM TESTAMENTO ANNEXO, ADMINISTRATOR (ADMINISTRATOR C.T.A.): With will annexed; an administrator c.t.a. settles an estate pursuant to a will in which he or she is not appointed.

DE BONIS NON, ADMINISTRATOR (ADMINISTRATOR D.B.N.): Of goods not administered; an administrator d.b.n. settles a partially settled estate.

DE FACTO: In fact; in reality; actually. Existing in fact but not officially approved or engendered.

DE JURE: By right; lawful. Describes a condition that is legitimate "as a matter of law," in contrast to the term "de facto," which connotes something existing in fact but not legally sanctioned or authorized. For example, de facto segregation refers to segregation brought about by housing patterns, etc., whereas de jure segregation refers to segregation created by law.

DE MINIMUS: Of minimal importance; insignificant; a trifle; not worth bothering about.

DE NOVO: Anew; a second time; afresh. A trial de novo is a new trial held at the appellate level as if the case originated there and the trial at a lower level had not taken place.

DICTA: Generally used as an abbreviated form of obiter dicta, a term describing those portions of a judicial opinion incidental or not necessary to resolution of the specific question before the court. Such nonessential statements and remarks are not considered to be binding precedent.

DUCES TECUM: Refers to a particular type of writ or subpoena requesting a party or organization to produce certain documents in their possession.

EN BANC: Full bench. Where a court sits with all justices present rather than the usual quorum.

EX PARTE: For one side or one party only. An ex parte proceeding is one undertaken for the benefit of only one party, without notice to, or an appearance by, an adverse party.

EX POST FACTO: After the fact. An ex post facto law is a law that retroactively changes the consequences of a prior act.

EX REL.: Abbreviated form of the term "ex relatione," meaning upon relation or information. When the state brings an action in which it has no interest against an individual at the instigation of one who has a private interest in the matter.

FORUM NON CONVENIENS: Inconvenient forum. Although a court may have jurisdiction over the case, the action should be tried in a more conveniently located court, one to which parties and witnesses may more easily travel, for example.

GUARDIAN AD LITEM: A guardian appointed by the court to represent a minor or incompetent person in a legal action.

HABEAS CORPUS: You have the body. The modern writ of habeas corpus is a writ directing that a person (body) being detained (such as a prisoner) be brought before the court so that the legality of his detention can be judicially ascertained.

IN CAMERA: In private, in chambers. When a hearing is held before a judge in his or her chambers or when all spectators are excluded from the courtroom.

IN FORMA PAUPERIS: In the manner of a pauper. A party who proceeds in forma pauperis because of his poverty is one who is allowed to bring suit without liability for costs.

INFRA: Below, under. A word referring the reader to a later part of a book. (The opposite of supra.)

IN LOCO PARENTIS: In the place of a parent.

IN PARI DELICTO: Equally wrong; a court of equity will not grant requested relief to an applicant who is in pari delicto, or as much at fault in the transactions giving rise to the controversy as is the opponent of the applicant.

IN PARI MATERIA: On like subject matter or upon the same matter. Statutes relating to the same person or things are said to be in pari materia. It is a general rule of statutory construction that such statutes should be construed together, i.e., looked at as if they together constituted one law.

IN PERSONAM: Against the person. Jurisdiction over the person of an individual.

IN RE: In the matter of. Used to designate a proceeding involving an estate or other property.

IN REM: A term that signifies an action against the res, or thing. An action in rem is basically one that is taken directly against property, as distinguished from an action in personam, i.e., against the person.

INTER ALIA: Among other things. Used to show that the whole of a statement, pleading, list, statute, etc., has not been set forth in its entirety.

INTER PARTES: Between the parties. May refer to contracts, conveyances, or other transactions having legal significance.

INTER VIVOS: Between the living. An inter vivos gift is a gift made by a living grantor, as distinguished from bequests contained in a will, which pass upon the death of the testator.

IPSO FACTO: By the mere fact itself.

JUS: Law or the entire body of law.

LEX LOCI: The law of the place; the notion that the rights of parties to a legal proceeding are governed by the law of the place where those rights arose.

MALUM IN SE: Evil or wrong in and of itself; inherently wrong. This term describes an act that is wrong by its very nature, as opposed to one which would not be wrong but for the fact that there is a specific legal prohibition against it (malum prohibitum).

MALUM PROHIBITUM: Wrong because prohibited, but not inherently evil. Used to describe something that is wrong because it is expressly forbidden by law but that is not in and of itself evil, e.g., speeding.

MANDAMUS: We command. A writ directing an official to take a certain action.

MENS REA: A guilty mind; a criminal intent. A term used to signify the mental state that accompanies a crime or other prohibited act. Some crimes require only a general mens rea (general intent to do the prohibited act), but others, like assault with intent to murder, require the existence of a specific mens rea.

MODUS OPERANDI: Method of operating; generally refers to the manner or style of a criminal in committing crimes, admissible in appropriate cases as evidence of the identity of a defendant.

NEXUS: A connection to.

NISI PRIUS: A court of first impression. A nisi prius court is one where issues of fact are tried before a judge or jury.

N.O.V. (NON OBSTANTE VEREDICTO): Notwithstanding the verdict. A judgment n.o.v. is a judgment given in favor of one party despite the fact that a verdict was returned in favor of the other party, the justification being that the verdict either had no reasonable support in fact or was contrary to law.

NUNC PRO TUNC: Now for then. This phrase refers to actions that may be taken and will then have full retroactive effect.

PENDENTE LITE: Pending the suit; pending litigation underway.

PER CAPITA: By head; beneficiaries of an estate, if they take in equal shares, take per capita.

PER CURIAM: By the court; signifies an opinion ostensibly written "by the whole court" and with no identified author.

PER SE: By itself, in itself; inherently.

PER STIRPES: By representation. Used primarily in the law of wills to describe the method of distribution where a person, generally because of death, is unable to take that which is left to him by the will of another, and therefore his heirs divide such property between them rather than take under the will individually.

PRIMA FACIE: On its face, at first sight. A prima facie case is one that is sufficient on its face, meaning that the evidence supporting it is adequate to establish the case until contradicted or overcome by other evidence.

PRO TANTO: For so much; as far as it goes. Often used in eminent domain cases when a property owner receives partial payment for his land without prejudice to his right to bring suit for the full amount he claims his land to be worth.

QUANTUM MERUIT: As much as he deserves. Refers to recovery based on the doctrine of unjust enrichment in those cases in which a party has rendered valuable services or furnished materials that were accepted and enjoyed by another under circumstances that would reasonably notify the recipient that the rendering party expected to be paid. In essence, the law implies a contract to pay the reasonable value of the services or materials furnished.

QUASI: Almost like; as if; nearly. This term is essentially used to signify that one subject or thing is almost analogous to another but that material differences between them do exist. For example, a quasi-criminal proceeding is one that is not strictly criminal but shares enough of the same characteristics to require some of the same safeguards (e.g., procedural due process must be followed in a parole hearing).

QUID PRO QUO: Something for something. In contract law, the consideration, something of value, passed between the parties to render the contract binding.

RES GESTAE: Things done. In evidence law, this principle justifies the admission of a statement that would otherwise be hearsay when it is made so closely to the event in question as to be said to be a part of it, or with such spontaneity as not to have the possibility of falsehood.

RES IPSA LOQUITUR: The thing speaks for itself. This doctrine gives rise to a rebuttable presumption of negligence when the instrumentality causing the injury was within the exclusive control of the defendant, and the injury was one that does not normally occur unless a person has been negligent.

RES JUDICATA: A matter adjudged. Doctrine which provides that once a court of competent jurisdiction has rendered a final judgment or decree on the merits, that judgment or decree is conclusive upon the parties to the case and prevents them from engaging in any other litigation on the points and issues determined therein.

RESPONDEAT SUPERIOR: Let the master reply. This doctrine holds the master liable for the wrongful acts of his servant (or the principal for his agent) in those cases in which the servant (or agent) was acting within the scope of his authority at the time of the injury.

STARE DECISIS: To stand by or adhere to that which has been decided. The common law doctrine of stare decisis attempts to give security and certainty to the law by following the policy that once a principle of law as applicable to a certain set of facts has been set forth in a decision, it forms a precedent that will subsequently be followed, even though a different decision might be made were it the first time the question had arisen. Of course, stare decisis is not an inviolable principle and is departed from in instances where there is good cause (e.g., considerations of public policy led the Supreme Court to disregard prior decisions sanctioning segregation).

SUPRA: Above. A word referring a reader to an earlier part of a book. (The opposite of infra.)

ULTRA VIRES: Beyond the power. This phrase is most commonly used to refer to actions taken by a corporation that are beyond the power or legal authority of the corporation.

Addendum of French Derivatives

CHATTEL: Tangible personal property.

CY PRES: Doctrine permitting courts to apply trust funds to purposes not expressed in the trust but necessary to carry out the settlor's intent.

IN PAIS: Not pursuant to legal proceedings.

PER AUTRE VIE: For another's life; during another's life. In property law, an estate may be granted that will terminate upon the death of someone other than the grantee.

PROFIT A PRENDRE: A license to remove minerals or other produce from land.

VOIR DIRE: Process of questioning jurors as to their predispositions about the case or parties to a proceeding in order to identify those jurors displaying bias or prejudice.

Made in the USA
Middletown, DE
17 August 2022

71621983R00157